Chumps to Champs

ALSO BY BILL PENNINGTON

The Winning Spirit

The Heisman: Great American Stories of the Men Who Won

On Par: The Everyday Golfer's Survival Guide

Billy Martin: Baseball's Flawed Genius

Chumps
to
Champs

How the Worst Teams in
Yankees History
Led to the '90s Dynasty

Bill Pennington

Mariner Books
Houghton Mifflin Harcourt
BOSTON   NEW YORK

First Mariner Books edition 2020
Copyright © 2019 by Bill Pennington

All rights reserved

For information about permission to reproduce selections from this book,
write to trade.permissions@hmhco.com or to Permissions,
Houghton Mifflin Harcourt Publishing Company,
3 Park Avenue, 19th Floor, New York, New York 10016.

hmhbooks.com

Library of Congress Cataloging-in-Publication Data
Names: Pennington, Bill, 1956– author.
Title: Chumps to champs : how the worst teams in Yankees history
led to the 90's dynasty / Bill Pennington.
Description: Boston : Houghton Mifflin Harcourt, [2019] | Includes bibliographical
references and index.
Identifiers: LCCN 2018046434 (print) | LCCN 2018051095 (ebook) |
ISBN 9781328849878 (ebook) | ISBN 9781328849854 (hardback) |
ISBN 9780358331834 (pbk.)
Subjects: LCSH: New York Yankees (Baseball team) — History — 20th century. | Baseball
players — New York (State) — New York — Biography. | Baseball managers — New York
(State) — New York — Biography. | BISAC: SPORTS & RECREATION / Baseball / History. |
HISTORY / United States / State & Local / Middle Atlantic (DC, DE, MD, NJ, NY, PA).
Classification: LCC GV875.N4 (ebook) | LCC GV875.N4 P45 2019 (print) |
DDC 796.357/64097471—dc23
LC record available at https://lccn.loc.gov/2018046434

Book design by Chloe Foster

Printed in the United States of America

DOC 10 9 8 7 6 5 4 3 2 1

To Joyce, Anne D., Elise and Jack,

the ultimate home team advantage

Contents

Introduction

IT WAS A sunny Sunday in Chicago, and Andy Hawkins, a journeyman pitcher with a career losing record, was only four outs from baseball immortality. Working briskly through the Chicago White Sox lineup that day, July 1, 1990, Hawkins had retired 23 batters without yielding a hit. There were two outs in the bottom of the eighth inning.

For Hawkins, in his second year with the New York Yankees, it was and would be the game of his life. And it had come out of nowhere. Just a few weeks earlier, he trudged off the mound after getting only one out in a starting assignment, trailing 5–0 in the first inning. In another game that month, he faced only 12 batters, with half of them getting hits and a third smacking triples or doubles. At that point, the Yankees planned to either cut Hawkins or demote him to the minor leagues. Only an injury to a teammate had kept him on the team.

But on July 1, the pitching gods had blessed Hawkins. It was shaping up as a milestone performance. Despite his 1-4 record, he flummoxed the White Sox lineup in a scoreless game.

It was a typically blustery afternoon in Chicago, and late in the eighth inning, wind gusts blew debris from the grandstand onto the infield. Play was halted as several white paper wrappers were gathered by field maintenance workers. Hawkins stood motionless on the mound throughout the delay.

"Everything was in control," Hawkins later said. "I felt good. I didn't sense anything else. It happened so fast."

The next batter slapped a crisp grounder to Yankees third baseman

Mike Blowers, who bobbled the ball for an error. Two walks and two mystifying errors in the windy outfield followed in quick succession.

It happened so fast.

Just like that, the White Sox led, 4–0. Hawkins retired his twenty-fourth White Sox batter soon afterward. The Yankees then went quickly and quietly in the top of the ninth inning. Game over.

The fans inside Chicago's rusting Comiskey Park, built in 1910, seemed giddy and confused at the same time. They were celebrating something they had never seen before: a no-hitter by the visiting pitcher and a home victory.

Hawkins's game of a lifetime, an everlasting memory, became baseball history and an undying nightmare.

A pitcher with an eight-inning no-hitter who *lost*? It had never happened before in the 114-year history of Major League Baseball. There had been lost extra-inning no-hitters, rain-shortened no-hit games lost and one nine-inning no-hit game when the home pitcher lost. But there had never been anything like what happened — and happened so fast — to Andy Hawkins.

But as a remarkably coherent Hawkins said afterward in the locker room: "It still counts. It's a no-hitter. They can't take it away from me."

Not so fast. In fact, Major League Baseball changed a record-keeping regulation the next season, requiring a pitcher to complete at least 27 outs for the game to count as an official no-hitter. The baseball gods had abandoned Hawkins yet again.

And so a new baseball decade that was just six months old began ignominiously for the Yankees, the most decorated American sports franchise of the twentieth century. The embarrassment of Hawkins's Chicago outing lingered, the omen for what was to come for the country's most renowned sports team.

It would turn out to be the dawn of the darkest period in Yankees history, a period willfully forgotten by Yankees fans — with good reason.

How had this happened to the team of Ruth, Gehrig, DiMaggio and Mantle?

By 1990, the Yankees had won 22 World Series and 33 American League pennants, both major league records. Twenty-six Yankees were already in the Baseball Hall of Fame or on their way there.

The Yankees had been the subject of countless books and motion pictures, television miniseries and Broadway shows. The franchise was likened to titans of American industry — compared to the Ford Motor Company in the 1920s and US Steel in the 1950s.

Yankees jerseys had been the best-selling brand in baseball, and a Yankees cap was still a fixture on streets, subway cars, bars and jet planes around the country. They were the favored team of celebrities, from Jack Nicholson to Bruce Springsteen to Jackie Onassis. The moneyed Yankees had cultivated a reputation synonymous with achievement and prosperity.

And yet, ten years away from a new century, the great Yankees run appeared all but over. Their empire had collapsed and seemed irreparably ruined. The minor league cupboard of budding young prospects was bare. The Yankees, by every measure, were broken.

From 1989 to 1992, the Yankees were the laughingstock of baseball, with a team that not only was at the bottom of the standings, but had the worst four-year record (288-359) since the team first became known as the Yankees, in 1913.

Attendance at Yankee Stadium was down 35 percent, TV ratings had plummeted, and the Yankees were in the midst of the longest World Series drought in team history, a stretch that lasted 14 seasons.

Those are the statistics. But it was so much worse than the numbers. How bad?

The team's owner, George M. Steinbrenner III, had been denounced as a stain on the game and banished permanently from baseball.

It was not the only bad karma shrouding the team after seven decades of mostly uninterrupted triumph.

It started with Hawkins's losing no-hitter. A year later, a prized Yankees draft pick with a 100-mile-an-hour fastball — in an era when almost no one threw that hard — got in a bar fight that ruined his career. Promising trades turned out to be embarrassing flops.

In the midst of four successive losing seasons, the entire Yankees roster had exactly one player, Don Mattingly, who had ever been to an All-Star game. But Mattingly's shining light was soon enveloped by a darker mood, too. An aching back was betraying him and would soon sap him of his greatest gifts.

At this juncture, the obituary for the once great, conquering Yankees was being written across the country. The Yankees were dated, worn and lacked new ideas or a modern operating philosophy. Their players had been sullied and humiliated. Even the team's physical plant appeared to be outmoded. The once groundbreaking Yankee Stadium, refurbished a generation earlier, was aging and had been surpassed by a host of newer, more imaginative and entertaining ballparks in Baltimore, Toronto, Chicago, Texas and Minnesota, outposts that now mocked the declining Yankees.

The Yankees were like a once proud transatlantic ocean liner or a too-big-to-fail corporation — a hearty symbol of a robust America in perhaps the country's greatest century — that was now slowly sinking or deteriorating brick by brick.

But in fact, and as hard as it was to see at the time, the seemingly vexed Yankees were about to embark on a revival that ended with the last great baseball dynasty of the twentieth century.

And so, this is a story of a wholly unexpected resurrection and rebirth. It is the story of the unlikely cast of characters — nobodies in the game of baseball at the time — who made it happen. They were baseball lifers, a mix of wandering scouts and their bosses, cubicle-bound analysts, untested coaches and junior executives led by the then obscure, first-year manager Buck Showalter and the team's general manager Gene Michael, two cogs buried deep in the organizational structure.

If Showalter and Michael were the duo who helped revive the Yankees, soon they were a trio. On July 9, 1992, I broke the story that George Steinbrenner would soon be reinstated by Commissioner Fay Vincent. It seemed impossible, and some of my colleagues called my scoop a bunch of hooey. But thirteen days later, Vincent announced that Steinbrenner could resume his Yankees ownership duties in March 1993.

Steinbrenner was going to ride a white horse into the Yankee spring training complex in Florida that day — like Napoleon returned from the Isle of Elba — but he changed his mind at the last minute, saying it was too showy. The mercurial shipbuilding magnate instead landed his private jet just beyond the outfield walls and walked through a gate near a sea of *The Boss Is Back!* placards.

That was George's idea of making a small entrance.

What transpired next is an untold story of ingenious, counterintuitive thinking that presaged baseball's analytics era. It is a story of stirring, plucky, startling triumph — a stunning rejuvenation that put a new face on an old franchise. It is also a story of heartrending disappointment, since the Yankees' rousing comeback, which brought them within sight of the pinnacle of the sport, ended in another devastating setback. The 1994 players' strike canceled the World Series and thwarted the most promising Yankees season in nearly a generation. It was one of many painful lessons absorbed, and these unheralded Yankees of the early to mid-nineties showed the perseverance to rally yet again.

And fail again in 1995.

Then, unbelievably, from 1996 to 2000, the Yankees won three of the next four World Series. From 1996 to 2012, they would play in baseball's postseason every year but one.

Even the Yankees of the 1920s, 1930s, 1940s and 1950s could not match that postseason streak.

The story of that unmatched success—the championship teams of Derek Jeter, Mariano Rivera, Andy Pettitte, Bernie Williams and Jorge Posada—cannot be told without understanding the underexamined, pivotal seasons that preceded it. With the hindsight of roughly twenty-five years, those seasons did indeed foreshadow what was to come, especially if you added a little good fortune.

I was a close witness to this period, as a Yankees beat writer and syndicated columnist at the *Bergen Record* in New Jersey and later as a sportswriter at the *New York Times*. I have remained in contact with the principals involved and spent the past two years revisiting them, to both help them recall their memories and listen to perspectives gained through the prism of history. In scores of interviews, they have helped me reconstruct an unobserved phenomenon that forever altered baseball's twentieth-century narrative.

The Yankees of 1990 were treated as a wasteland by the baseball community. But surreptitiously, the quietest of revolutions was taking place, an uprising that would conquer every unsuspecting opponent in the sport and install a new ruling force in baseball for years thereafter.

It is the dynasty no one saw coming, spawned by the worst teams in New York Yankees history. It was a time when a phoenix rose unforeseen from the ashes.

Part One

The Long Decline

1

Yankee Circus

"WE WERE THE best team in baseball in the 1980s," George Steinbrenner said at the dawn of the 1990 season. "We just didn't win very much."

Steinbrenner was, as he often could be, both right and wrong. The Yankees were indeed the best team in major league baseball from 1980 to 1989, if the measurement is the total number of victories (854). The Yankees also had the best winning percentage (.547) of the 26 major league teams playing at the time.

And yet, when the baseball community looks at the Yankees in the 1980s, it sees only what those teams did not win: a World Series.

It's a high standard, but the Yankees created it. The 1980s were the first decade since 1910 to 1920 that the Yankees did not win at least two World Series, if not five or six. And people took notice of that, especially because the Yankees began the 1980s with such boundless promise. They seemed on the verge of another era of preeminence.

The 1980 Yankees, for example, won 103 games, which was, by three games, the best record in baseball. They were a deep, balanced team, led by Reggie Jackson, who hit .300 for the only time in his career and slugged 41 home runs. They were a mix of young and old, from the twenty-six-year-old catcher Rick Cerone, who drove in 85 runs, to the thirty-four-year-old first baseman Bob Watson, who hit .307. The pitching staff had two future Hall of Famers (Rich Gossage and Gaylord Perry) and four starters (Tommy John, Jim Kaat, Ron Guidry and Ed Figueroa) who collectively would end up winning more than 800 major league games.

The roster was also filled with prominent leaders. Shortstop Bucky Dent and outfielder Lou Piniella would end up Yankee managers, with

Piniella also managing four other major league teams, including Cincinnati, where he won a World Series. Second baseman Willie Randolph would become the New York Mets' manager and be a longtime Yankees coach for four World Series champions. Watson was destined to be the Yankees' general manager sixteen years later.

The off-the-field leadership was as impressive and experienced. Manager Dick Howser and general manager Gene Michael both had been with the Yankees since the mid-1960s, when they were infielders for the team. Each had held a variety of central roles in the franchise as it won three American League pennants and two World Series in the late seventies.

But after a superlative regular season, the 1980 Yankees were swept in what was then a best-of-five American League Championship Series, losing to George Brett's Kansas City Royals, who had won 97 regular-season games.

There was no shame in being upset by the Royals, who were more than worthy opponents. But the defeat turned out to be more than a simple setback.

In many ways, it set in motion a decade of Yankee baseball that was simultaneously successful and dysfunctional. Year after year, the team won a ton of games and were regularly in sight of a World Series championship — much more than fans remember.

In fact, had today's current wild-card postseason system been in place in the 1980s, the Yankees would have qualified for the playoffs seven times. But it is just as true that every time the Yankees made a charge toward the top, the team's organization, in a variety of ways, did something to shoot itself disastrously in the foot.

This pattern of achievement coexisting with disorder became a Yankee calling card in the 1980s, one that portended the comprehensive folly of the early 1990s. And the genesis of the Yankees' decade-long template of accomplishment mixed with chaos — the very moment it all began — can be traced to one critical play of the 1980 playoff series with Kansas City.

The crucial, decisive sequence happened in the eighth inning of Game 2 at Kansas City when Randolph was thrown out at home plate trying to tie the game on a Watson double. George Steinbrenner was fifty years old at the time and still feisty and defiant enough to sit in the stands with the Royals fans. As Randolph was called out, he immediately began waving his arms at the field in disgust as he shouted at Yankees third-base coach Mike Ferraro.

In the seat adjacent to Steinbrenner, Gene Michael tried to calm his boss, who felt (at least after the play) that Ferraro should have held Randolph at third base. But Steinbrenner's hissy fit was not to be bridled, and it was broadcast on national television. Also, Steinbrenner's presence — he was wearing a bright white sweater — was unmistakable to Royals fans near him, who began to goad the Yankees' owner with catcalls and jeers. George responded in kind, engaging the crowd in ways that only fanned the incendiary atmosphere.

Randolph had been shaken up on the play, his head having slammed into Royals catcher Darrell Porter, and he rose from the dirt around home plate slowly. The Yankees were staggered. It was hectic on the field and maybe crazier in the stands near Steinbrenner. "I looked up and saw Mr. Steinbrenner gesturing and waving at the field, giving it that disgusted dismissal wave he did — I used to call it the big shake," Randolph said in 2017. "He was getting into it with the fans. There was wild commotion. And I thought, 'Oh boy, I know what's coming.'"

The Yankees lost the final game of the series two days later, when Gossage came on in the seventh inning to protect a one-run lead and instead gave up a three-run homer to Brett.

Although Howser and Ferraro were not to blame for Brett's home run, Steinbrenner wanted both fired immediately. Under pressure, Howser resigned, only to resurface with the Royals, whom he led to a World Series title in 1985.

While the volatile Steinbrenner had already changed managers six times since buying the Yankees in 1973, there was something preposterous and shameful about forcing Howser out of his job. Howser had inherited a fourth-place team, one that was rudderless and reeling from the tragic 1979 death of catcher Thurman Munson. Howser had resurrected the Yankees with compassion, baseball acumen and a calm but authoritative managerial style.

The 1980 season was Howser's first as a major league manager, and his team's winning percentage (.636) was the highest of any Yankees manager in seventeen years. Now he was gone.

It was proof that Steinbrenner might do anything after a season that did not end with a Yankees World Series victory. And that proved to be true. Howser's departure was just the first of 13 managerial changes Steinbrenner made in the 1980s.

The early 1980 playoff exit set a future course that became wearisomely familiar by the end of the decade. It was far from entirely Steinbrenner's fault. There was little consistency to the team's management structure and no overarching Yankee philosophy of how to build continuity. The minor league teams fared well, which spoke to astute drafting and amateur-free-agent purchases, but the young talent was regularly traded away for existing big league stars, usually ones past their prime. The youngsters blossomed for other teams. The Yankees were left with fading also-rans.

Worse, the Yankees' ceaseless pursuit of prominent major league free agents cost them picks in the amateur draft as compensation for their unrestrained spending.

"We were denied eighteen draft picks in the 1980s," Bill Livesey, the team's scouting director at the time, said, looking back more than thirty years later. "We only had one first-round pick in the entire decade."

But the Yankees of the eighties could not change their heedless ways. The team and its fans, intoxicated by the two World Series wins in the late 1970s when Munson, Jackson and Billy Martin owned the city, were chasing an unsustainable ambition to contend for the World Series every season. And that never permitted the Yankees to rebuild or nurture from within.

"In some ways, the success George Steinbrenner and the Yankees had in the 1970s laid the path for the bumpy ride the team had in the 1980s," Lou Piniella, who played for the Yankees in both decades and eventually became the team's manager, said in a 2017 interview.

"George made a bunch of good free-agent signings in the 1970s, like Reggie and Catfish Hunter. And he thought he could just keep that up. But free agency was new in the 1970s, and George succeeded by jumping in before other teams. By the 1980s, there was a lot of competition for the top free agents and George didn't always get the top-tier guys anymore. But he kept signing free agents anyway — and some of them were failures. And that meant signing more free agents to make up for the mistakes. What the Yankees needed to do was step back and say, 'Hey, what are we doing here?' But that didn't happen for a long time."

This endless Yankees pursuit of yearly greatness became a relentless, exhausting marathon in the eighties that left no time to ponder and devise a coherent, articulated vision of the future. This was most apparent in Steinbrenner's incessant meddling with the managers, general managers and eventually the roster, and that helped sabotage season after season.

The impulsive purge of Howser was the first warning signal. It was not the last.

In 1981, Michael reluctantly replaced Howser as manager, under the new general manager Bill Bergesch (one of eight Yankees general managers in the 1980s). Michael had another skilled Yankees team, which included newly signed free agent Dave Winfield, and the team was in first place when the 1981 season was interrupted by a strike. When the season resumed, 38 percent of the regular-season games had been canceled, and baseball decided to split the season into two halves, prestrike and poststrike, with a champion named for each half.

The first-place teams from each half, in each division, would then meet in a best-of-five playoff series, with the surviving teams advancing to the American and National League Championship Series. If one team won both halves, it would still have to play an extra playoff series against the runner-up from the second half of the season.

This flawed, ill-conceived setup left the first-half winners, like the Yankees, with no incentive to win the second half of the season, and, not surprisingly, none of them did. But before the second half was concluded, Steinbrenner fired Michael for not being able to motivate his team as he did in the first half.

Under Bob Lemon, who had led the Yankees to a 1978 World Series victory, the Yankees charged through the playoffs and won the first two games of the 1981 World Series against the Los Angeles Dodgers. But then the Yankees lost the next three games.

After Game 5, Steinbrenner said he got in a fistfight with two Dodgers fans in his hotel elevator. "I clocked them," he said of the altercation. "There are two guys in town looking for their teeth."

The Yankees lost the next game, and the World Series, anyway.

Steinbrenner issued a statement after the final game. "I want to sincerely apologize to the people of New York and to the fans of the New York Yankees everywhere for the performance of the Yankee team in the World Series," it read. "We'll make the necessary changes to make sure it doesn't happen again."

The "necessary" changes soon included firing Lemon 14 games into the 1982 season. Gene Michael was back again, albeit unwillingly. He survived 86 games before he was replaced by Clyde King, a longtime scout and Yankees adviser.

Three managers for one team in one season? You bet.

That season, *Boston Globe* columnist Leigh Montville wrote a satirical piece in which he imagined that he was the last person on earth who had not yet managed the Yankees. He got up for breakfast and his teenage son comforted him by saying, "Don't worry, Dad, you'll get your chance to manage the Yankees. I remember when I was the skipper of the Yankees . . ." Montville went to a gas station and was met at the pump by an attendant, who counseled, "Don't worry, Leigh, I remember when I managed the Yankees . . ." He went to church and the pastor opined from the pulpit, "Now when I was manager of the Yankees . . ."

This is what the Yankees had come to.

The three-manager charade of 1982 led to only 79 victories and a fifth-place finish — the first losing season for the Yankees since Steinbrenner bought the team nine years earlier.

Billy Martin returned to skipper the Yankees to a respectable 91 wins the next season, but still no World Series victory, so he was let go again. The Yankees lineup had become a hodgepodge of noncomplementary talents. It especially lacked reliable pitching depth, since the Yankees put a priority on acquiring power hitters, on the premise that a high-scoring team attracted fans to the ballpark. And the Yankees, for the first time in a decade, were beginning to have trouble keeping the home stadium even half full.

The calm, reserved Yogi Berra was named manager in 1984, but never-ending turmoil had by now bled into the fabric of the franchise like the pinstripes on the uniforms. Berra was fired 16 games into the 1985 season, and while Martin returned to lead the Yankees to a stunning and remarkable 97-win season in 1985, they were still two wins short of a division title. Again, without a wild-card playoff system, the Yankees went home. Martin, his right arm still in a cast because he broke it fighting one of his own pitchers, was dismissed.

By 1986, Piniella had made his managerial debut. He lasted two successful seasons, winning 90 games his first year and 89 games the next season, but Piniella was then supplanted by Martin. Yes, again.

"People have said that the Yankees have become a circus," the influential syndicated newspaper columnist Jerry Izenberg wrote at the time. "That's not fair. Nothing in the strangest circus anywhere on God's green earth is as bizarre as what's going on with the Yankees."

In June 1988, though the Yankees were in first place in the American League East, Martin was fired for the last time after a brawl in a Texas strip club left his ear nearly torn from his head. Piniella came back yet again, leaving his post as the Yankees' general manager to do so.

It did not go well. Piniella was fired, too.

The eighties were coming to a close, and the Yankees, as an organization, were crumbling from top to bottom. There were good baseball minds running things down on the farm, and good scouts providing top-notch players for the indispensable talent pipeline. But at the lowest levels, morale was lagging.

What good did it do to find gifted young talent if it was constantly being traded away in shortsighted deals meant as quick fixes that ultimately failed? "By the end of the 1980s, we had traded away so many future All-Stars I lost count," said Livesey, the scouting director.

There were two examples: slugger Fred McGriff and starting pitcher Doug Drabek, who were each traded by Steinbrenner and his general managers. The players, all in their thirties, the Yankees got in return for McGriff and Drabek lasted about a year with the team. McGriff would go on to hit 493 home runs, most for the Atlanta Braves. Drabek won a Cy Young Award in Pittsburgh, had eight seasons with a winning record and won 155 games overall.

By 1989, the Yankees minor league system, filled with accomplished managers and coaches, had been stripped of talent.

The magazine *Baseball America,* which chronicles and studies the minor leagues comprehensively, ranks each of baseball's franchises every year in terms of how many quality prospects they have outside of the major league roster. In 1989, the Yankees ranked 22nd of 26 teams.

At the time, *Baseball America* also ranked the top 100 individual prospects. The Yankees did not have one minor leaguer in the top 40, the only club shut out in that category.

The drumbeat of recurring setbacks and organizational disarray left the 1989 big league Yankees staggering into spring training, where they were greeted by a bold new sheriff in town. Breaking with tradition, the Yankees had turned to an outsider and directed him to shake things up as only an outsider might. The new manager was Dallas Green, the brassy, former Philadelphia Phillies skipper. As directed, Green took charge with authority and influence. He imported a slew of National League players and shoved out several Yankee mainstays, particularly the popular Willie Randolph.

Green was a smart, honest leader, but after a few months, he warred with Steinbrenner, too. And the Yankees didn't win much — too many aging players and not enough youthful athleticism. Green was gone by mid-August. Chastened, the Yankees once again reached into their past, hiring the shortstop from the team's late-1970s heyday, Bucky Dent, the hero of the 1978 one-game playoff victory at Fenway Park.

Under Dent, the team did its best to reverse all the changes Green had been allowed to make, hoping to restore the roster to its former American League and Yankees-centric look — whatever that meant at this point.

It came off as more window dressing, the Yankees changing course yet again with no clear destination in sight. It fooled no one, most of all the players in the clubhouse, who were the people who had to put on the historic Yankee pinstripes and try to recapture the magic.

At the close of the 1989 season, Winfield, wistful and contemplative, assessed the Yankees as he now saw them. He was approaching another long, unfulfilled off-season. In his first year as a Yankee, he had played in the World Series. To Winfield, that now seemed as far away as grammar school. "I've been here nine seasons," Winfield said wearily, collapsing his thirty-seven-year-old, six-foot-six, 225-pound frame into a tiny folding chair. "I thought I was coming to an organization with all this famous tradition. You know, where the ghosts of Ruth, DiMaggio, Mantle and all those cats just made the World Series happen year after year. My first year here, that did happen. It was like the cheering never stopped.

"But let me just say this: That's not what's happening around here these days."

2

Adrift

GEORGE STEINBRENNER HAD many unique abilities, and one of them was that he could smile and frown at the same time. It was as if he could split his face in half. Above his nose, his brow would furrow. Almost simultaneously, he would force his lips into a grin. He did it most often when confronted with disconcerting facts about his Yankees that he refused to acknowledge.

When something that cast the Yankees in a poor light was presented to him, George looked pained, but he might instead add a wide-mouthed chortle.

Derogatory statements about the Yankees were to be turned into positives. Those who knew the complicated, multifaceted Steinbrenner did not necessarily view this as spin. It was, more likely, how Steinbrenner's brain was wired, which worked like this:

The Yankees weren't doing anything wrong; things had just not turned out right.

But as 1990 dawned, even George's well-honed scowl/smile reflex was being challenged. And he was not in an especially good mood because of it.

The Yankees might have won more games than any other major league team in the previous decade, but each victory cost roughly $161,500 in player salaries.

The Yankees payroll in the 1980s, which ballooned with the nearly annual restructuring of the team's roster, was $137,883,665, which was nearly $22 million more than any other major league team's payroll. The average player's salary was about $485,000. That may seem like a steal today, but not in 1990, when the average salary for all of baseball was $153,000 less.

Making matters worse, the collective bargaining contract between the players' union and the owners had expired, and players were balking at the owners' proposal for a salary cap.

In response, the owners forbade players from coming to spring training, locking them out of their workplace.

Steinbrenner, meanwhile, was fighting fires on multiple fronts.

Yankee Stadium lacked corporate luxury boxes, a bountiful revenue stream already in place in the new baseball palaces that were sprouting up in other cities. This irked Steinbrenner mightily. How could the little-market, small-city Baltimore Orioles be taking in tens of millions of luxury box dollars when the Yankees, a baseball monolith, were not?

It filled Steinbrenner with stadium envy. He, like other sports team owners around the country, ramped up the pressure on municipal leaders for stadium improvements. New York City owned Yankee Stadium, which had been almost entirely reconstructed in 1976. Steinbrenner wanted more upgrades — new highway exit ramps and a sophisticated train station — if not a new stadium altogether.

Desperate, the borough president of the Bronx, where the Yankees first put down roots in 1923, proposed a new stadium in the little-used Ferry Point Park, at the foot of the congested Whitestone Bridge connecting Queens and the Bronx. A stadium in that spot would create a traffic nightmare, something Steinbrenner already had in his current location. The Ferry Point Park baseball project never gained traction. About twenty-five years later, the site would instead become an elite golf course, built and operated by Steinbrenner's friend Donald Trump.

But in 1990, Steinbrenner knew a bad idea when he saw one. Huffing his disapproval of the Ferry Point plan, Steinbrenner did what was then unthinkable in New York: He suggested that the most famous sports franchise in the world, a team as emblematic of New York as the Statue of Liberty, be moved to New Jersey.

Steinbrenner initiated talks with New Jersey officials about a new Yankee Stadium next to Giants Stadium, in northern New Jersey's Bergen County, which had become the prosperous home to the NFL's New York Giants and New York Jets.

In the early nineties, flying over northern New Jersey in his private jet with a New Jersey reporter, Steinbrenner peered out the window and pointed toward Giants Stadium and the hundreds of acres of undeveloped land near it. He smiled and said: "We're going to put the new stadium right there. There's plenty of room for parking and major highways all around."

When Steinbrenner's comments were published the next day, New Yorkers revolted. The *New Jersey* Yankees? It was inconceivable. What next? The New York Stock Exchange in Hoboken?

Steinbrenner refrained from further comment on his relocation plan — at least initially — but the stadium firestorm raged throughout the nineties. New York City's leaders, and Yankees fans, had been forewarned. And it quickly made Steinbrenner the least favorite team owner in New York.

But Steinbrenner had other, far more substantial and lasting worries. On March 18, 1990, the day that season's baseball lockout ended, the *New York Daily News* uncovered shocking information about Steinbrenner. In January that year, he had paid Howie Spira, a former quasi-employee of Dave Winfield's charitable foundation, $40,000 for damaging information — "dirt," to use Spira's word — on the workings of Winfield's foundation.

Steinbrenner had been warring with Winfield for almost a decade, mostly because he felt Winfield had duped him when the two agreed to a record-setting, ten-year, $23 million contract before the 1981 season. The contract had a cost-of-living escalation clause — one not calculated correctly by the Yankees front office — that could inflate Winfield's pay dramatically.

The contract had been a sore point between the two men ever since, especially after Winfield had just one hit in 22 at-bats during the team's loss in the 1981 World Series, and also failed in the 1980s to lead the Yankees to a championship, like Steinbrenner's other headline free-agent purchase, Reggie Jackson. In the middle of an important game in September 1985 that the Yankees were about to lose, Steinbrenner stood in the back of the Yankee Stadium press box and noted that Jackson was so productive in late-season clutch games, he was nicknamed "Mr. October." He added, "Now I've got Dave Winfield — Mr. May."

But the dispute between the owner and one of the best players in baseball was more acrimonious than simple insults. Part of his contract with Winfield called for Steinbrenner to make annual payments of about $300,000 to Winfield's foundation, which was set up to benefit impoverished youth. According to the contract, Winfield was also required to make regular payments to the foundation, which was to be operated in certain stipulated ways.

By the mid-eighties, Steinbrenner and Winfield had clashed repeatedly over these terms and whether the foundation was doing what it was intended to do. The Yankees had also been complaining that the foundation was a front for employing Dave Winfield's relatives. To which Winfield said, "Look at the Rockefeller foundations. Are you telling me there are no Rockefellers working there?"

By 1986, Steinbrenner had dug in his heels and refused to make his mandated payments to the foundation. It was not an act of stinginess. Steinbrenner was one of the most generous of all sports team owners. He founded the Silver Shield Fund in 1982, which benefits the children of New York–area police officers and firefighters who die in the line of duty. Thirty-six years later, the charity continues to financially support hundreds of children annually. And for decades, Steinbrenner quietly paid for the college educations of countless children whose lives intersected with his in one way or another.

In the early nineties, I was staying at Steinbrenner's Tampa hotel and struck up a conversation with the restaurant lounge's bartender. The bartender, who did not know she was speaking to a reporter, had been complaining to a waitress about Steinbrenner's presence in the hotel that night. Having the Boss, as he loved to be called, in the house put every employee on edge, because Steinbrenner would sometimes barge into the kitchen to inspect the silverware or scrutinize the food prep. He might do a uniform check.

"Everyone is so goddamned relieved when he leaves for the night," she said.

Added the waitress: "Such a pain in the ass."

The bartender smiled. "But I guess I should be nicer," she said. "When my husband got sick and couldn't work last year, Mr. Steinbrenner heard about it and said he would put my son through grad school."

The waitress piped up as well. "He did the same thing for my daughter. Paid all of her tuition so long as she got A's and B's. She had to bring him a report card, but a few days later, her college got a check."

So Steinbrenner's refusal to pay the David M. Winfield Foundation was not a case of the Boss being miserly. It was another chapter in the bitter, costly Winfield-Steinbrenner feud.

The impasse soon led to a series of suits and countersuits between Winfield and Steinbrenner. It was at this moment that Howie Spira, the former foundation employee, called Steinbrenner's office and offered "dirt on Winfield" that would presumably help the Yankees' owner win his dispute with his star outfielder.

Spira was an odd, nebulous character, a thin, gangly twenty-six-year-old from the Bronx who, it turned out, had considerable gambling debts. Spira was often at Yankees home games with a radio reporter's credentials, although few of the regular media members had any idea what he did. He had been a publicist for the Winfield Foundation, although Winfield later called him more of a "go-fer." Most of all, Spira was quiet, someone seen but seldom heard.

But in the spring of 1987, Spira met with Steinbrenner several times and convinced him he could prove various Winfield Foundation improprieties. In June, Spira, Steinbrenner and Yankees lawyers took their allegations to the Manhattan district attorney.

The legal maneuvering that followed clouded three Yankees seasons, a time when Winfield, along with Don Mattingly, was the team's most respected player — in the Yankees' clubhouse and around the league.

Finally, on September 6, 1989, arbitration resulted in a settlement of the Steinbrenner and Winfield lawsuits, with Steinbrenner paying the $600,000 he had withheld from the foundation and Winfield agreeing to pay about $200,000 he had not contributed.

One long, disruptive Yankees distraction had come to an end.

Or so it seemed. The détente between Winfield and Steinbrenner was short-lived. In January 1990, Spira began pestering Steinbrenner for money, insisting that Steinbrenner had reneged on a promise to give him a job. Spira threatened to disclose tape recordings of their telephone conversations about Winfield. He also contacted several newspapers, promising to relate his story, with the tapes, for $50,000. No publication took him up on his offer. But eventually, Steinbrenner wrote Spira a check for $40,000. At first, Steinbrenner said he had given Spira the money "out of the goodness of my heart," because he was trying to help the financially strapped Spira. Later, Steinbrenner said he had paid to keep Spira from reopening the details of the battle with Winfield and to prevent Spira from disclosing embarrassing information about former Yankees employees.

Whatever Steinbrenner's true intentions were, he also contacted the

FBI and asked it to investigate Spira. And indeed, five days after the *Daily News* story in 1990, Spira was indicted by a federal grand jury for trying to extort money from Steinbrenner, and from Winfield as well.

The next day, in an ominous revelation, baseball commissioner Fay Vincent, who a year earlier had assisted then commissioner Bart Giamatti in the investigation that led to Pete Rose's permanent expulsion from baseball, said his office had begun looking into the Steinbrenner-Spira connection.

"We're happy to have it looked into," Steinbrenner said of Vincent's inquiry. "I understand he's going to look at the whole picture where Spira's concerned, not just my involvement."

Asked by the *New York Times* if he thought there might be a chance he would be disciplined for his dealings with Spira, Steinbrenner responded: "None whatsoever, according to my people. From what I understand, we're not worried about it."

Since the interview was conducted over the telephone, it is not known if Steinbrenner's frown/smile reflex had kicked into gear during his answer.

What is known is that a week later, John Dowd, a Washington lawyer who conducted the six-month Rose investigation and compiled a dossier that filled seven volumes, began interviewing various parties associated with the case, including Spira.

At roughly the same time, the 1990 Yankees, no longer locked out of their spring training home in Fort Lauderdale, were finally convening for the first time.

At least most of them were there. The team's best pitcher, Pascual Pérez, could not leave the Dominican Republic because of visa and legal problems. Or something like that. Pérez earned the nickname "Wrong-Way Pérez" after a 1982 incident when he missed an Atlanta Braves home game as he circled — three times — a beltway interstate looking for Atlanta–Fulton County Stadium. Pérez had also twice been suspended for cocaine use in the eighties. In 1990, he would arrive in Fort Lauderdale a week late.

Pérez, who had the comical habit of checking a runner on first base by bending over and peering through his legs, was easily the riskiest of the bets the Yankees were making in 1990. But he was not the only one.

Another veteran starting pitcher, Tim Leary, had been acquired from the Cincinnati Reds. Leary had been brilliant in 1988, when he had a 17-

11 record. But in 1989, he had slumped to 8-14. Which pitcher were the Yankees getting?

Dave LaPoint was the third starter, and he was coming off shoulder surgery after a season when he had a 5.62 earned run average. LaPoint's record was 38-53 in the previous five seasons.

Andy Hawkins, the fourth starter, had been a steady workhorse for the Yankees in 1989, winning 15 games and losing 15. Chuck Cary, the fifth, was thirty years old but had just 14 career decisions, eight of them defeats.

The strength and reliability of the Yankees' bullpen was similarly uncertain. Dave Righetti, the team's All-Star closer since 1984, had worried the Yankees with his inconsistency in 1989.

As for the batting order, there were an equal number of paradoxes and enigmas. The right fielder Jesse Barfield had once hit 40 home runs, but that was four years earlier. Barfield still had power, but his batting average had slumped to .234. Winfield had been an All-Star selection every year in the 1980s except for one, and that happened to be 1989, when he did not play a game because of major back surgery.

No one knew what to expect from Winfield in 1990, including Winfield himself. "I feel fine and you see me out there swinging the bat and playing the field," Winfield said in spring training. "So it looks like me. But I've got a long way to go until I am actually me again."

In many ways, the 1990 Yankees were still lurching from the 1989 trade of Rickey Henderson, the team's most versatile, explosive, talented — and irrepressible and disruptive — player.

Henderson had never truly been happy as a Yankee unless his long-time mentor Billy Martin had been the manager. In other years, Henderson was finicky, moody and mercurial. In 1989, he was particularly in a funk — oft-injured, listless and underperforming. He, too, seemed worn out by the nonstop turmoil. So, as gifted as Henderson was, the Yankees felt compelled to deal him to the Oakland Athletics. The problem was that the Yankees received almost no one of prominent value in return, acquiring pitchers Greg Cadaret and Eric Plunk and outfielder Luis Polonia. Cadaret would end up compiling a 22-23 record in four seasons with the Yankees. Plunk would be 15-13 in three Yankee seasons. As a Yankee, in 1989, Polonia had been arrested and jailed for having consensual sex with a fifteen-year-old in Milwaukee.

The deal was crafted by then Yankees general manager Bob Quinn, who was also on his way out of the Yankees organization.

Henderson's departure left a gaping hole in the Yankees lineup and diminished their defense, but most of all, it meant the Yankees were no longer feared by American League teams. Opposing teams viewed Henderson, who would eventually score more runs and steal more bases than any player in major league history, as a dreaded pest. He especially unnerved pitchers.

With a career on-base percentage of .401, Henderson, who ranks second all-time in walks, was a constant presence on the basepaths for the Yankees from 1985 to 1989. It seemed like Henderson was standing on first or second base about half the time that Winfield or Don Mattingly came up to bat in that period. And since Henderson led the major leagues in runs in three of those seasons, it seemed as if either Winfield or Mattingly always drove the speedy Henderson home with a hit.

It was the Yankees' only established formula for success. In Henderson's absence, a new formula for success had yet to be developed.

Winfield lamented Henderson's exit, but he was far too busy trying to rebuild his body from a year's layoff and serious back surgery. The Yankee who missed Henderson the most — on the field at least — was Mattingly, the heart and soul of the team.

Mattingly, as captain of the team, and because he was an ultrapolite Midwesterner, was not one to decry or belittle the players remaining in Yankee pinstripes. But when he came to the plate, he knew Henderson was no longer on the bases to harass the opposing pitcher into a mistake. He knew the Yankees lineup was now more toothless. Randolph, a shrewd number two hitter behind Henderson, was also gone. Mattingly, who had recently signed a five-year, $19 million contract that made him the highest-paid player in baseball, knew that Henderson's daring swagger and Randolph's competent batsmanship were no longer setting the table for him and other Yankees hitters.

Mattingly saw a team that was losing its bite and beginning to doubt itself. The Yankees, lacking direction, were a team cast adrift. "The lack of a plan, the constant changes, the impact of all that had been building," Mattingly said in 2016. "But something in and around 1990 was worse. There wasn't the right plan.

"Or there wasn't a plan. Maybe that was the real problem. We needed a plan. We needed someone who could plan."

3

Buck Naked

FOR THE FIRST Yankees game of the 1990 season, there was a new presence, one altogether out of place, sitting in the last row of the press box. The new face was neither a member of the news media nor a front-office employee.

It was thirty-three-year-old William Nathaniel Showalter III.

He was a new invention in baseball: the eye in the sky.

The Yankees were one of two teams that used this novel scouting tool. It meant placing a coach behind home plate and about 50 feet above the field — roughly at the mezzanine level in a baseball stadium — where the coach could better observe the positioning of the players and the signals from the base coaches and managers in the dugout, and also take notes on the strengths and deficiencies of both teams as they reacted to various game situations.

By Major League Baseball rules, Showalter was forbidden from communicating with the rest of the coaching staff during games, but he wrote elaborate, copious reports on what he saw from his perch above the diamond.

The job paid $50,000 a year, or half what the other coaches were earning. "And in New York City, $50,000 didn't go far — I was losing money," Showalter said.

Years later, Showalter had his doubts about whether manager Bucky Dent — or anyone — was reading his detailed, meticulous accounts of the movements he perceived during games. But as it turned out, someone named Steinbrenner was intently scouring Showalter's missives on his view of the game within the game.

And that someone was not George Steinbrenner, but George's elder son, Hank. And that mattered a great deal down the road.

Buck Showalter had been a Yankees minor league manager and player —he picked up his nickname in the minors because teammates said he liked to walk around the locker room "buck naked." When called up to be the eye in the sky in 1990, Showalter would be in uniform and on the field before games, pitching batting practice or hitting ground balls to infielders. Then he would shower and change into civilian clothes and take an elevator to the press box.

Most press boxes are loud, jocular places where the repartee is mostly nonstop—at least until late in games, when the noise of fingers pecking at keyboards replaces the banter. But Showalter in this setting generally kept to himself, sitting as far from the working press as possible. He wasn't antisocial or distrustful; Showalter actually enjoyed interacting with reporters. He is a gifted storyteller who would have been at home in Casey Stengel's 1950s prime.

But the eye-in-the-sky assignment was a crucial gig to Showalter, and like the high school principal's son that he was, he took it somberly and seriously. When the game commenced, Showalter would grow quiet and intense. He stared straight ahead with a determined, fixed mien, and his eyes would dart around the field even as his head and body would remain motionless. He sometimes held a stopwatch, and he wrote continually in one of two loose-leaf notebooks. One of the notebooks had drawings depicting the infield diamond and the outfield configurations. In the other, he would make X's and O's with sketched lines showing the paths of base hits, ground balls and throws.

Nowadays, every team has a gaggle of employees who analyze the same game data as it is gathered by sophisticated, baseball-specific software programs that collect statistics on launch angles, bat speeds and vector mathematics, which would have seemed unimaginable to Showalter at the time. In 1990, he was helping the Yankees get started by doing it the hard way: in longhand notes as the newly minted eye in the sky.

After games, Showalter would descend to the clubhouse, to quiz his fellow coaches about why certain strategies unfolded as they did in the game. And then, since Showalter also kept his own journal on a baseball season, he would make more personal notes, mostly on things to remember and lessons to absorb. He sometimes awoke at night to jot down a new observation that popped into his head.

There was much to absorb, catalog and process — for a very good reason. Showalter had never been in the major leagues before.

Showalter was born in 1956 in DeFuniak Springs, Florida, and he forevermore spoke with the Southern accent of someone whose Florida panhandle hometown was five miles from the Alabama border.

He was a sports star in a racially mixed community that was segregated, not by law but by custom. Showalter's father was known as Bill, and his only son was called Nat. Bill Showalter had been a football star at Milligan College in Tennessee. When World War II began, he enlisted in the US Army, where he was assigned to the famed 1st Infantry Division, a combat unit immortalized in the film *The Big Red One*. Bill Showalter was part of three monumental invasions, at Normandy, Sicily and Algiers. He was awarded a Bronze Star for bravery, a character trait he did not exhibit only on the battlefield.

As principal of the middle school and then the high school in the tiny Florida town of Century, where Bill lived with his wife, three daughters and son, he knew what federal laws said about the mandated racial makeup of schools across the land. Century had not been in accord with those laws, and Bill took it upon himself to lead the fight to desegregate Century's schools. As just one example, when the town's schoolteachers, hell-bent on reform, went on strike, Bill went on strike with them.

It was not a popular stand in many parts of Century.

The Showalters' household phone rang throughout that first night of the strike, and Bill took the calls and listened to the threats. But when the strike ended, he went back to enforcing the desegregation plan he had helped devise.

When his son was eleven years old, he put him in the front seat of the family pickup truck and drove to an all-black neighborhood to play in organized baseball games, even if it meant that there was just one white face on the field. "There's another world out there, son, and the more you know about it, the better off you'll be," Bill Showalter said.

One Sunday morning, he took his entire family to the black church in town. "I'll never forget all of us walking down the center aisle of the church and seeing the shocked expressions on the faces of people turn into smiles," Buck Showalter said in a 2016 interview in the small office of his Dallas home. "I was never so proud of my father, and I knew right then what it meant to have honor and conviction."

Bill had his son accompany him to watch University of Alabama football games and encouraged him to observe Bear Bryant closely throughout the contests. On the drive back to Florida after one game, Buck told his father that he was surprised because Bryant was remarkably stoic on the sidelines.

"Beware of coaches who do too much active coaching during games," Bill Showalter said. "It means they didn't do their jobs before the game."

Then Bill Showalter asked, "But do you think Bear was watching every single thing that happened on the field?"

Answered Buck: "Like a hawk."

Bill Showalter smiled.

As a lefty quarterback who mostly ran the football, Buck Showalter scored a lot of touchdowns for his high school team. He was also known for changing plays that his coach sent in from the sidelines. He did it at the line of scrimmage after assessing the defense, using code words he had explained to teammates in the huddle. It was a system rarely used in high school football in 1973, and at first Showalter's coach protested.

But on films of the games, the coach noticed that the revised plays Buck was calling were based on sound strategy and highly productive, too. He encouraged his quarterback to continue his role as a play caller, and the Century High School team lost only one game all season.

But at five-foot-nine and 155 pounds, Showalter knew his future wasn't in football. He instead accepted a baseball scholarship to Mississippi State, where he set the school's record for batting average one season when he hit .459.

Sometimes after a college game, a teammate would tell Buck he saw his father at the game, which was news to Buck.

"He didn't want to distract me or put pressure on me," Buck said of his father. "So he would drive three or four hours to watch me play — standing way out by right field or somewhere I wouldn't see him — and then drive home afterward."

Buck graduated from Mississippi State with a bachelor of science degree in education, in tribute to his father.

The Yankees made Showalter a fifth-round draft pick, even though he was a lefty-hitting and lefty-throwing first baseman without much power. He became a lifetime .294 batter in seven minor league seasons. "He'd get 150 hits in 500 at-bats and every one would be a single," said one of his minor league managers, and the future Yankees manager, Stump Merrill.

And Showalter was known for sitting next to the manager during games so he could pepper him with questions. "He was very inquisitive about everything," Merrill said. "He'd say, 'Why'd we hit-and-run here?

Why'd we steal there? Why aren't we pitching around this guy? Why is the outfield playing back? Does it really make sense to bunt with a runner on first base and a lefty on the mound? Because the runner is going to get a bad jump.' I'd wonder how he had time to do all that thinking and asking and play the game, too."

But questioning every baseball tenet was part of Showalter's DNA. He wanted to try to verify with statistics or personal insight every strategy, theory or bromide the game had handed down through the years. Once, when he laced a blistering line drive right at an infielder for an out, he returned to the dugout and heard a familiar, age-old baseball maxim: "Don't worry, Buck, the line drives and seeing-eye base hits even out over the season."

The adage is meant to describe how a batter, in the course of a season, will be credited with a certain number of base hits he does not deserve — weak grounders that nonetheless dribble into the outfield, for instance — and they will be offset by all the well-struck liners, long fly balls and hard grounders that become outs because of good fielding plays, good positioning by the defense or simple dumb luck.

"I decided to keep track of every one of those incidences that happened to me one season to see if they did in fact even out," Showalter told me years later.

For the 1979 season, with the West Haven Yankees in southern Connecticut, Showalter had 526 plate appearances. He batted .279, with 51 runs batted in — a decent year. "But things did not even out," Showalter said. "I had 15 more instances of bad luck. Give me those 15 hits, and I hit .311."

The next year, Showalter kept track again. He batted .324 with 82 RBI for the Yankees' team in Nashville. "Everybody in the organization said I had rebounded with a great year," Showalter said. "And it was a great year."

He laughed, then added: "But guess what? Things didn't even out again — this time I got lucky 21 more times than I got unlucky. Take those away, and I hit .285, or pretty much the same as the season before."

Showalter wondered what other diagnostic tools or statistical analysis — quantifiable data — could help explain what was happening on a baseball diamond, and whether it would help predict the performance of a team or any given lineup of players. He started recording his findings in a notebook. "It taught me not to accept conventional wisdom," he said. "I listened to everything my baseball elders told me — I even kept journals about what was said — but I wondered about all the things said that had gone unproven. Or the things nobody ever said or never thought of."

Meanwhile, his status with the Yankees was sagging. He was also behind two future stars on the Yankees' first-base depth chart: the graceful, future American League MVP Don Mattingly and the lumbering but powerful Steve Balboni, who would end up hitting 181 home runs in the big leagues. Showalter probably could have latched on as a utility infielder, had he thrown right-handed.

As Merrill said: "Buck was sneaky good. Once he weaseled his way into the lineup you couldn't get him out of the lineup because he would get two or three hits every night. The next thing you know he's played the whole year for you — and once he led the league in hitting.

"But he didn't have a natural position for a big league prospect because he didn't hit enough home runs for a first baseman or a corner outfielder. And he wasn't fast enough to play center field. But he surely knew how the game should be played. He was never surprised by any signal I'd give him — suicide squeeze, hit-and-run, whatever. He was way ahead of you. He was thinking along with the manager."

But Buck could also recognize who the truly gifted prospects were in the major leagues. Once, in a Class AA minor league game, he faced lefty starter Mark Langston, who was on his way to a sixteen-year major league career. Langston struck out Buck with a slider that broke so sharply he missed the ball by a foot.

Buck called his father and said, "Dad, don't sell the mules yet. I'll be home shortly."

Or so he likes to tell the story, always with a self-deprecating laugh.

But the reality was that in 1983, Buck's batting average had dropped to .269 and Mattingly had already made an impressive debut at Yankee Stadium. The writing was on the wall. There were 21 position players on the Yankees' top minor league team that year; all of them eventually made it to the major leagues except one. And that player, Buck Showalter, was released by the Yankees at the end of the season.

"The year was not a total loss," he said years later. "I got married that spring."

In early 1983, Buck had been demoted from the Yankees' affiliate in Columbus to the team's Class AA team in Nashville. Hours before one of his first home games that year in Nashville, he approached a pretty young blond woman named Angela McMahan, who was selling programs for the team.

"He said he was new to the team and needed the program to learn the names of his teammates — what a line, huh?" Angela Showalter said, retelling the story. "Then he asked for the program for free. I said no. And he went into the clubhouse and got money.

"I didn't think too much of it — these minor league ballplayers come and go. But not long after, one of his roommates had a birthday party and I went to it. I saw him there, and the rest is history.

"But I'll tell you what. I was thrust into the baseball life right away. When we got married, I remember we left our church wedding reception, got in Buck's car and drove to spring training. We left that afternoon."

While the Yankees in 1983 had cut Showalter loose as a player, they did ask him to work in the franchise's instructional league for a year and then offered him a job as manager at the lowest level of the team's minor league system. "I had watched Buck as a player since he was in college," said Bill Livesey, the team's scouting director in the early eighties, who had been promoted to vice president of scouting and player development. "The way he played, he was a coach out there already. He was that cerebral."

With Livesey's urging, in 1985, the twenty-eight-year-old Showalter agreed to take over a ragtag team of first-year pros in the rolling hills of a flagging, former railroad town: Oneonta, New York.

"We had a small little apartment in Oneonta and not much money, but I remember we bought a fairly new invention, the VCR," Angela said more than thirty years later, referring to the videocassette recorder, which in the mid-eighties still cost a pricey $400. "We needed the VCR because Buck wanted to tape all the New York Yankees games. He would manage an Oneonta Yankees game, stick around in the clubhouse until all the players left and then come home."

Angela would make her husband a bologna sandwich, and Buck would sit up and watch the entire Yankees game on the VCR, because he felt it was important to understand where the top of the organization was headed. Also, the Yankees' manager in 1985 was Billy Martin, who was already a dugout legend. Showalter studied him.

Then, after dissecting the Yankees, Showalter would turn his television to another relatively new phenomenon: ESPN. There, in the dead of night, he could watch the cable network's highlights of baseball games from around the country.

Years later, Angela Showalter was asked if Buck had a favorite song.

"The theme from *ESPN SportsCenter*," she answered.

Showalter's Oneonta team had only two position players who would ever make it to the major leagues, and that duo combined to suit up a total of 58 big league games. The roster was a mix of raw kids out of high school, college prospects and castoffs from other organizations. The team sometimes had a *Bad News Bears* feel to it. Visiting Oneonta that summer, I thought I heard the players discuss batting technique around the pregame batting cage. There was talk about pulling your wrist in one direction as you moved your head and chin in the opposite direction.

But it was not a baseball conversation. It turned out that the eighteen- and nineteen-year-olds were talking about something else they were learning: shaving their faces.

The team was full of dreamers, including catcher Todd Ezold, who thought his future was not behind home plate but on the mound as a pitcher.

Showalter told Ezold he would let him pitch at some point, but first he wanted to see him throw in the bullpen before a game. Ezold began to warm up, throwing from the bullpen mound to a teammate. Buck walked over and stood next to the catcher, as if he were in a batter's box alongside the bullpen home plate. It was the best way to see what Ezold's fastball looked like to a hitter. Buck didn't see any danger in that. He'd made 3,292 plate appearances in the minor leagues and had been hit by a pitch just 15 times.

But Ezold's first pitch with Buck standing near the plate sailed inside and struck Buck just above his right ear. He was not wearing a helmet.

As Showalter lay on the ground, he heard his salty pitching coach, Russ "Monk" Meyer, who'd had a long stint with the Brooklyn Dodgers in the 1950s, say: "Don't get up, Buck, there's blood coming out of your ear. You're pretty fucked up."

Showalter was whisked by ambulance to the nearest hospital, which was in Cooperstown, home of the Baseball Hall of Fame.

"It was not exactly how I planned to get to Cooperstown in a baseball uniform," he later said.

He was back with the team a few days later. But to this day, he has some trouble hearing out of his right ear. If someone is speaking to him in a crowded, noisy place, he will crook his head so that his good ear is free to hear the conversation.

If the 1985 Oneonta team was an irregular bunch, the players none-theless listened to their young skipper. He treated them like men, even if many were still boys, and he was still Bill Showalter's son, which is to say he was a disciplinarian. He might have been close enough in age to be their older brother, but he wanted to lead his charges, not be their friend.

And Showalter's band of young misfits won more than 70 percent of their games and the league championship. The next year at Oneonta, with different players, Showalter's Yankees won more than 76 percent of their games and another championship. Promoted to the Yankees' Class A farm affiliate in Fort Lauderdale in 1987, he won another minor league championship. Sent up the ladder again, this time to Class AA Albany, New York, he set a record for wins in a league that had been around for seventy-five years. And he won yet another league title.

Decades later, Showalter would point to his five seasons as a minor league manager as a formative period when he was allowed to develop his own style of managing. "You're in a little town in upstate New York and you're really there all by yourself," he said. "Especially back then, before the widespread use of video. What you are doing or what you were trying to do was unseen by your bosses. They got reports, but as the manager, as the guy sitting in the front of the bus, you're all by yourself.

"But I learned that it's really about what you do when nobody is looking that shapes you. You get a lot of opportunities to do the right thing or the wrong thing when nobody's looking. And how you respond to that, it can set the course for everything to follow."

Showalter's record as a minor league manager was 360-207, a winning percentage of .635. His teams won 14 of 18 postseason games.

Clete Boyer had been a Yankee All-Star infielder who became a roving instructor in the team's minor leagues and was a coach for Billy Martin in 1988. In 1990, Oakland Athletics manager Tony La Russa was widely considered the greatest baseball mind working in a dugout. Said Boyer that year: "I wouldn't say Showalter is better than Tony La Russa. But I'd say he and La Russa are the two best managers around. He's just got a great knack for the game. He's like Billy Martin. He keeps other guys off balance."

Boyer also knew that Martin was fond of Showalter and had taken him under his wing during spring training in 1988.

Granted, Showalter, who did not drink much, was the perfect designated driver for Martin's hard-drinking crew during their late-night escapades. And Showalter still tells stories of dumping half a dozen drinks in potted plants when no one was looking, so he could survive trips to "dinner" with Martin that, in fact, never included eating.

But during the day, Martin also had Showalter walk around the Yankees' training complex with him, schooling him on finer points of the game. He had Buck sit next to him during exhibition games, and Martin never turned away a question. "I thought I was pretty observant," Showalter said. "Billy opened my eyes to all the other things I wasn't seeing from the dugout. He talked about reading a pitcher's front foot to know when a base runner could break for second base on a steal. He talked about not just following the ball on a play but watching the fielders.

"Take a ball that one of your guys hits into the right-center-field gap. Billy said don't watch the ball; you know it's going to be a double or a triple. Watch to see if the pitcher is backing up third base. Is the left fielder moving? Are the relay guys in the proper order? How are the outfielders' and infielders' arms? You have a checklist of things to look for that might tell you something that you can use later."

Martin taught Showalter one of his favorite managerial sayings: Preparation always shows itself in the spontaneity of the moment.

And Billy Martin schooled Showalter in a manager's most magical advantage: stealing the other manager's signs to his players and coaches.

"Every team has the batter give a return signal to the third-base coach that acknowledges that a bunt or a hit-and-run is on," Showalter said, recalling part of Martin's sign-stealing advice. "If you watch, you can pick up the return signal — the batter taps his cleats or touches the brim of his cap. The key is to watch closely early in the game when they're not doing any of those things, then notice the difference later in the game when more of those kinds of plays are going on."

Others in the Yankees chain of command started to recognize Showalter's skill at stealing signs. "Buck was probably the best I've seen other than Billy, who was just a genius at it," said Gene Michael, who was then a team scout and an adviser to George Steinbrenner. "Buck's baseball IQ was extremely high; he was way ahead of the curve for someone so young. More than that, you could just see that the wheels were always turning in his head. He was kind of plotting a course, always thinking ahead."

Michael would know, since he was doing the same thing. The Yankees needed all the help they could get when it came to someone making a plan and having the fortitude to stick to it.

And as it happened, the Yankees brass had plans for their precocious strategist from the Florida panhandle. Buck Showalter just didn't know it yet.

4

Stumped

SIX WEEKS INTO the 1990 season, the Yankees were already in last place, six games under .500 and seven games out of first place. Pascual Pérez, the team's enigmatic ace, pitched five shutout innings and won his first start of the year, but left his third start with a shoulder spasm. A day later, he was on the disabled list, where he would remain for the rest of the season.

In late April, reeling from a string of losses, the team traded for Claudell Washington, who at thirty-five years old was in the last of his 17 major league seasons. The lefty-swinging Washington was there to platoon in left field with Winfield, who had recently gone 0-for-20.

Washington turned out to be a dreadful experiment. He went 8-for-55 in his first month as a Yankee.

The team's defense was no more efficient. The rookie third baseman Mike Blowers made four errors in one game, which led to five unearned runs and another defeat.

Everyone in the American League seemed to be beating up on the Yankees. The defending World Series champion Oakland A's, with Rickey Henderson leading the way, were already 6-0 against the Yankees.

In late May, Winfield was traded to the California Angels for pitcher Mike Witt, who, in keeping with recent Yankees tradition when it came to trades, was a couple of seasons from ending his career. Winfield was less than two years away from hitting .290 and driving in 108 runs for the Toronto Blue Jays. He also had an extra-inning RBI double that won the 1992 World Series for Toronto. Winfield would play until he was forty-three years old.

Dent had pushed for the Winfield trade, something not forgotten by the team's owner.

Early in 1990, most everything the Yankees did came off as clownish. Late in one game, Dent used a pinch hitter for his last available infielder, then had to play backup catcher Rick Cerone at second base, where Cerone had never before played. A miscue by Cerone as he tried to turn a double play led to another Yankees defeat.

The dynamic rookie Deion Sanders, the future pro football Hall of Famer, was inserted into another game when the Yankees needed a stolen base. And Sanders did steal second base, to set up a potential game-tying hit by the next Yankees batter, Steve Sax. Except Sanders, on his own, broke for third base before Sax could swing the bat. The inning, the scoring threat and, in essence, the game ended when Sanders was thrown out at third.

The bad news was piling up on the beleaguered Dent, whom Steinbrenner never expected to last the 1990 season anyway. In late 1989, Steinbrenner had told Billy Martin to stay ready, that he would be back for a sixth tour as Yankees manager, "when Bucky screws up."

That idea expired with Martin when he died in an auto accident on Christmas Day in 1989. But Steinbrenner's faith in Dent remained just as shaky.

On Monday, June 4, the Yankees went to Boston's Fenway Park and lost their third consecutive game. They lost again to the Red Sox the next day. The Yankees had the worst record in baseball.

Not surprisingly, George wanted to make a change in the dugout. But the usual suspects were not available. Piniella was succeeding in his first year as manager of the Reds. Michael had long ago adamantly refused to manage again. Bob Lemon was long retired. Davey Johnson, a proven winner, had recently been fired by the Mets, but he was known as a players' manager who did not enforce strict rules — one of the reasons the Mets let him go — and that turned off Steinbrenner.

The New York newspapers could not figure out who Dent's heir apparent would be. But George had already hatched a secret plan for Dent's successor, one that few in the Yankees brain trust knew about until the early days of June.

George had been thinking about it for weeks.

In 1990, the manager of the Yankees' Class AAA minor league team in Columbus, Ohio, was Carl Harrison "Stump" Merrill. Columbus was the

home of George's wife, Joan, and George made frequent trips to Columbus to see his in-laws.

This was Merrill's second term as Columbus manager, and he had first
met Steinbrenner in 1984.

"George came to one of our home games and he was sitting right next
to the dugout," Merrill said in 2017, sitting in the lobby of his hotel a
mile from the Yankees' Tampa spring training complex, where he acts as
a special instructor. "I forget which player it was, but one of the players
hits a single and tries to stretch it into a double. He slides into second but
he's out. That ends the inning, and the player heads to right field for the
next inning.

"Back then, George had a strict rule that our pant legs had to be
bloused, which means the socks and stirrups must show at least to the
shins. This kid, when he slid into second, one of his pant legs unbloused,
so he's standing in right field with one pant leg down to his shoes.

"About three minutes later, I was told to go over to where Mr. Steinbrenner was sitting, and I said to myself, 'This is great. I'm going to get
to meet the boss. Maybe he wants to tell me what a good job I'm doing.'

"I get over there and George asks, 'Who the fuck is your right fielder?'"
Stump gave George the player's name.

"Well," George said, "you tell him if he doesn't fucking blouse his pants
he'll be on the next fucking plane out of here. You got that?"

Stump laughed telling the story, adding, "I just said 'Yes, sir.' And that
was my introduction to the world of George Steinbrenner."

But Stump, who is five-foot-eight and picked up his nickname as a star
catcher at the University of Maine in the mid-1960s, became something
of a Steinbrenner favorite, at least for a minor league manager. And with
good reason.

Beginning in 1978, Stump managed at four different levels of the Yankees' farm system, from rookie league to Class AAA. His teams had finished in first place at each level, including a streak of seven consecutive
regular-season championships, from '78 to '84. And George Steinbrenner
liked winning at everything.

Stump had also won a championship in 1989, and his Columbus team
was humming along at the top of the standings in May 1990 when George
was a frequent visitor. George's father-in-law, who had been a prominent
real estate developer, had died, and it took several trips to Columbus to
settle the estate. Steinbrenner became a regular in Merrill's office.

"One day George leaned forward and said to me, 'Do you think you could handle our major league team?'" Merrill said. "And I said, 'I think I can.' And he says, 'Don't be watching the scoreboard for our results, but if we keep losing, we're going to make a change. And I'm talking to you about that now.'"

Stump admitted that he could not help but watch the Yankees spiraling down the American League East standings. And sure enough, he got the call on June 5 to meet the Yankees in Boston the next day, because he was going to succeed Bucky Dent.

The mercilessness of firing Dent while he was in Boston, the scene of Dent's greatest triumph, apparently did not occur to the Yankees' owner.

But Merrill almost did not make the Boston news conference that would name him the new manager — the eighteenth managerial change in the eighteen years Steinbrenner had owned the team.

"The Yankees had arranged to leave an airline ticket for me at the Columbus airport so I could fly to Boston," Merrill said. "But the ticket said 'Stump Merrill.' And I needed an ID to pick it up and my driver's license reads, 'Carl Merrill.'

"They won't let me on the plane. They kept talking about my alias. The airline was adamant: 'No, sir, no way you're getting on the plane.' And I'm thinking that if I don't get on that flight I'm going to be the first Yankees manager fired before he even gets to his first game."

Eventually, someone at the Columbus airport got in touch with the Yankees and Stump boarded his flight. His welcome in Boston was rocky. Inside the visiting manager's office at Fenway Park later that day, reporters were disbelieving.

One reporter asked Merrill how long he thought it would be before he was fired.

"Really? On the first day you ask that?" Stump said.

A New York tabloid the next day had a headline that read, "Stump Who?"

It was a reasonable question, especially since every recent Yankees manager had been a prominent baseball figure and every Yankees manager since 1965 had at least played in the major leagues.

Stump had underwhelming playing statistics: a lifetime .234 batting average in six minor league seasons.

A Maine native and born on the coastline, he speaks with the same thick accent as the local lobstermen he worked alongside as a boy when he wasn't playing baseball and football. Recruited by the University of

Maine, where he played both sports, he was at practice one day, walking with a six-foot-six teammate. His college coach, Jack Butterfield, was the one who remarked that his catcher, beside his tall teammate, looked like a stump.

"And nicknames stay with you in baseball," Stump said. "The only people who call me Carl are the ones I went to high school with."

Those are the folks who recall Merrill as a talented athlete who played with a scrappiness that seemed to have intensified after his father died, unexpectedly, of a heart attack when Merrill was a high school freshman. "I never thought I was that close to my father," Stump said many years later. "I found out how wrong I was."

He attended the University of Maine in part because Butterfield, aware that Stump's mother was working two jobs to support her four children, arranged for cheap lodging, at $30 a month. One year, Butterfield let Stump stay at his own home.

As a junior at the 1964 College World Series, Stump led Maine to upsets of Southern Cal and Arizona State and a third-place finish, a rare feat for a Northeastern institution, let alone one with a campus where the snow did not melt until April.

Stump became a second-round draft pick of the Philadelphia Phillies, but a knee injury stalled his career. He did play in six leagues and five states in a minor league odyssey that was highly educational for the perceptive and quick-witted Merrill. He played for several managers, trying to pick up something from every one, including his last, Lou Kahn, who had played an astounding seventeen years in the minor leagues, from 1936 to 1953.

But it was Butterfield, who became the Yankees' director of player development and scouting in 1977, who brought Merrill into the Yankees fold. And that, too, was something that always endeared Merrill to Steinbrenner, because Steinbrenner personally recruited Butterfield to the Yankees after Butterfield left Maine to coach at the University of South Florida.

Butterfield died in an auto accident in November 1979, just after Merrill's second year of managing in the Yankees minors. Showalter was on that team, as was future Yankees starter and closer Dave Righetti.

Showalter went with Merrill when he was moved on to the Nashville Sounds, where the roster included Mattingly. But by 1981, the big star on that team was a fleet, switch-hitting outfielder, Willie McGee, the Yankees' 1977 first-round draft choice, who batted .322 with 63 RBI.

Merrill nurtured a lot of top Yankees talent in those years and gritted his teeth when they were traded away. McGee, for example, was traded in 1981 to the St. Louis Cardinals for pitcher Bob Sykes. McGee would go on to win two National League batting titles and the 1985 NL Most Valuable Player award before retiring after eighteen major league seasons with 2,254 hits and 352 stolen bases. Sykes never pitched for the Yankees but did eventually compile a forgettable 23-26 career major league record.

As McGee said in a 2016 interview: "In the Yankee organization as a minor leaguer, we were always told that if you were good enough, you'd make it. But back then everybody knew that getting traded somewhere else was your best bet because the Yankees then were signing free agents instead of going with young players."

Toiling away in the minors, Merrill tried to remind himself that he was still helping the big league club by developing the down-on-the-farm Yankees. But he scratched his mostly balding head from time to time in befuddlement. "There were some frustrating trades of young talent we had nurtured," Merrill said of his time in the minors. "You hoped we'd learn our lesson eventually."

He kept his head down and stayed busy. Every fall, he returned to Maine, where he refereed high school basketball games, helped coach the football team at tiny Bowdoin College and jogged through the often snow-covered streets of his hometown of Topsham (population 9,000), where he lived on Merrymeeting Road, across the street from his brother.

"It was a good life," he said in 2017, looking back. But he also recalled that his wife, Carole, spent every winter trying to persuade him to use his two college degrees to become a teacher instead of a baseball lifer.

He would argue: "But I'm already good at what I do. I loved what I was doing."

Replied Carole: "Just so you know that you'll never manage the New York Yankees. You have to be famous or a great ex–major leaguer to do that."

"I don't care," Stump said. "It's not on my bucket list."

Still, summer after summer, the victories kept piling up for Stump's minor league teams. Finally, in 1985, he was promoted to Yogi Berra's Yankees coaching staff. But Steinbrenner fired Berra after just 16 games that season, and Billy Martin, the new manager, sent Stump back to the minors.

Stump was back with the Yankees when Lou Piniella became the manager in 1986, and coached first base for parts of the next two seasons. He was expecting to return to that job in 1988, but Steinbrenner fired Piniella and hired Martin again. Stump was out. "George fired Billy five times, but I might be the only guy that Billy fired twice," Stump said with a smirk.

Back in the minors, he was dispatched to the Yankees' affiliate in northern Virginia, where the team was floundering and 10 games under .500. By the season's end, Stump had another championship team.

And then, one June day in 1990, he was the forty-six-year-old Yankee skipper in the visiting clubhouse at Fenway Park.

Carole Merrill drove down from her modest home on Merrymeeting Road and stood beneath the Fenway grandstands that evening with a look of shock and wonder. "Never in a million years," she said, shaking her head with a smile. "Never dreamed this."

Earlier that day, in a room at the Sheraton Boston Hotel, Buck Showalter's wife, Angela, was sobbing. Buck had just told her that Dent was going to be fired. Word had leaked that Stump was on his way to Boston, but none of Dent's coaches — and that included the eye-in-the-sky coach — knew of their fate.

Buck expected to be let go along with the rest of the coaching staff, which was customary. Angela quickly recalled the June rent she had already paid back in New York, money she could barely afford even when Buck had a job. She had considered the trip to Boston a fun perk; she wanted to show the city's historic sites to her four-year-old daughter, Allie. Now, in tears, Angela started packing to check out of the hotel, wondering where they would be going next.

Back to the minors? To another organization? To what?

Buck, the son of a decorated Army veteran, was not going to be dismissed out of uniform. "I went to Fenway at 11 that morning, put on my uniform and sat at my locker," he said. "I figured, I'm going to be at work if they come to fire me. I'm not going to be sitting around somewhere."

George Bradley, one of the team's front-office executives, approached his locker to tell him that he was soon going to be named the new third-base coach under Stump — and he would be the hitting coach until another hitting coach was hired. Oh, and his salary would be doubled.

"I went from not having a job to making $100,000 and having to work in the third-base coaching box at Fenway Park that very night," Showalter said twenty-seven years later, his eyes widening as he told the story.

It was about five years before cell phones would be ubiquitous, so Buck had no easy way of reaching Angela. There was a phone in the manager's office — not available amid the tumult of the day — and one other phone in a hallway near that office, but that was in constant use by Yankees officials as they arranged Dent's exit news conference and Stump's first briefing with New York and Boston reporters.

The clubhouse was soon a madhouse. And Showalter had a new job to prepare for.

"I was scared shitless," he said.

He never did phone Angela.

"I didn't know what was going on, but I had a ticket to the game so I figured I better go," she said, recalling the day many years later. "No news was good news, right?"

At her seat with Allie, she looked onto the field as the game was about to begin and saw her husband in uniform on the top step of the Yankees' dugout. That had never happened before. Not at game time.

Then Buck jogged across the diamond and stood in the third-base coaching box. And that's how she learned that Buck had not been fired — and he had a new, prominent job, too.

"When I got back to the hotel I told her that my salary had been doubled," Buck said. "We almost went crazy."

In his pregame press briefing, Stump had said: "My main concern is to get them to playing and having fun. I'm not saying anything against Bucky — I don't want to throw darts — but from watching them, it looked like a listless ball club from what I saw."

He added, "But I'm not someone thrown here from outer space that's going to perform a miracle."

Indeed. The Yankees went out and lost the game that night. And three more after that, extending the team's losing streak to eight games. They had also lost 12 of their last 13. That led to a streak of 18 defeats in 22 games. By the last days of June, the Yankees were 15 games out of first place and 17 games under .500. Some Yankees home games were now drawing about 10,000 or less, though the official paid attendance was announced as closer to 20,000.

That might not have been the worst news for George Steinbrenner. Baseball commissioner Fay Vincent had recently received the report of John Dowd, the Pete Rose investigator, who was looking into Steinbrenner's $40,000 payment to Howie Spira for incriminating evidence on Dave Winfield's foundation. Vincent now wanted Steinbrenner to appear at a hearing in his office on July 5, one day after Steinbrenner's sixtieth birthday.

One New York newspaper wrote that Vincent had already decided to ban Steinbrenner for one year, which Vincent denied. "George has yet to make his presentation," the commissioner said.

But there was an unmistakable uneasiness enveloping the 1990 Yankees, an almost palpable cloak of doom. The bad karma was mounting.

5

Dazed and Confused

ANDY HAWKINS WAS never supposed to be the Yankees' starting pitcher on July 1 in Chicago. He wasn't even supposed to have a Yankee uniform.

On June 5, the day before Stump Merrill was hired, Hawkins had pitched miserably — again. His 1990 ERA had ballooned to 8.56. His ERA in his last two starts was 45.00 (10 earned runs in two innings pitched).

So the Yankees offered Hawkins a choice: be demoted to the minor leagues or be released. As a nine-year veteran, the team could not demote him without his permission.

Hawkins, who would still receive the $1.2 million the Yankees agreed to pay him in 1990, chose to be released. He had packed his bags and was awaiting a flight home to Texas.

Then Mike Witt was injured, again. The Yankees needed Hawkins after all. Unpack your bags, they told him. He was still under contract.

Hawkins rebounded with four good starts in succession. Same guy, different results.

So Hawkins was confident when he took the mound at Comiskey Park before 30,642 fans on July 1. It was 70 degrees. As the day went on, the wind blew in from the outfield with gusts up to 25 and 30 miles an hour.

"First of all, there might have never been a no-hitter — we wouldn't be talking about this game if not for the wind," Hawkins told Steve Politi of the *Newark Star-Ledger* on the twenty-fifth anniversary of the game in 2015. "Because in the third inning, Sammy Sosa hit a fly ball that might have gone five hundred feet. It was a certain home run. But instead, the wind blew it back into the ballpark and it was caught for an out."

Jim Leyritz, a catcher/third baseman by trade, who was making just his third start in left field for the Yankees that season, zigzagged his way under the Sosa fly ball and caught it a few feet in front of the wall separating the field from the Comiskey Park picnic area, where fans ate barbecue and drank beer in a courtyard.

In the Yankees' broadcast booth, Phil Rizzuto, the Hall of Famer whose first professional baseball game was in 1937, watched the flight of Sosa's fly ball and said, "That was one of the craziest things I've ever seen."

Actually, the crazy was only beginning.

Hawkins breezed along for several innings, needing only seven pitches to induce three ground-ball outs in the fourth inning and overcoming two walks in the fifth inning without letting a Chicago base runner past second base. "I knew I was pitching a no-hitter," Hawkins said, admitting that he wasn't used to looking at the scoreboard and seeing all zeros, "because Greg Hibbard was pitching a no-hitter for the White Sox, too."

The Yankees' first hit came with one out in the sixth inning. Hawkins retired Chicago in order, with 10 pitches, in the bottom of the sixth and threw just 17 pitches in a hitless seventh inning. The game was scoreless entering the bottom of the eighth.

The first two White Sox batters in the eighth hit pop-ups over the infield. Yankees second baseman Steve Sax wobbled as he tried to stay with the pop-ups in the windy conditions but corralled each one into his glove.

Rizzuto's comment at the time? "Everything in the air is an adventure out there right now."

So it was perhaps a blessing that Sosa, the next batter, rapped a bouncing grounder right at Yankees third baseman Mike Blowers.

It was a routine play for a major league third baseman, and Blowers backhanded the ball, but it popped out of his glove and fell at his feet. He snatched the baseball from the infield dirt and fired a strong throw to first base, but Sosa, who was about 35 pounds lighter than he would become in baseball's approaching steroids era, clearly beat Blowers's throw with a head-first slide.

It was initially called a hit by the official scorer, Bob Rosenberg. Protests in the press box and in the Yankee dugout — the howling of players and coaches could be heard one level up, in the open-air press box — led to a reversal: It was an error. Forevermore.

Blowers had made 106 errors in four seasons as a minor league infielder, or about one every four games. But he had some power and the Yankees stuck with him. Now he had opened a door for the White Sox. "I didn't know what to say or do," Blowers, a rookie, said. "It was a no-hitter. I had never been through this before."

Hawkins was not concerned. "No big deal — two outs," Hawkins, who has replayed the game for countless reporters, said in an interview many years later. "I was feeling good. No fatigue. I felt great."

His apparent calm was believable. At thirty years old, Hawkins was far from a greenhorn. The July 1 start was the 220th of his major league career. Before joining the Yankees as a free agent from San Diego in 1989, he had three seasons with 10 or more victories. He won a game for the Padres in the 1984 World Series, the first World Series victory in the franchise's history.

Hawkins was seasoned enough to be careful with the next Chicago hitter, the pesky, clever shortstop Ozzie Guillén, who would be playing in the All-Star Game in another nine days. Hawkins worked Guillén to a 3-2 count, but eventually walked him.

As the tension mounted, Hawkins walked the next batter, Lance Johnson, on four pitches, to load the bases.

Leyritz was an undrafted rookie who had played 363 games in the Yankees minor leagues — most of them for Buck Showalter. In just 32 of those games he had been asked to play the outfield. "Jim usually was in the outfield because of an injury or a substitution," Showalter said. "He was an athletic guy, but we didn't try him in the outfield at all until 1989." But it is also true that Leyritz had made a dandy sliding catch on the first play of the bottom of the first inning. Then again, no one at the time thought of it as saving the no-hitter.

The situation, and the pressure, was different now. The bases were loaded in a scoreless game that was also a no-hitter.

Hawkins's first pitch to Chicago's lefty-swinging Robin Ventura was slapped toward Leyritz. It was a high, lazy fly ball ten feet short of the warning track. In his pursuit of the ball, Leyritz at first turned his back to the infield and started running to his left as he looked over his right shoulder. Then he spun to his right with a crossover step and faced the ball as he backpedaled.

But the wind gusts were pushing the fly ball around in the sky. Soon Leyritz had turned again, running toward his right and looking over his left shoulder.

Finally, Leyritz appeared to have squared up and zeroed in on the descending ball, pausing as he raised his glove to about head high. The whole sequence, from contact with Ventura's bat to contact with Leyritz's glove, took 5.3 seconds. And at the end, the ball sharply ricocheted off the top of his glove, as if the mitt were made of steel, not soft leather. Leyritz amplified the sense of tragicomedy with a pratfall that sent him to his knees. In an instant, the ball was a dozen feet from Leyritz, bounding through the grass toward the left-field foul line.

Most of the fans in Comiskey's left-field picnic courtyard threw up their hands. One dropped his beer. Another put both hands on the top of her head, as if aghast at what she had just witnessed.

Rizzuto's call was classic. "Leyritz going back," he said, then yelped, "Don't fall!"

Finally: "Whoa, he dropped it."

Leyritz had a good postgame explanation. Even if it revealed his confusion, or the effect of the wind. "I thought it was to my left, then I thought it was to my right, and then I didn't catch it," he said.

Three runs scored on the play.

Iván Calderón was the next hitter, and he looped a soft fly ball to right fielder Jesse Barfield, who was one of the league's best outfielders and had already won two Gold Gloves.

Barfield did not have trouble with the wind. But he did struggle to find the ball in the sun. Barfield tentatively tracked the fly ball, then turned and shied away from it as he raised his hand to shade the sun. At the last minute, he stabbed at the orb going past him and the ball deflected off his glove for the third error of the inning.

Ventura scored. The White Sox were ahead, 4–0. They had not hit one ball hard in the inning.

As Rizzuto said after Barfield's miscue: "What's coming off here? It's still a no-hitter."

Dan Pasqua, an ex–Yankees phenom, popped up in the infield for the third out.

Hawkins walked off the field still throwing a no-hitter.

In the dugout, Hawkins found Leyritz and told him to forget about his gaffe, blaming the wind. Then he went to Barfield and blamed the sun.

"Classiest thing I'd ever seen," Stump Merrill said of Hawkins's reaction.

Only three Yankees batted in the ninth inning, with the last two outs coming on a double play.

Hawkins was immediately congratulated for his no-hitter in the Yankees' dugout afterward, shaking hands with nearly every player. Interviewed on the field by local broadcasters, Hawkins was cheered by the

White Sox fans who had remained in the stands. Which led to something that may never have happened before: The visiting, losing pitcher who held the home team without a hit doffed his cap to the home fans, thankful that they were cheering him.

Hawkins admitted to being thunderstruck afterward. "Reporters were asking me how I felt, and frankly I didn't know how I felt," he said during an interview in 2015, on the twenty-fifth anniversary of the game. "I felt kind of in shock about the whole thing. What are you supposed to feel?

"It's not how I envisioned a no-hitter. Obviously, you expect to win in that situation and come off the field in jubilation. That's not what happened."

When his playing career ended in 1991, Hawkins became a pitching coach for the Texas Rangers. Like a lot of coaches, his assignment kept changing. By 2010, he had been a pitching coach for several Class AAA minor league teams affiliated with various major league clubs.

In a 2017 interview, he conceded that the no-hitter in a loss has come up often during his coaching career. Minor league pitchers Hawkins has tutored will inquire about his major league career, and he will talk about winning a World Series game for the San Diego Padres and his 18-8 record in 1985.

But those same young pitchers will eventually go to social media or Google to look up Andy Hawkins and come across the eight-inning no-hitter. "They usually ask about that game at some point," Hawkins said. "And I tell them about it. I mean, it did happen. It's part of baseball history."

But at the time, in the wake of the game on July 1, 1990, Hawkins remained dumbfounded by the circumstances. As he entered the clubhouse after the game, his teammates gave him a standing ovation. Hawkins offered an uneasy smile. "I feel dazed," he said.

The next day, George Steinbrenner called and offered to buy him a car. Hawkins said thanks, but declined. The TV shows *Good Morning America* and *Late Night with David Letterman* each called and wanted to have him as a guest. He said thanks, and declined again.

"It didn't feel like I was being recognized for the right thing," he said.

In Hawkins's next start, he fared almost as well as he did in Chicago, pitching 11⅔ innings before losing to Minnesota, 2–0.

The next time Hawkins pitched, again against the White Sox but at Yankee Stadium, Chicago starter Mélido Pérez — the brother of the Yankees' Pascual Pérez — pitched a rain-shortened, six-inning no-hitter as the White Sox won, 8–0. "It bothers me a little because I think I could have pitched a whole game without a hit," Pérez said. "But it's still a no-hitter." (Until, that is, baseball changed its definition of a no-hitter the next year, with a new ruling that required the pitcher to pitch nine innings.)

But in the wake of Pérez's rare performance, and given that he was part of another no-hitter that left a bad taste in his mouth, Hawkins, whose record was now 1-7, seemed understandably stunned. "I don't know what to say — this has been a crazy year," he said in the Yankees' locker room, tossing his cap in his locker and running his hands nervously through his hair. "I mean, what else is going to happen?"

6

Banished

GEORGE STEINBRENNER CELEBRATED his sixtieth birthday on the weekend before his actual Fourth of July birthday, at a lavish gala in a hotel outside Ocala, Florida, where he owned a prosperous horse farm. More than two hundred guests attended. At one point, a large video screen showed the opening scene from the movie *Patton,* which was perhaps Steinbrenner's favorite film.

The scene shows Patton in uniform and wearing a helmet in front of an enormous American flag, which became the lasting image of the 1970 Academy Award–winning movie. On this night, however, when the camera zoomed in on the general, everyone in the room saw Steinbrenner's face under the helmet, not Patton's.

It was a rare, carefree, lighthearted highlight for Steinbrenner in 1990. On his birthday, the Yankees lost again, 13–6, to Kansas City, which dropped their record to 28-48.

George also flew to New York that day. He was to report for a hearing before Fay Vincent in Manhattan the next morning.

The two men were actually old associates, if not quite friends. Both had graduated from Williams College, an elite liberal arts institution in the Berkshire Mountains of western Massachusetts. They had communicated and did small favors for each other over the years, as Steinbrenner took over his father's American Ship Building Company and bought the Yankees, and Vincent became a finance lawyer for the Securities and Exchange Commission, the chief executive of Columbia Pictures and the executive vice president of Coca-Cola.

But they were also very different men from disparate backgrounds.

Francis T. Vincent Jr. was the son of a Connecticut telephone company employee who dug the holes for telephone poles. His father, also called Fay, had grown up poor but had been a western Connecticut baseball and football star who attended the refined Hotchkiss prep school and Yale University on what amounted to athletic scholarships. Graduating during the Depression, Fay Sr. felt lucky to have a secure job at a utility company, even if it meant his family lived a frugal life. On weekends, he worked baseball and football games, even NFL games, as a respected umpire and referee. He was the man who made the rulings that changed games, the arbiter of right and wrong.

His son, called "Little Fay" despite being six-foot-three and 230 pounds as a young teen, revered his father and tagged along to the weekend games, developing an affinity for the tough job that officials of all kinds in sports face when they have to make important decisions. Fay Jr. also became an ardent Yankees fan. He made pilgrimages to Yankee Stadium from his New Haven home and grew to idolize Joe DiMaggio.

Fay Jr. was a football prospect at Hotchkiss who spurned Yale — and the shadow left there by his father, who had been captain of the football and baseball teams — to attend Williams.

At Williams, Vincent played tackle on the freshman football team in 1956 and looked forward to his time with the varsity. (Freshmen were not eligible for NCAA varsity football until 1972.) But that winter, a roommate, in a prank, locked Vincent in his third-floor dormitory room. Fay climbed out a window, planning to tiptoe three feet across a narrow ledge to an open window of a neighbor. But the ledge was icy and Vincent fell forty feet, crushing two vertebrae. The mishap left him temporarily paralyzed and ended his athletic career. He kept a cane at his side forevermore. It was the only way he could walk.

Steinbrenner, who was eight years older than Vincent, literally sprinted through his time at Williams. His father, Henry, had been an Olympic-level hurdler and insisted that his son run the same grueling race, periodically arranging for the four-time Olympic gold medalist Harrison Dillard to train George.

George had come to Williams from Cleveland by way of the Culver Military Academy in northern Indiana. His father, who was also a marine engineering scholar at the Massachusetts Institute of Technology, was strict, austere and domineering — a dictatorial style that exasperated

George, even if he nonetheless adopted it himself as an adult. "George was not touchy-feely," Hal Steinbrenner, George's son, said in 2017. "And he got that from his father."

Besides being a fixture on the Williams track team, Steinbrenner spent one season as a halfback on the football team. He wrote a sports column in the college newspaper, played the piano in the band and sang with the glee club, standing one row in front of Stephen Sondheim, who would go on to become perhaps the best-known composer in American musical theater.

"I had a better singing voice than Stephen," Steinbrenner insisted in a 1980 *New York* magazine story.

George did not join his father's shipbuilding empire after his college graduation in 1952 but instead spent four years as an assistant football coach for Northwestern and Purdue universities. (After a winless season at Northwestern, Steinbrenner was fired.) George also coached football at an Ohio high school.

By 1957, his father reminded him that he had not financed a privileged, private education to produce an assistant football coach. The family business beckoned, and George threw himself into it.

He was a success and well known in the capitals of commerce along the Northeastern seaboard. In the early 1970s, *Penthouse* magazine called him "the best-dressed businessman in America."

He maintained his interest in sports, becoming a part owner of the Cleveland Pipers basketball team, which played in a professional league meant to challenge the NBA. In the seventies, with a consortium of business associates and Williams College–related investors, he tried to buy the Cleveland Indians. When the Indians purchase failed, one of his financial partners told him the Yankees were likely for sale.

Steinbrenner expanded his circle of investors to raise additional funds and secure some loans to purchase the Yankees in 1973 for $10 million. George had contributed about $170,000 to the effort, which was the principal share.

From then until 1990, Steinbrenner and Vincent had interacted only occasionally, even after Vincent was named deputy baseball commissioner in 1989 by his friend Bart Giamatti, the Yale president who had become the baseball commissioner. "But in that time he had been supportive of me and I of him," Vincent said in a 2017 interview.

Still, based on observations he made in his 2002 memoir, Vincent clearly regarded Steinbrenner warily. Steinbrenner also had harshly scolded Vincent in a bizarre phone call after a deadly earthquake interrupted the 1989 World Series in San Francisco. A month earlier, Vincent had been promoted to baseball commissioner, days after Giamatti's sudden death.

The morning after the earthquake, with most of San Francisco without electricity or running water and some of the city still in flames, Vincent had done a national television interview. He was unshaven, his hair was untidy, and he did not wear a tie.

"You looked like a bum," Steinbrenner told Vincent over the phone. "Don't do that again. You represent all of us in baseball."

Vincent was offended. He had been up all night. His hotel did not even have functioning toilets.

So, entering the hearing on July 5, 1990, Vincent and Steinbrenner were not adversaries, but they were not chummy either. That became resoundingly evident early in the meeting, which would last about four hours and then continue into the next day. Almost from the outset, Vincent personally and pointedly interrogated Steinbrenner in great detail about his dealings with Howie Spira, who in March had been indicted by a federal grand jury on eight counts of trying to extort money from Steinbrenner and Dave Winfield. The two days of Steinbrenner's testimony in the commissioner's office would produce a 392-page transcript, which was leaked a few days later to the *National Sports Daily*, a new publication that would last only eighteen months.

A day after the *National* printed excerpts of the transcript, Vincent's office released the full document, although parts were redacted. The editing of Steinbrenner's comments prompted one of several disputes between Vincent's office and Steinbrenner's lawyers.

In the released transcript, Steinbrenner did not come off well. Twenty-five years later, his lawyers admitted that their client was not a convincing, robust or resilient witness in the face of Vincent's grilling. Steinbrenner's performance surprised the attorneys, but they had also not been able to prepare their client for Vincent's likely line of attack, since the commissioner had refused to give Steinbrenner's legal team a copy of John Dowd's investigative report, which would have been required in a court of law.

But this was not technically a legal proceeding.

"It is a private proceeding," Vincent wrote in his memoir, *The Last Commissioner*. As such, he continued, "the accused in a baseball hearing doesn't have much in the way of civil rights . . . no different from a private men's eating club kicking out a member for chewing gum in the dining room."

And in this proceeding, Steinbrenner, Vincent said, would not be allowed to call other witnesses to buttress his defense. He alone was left to expound on his bewildering contacts with Spira. He was not his own best witness.

Steinbrenner's explanation for giving Spira $40,000 — and having him paid circuitously through two law firms — seemed mendacious, or at least wholly mystifying. George said he gave Spira the money for a variety of reasons: compassion for Spira's financial plight (he had a sick mother and a gambling problem); fear that Spira might harm him or his family or reveal something embarrassing about their personal dealings; and worry that Spira would expose shameful lifestyle choices about, of all people, Lou Piniella, the ex–Yankees' manager.

What Steinbrenner did not do was admit to making the payment for what seemed the most obvious reason, which was also what Spira alleged: so that Spira would turn over damaging information on Winfield and his foundation.

In the hearing, it did not appear that Vincent believed any of Steinbrenner's justifications for the payment. At one point, Vincent incredulously asked George if there wasn't an obvious, singular reason he gave Spira the money — that is, to get the dirt on Winfield.

George wouldn't bite.

"This guy was a bad guy," George said. "He scared me and he really scared my children . . . I wanted him to get away from me and get away from here . . . And then there was the Lou Piniella situation. He [Spira] said that he threatened to sell information, as I recall he told me, on Lou Piniella and his sports betting habits. I didn't want to see baseball or Lou Piniella dragged through something the way it would have been sensationalized. We couldn't take it."

Piniella's only offense, if it was an offense, was that he liked to visit the horse-racing track occasionally, as he later testified to Vincent. He placed legal bets for between $20 and $50 and incurred no significant debts. Vincent later cleared Piniella of any wrongdoing.

But some of the most damning testimony in Steinbrenner's hearing with Vincent came as the result of an exchange about why George, if he feared Spira so much, did not immediately contact law enforcement authorities or the baseball commissioner's office. To quote from a portion of the hearing transcript:

VINCENT: This is really the guts of it, from where I'm sitting. I'm putting myself in your shoes . . . I'm sitting in Tampa and I'm talking to my advisers, as I assume you were. Indeed, you've testified that they told you —

STEINBRENNER: Not do it.

VINCENT: To not do it?

STEINBRENNER: Absolutely.

VINCENT: And you're a smart fellow and have been around baseball. And here is a guy we know has been involved in some bad things. We know he's a gambler or a former gambler. We know, to put it in your terms, that he may be involved in extorting money from you.

STEINBRENNER: Threatening me.

VINCENT: Yes. Why didn't you behave differently? Why didn't you call authorities? Why didn't you surround yourself with people who could protect you, both physically and legally? You might have called me . . . If it were me, I certainly would have gone to baseball and said, "Look, I'm in a very tough spot." Even if you wanted to make the payment over your advisers' recommendation, why wouldn't you have come to me to say I'm going to make a payment? You did quite the reverse. You made the payment in a way that wasn't direct. You did it through a law firm with a bunch of steps — I'm being critical here — that were not straightforward.

George's response was that he didn't know if anyone could protect him from Spira's wrath. "I mean, they shot the President of the United States and they shot the Pope," he told Vincent. "If somebody wants to shoot you, they are going to shoot you."

Later, Vincent wondered why Steinbrenner didn't realize how much he was undermining his place in baseball if he gave money to a known gambler.

VINCENT: Did anybody say to you: "George, suppose this guy takes the money and pays off gambling debts. You are now an owner in baseball financing a gambler?"

STEINBRENNER: I didn't — I never thought of that.

But Vincent had most definitely thought of it. Moreover, he knew that George Steinbrenner might never have given Howie Spira the time of day let alone met with him and instructed subordinates to talk with him

— if Spira had not floated the notion that he could prove that Dave Winfield's foundation was guilty of some malfeasance.

The hearing in Vincent's office ended. The commissioner said he would probably decide whether to discipline Steinbrenner within a few weeks.

Seven days later, George's lawyers said they were preparing to sue Vincent if he suspended their client, because the hearing had been biased and unfair. "We were prevented from presenting any case at all," Paul Curran, a Steinbrenner lawyer and a former US attorney, told me in an interview in 2000. "It was one-sided. Looking back, George wasn't given an equal chance."

Another week passed. Vincent was holed up at his summer home on Cape Cod, along with his deputy commissioner Steve Greenberg, who, like Vincent, was a Yale Law School grad. The duo, along with John Dowd, reviewed the many depositions that had been taken from scores of baseball figures, including Winfield and multiple Yankees employees.

George didn't like the quiet or the fact that the New York newspapers were speculating that he was soon going to be suspended for not one, but two years. So George decided to invite a gaggle of newspaper writers to his suite on the twelfth floor of the Regency Hotel on Manhattan's Park Avenue. (For all his time in New York, Steinbrenner never bought a home or established a permanent residence in Manhattan, preferring to stay in various refined midtown hotels.)

Meeting with reporters, Steinbrenner was a mix of defiant and vulnerable as he talked for an hour and twenty minutes. He sat in a large, flower-embroidered chair and wore an open-collared dress shirt and slacks, without a tie or jacket, which was rare for him in public.

At various times in the interview, he frowned and smiled at the same time.

"There's something to be concerned about," George said. "It's a worry when you're in a situation where you're sitting there and you want to stay active in baseball and somebody may come down and say no to you about that.

"I'm worried. But I am very comfortable with the facts in this case . . . I believe there will be no suspension."

A minute later, he conceded a suspension might happen.

"It would be very difficult," he said. "Two years?"

He had been suspended before, in 1974, by then baseball commissioner Bowie Kuhn for illegal contributions to President Richard Nixon's reelection campaign. Would this be a harder penalty to accept?

"I was younger then," Steinbrenner responded. "There's less time. It's tough; I'm sixty. That's getting up there."

The next day, at a news conference, New York governor Mario Cuomo suggested that Steinbrenner might have to sell the Yankees. Cuomo said the state might be a bidder for the team. "I wish he would talk to us," the governor said.

Representatives of New York City's legislative body read Cuomo's comments and said the city would consider buying the team, too. After all, it already owned Yankee Stadium.

Not surprisingly, Steinbrenner's mood was not improving. "I'm not selling the Yankees," he roared when approached after another Yankees loss.

Vincent remained on Cape Cod, giving no exact timetable for when he might deliver his ruling on the matter.

In late July, Steinbrenner's lawyers requested that Vincent reopen the hearing. They wanted to call forty-eight witnesses in Steinbrenner's defense. The list of potential witnesses included everyone from broadcaster Howard Cosell to Spira's mailman in the Bronx.

Vincent rejected the request. "No more witnesses," he said, adding that Steinbrenner's lawyers could submit to him any additional information or testimony in writing.

Which Steinbrenner's lawyers did. But all of the wrangling, public relations efforts and negotiations did not predict what would transpire on July 30, when Steinbrenner arrived at Vincent's Park Avenue office at 9 a.m.

Steinbrenner would not leave for eleven and one-half hours, and when he did, he was neither suspended nor told to sell the team. But he could have nothing to do with baseball or the day-to-day operations of the Yankees. For the rest of his life.

He also agreed not to sue the baseball commissioner.

And in the strangest twist of all, the penalty was Steinbrenner's idea.

Leaving the meeting, Steinbrenner said, "I will not comment on the decision."

Of course, he nonetheless commented on it. "I'm very happy it was resolved. I'm very satisfied with the resolution," he said.

The outcome of the meeting shocked the American sports community. And George's reaction to it was astonishing.

Vincent, in a statement and at a news conference, explained his decision on punishing Steinbrenner under baseball's Rule 21(f), which allows
the commissioner to act in the "best interests of baseball." Vincent's con-
clusions would be fairly obvious to anyone who had read the transcript
of the interview, since Vincent was highly skeptical of Steinbrenner's explanations for paying Spira.

He chastised Steinbrenner for the payment and the private investigation into Winfield and his foundation based on Spira's allegations. He
insisted that no baseball owner was allowed to have a secret, working
relationship with a known gambler.

And then, as if he were talking about Watergate, Vincent talked about
the cover-up. "I am able to discern an attempt to force explanations in
hindsight onto discomforting facts," Vincent wrote. "And I am able to
evaluate a pattern of behavior that borders on the bizarre . . . He knew
the payment, if exposed, would look bad and he knew, or at least should
have known, that, if the payment were exposed, it would bring disrepute
to him and therefore to baseball. As a result efforts were made to cover
it up."

As for the claims made by Steinbrenner's lawyers that the hearing was
biased, Vincent said, "In my view, Mr. Steinbrenner's dilemma is not with
the procedures I have utilized, but with his inability to rewrite history."

Fay Vincent has had decades to review what happened in his office on
July 30, 1990. In an interview at his Connecticut home in 2017, he sighed
when recounting a long day of negotiating, but he remembered minute
details as if they had occurred the previous day. He conceded that the
back-and-forth might have remained fresh in his mind because it was so
peculiar that Steinbrenner chose the terms of his own banishment.

Vincent came to the July 30 meeting intending to suspend Steinbrenner for two years. He and his deputy Steve Greenberg had prepared an
alternative punishment in the unlikely scenario that George wanted
something other than the suspension. Nonetheless, Vincent was more or
less dumbfounded when Steinbrenner actually asked for an alternative,
which turned out to be a permanent prohibition from having any involvement in the management of the Yankees, except for certain business
or financial decisions (but not player transactions, trades or free-agent
signings).

Steinbrenner had a couple of overarching goals. He was desperate not
to be suspended again, which he felt — incorrectly — would be a worse
stain on his legacy. He also worried that if he was suspended by baseball

he would lose his coveted position as vice president of the United States Olympic Committee. Steinbrenner, the former college hurdler and the son of a top champion hurdler, prized his Olympic duties. At the July 30 meeting, Vincent quoted Steinbrenner as saying that the Olympic Committee position was "the most important thing to me in my life right now."

So George was insistent.

"He had a conniption over one word in particular," Vincent said in 2017. Steinbrenner did not want the commissioner in any way to use the word "suspended," and Vincent did not.

"But he was essentially bargaining a two-year suspension into a lifetime ban," Vincent said. "And that was a silly deal. I tried to talk him out of it. I said, 'You'll go on the permanently ineligible list.' But I don't think he understood that it was actually a lifetime thing. It was a terrible mistake.

"But George said the Olympic Committee wouldn't let him in if I suspended him. He said, 'I want to leave baseball. I'm fed up.'

"I said, 'George, you don't realize what that means.'"

George's lawyers had used stronger words in private with their client at the July 30 meeting. "We begged him not to take the lifetime ban," Curran said. "Everyone in the room took a run at convincing him. But we could not get him to see the gravity and terms. And he gave away his right to sue as well."

Why would George prefer an exile, which meant he could not set foot in the Yankees' offices, clubhouse, press box or any other team property? Why would he make such a choice?

In George's mind at the time, and within a few months he had a change of heart, he could get around most of the ban. He would still be able to attend quarterly ownership meetings, and in those meetings he could express his opinions about how the Yankees should be run, including the free agents they should or should not sign, or who should be in the starting lineup, or who should be managing. Surreptitiously, he could probably communicate his wishes in other ways.

"You have to put yourself in George's position in 1990," Vincent said in 2017. "I think at every step of his life to that point, he thought he was the smartest person in the room. And in many respects, he was right. He had been successful. He thought he could come out ahead again. He was also a little fed up with the day-to-day baseball business. He's thinking, 'Things aren't going very well for us. We're not doing very well. I'll turn it over to my family. I can stay involved from afar.'"

In fact, in time, weighing in on team issues every three months would not prove to be effective — or satisfying to Steinbrenner. Moreover, Vincent imposed strict prohibitions on George's direct contact with Yankee decision-makers, like the general manager, manager, scouting director and others. Those employees had to periodically sign affidavits stating they had not been in contact with Steinbrenner in any way.

But even with those encumbrances, George figured he had another, easy way to get around the limitations of his ban. He would put his thirty-three-year-old son, Hank, in charge of the team. And his other son, Hal, then twenty-one, would soon come into the Yankees fold.

"George felt he could cheat," Vincent said. "His thinking was something like, 'I'll be able to have dinner with my boys and they'll be running the team and I'll tell them what I want. And they'll do it.'"

It would be as simple as that.

Except it would not be that simple. While Steinbrenner's lawyers said on July 30 that Hank Steinbrenner would take over the ownership duties of the Yankees, less than two weeks later, Hank decided he did not want to run the Yankees. He had been a team executive once before, traveling with the Yankees as a kind of special adviser in the mid-1980s. He saw what it was like to be under his father's thumb then. Hank has never spoken at length about his decision not to succeed his father in 1990, but he has told others in the organization that he viewed the arrangement as a titanic, stressful travail.

In the late eighties, Hank had stepped away from the Yankees to run the family's 860-acre horse farm in central Florida. He preferred that job expressly because it was away from the limelight. Asked once why he liked being around horses instead of baseball players, he answered, "Because the horses don't talk back."

Hank wanted to remain in the background. And what bigger spotlight could there be at this juncture in New York sports history than to be the new chief officer of the downtrodden Yankees?

No, Hank would not run the newly rudderless Yankees. Besides, Hank understood the obvious — that Vincent would have worries about the easy collusion of a father-son tandem at the top of the Yankees leadership. And Vincent could investigate the Steinbrenners based on his suspicions. The whole idea of leading the Yankees was just not worth it to Hank.

And that called for a new Steinbrenner plan. Vincent's decree gave George until August 20 to find his successor, not as the Yankees' owner, which he still was, but as the team's chief executive, which baseball officially called the "general partner."

It was all semantics to George. Or so he thought at the time. But in fact, his influence on the Yankees, despite his attempts to subvert his self-imposed exile, would be greatly diminished for at least two years. Steinbrenner, who always thought big, still had grander plans. He might be mostly stepping away — for now.

But leaving Vincent's office on July 30, George asked this question about the lifetime ban he had just agreed to: "How long does this last?"

7

"Goodbye, George"

THE YANKEES WERE playing the Detroit Tigers at Yankee Stadium on July 30, the night that George Steinbrenner was told to stay away from the Yankees, seemingly forever.

The smartphone was years from being invented, so there was no Twitter or texting, but it was not uncommon in 1990 for fans to bring transistor radios to games so they could follow the broadcast announcers' commentary. And in the fourth inning, it was that cultural artifact, the transistor radio, that helped spread the news of Steinbrenner's ban from section to section in the stadium grandstand and into the Yankees' dugout.

Fans were jubilant, and several times a chant of "No more George" resounded in the ballpark. Even during the seventh-inning stretch, when the PA system began to play "Take Me Out to the Ballgame," fans drowned out the song with another chant of "No more George."

Then they switched to a different singsong chant: "Goodbye, George."

After the game, which the Yankees won, 6–2, the atmosphere was funereal in the home clubhouse. "It's a shame the fans made a party out of things," said the winning pitcher, Dave LaPoint. "For us guys playing for his team, it wasn't a good feeling out there."

Said Dave Righetti: "I know I wasn't cheering. I was sad."

Stump Merrill was somber as well, saying that Steinbrenner had meant a lot to his family. When quoting Merrill, the *New York Daily News* wrote that Merrill would forever have the distinction of being the "last Yankees manager in the Steinbrenner era."

Fans leaving Yankee Stadium were stopped by reporters who descended on the South Bronx to do the classic man- (and woman-) on-the-street interviews. "I wish he had lost the team completely," said Wendy Schmid of Westport, Connecticut. "He should be banned from baseball for life." Don Duncan of Westwood, New Jersey, said Steinbrenner should have been banned for "gross incompetence."

At Mickey Mantle's restaurant and sports bar, on Central Park South in midtown Manhattan, patrons had been confused when, around 9 p.m., the loud music being played through speakers was silenced and every television was tuned to Fay Vincent as he read the details of his decision on Steinbrenner.

Soon someone yelled, "He's outta here." And cheers filled the bar.

"This is so sweet," Mike Nisson, a thirty-year-old dentist from Connecticut, said. "Maybe it'll save the team. Now they can build a dynasty again."

Others had short-term goals. "If somebody besides George is making the decisions, maybe we can get out of last place," Rudy Rummels of Staten Island said.

And in the two weeks after Steinbrenner's banishment was announced, the Yankees had played .500 baseball. They no longer had the worst record in the major leagues. But things were far from rosy. Don Mattingly had not played in weeks, resting his now chronically sore back. Pascual Pérez had recently had shoulder surgery; his career was all but over. Righetti's Yankees career would soon end when he chose to sign as a free agent with the San Francisco Giants. Jesse Barfield was begging to be traded. Deion Sanders, who was hitting .158, left for the National Football League's Atlanta Falcons. Released by the Yankees, Sanders resurfaced in the Atlanta Braves outfield and by 1992 was hitting .304 and was a World Series star.

But the Yankees' ongoing adversity was background noise, since all eyes were on Steinbrenner during what was perceived as his final days as the boss, or the Boss, as he preferred to be called. And George was indeed busy.

On August 15, he surprised the baseball community by naming Robert E. Nederlander, one of the Yankees' minority owners and a member of a prominent New York theatrical family, the team's new leader. Nederlander, one of nineteen minority owners, was president of a group that owned thirty theaters in the United States and Great Britain.

Nederlander, who was fifty-seven, admitted he knew little about baseball.

During a 1984 meeting of the Yankees' ownership, Nederlander had famously reviewed the team's batting statistics and asked, "Where's Reggie?"

"Reggie Jackson?" another owner responded.

"Yes," Nederlander said. "You know, Mr. October."

He was told that Jackson had last played for the Yankees in 1981.

Nederlander was viewed as a benign caretaker who wouldn't interfere in some of George Steinbrenner's other plans, which already included trying to get himself reinstated as chief executive in a year or two. At the least, Nederlander could shepherd the Yankees in a nonthreatening way until Hal Steinbrenner, George's youngest child, or one of his sons-in-law could assume control of the team.

Next, George turned to the matter of Stump Merrill's contract, which was to expire in October. Steinbrenner called Merrill and told him the team was extending his contract through the 1992 season.

It was the first time in Stump's fourteen years with the Yankees that he had been offered anything but a one-year contract. "Believe me, I'd have taken anything they offered," he said when asked for his reaction to a two-year extension.

Merrill celebrated over light beer(s) that evening. And told his wife he was going to buy the Mercedes-Benz he always wanted.

On Monday, August 20, his final day in power, Steinbrenner hosted about one hundred employees at a farewell lunch at Yankee Stadium's elegant Diamond Club. His guests ate chateaubriand and green beans amandine. The meal was capped off with a dessert of strawberries and whipped cream.

Steinbrenner spoke to the gathering for several minutes. "I've stepped down because maybe it's time to move on," he said evenly, although at one point he appeared to wipe away tears. "Things might even be better under the new people. I will still be involved in many ways. And the Steinbrenner family will be a part of the Yankees for a long time to come. We are still the owners."

Steinbrenner had nosily run the Yankees for 17 years and 229 days. In that time, the team had 19 managers, 14 general managers and 29 pitching coaches, because George especially liked to blame, and fire, pitching coaches.

George said he did not plan to watch that night's game against Toronto. The next time he wanted to watch a Yankees game in person, he would not be allowed to do so from his owner's private box adjacent to his office. If it was a Yankees road game, he would not be permitted to sit in the opposing owner's box.

In either case, he could sit in the stands.

"I hope the fans will get along with me," he said in a brief news conference.

He was asked if it was a sad day for him. "No," he replied.

What was his state of mind? "It's fine," he said.

At about 4 p.m., Don Mattingly arrived at Steinbrenner's office. Mattingly had requested the meeting and stayed for ten minutes. "It was definitely strange," Mattingly said afterward in the players' clubhouse. "I mean, the man has been a huge presence here."

At 5:30, two hours before the start of the game, a fan had draped a banner across the front of the Yankee Stadium upper-deck wall that read: *Aug. 20, 1990. A Great Day For The Yankees.*

In his last official act that day, George appointed a new Yankees general manager. There had been much speculation that the existing general manager, Pete Peterson, was going to be jettisoned. The leading candidates were expected to be former St. Louis Cardinals manager Whitey Herzog and Tom Seaver, the ex–New York Mets star who was now a Yankees broadcaster.

Instead, George went back to his Yankees past, promoting Gene Michael, whom he had first met in 1973, when he bought the team and Michael was its shortstop. Theirs had been a long, tangled relationship ever since, with Michael serving under Steinbrenner at various times as manager, general manager, coach, administrative assistant, minor league manager and player. He had most recently been a scout for the Yankees. He knew its minor league system rosters well.

"No one is more knowledgeable in or about the organization," Steinbrenner said.

Michael, who was fifty-two, insisted he had not sought the job. George had called and asked him to take it.

Many years later, Michael added a caveat: "He called to ask, but he already knew I would take it. He knew me. He knew I saw opportunity."

At the same time that Michael was promoted, George Bradley, a Yankee executive normally based in Tampa, also moved up the team's chain of command and relocated to New York to assist Michael.

At an impromptu news conference at Yankee Stadium — Steinbrenner was to leave the building in twenty minutes — Michael called his job "a good challenge." "I know we're not winning now and I'm not a know-it-all, but a team can turn things around within two years," he said. "It can."

Michael, fired by Steinbrenner three times already, was asked if he would have taken the general manager's job if Steinbrenner weren't going into exile. He smiled and then laughed. "That's not a fair question. I wasn't offered that," he said.

Michael was asked if he planned to communicate with Steinbrenner and pledged that he would not. Michael was a scout at heart. He had done some digging around the edges of his new responsibilities. Many years later, he acknowledged that he knew about the affidavit requirement before he took the job. At the time, he said he wasn't going to let George get him kicked out of baseball.

"I read the papers," he said. "I know the rules."

But what if George were to call him?

"Naw," Michael said. "George wouldn't call. Besides, I'm going to be pretty busy."

Steinbrenner left Yankee Stadium on the home plate side around 7 p.m. with news photographers walking backward in front of him, their camera shutters snapping as they backpedaled. There were about a dozen of them, taking pictures in the gloaming of a hot August evening as the most famous sports owner in America got into a long, black town car.

Hal Steinbrenner was not at Yankee Stadium that day. But he was around his father in the immediate aftermath and for many months. In 2017, seated in a conference room high above the Yankees' spring training complex, a space dominated by a life-size oil portrait of George Steinbrenner that, with its ornate frame, occupies almost an entire wall, Hal was asked to describe how his father took his 1990 expulsion from baseball.

"He was as passionate as a man could be about the business, and very hands-on, and to be out of it like that had to kill him," Hal said. "It's nothing he told me. He never would have told me something like that. But it just had to have eaten him up."

Hal, who in 2008, at the age of thirty-nine, ascended to the role of chief executive of the Yankees, still sometimes refers to his father in the present tense, as if he were still alive. "He is — I mean he was — a strong guy," Hal said. "But you could tell his frustration. He would not admit that he was hurting. But I was around him my whole life, so I could tell just by looking at him. I think it ate him up for quite a while.

"It was a chapter in his life he had to endure. One way or the other."

8

The Architect

THE MAN ENTRUSTED with rebuilding the Yankees, as the disastrous, tumultuous 1990 season wound to a humiliating close, never planned on a career in baseball. He expected to be a basketball player. Or maybe an architect.

Eugene Richard Michael, in 1955, attended his hometown university in Ohio, Kent State, on a basketball scholarship. Baseball was a second sport. Astute, thoughtful, perceptive and wily—he almost never lost money at a card table—Michael also considered opening his own business. He took college classes in architecture. Why?

"Because I liked to design and create things," he said.

He was six-foot-two and a rail-thin 175 pounds, and had an upright, ostrichlike running style, so teammates in both sports started calling Michael "Stick" early in his career. It was a time when a majority of sportsmen, and sportswomen, had nicknames, and many of them outlasted the athletes' playing careers. So it was for Stick Michael.

A basketball star at Kent State, he then played professionally for the Columbus Comets of the North American Basketball Association and was approached by several teams for the nascent National Basketball Association. But baseball was America's pastime, and for all his basketball prowess, Michael switched sports in 1959 when the Pittsburgh Pirates offered him far more money than any basketball team could.

It was the beginning of a ten-year major league career, with occasional winter sojourns on the semipro basketball circuit.

Michael was a slick-fielding, weak-hitting shortstop—a common combination of skills for a professional shortstop in the 1960s and 1970s

— and he spent seven years in the minor leagues before Pittsburgh called him up in 1966. That first season, in 30 games, he hit just .152 and was summarily traded to the Los Angeles Dodgers, who kept him just one season (.202 batting average) before shipping him off to the Yankees in 1968.

Stick, as he was known to everyone in baseball from the 1960s to the 2000s, managed to raise his batting average to about .240 in his seven years with the Yankees. But he knew he was no prized batsman. As he once joked, "The bat really jumps off my ball."

And he was forever overshadowed in the American League by the luminous Baltimore shortstop Mark Belanger, another rangy, reedy fielding maestro who won eight Gold Gloves and was a defensive standard-bearer of the Orioles' meticulous championship teams. Belanger's batting average was even lower than Michael's, but Belanger was fortunate to be playing for the equivalent of baseball royalty in the sixties and seventies.

Stick Michael's timing was not as providential. When he joined the Yankees they were in the throes of a stormy restructuring on the field and an upheaval of the ownership group. The CBS Corporation, which had never ventured into professional sports, had bought the Yankees in 1964, just as all the team's aging stars, like Mantle, Berra and Whitey Ford, were on their way out of baseball.

It was a turbulent, humbling time for the once great Yankees, who were suddenly a second-division team. Still, Michael did not have to wait long to witness a Yankees revival, one fueled by the promotion of young minor league talent and shrewd trade acquisitions. By 1970, when the team finished in second place, the attentive, insightful thirty-two-year-old Michael was the team's elder statesman. He had been in New York City long enough to become something of a man-about-town, welcomed in the best restaurants and a jocular, familiar presence in the most important Manhattan saloons, which always treated Yankees like royalty.

Michael became a big brother to the Yankees' biggest homegrown star, twenty-three-year-old Thurman Munson, who had also attended Kent State. He also developed lasting, lifelong relationships with a number of players who made up the core of the late-1970s Yankees championship teams, including Munson, Lou Piniella, Graig Nettles, Chris Chambliss and Sparky Lyle. Moreover, Michael was a close witness to how those superlative Yankees teams were built after several losing seasons. (The late sixties and early seventies were the second-darkest period in the team's modern history — only the teams from 1989 to 1992 were worse, and for longer.)

In contrast, they were vastly different periods in big league baseball, but some of the principles of recasting a roster were similar nonetheless, and Michael, who did not retire until after the 1975 season, observed with keen personal interest how the Yankees' pennant-winning teams of 1976–78 were reconstructed. It was another way to learn how to create and produce a successful product.

He was already used to winning at most things. His card-playing skills were legend. When Stick joined the Yankees in 1968, Mantle had already privately told the Yankees it would be his last season as a player. By the end of it, Mantle said he owed Stick so much money that he could no longer afford to retire.

It was — mostly — a joke. And yet, when Manhattan's St. Moritz Hotel, where Mantle lived, sent him its bill from April to October, he told the hotel manager: "Call Gene Michael. He's got all my cash. He can write a check."

Michael was more than a polished fielder; he may have been the best practitioner of baseball's hidden-ball trick in the history of the game. With a runner on second base, Michael would often visit the pitcher on the mound and furtively take the baseball from him. Or he would take a throw from the outfield with a runner at second base and casually pretend to throw it back to the pitcher. Except that he palmed the ball like someone doing a magic trick, then surreptitiously slipped the ball into his glove. When the runner took his lead off second base, Michael would wait and then pounce, tagging him out. He did it nearly a dozen times as a minor leaguer and another five times in the majors, once tagging a runner at second base for the final out of a one-run Yankees victory.

"I could have done it another thirty times, but the guys who got tagged out were so embarrassed and furious it was almost dangerous for me," Michael said. "Later, they would come sliding into second base on double plays trying to kill me.

"The other problem sometimes was the second-base umpire. I'd have to tell him in advance so he'd be watching, but once in a while, the umpire would start laughing and give it away.

"And at least another ten times, I was in place to do it, but the manager happened to come to the mound to take the pitcher out. He would ask where the ball was and blow the whole thing."

By the time Michael's playing career quietly ended, he had already become a confidant and favorite of fellow Ohioan George Steinbrenner, who had bought the Yankees in 1973.

One of Steinbrenner's first acts as owner was to order certain players — Piniella, Munson and Michael — to get haircuts.

Michael approached Steinbrenner and said he would gladly trim his locks. "Are you going to pay for the haircut?" Michael asked.

Steinbrenner said he would.

Stick added: "Well, the least you could do is buy us all new suits, too. I mean, if the goal is for us to look more presentable."

Steinbrenner was incensed, until Michael broke into a wide grin. For decades thereafter, the Yankees' owner privately relished Michael's cheekiness and never-ending desire to poke fun at his boss.

The two men built a close bond, not quite like father and son but maybe something like an uncle and his favorite nephew. They also gravitated toward each other because they had mutual friends, most notably a former Heisman Trophy winner from Ohio State named Howard "Hopalong" Cassady, who had been Steinbrenner's idol growing up and who had introduced Steinbrenner to his wife, Joan.

Steinbrenner was not especially close to many of the 1973 Yankees. He kept his distance. But Michael was different, a well-spoken, dapper and studious presence who at first blush looked and acted more like a bank president than a professional athlete.

Michael had diverse interests outside baseball. He devoted many hours to charities and read extensively, especially history. Once, after Steinbrenner's death in 2010, he was asked whom he would invite to dinner if he could host any three figures from the past. Michael named three Georges: George Herman "Babe" Ruth, George Patton and George Steinbrenner.

Asked why he included Steinbrenner, Stick, ever the scamp to the haughty Steinbrenner, laughed and said, "I'd want him there just so I could tell him off one more time."

But in truth, the two were exceedingly close, and Michael often called Steinbrenner one of the most important, influential people in his life. "I taught him a lot of baseball, and there was no one he listened to more than me when the topic was baseball," Stick said in one of several 2017 interviews, not long before he died of a heart attack at seventy-nine. "But at the same time, he taught me a lot about hard work and how to use your strengths. He was impatient, difficult and a pain in the butt, but he was a teacher and a mentor, too."

In Michael, Steinbrenner saw a baseball savant who was in many ways more useful away from the field. Michael did his best work sitting quietly in the stands, where like a crafty poker player he silently observed and noted tendencies, trends and subtle, small movements that added up to big things.

"My father knew that Stick had one of the best sets of eyes in baseball — he saw it all," said Hal Steinbrenner. "We're all indebted to Stick. He has vision, and not just in the obvious sense of the word."

Said Buck Showalter of Michael: "He was the best at evaluating and understanding the inner, less seen qualities of a player. He could read the person and the player, which is a gift. And he could discern opponents' weaknesses. It was almost like reading minds. That's why no one liked to play cards with him."

One example: Stick was an advance scout for the Yankees in the fall of 1977, traveling with the Yankees' likely postseason opponents to compile reports for use by manager Billy Martin and the team's players. On October 18, before the sixth game of the World Series between the Yankees and Los Angeles Dodgers, Reggie Jackson put on a prodigious display of power hitting during batting practice.

Then he went inside the clubhouse and called Michael in the Yankees' executive offices. "What should I look for tonight?" Jackson asked Stick.

"Fastballs in — you should back up in the batter's box a little bit," Michael answered.

The first pitch to Jackson, who was dug in at the back of the batter's box, was an inside fastball that Reggie belted deep into the right-field stands. The next pitch he saw, an inning later, was also inside and ended up in the right-field seats as well. By the eighth inning, when Jackson came to the plate again, the Dodgers had inserted knuckleball pitcher Charlie Hough. The catcher set up inside, but Hough's first knuckleball floated over the middle of the plate and became Jackson's third home run.

But Reggie had not forgotten the scouting report. When he saw Stick in the clubhouse after the Yankees' 8–4 victory, he pointed and yelled: "Right on! It was just like you said."

By 1979, Steinbrenner had installed Michael as manager of the team's top minor league club. As a rookie manager, Michael proceeded to win nearly 62 percent of his games and the league championship.

Michael took over the big league club in 1981, won a division title and 59 percent of his games and was still fired by Steinbrenner. Michael came back to manage the Yankees in 1982, only to be fired again (with a winning record). After that, whenever Steinbrenner tried to persuade Michael to manage his Yankees — as he did in '84 and '86 — Michael refused.

"We didn't get along when I managed," Stick said. "He knew me too well. He was constantly in my office, talking and arguing about things. Other managers he didn't know quite as well and he wouldn't bug them quite as much. But he thought nothing of calling me ten or fifteen times in a day. As I said, he knew me too well. Finally, I said, 'I'll work for you, but I'm not ever going to be your manager again.'"

Besides, Michael preferred being involved with the off-the-field-personnel side of the organization. He liked finding talent, nurturing it and molding a group that was greater than the sum of its parts. The former school kid who liked to create things would happily sit in the bleachers during a high school or college baseball game and watch players he envisioned as the pillars and interlocking parts of a great edifice he would build in New York: a World Series winner.

Better than that, a team that won multiple World Series.

So rather than manage, Michael stayed in the organization in various roles, mostly as Steinbrenner's counsel. He disdained Steinbrenner's outbursts and off-the-record media machinations. But he also noticed that George routinely worked twelve-hour days. He knew he himself would have to work similar hours if he was going to get the Yankees out of the abyss they had descended into by the final days of the 1990 season.

When George was banished from baseball, Stick knew it was a blemish on the franchise he had come to think of as home. But privately, even secretly, he was relieved. He knew how it devastated George, his benefactor and biggest supporter. But he finally saw the opportunity he had been longing for.

"The Yankee organization needed a break from George at that time," Michael said. "Sometimes you need an abrupt change. It was like a timeout. It was a time to rethink things."

Stick did not have a specific strategy, but he did have a set of overarching tenets and various baseball principles he valued. He knew the kinds of hitters and pitchers he wanted, and he would assiduously look for certain obscure but identifiable attributes in those players, whom he would draft, promote from the minors and trade for in the big leagues. Many of the abilities he sought were skills later associated with what became known as Moneyball. They were the doctrines of modern baseball's analytics era.

"Gene Michael was Moneyball; they just didn't have a title for it yet," said the Yankees broadcaster Michael Kay, a beat writer and radio or TV commentator with the team since 1987.

It was thirteen years before Michael Lewis's book *Moneyball* would be published, but Gene Michael had developed his own evidence-based, sabermetrics approach to assembling a baseball team. The high priest of that movement, the Red Sox and Cubs wunderkind Theo Epstein, learned the fundamentals on a laptop. Stick Michael, born in 1938, learned them as a kid at Kent, playing a version of the Strat-O-Matic board game, which became popular in the 1960s.

"It all goes back to that baseball board game in my childhood," he said, recalling summer afternoons sixty years earlier as he sat in the grandstand behind home plate at the Yankees' Tampa minor league complex, where he continued to work as a special adviser in his final years. "There used to be a game where you had these disks and a spinner you used to get a number, and together with the disks you'd land on a base hit, walk, error, fly out, pop out, home run, double, etc.

"It was all about percentages based on the real statistics of actual players, who would have individual cards with their percentages on getting a hit or walk. I would always pick the guys who got a lot of walks, guys with high on-base percentages. I'd get Ted Williams every time if I could. And I won a lot at that game with that approach.

"We also kept our own stats on how certain teams did, and I studied what kinds of hitters were on those teams. It was all about on-base percentage — walks and runs and extending innings — never mind pure batting average.

"This was in high school. I'm still friends with my buddies who played that game with me. We joke about it now. They say: 'Gene, you were accumulating those pesky little guys who got on base in 1952. And now they say it's a modern baseball invention. It's sabermetrics.'"

Michael laughed. "I was just a kid trying to beat my friends at a card game," he said. "But my theories stuck with me."

Stick understood that there's a difference between board games and modern algorithms. "Obviously, it is more advanced now because they can break the numbers down to identify every advantage," he said. "But back in 1990, and even before when I was managing in the minors, I was always explaining to our scouting people that we need guys with high on-base percentages.

"Not only that, but I'd say, 'Get me guys who take a lot of pitches and foul off a lot of pitches.' Because I want to wear out their starting pitchers and get to the middle-relief pitchers, the weakest part of any team.

"I used to call it the vulnerable underbelly. Every team has five starting pitchers and maybe three late-inning bullpen guys. But get the starter out early and you're facing that team's ninth-best pitcher and maybe their weakest pitcher. Do that and you can pull away in a game. A 6–2 lead in the sixth or seventh inning leads to a lot of victories." On the flip side, Michael championed a new pitching stat: innings per start. He instructed his staff and scouts to look for pitchers with the highest innings-per-start numbers. He did not want opposing teams attacking the Yankees' vulnerable underbelly.

But Michael's approach was more complex than simply finding guys who got on base often and took a lot of pitches. Or starters who worked into the seventh inning. He also scouted personalities and not just athletes. As someone with a career batting average below .240, he knew that baseball was a game of failure. Even the best hitters would fail seven out of ten times at the plate. The best pitchers gave up three or four runs every nine innings. He wanted players who knew how to handle disappointment or adversity, and who found ways to rebound. Scouting players, even ones who had already made it to the major leagues, Michael asked about family backgrounds and obstacles the player had overcome in his life or career — or both. He needed not only dependable players, but players who, under the harsh scrutiny of George Steinbrenner or the glare of an unblinking, unforgiving New York media machine, would not cower or fold.

He needed to find sparkling gems where others saw rough-cut stones, and he knew the first place to look was in baseball's bushes — the least examined reaches of amateur baseball as well as the Yankees' multitiered minor league system.

"It was a total rebuild, but I knew that down the ladder, down on the farm, we already had some good players because we had good scouts who for years had found players," Stick said many years later. "The problem was that we just kept trading them all away. It was time to go find those guys and figure out which ones to keep."

9

Prospecting

MARIANO RIVERA HAD no idea why the Yankees would give him $2,000 to pitch a baseball, something he had rarely done. But the money represented nearly a year's pay in Rivera's current job, so he signed the Yankees contract presented to him in his family's congested, two-room concrete house in the tiny Panamanian village of Puerto Caimito.

It was 1990, and until then Rivera had been working twelve-hour days on his father's fishing boat alongside his uncle Miguel. Rivera hated the fisherman's life, which meant being at sea six days a week. His only day off was Sunday, when he went to church in the morning and played sports in the afternoon and evening. He was a 155-pound shortstop and twenty years old — ancient for a prospect from Latin America.

A Panamanian cab driver who moonlighted as a baseball scout, Chico Heron, was at an All-Star game when Rivera had unexpectedly been asked to pitch. He threw only fastballs, at about 87 miles an hour, but Rivera could throw it wherever he wanted — outside corner at the batter's knees, inside corner, up and in. His control was effortless.

Heron coaxed the Yankees' Latin American scouting director, Herb Raybourn, an Anglo who was Panamanian and spoke Spanish, to watch Rivera in a tryout. Raybourn became enamored of Rivera's minimalist, graceful pitching motion. He knew Rivera was raw and unproven, and he certainly knew that Panama had a limited history of producing major league players — in the past fifty years, there had been only a couple of dozen.

But the Yankees were known for taking risks internationally. Maybe with better nutrition and tutelage, the Yankees thought, this waif of an infielder turned pitcher, who hailed from one of Panama's poorest districts, could become something.

Still, it was a mighty gamble. Rivera did not speak English, had left school in the ninth grade and had never been outside Panama. He had never flown in an airplane. He could name only a few major league teams. When the Yankees talked to him about their minor league training complex in Tampa, he asked, "What's a Tampa?"

Rivera himself sensed the long odds against him. He wondered if he shouldn't just stay at home. "I wasn't even a pitcher," he said. "I was scared."

The alternative was to head back to sea, where only a few months earlier his uncle Miguel had been fatally injured in an accident with the rigging on his father's boat.

Mariano Rivera signed and boarded his first flight to Tampa.

Fast-forward several months. The New York Yankees were going down in flames, their pitching staff on its way to 95 losses, the most in Yankees history. (The 1912 New York Highlanders, who were one year from being recast as the Yankees, lost 102 games.)

But down on the farm, in the Gulf Coast League, Rivera had the lowest earned run average in the league. Sure, it was a rookie circuit that played about sixty-five games in a season, but Rivera was still averaging more than a strikeout per inning and allowing roughly one base runner every three innings.

At the time, the Yankees handed out $500 bonuses to minor leaguers for winning certain statistical titles, like having the lowest ERA in a league during a season. And Rivera surely wanted his bonus. There was only one problem. Rivera, used exclusively as a reliever, had pitched just 45 innings, and the Gulf Coast League regulations required pitchers to have at least 50 innings to qualify for the ERA title.

But Rivera made it plain to his manager, Glenn Sherlock, that he really needed that $500.

"I went to my pitching coach, Hoyt Wilhelm, and said we have to do something for Mariano," Sherlock said in an interview decades later. "He was such a dedicated guy and good teammate. You wanted to make him happy. Heck, I always thought Mariano could have been a great outfielder and decent hitter if he hadn't been a pitcher."

In 1985, Wilhelm had become the first pitcher who had appeared almost exclusively in relief to be inducted into the Baseball Hall of Fame. He told Sherlock that he wasn't going to let a fellow bullpen ace be deprived of an honor. Rivera got to start the Gulf Coast Yankees' last game of 1990. Perhaps if he pitched well enough, Rivera would get to 50 innings, win the ERA title and collect his bonus.

Except until that point in 1990, Rivera had not pitched more than three innings in any game.

Nevertheless, he started the final game of his first professional season. And pitched a seven-inning no-hitter. He finished the year with an ERA of 0.17, with 58 strikeouts in 52 innings. He averaged 0.46 walks and hits per inning, and his strikeout-to-walk ratio was 8.29.

Not bad for a prospect who just a few years earlier was using discarded cardboard for a baseball glove because he could not afford a real mitt. He also wrapped up snippets of fishing nets and bound them with electrical tape to fashion a makeshift baseball. Rivera and his friends used tree limbs for bats.

"Raw baseball background for sure," said Mitch Lukevics, the Yankees' farm director at the time. "But his delivery was fluid, unforced and unnaturally accurate. That skinny guy could throw a baseball into a teacup."

Bill Livesey went further. "Mariano could throw it into a thimble."

Stick Michael had read the reports on the obscure, $2,000 pitcher from Panama. "I knew of Mariano in 1990," he said many years later. "But a lot of kids tear it up in rookie league. You didn't know what it meant yet. We kept him in A ball the next year. But yeah, you kept your eye on him.

"We had decided to keep our eye on all of them. We were definitely going to need some of them. We were going to need them in a big way."

The Yankees were also closely, quietly watching players who were not yet Yankees.

One was a tall, reedy shortstop in western Michigan who had been wearing a Yankees necklace, and even Yankees boxer shorts, since he'd spent summers at the New Jersey lake house of his grandmother, a devoted Yankees fan. And the Yankees had been aware of Derek Sanderson Jeter since a scout, Dick Groch, saw him as a fifteen-year-old playing on a top summer travel team.

"Catlike movements, the personification of athleticism," Groch said nearly thirty years later, recalling his first view of Jeter in the infield. "It was a moment I have never forgotten. Scouts watch thousands of players, waiting to see a special player. You wait to see a kid who has it all.

"I saw that in Derek Jeter."

Groch felt Ken Griffey Jr. was the best player he had ever scouted. In Groch's eyes, now Griffey had an equal.

Groch filed a report to the Yankees about the lean and not fully developed Jeter, who Groch said already had an outstanding arm, good range, speed and a quick bat. The scout called him a five-tool player and wrote, "Will be a ML Star!"

As in Major League Star.

The Yankees scouting brain trust believed the reliable Groch, whose territory included Kalamazoo, Michigan, where Jeter was in high school. The Yankees also knew not to tip their hand. Stick Michael, the poker ace, had stressed that.

Part of being a good scout was recognizing whether other scouts were looking at your prospect, too, and Groch knew he was not the only person traveling all the way to frigid Kalamazoo to look at the tall, rangy shortstop.

Per the Yankees' instructions, Groch did not introduce himself to Jeter or to his high school coach, Don Zomer. (Twenty-five years later, Zomer had still not met Groch.)

To watch Jeter play, Groch sometimes stood on the hill of an adjacent field or in the shade of a shed far down the left-field line. Even then, Groch would seem like an apparition, one that disappeared after a single Jeter at-bat and a couple of innings. He did this to feign disinterest in Jeter, as if Groch had other games to get to and other players to see.

In fact, Groch had not left the scene but instead retreated to the tree-shrouded Grand Prairie Cemetery just beyond the right-center-field fence. From there, sometimes with the help of binoculars, he could observe Jeter for dozens of innings — and more importantly, not be observed by other scouts or by Jeter himself.

The cemetery also gave Groch a good view of the subdivision where Jeter had grown up. A collection of low-slung, mostly split-level homes backed up to the Kalamazoo Central High School athletic fields. The houses, built in the mid-twentieth century, were on small lots on tree-lined streets. It was a cozy neighborhood — neat but not fancy. But what Derek Jeter liked most about his split-level home at 2415 Cumberland Street was that he could jump over the five-foot backyard fence and be practicing on the high school baseball field in less than three minutes. It became a ritual.

For the Jeters, a typical family weekend or evening out was Charles and Dot, Jeter's parents, hitting ground balls and fly balls to Derek and his sister, Sharlee, who was a softball star.

Groch heard from the locals that the Jeters were fixtures on the Kalamazoo Central High fields. The scout also heard about how Charles and Dot made their children sign behavioral contracts with provisions that covered homework, grade point averages, curfews, drugs and alcohol, phone calls, television hours, conduct in public and respect for others. Jeter ranked twenty-first in his class, was a member of the National Honor Society and volunteered to tutor his younger classmates.

It all went into Groch's report to the Yankees scouting office.

That same year, Bill Livesey, the scouting director, had traveled with Joe Robison, another Yankees scout, to look at about a dozen potential draft picks in Texas, a baseball hotbed. Robison had been hired by George Steinbrenner in 1985 after a chance meeting at the Air Force Academy in Colorado, where Robison was the baseball coach and Steinbrenner was making a speech. During his visit, Steinbrenner was impressed when other athletic department employees talked glowingly about Robison's knack for finding top high school players that other college coaches overlooked. Steinbrenner offered Robison a job as a scout on the spot — with a big raise.

"Joe Robison tells me he wants to go to a regional playoff game so I can see a kid that's not on our list," Livesey said of his 1990 Texas visit. "I said, 'OK, Joe, but we're going to get to the other games, right? That's what I'm here for.'

"But Joe was insistent, and I go watch this stocky left-hander named Pettitte. I also noticed that there's not another scout in the stands anywhere. Pettitte is throwing like an 88-mile-an-hour fastball, but he doesn't have another quality pitch. Granted, he was very competitive and had great mound composure. And at Yankee Stadium, which was friendly to lefty hitters, we were always looking for left-handed pitchers.

"But I said, 'Joe, I see what you see, but if we took this kid to our lowest minor league team he couldn't survive.' And Joe agrees with me but says he sees something. It's like he has a hunch that the kid will improve. Best of all, Pettitte is going to San Jacinto Junior College."

That became something of a game changer for Livesey. San Jacinto had the preeminent junior college baseball program in the nation. The future seven-time Cy Young Award winner Roger Clemens had blossomed from a nondrafted high schooler into a major prospect at San Jacinto under its coach, Wayne Graham, who had never had a losing season as a high school or college coach.

Graham, who went on to build a powerhouse baseball program at Rice University, had turned the once rotund Clemens into a feared mound presence, and he told Robison he thought he might be able to do the same for Pettitte.

In 1990, in the twenty-second round, the Yankees selected Andy Pettitte, and the team kept in constant touch with him, although they did not push to sign him. They wanted to see his progress under Graham. And Pettitte did not seem in any hurry to sign with the Yankees either. He knew that he was the fourth left-handed pitcher the team had taken in that year's draft — the others went in the fourth, eighth and twenty-first rounds. He was not an immediate priority.

In the twenty-fourth round that year, the Yankees had also drafted Jorge Posada, a switch-hitting shortstop with a rifle for an arm who played for Calhoun Community College in Decatur, Alabama. Posada was born in Puerto Rico to a Cuban father, a talented ballplayer who had fled his home country to escape the Fidel Castro regime, and a mother who was from the Dominican Republic.

Posada, like Rivera, was not a dedicated student. He had hoped to play major college baseball in the States, but scored too low on the SATs to qualify for an American college baseball scholarship. But his father, Jorge Sr., had become a scout for major league teams in the United States, and through some of his contacts, word was passed to Fred Frickie, the coach at Calhoun Community College. Frickie, who needed a shortstop, called the Posadas' home in Puerto Rico. A neighboring aunt who spoke English came over to interpret for the two parties.

Frickie made his pitch for Jorge Jr. to come to Alabama.

Said Jorge: "Where's Alabama?"

Posada came from a baseball family and had been intensely tutored in all the nuances of the game by his father. In fact, the entire Posada family had a high baseball IQ. Leo Posada, Jorge's uncle, had played for three years for the Kansas City Athletics in the early 1960s.

Jorge Jr., who was naturally right-handed, was also taught to bat left-handed by his father at a young age. Jorge Sr. knew that a switch-hitting but right-hand-throwing infielder was always a valuable commodity, in any league. Jorge's father insisted that he use wood bats as a youngster as well, even though all his contemporaries were using the easy-to-swing aluminum bats. Major leaguers only swing wood bats, said Jorge Sr.

But as a young teen, Jorge was only five-foot-six and 135 pounds. He was never an All-Star and never the best kid on his team. He would spend hours hanging upside down from a bar affixed to a doorframe at home, hoping it would make him taller.

In time, he did grow, and landed at Calhoun, but the transition was challenging. Since he did not speak English, Posada was noticeably out of his element in Decatur, Alabama.

In a 2017 interview, he related a story about his first trip to the Decatur Walmart, looking for bed sheets. Conjuring his best English, he asked a woman clerk for some "shits."

Eventually, the clerk deciphered what Posada wanted and corrected his pronunciation.

On the field, the universal language of baseball was more familiar. And with the help of several teammates, Posada's English gradually improved. He was a popular teammate, especially since he was batting over .350.

"And we had a scout down there, Leon Wurth, and he found Posada," said Mitch Lukevics. "He had good hands and a strong arm. We weren't sure where he would fit in. His leg speed and quickness wasn't quite the major league level for a shortstop. At first we thought he could be a power-hitting second baseman — a Jeff Kent type, if you look at the ideal."

Kent played 17 major league seasons and hit 377 home runs with more than 1,500 RBI.

Still, the Yankees obviously did not assess Posada as a bona fide prospect. He was the 646th pick of the 1990 draft. But there was one other thing about Posada that piqued the Yankees' interest.

Wurth, going the extra step like a sage scout, happened to be observing a Calhoun game when the regular catcher did not show up. Posada, who had been the backstop on his father's fast-pitch softball team, volunteered to catch the game.

The word got out that the 646th pick, the infielder with the strong arm, might be a catching prospect down the road.

"We used to have a saying for guys who didn't have the greatest range in the field," said Livesey. "We'd say, 'If you can't get to the ball, we've got a place where the ball comes to you.'"

If he could be converted to catcher, the Yankees would like their pick of Posada even better. But like Pettitte, Posada did not sign with the Yankees in 1990. The team would retain the rights to both players for one year. If neither player signed by May 25, 1991, they would reenter the draft pool and could be drafted by any team.

The clock was ticking. But Gene Michael had a lot of draft picks and minor leaguers to assess. And he had a major league team that had become a daily embarrassment.

The 1990 Yankees not only finished with the most defeats of any team since the franchise changed its name to the Yankees, they also had the worst record in the American League and finished 21 games out of first place. The defending world champion Oakland Athletics went 12-0 against the Yankees, the first time in franchise history that an opponent had been undefeated throughout a season against the Yankees. The Yankees had a winning record in just one month, and that was August. But it did not portend an uplifting end-of-season rally. In September and October, they lost 19 of 30 games.

Statistically, the Yankees were harrowingly bad. They were 30-51 on the road, and the team's batting average of .241 was the lowest in the major leagues. They had a team earned run average of 4.21, the fifth worst in baseball, and only four other teams gave up more runs. The Yankees led all of big league baseball in just one statistical category, and even that hurt: They had 53 batters hit with a pitch.

The stat that Stick Michael noticed more than any other was the Yankees' on-base percentage. It was only .300, the worst in the American League in nine years. The AL East champion Boston Red Sox had an on-base percentage of .344. "I knew we had to do something about the on-base percentage as fast as possible," Michael said. "That stat jumped off the page. No wonder we lost 95 games."

Individually, there were some troubling story lines. Mattingly's bad back limited him to 102 games, and he hit .256 with five home runs and 42 RBI. It was a precipitous drop-off. In the previous six seasons, Mattingly had hit .327 and averaged 27 homers and 114 RBI.

Steve Sax, the onetime All-Star at second base, hit .260 and slugged just four home runs in 1990. The team's top four starting pitchers were a combined 27-53.

"That season just petered out and you left with a little dread," Buck Showalter said. "It was a little frightening, like a cliffhanger movie where you're waiting for the last scary thing to happen.

"I was happy to be on the field and I enjoyed coaching at third base, but when I went home for the off-season I really had no feel for what we were going to be next year.

"George was gone and no one knew what that was going to mean. Fortunately, I think Stick was a little scared about the future, too. And he was absolutely defiant that he was going to start doing things to make us better. But George's absence was still weird."

It would get weirder. On October 20, minutes after Lou Piniella's Cincinnati Reds swept the Oakland Athletics to win the World Series, Steinbrenner walked onto a sound stage in Rockefeller Center as the host of NBC's *Saturday Night Live*.

The *SNL* writers, who included future US senator Al Franken, lampooned Steinbrenner at every turn. In the first sketch, George appeared in a lineup of famous men who had lost weight by following an Ultra SlimFast regimen. It was set up as a spoof of diet television commercials that had come into vogue, but the real ruse was that George was giving his diet testimonial alongside *SNL* actors playing African tyrant Idi Amin, Cambodian despot Pol Pot and Iraqi dictator Saddam Hussein.

As the skit played out, George finally got the inference of his so-called peers and interrupted the sketch to complain to the show's producer, Lorne Michaels. "Why am I with these guys?" he protested. "I mean, they're ruthless dictators. I'm a baseball owner. Is that the joke, linking me with these guys? I'm getting the feeling that this whole bit is just to humiliate me."

Said Michaels: "Why would we do that? We're all Yankees fans."

That was intended as joke number one.

Franken was called from backstage to explain the skit, but what he really did was con George, which was joke number two. He said that the skit was a parody of the obsession with losing weight, especially since there were so many other grave problems in the world, as represented by Pol Pot, Amin and Saddam.

"So what am I doing up there?" George asked.

Franken said: "You're here as the everyman, someone who our audience identifies with. You're an average Joe American. The joke is that you're the antithesis of a dictator like Pol Pot or Saddam Hussein."

Added Michaels: "The very opposite."

George smiled and went along. "Funny bit, Al," George said as Franken turned to the camera to smirk and wink at the viewers and the live audience. Laughter filled the studio.

To finish off the sketch, and to further prove its intended point, Michaels asked George to wear a spiked Prussian helmet during a closing statement.

More laughs.

Steinbrenner's appearance, however, was generally praised.

Asked if he thought *SNL*'s writers had been too hard on him, George answered, "No, come on, if you can't laugh at yourself there's something wrong with you."

Without question, everyone in America noticed that George was not exactly hiding in Tampa during his exile. He was yukking it up on late-night television.

He might not be in baseball. But he was not going away.

Others in the Yankees family, meanwhile, were most definitely trying to get away.

The day after the team's final 1990 game, Stump Merrill went back to Maine and started running eight miles a day in an effort to lose the twenty pounds he had gained during the season. Postgame light beers, imbibed to dull the pain of a 95-loss season, had certainly been a contributing factor. By early November, Merrill had dropped twenty-five pounds.

He organized a Sunday-morning 10-kilometer road race in his home-town that was called "Stump's Revenge." The name referred to a similar race a year earlier, when Stump had been beaten by almost every contes-tant.

The 1990 race was run on a bitter-cold day. Stump addressed the en-trants at the start, with snow flurries floating from the sky. "We've put water out at the halfway mark," he said, "unless it's frozen."

In the afternoon, Stump tailgated before a Bowdoin College football game and stood near the end zone with family and friends, including some he had known since childhood. Former Yankees pitcher Tommy John drove from New Jersey to Maine in a van with his wife and four children to run in the race.

In the evening, Stump ate fish stew with more friends at a tiny lobster shack on the coast of Bailey Island, just south of his home.

"I'm living the dream," he said as he drove himself home in his Mer-cedes.

Twenty-seven years later, Stump amended that sentiment.

"I was living the dream," he said. "But I also knew our team wasn't very good. And with the old man banished, I wasn't sure we would be able to get good enough fast enough. The one thing you always knew about George — you knew that he hated to lose. And if you were losing, he would spend money to try to get better. But shit, now he was gone. It kept me up some nights. What's going to happen?"

Michael did not wait long to show that he wasn't sitting still. Many things happened in the immediate aftermath of the worst Yankees season in seventy-seven years.

Michael promptly cut Claudell Washington and veteran infielder Wayne Tolleson. They were the first two of 14 Yankees that Michael released, traded, demoted or declined to re-sign between the end of the 1990 season and the beginning of the 1991 season.

It was only the beginning of the purge. By 1992, 25 players from the misbegotten 1990 Yankees were no longer with the team.

Brian Cashman, who in 1998 would take over as Yankees general manager, was a newly hired assistant farm director in 1990. And within a year, he would become Michael's assistant general manager.

But in 1990, Cashman was convinced that with Steinbrenner no longer involved in day-to-day operations, the Yankees were about to entirely overhaul the organizational philosophy.

"Look, we were embarrassed, no doubt about it — the big league club couldn't compete," Cashman said in 2017. "We were not something to be proud of. But George gets thrown out of the game for that period of time. Everything changed. When the boss left, he took his money with him. At the same time, Gene Michael said, 'We're going to go find good young players and we're going to hold on to them for a change.'

"I would hear Stick on the phone saying no to trades hundreds of times after that. Over and over, he'd say, 'He's not available; we're not trading him.' So we became more of a pure baseball operation with an established strategy rather than a constant assembly line of short-term-interest decisions and quick fixes at the expense of the future."

Michael saw 1990 in much of the same way. Except he also knew he had to clean house. "There were guys in that big league clubhouse that had to go, and there were guys we had to make room for who were down in the minors," he said.

It was vital to the Yankees that they promote some of their young talent to the team's 40-man roster. While big league teams carry only 25 players on their active roster, everyone listed on the 40-man roster is protected from being poached by other organizations.

Late in 1990, the Yankees swiftly put two of their coveted prospects on the 40-man list: outfielders Bernie and Gerald Williams.

The two players were not related, but the Yankees were convinced that one of the two would be a starting outfielder for many years to come. More than that, everyone in the Yankees high command was certain that one of the Williams outfielders would be a linchpin in the team's success in the nineties.

But the argument was just beginning about which Williams it would be.

10

Finding One Williams,
Hiding the Other

GERALD WILLIAMS WAS drafted by the Yankees in 1987 from Grambling State in Louisiana, where he had exhibited extraordinary speed on the basepaths, a cannon for an arm in the outfield and a slashing, powerful stroke in the batter's box.

He also showed up at the first Yankees workout after he was drafted with an ever-evolving batting grip that confounded his new employers. Sometimes Williams's hands were inches apart. Once in a while they were upside down, at least from the traditional way players grasped a bat. Williams, who batted right-handed, seemed to be experimenting with having his hands reversed, with his left hand higher on the bat than his right hand.

"He was the rawest of raw prospects," said Mitch Lukevics, the Yankees' director of minor league operations.

Williams was sent to the team's Class A Oneonta farm team that year and promptly hit .365, leading the team in on-base percentage (.447) and slugging percentage (.504), and he had 29 RBI in 29 games played. What to do about the changing batting grip now?

It was neither the first time nor the last that the Yankees were happily surprised, but nonetheless perplexed, by the gifted Gerald Williams.

Gerald played at Oneonta alongside eighteen-year-old Bernie Williams, who hit .344. Bernie, born and raised in Puerto Rico, was one of the Yankee scouting department's greatest, stealthiest free-agent coups — a gifted gem covertly signed to a Yankees contract while other major league teams, who wanted Bernie as well, futilely hunted after him as if he were a ghost.

Bernie was considered a blue-chip prospect, a crown jewel. And yet, by 1987, when he teamed with Gerald Williams, he had already bounced around three minor league teams and been demoted.

The Yankees often wondered what ever would become of the *über*talented Bernie Williams.

The two were linked for years, despite their many differences. Gerald was gregarious, playful and bursting with pride. His nickname was "Ice." Bernie was shy, reticent and sensitive. An appropriate nickname might have been "Nice." Eventually, his teammates came up with another moniker for him, "Bambi."

Gerald always expected to be a professional athlete. Bernie had made plans to study medicine; athletics were a hobby. Gerald played loud hip-hop music that blared from his locker. Bernie sat facing into his locker, quietly strumming jazz riffs on a guitar.

At one time, the Yankees thought that maybe the two Williamses would one day be a center-field and right-field tandem at Yankee Stadium. But it took many years to sort that out. The debate about the merits of the duo would consume countless hours in team personnel meetings and continued until 1993. And throughout, two overarching questions remained the same: What to do with Bernie? What to do with Gerald?

The choices made about the two outfielders, and the choice made between the two, ultimately helped shaped the course of the last baseball dynasty of the twentieth century.

Bernie Williams arrived first, a wide-eyed, tall teen. When brought to Yankee Stadium not long after he signed a free-agent contract on September 13, 1985 — his seventeenth birthday — he confessed that just months earlier he had no intention of ever being a big league ballplayer. "It all happened very fast," said Williams, looking a reporter directly in the eye as he had been taught to do by his mother, a high school principal and college professor. "I'm still not sure how this happened."

Williams grew up in an upper-middle-class family and graduated from a private music school, where he studied classical guitar and had a 3.8 grade point average. He was a track star, winning international junior races in the 200 and 400 meters. He played baseball, but never at the highest levels, in Puerto Rico, where the best All-Star teams of teenagers toured the country. Instead, Williams was on a champion regional team near his hometown of Vega Alta.

A Yankees scout, Roberto Rivera, was at the regional championship. He saw two outfielders who intrigued him. The first was the younger of the two, just fifteen years old. Between innings he would dance in the out-field, which Rivera found off-putting. The scout crossed that outfielder off his list — he would recommend only serious players to the Yankees.

But Rivera liked the older boy, sixteen-year-old outfielder Bernabe Figueroa Williams, who had an elegant manner on the field, gliding after fly balls with the long, smooth strides of a sprinter. He had a silky swing at the plate, and when Rivera spoke with him afterward, Williams, in braces and eyeglasses, was respectful, polite and humble.

He did not talk that day to Bernie's friend the outfield dancer, Juan González, who would eventually sign with the Texas Rangers and hit 434 home runs in a seventeen-year major league career.

But Rivera did watch Williams play several more times and then called the Yankees' scouting director at the time, Doug Melvin. Rivera told Melvin that if Williams filled out and developed, he could one day become a multidimensional talent like the Yankees' current outfielder Dave Winfield. Melvin did not have to be told that information twice. He wanted such a player.

But there were two important considerations to weigh. The rules governing international players at the time forbade any major league team from signing a player younger than seventeen. And Rivera told Melvin that other teams, especially the Rangers and the San Diego Padres, had seen Bernie play as well. Their interest was intensifying.

The Yankees, with Rivera's urging, hatched a plan that took both factors into consideration. They would hide Williams in the United States until his seventeenth birthday. In the summer of 1985, the Yankees whisked Williams to a baseball camp in Connecticut.

Why Connecticut?

It happened to be not far from Melvin's home, which made it convenient for Bernie to have occasional dinners with the Melvin family and made it easy for Melvin to keep tabs on his prospect, who was in the baseball equivalent of a witness protection program.

"We talked to Bernie's parents and told them a few things," Melvin, who would leave the Yankees in 1987 to become a top executive with the Baltimore Orioles, Texas Rangers and Milwaukee Brewers, said years later. "It would be good for their son from a developmental baseball standpoint; it would be good for him to get a little bit acclimated to life in the continental US; and it would be a chance for him to improve his English, although truthfully that was already pretty good."

Bernie's parents agreed with the plan, and Williams prepared to fly to New York for the short drive to Connecticut. Unsure and a little frightened about leaving home, Bernie asked Roberto Rivera if he could bring a teammate along to the baseball camp. It was González. Again, Rivera declined to bring González into the Yankees fold.

Williams was tutored in baseball drills on weekdays and played with an informal team of former professionals on the weekends. He watched Yankees games on television, made visits to the Melvin home and took a rare trip to Yankee Stadium, which was kept something of a secret.

Back in Puerto Rico, the island's many baseball scouts were wondering what had happened to Bernie Williams. Manny Batista, a Rangers scout, had been looking forward to watching Bernie's development that summer. But Batista could not find him.

Just before his birthday, Williams returned to Puerto Rico. The day he turned seventeen, he signed the contract that made him a Yankee for a bonus of about $16,000.

"It was kind of a whirlwind and I had to commit to baseball and make music or medicine a secondary thing — at least for a while," Williams said. "Still, my adjustment to a full-time baseball player — a professional baseball player — was not entirely smooth."

That is a monumental understatement.

As a seventeen-year-old, Williams had a respectable professional debut in the late-season Gulf Coast League, but the next year, playing for Buck Showalter's Fort Lauderdale Yankees, Williams looked lost. It did not help that the Yankees were turning him into a full-time switch-hitter, something Williams had done only occasionally in Puerto Rico. He was primarily a right-handed hitter.

In 25 games in Fort Lauderdale in 1987, Williams batted .155 with four runs batted in. On average, he was striking out once every three at-bats, and he sometimes looked listless chasing after line drives in the outfield. On the bases, he made mental errors.

At that point, Williams stormed into Showalter's office.

"He charged in and said he wanted to go home," Showalter said. "He was mad at me for continuing to insist that he switch-hit. 'I can't hit left-handed,' he said. He was unhappy with how everything was going."

Telling the story more than thirty years later, Showalter said he opened a drawer in his desk and pulled out a small piece of paper with writing on it. At the start of 1987, Williams's parents had given Showalter their phone number in Puerto Rico.

"They had said to me, 'Bernie hasn't been away from home very much, and if he ever gets homesick or wants to quit, call us,'" Showalter said.

When Williams told Showalter he wanted to go home, Showalter responded, "That's fine, Bernie, but I've got to make a phone call first."

Showalter had the piece of paper in his hand as he reached for the phone on his desk.

"Who you calling?" Bernie asked.

"I'm calling your mom and dad because they told me you might want to go home," Showalter said. "And they gave me their phone number and asked me to call them if that happened."

Said Bernie: "You don't need to call them."

"Yes, I do, Bernie. I promised them I'd take good care of you, and I'm going to call and let him know you're quitting and coming home."

Williams stood. "Just wait," he said. "Let me think about it."

Williams's play improved. He continued to switch-hit.

"I told him, 'Bernie, one day you will thank me for forcing you to switch-hit,'" Showalter said. "When you're seeing all these breaking balls and you can just go to the opposite side of the plate and handle them easier from the other side — you're going to love that. Trust me, it's a process. Just stay with it. We know what we're doing."

Williams put his faith in the Yankees. Although their faith in him wavered considerably. In some quarters, he was a constant source of consternation. He was a good teammate and well liked, but his inconsistency befuddled the Yankees executives. His progress followed no predictable track.

After hitting over .300 twice in Class A, he was promoted to Class AA but hit just .252 with little power. When he played 50 games at AAA Columbus, he was overmatched, batting .216 with nearly four times as many strikeouts as extra-base hits. In 1990, he was still at Class AA Albany, doing well (.281, 8 homers, 54 RBI) but not necessarily spectacular for someone in his fifth minor league season. His bosses wondered about his devotion to the craft, especially when they would look in the outfield between pitches and see him strumming an air guitar.

Williams had entered the Yankees organization to much fanfare. Now some thought he was going to be a bust. "We were in a meeting that year and someone from the big league side of the organization said Bernie was a disappointment," Livesey said. "And I asked him who he liked better in our minors. He mentioned an outfielder at Oneonta.

"I said, 'That guy is twenty-two years old trying to make it in rookie ball. Bernie is twenty years old trying to make it in the Eastern League, the best AA league in baseball. Give him some time.'"

That earned Bernie Williams a reprieve, but it was a conversation Livesey would have time and again in personnel meetings. The doubts ran deep. Williams would remain potential trade bait in seemingly every deal the Yankees considered as late as 1993.

And if Bernie wasn't the one in the middle of those trade talks, it was Gerald Williams instead.

Gerald was the ninth of Dorothy Williams's thirteen children in La-Place, Louisiana, a dreary Mississippi River town 25 miles west of New Orleans. Williams's father left the family home when he was an infant. His mother was the sole means of financial support. "It was hard at times, just like any other life," Williams said. "We struggled, but she always was able to make ends meet. Basically, my mother was everything I needed. I never actually missed my father.

"But I did have to grow up quicker. I didn't have any time to make young, bad decisions. I wasn't going to get many second chances."

Gerald, like Bernie, was six-foot-two and 190 pounds. Gifted athletically, he starred at Grambling, a historically black college. He was raw but widely known to scouts, and the Yankees selected him in the fourteenth round.

"Gerald had a lot of tools but so little high-level experience," said Mitch Lukevics, the Yankees' minor league director. "He came from a backwoods Louisiana town. He had a lot to acclimate to once he turned pro."

After his successful first minor league season in Oneonta, Williams found himself playing for Showalter in Fort Lauderdale in 1988. He had settled on a traditional grip of the bat, with the left hand near the knob, but there were many other unusual habits to break. And new, beneficial habits to learn.

"I remember writing up a report on all the players for Bill Livesey, and when I got to Gerald I pointed out all the things that Gerald still couldn't do — he swung at too many bad pitches, didn't understand the various outfield relays and choices to make in the field, didn't hit the ball the other way — stuff like that," Showalter said. "So a couple days later my phone rings and it's Livesey.

"He says to me: 'Listen, Buck, we don't need your scouting reports. We scouted all these guys for years. We know what they can't do. But let me ask you something. This Gerald Williams, can he run fast?'"

Showalter answered, "Like the wind."

"Does he have a good arm?"

"Yes, sir, one of the best."

"Is his bat alive? Does he have power?"

"Yes, the ball explodes off his bat when he makes contact."

"Is he aggressive? Is he a competitor?"

"Absolutely."

Livesey paused, then roared: "Those are the reasons he's on your team! It's your job to teach him all the other stuff. It's not your job to tell us what he can't do."

Showalter heard a click on the other end of the line, but not a goodbye. "I'm glad Livesey hung up, because I was speechless and about to shit my pants."

Showalter rethought his approach. But he still had his hands full. Williams hit just .189 that season and not much better the next. By the end of the 1990 baseball season, he was still a prized, highly rated prospect. But he was stuck in Class AA Albany, playing alongside Bernie Williams.

Both players would make spectacular plays one night and then butcher a routine fly ball the next night. They might hit a long home run in an opening at-bat of a game and then strike out, and look bad doing so, in every other plate appearance.

The Yankees didn't know what to do with either man. The one thing they knew was that it seemed like each of the other 25 major league teams had keen, fervent interest in acquiring one of what had become known, inaccurately, as the Williams brothers.

Privately, Gene Michael believed that sooner or later he would probably have to trade one or the other. But trading the wrong one might cost him his job and permanently derail any recovery the Yankees' future might hold.

"I knew we could be a little patient with Bernie and Gerald," Michael said, grateful — not for the last time — that in late 1990 George Steinbrenner was no longer calling the shots directly. "We were just getting started with the rebuild. I wanted to believe that things were looking up — at least in the minors, where not many people were actually paying attention."

Some were taking notice, though. The minor league publication of record, *Baseball America,* ranked the Yankees farm system as the ninth best in baseball, up from twenty-second one year earlier. Bernie Williams was rated the eleventh-best prospect in baseball. Gerald Williams would not crack the top-100-prospects list for two seasons.

11

Scouting and Hope

IT WAS NOT of any real consequence, but just to prove that not much had changed by the time the Yankees opened their spring training camp in 1991, Bernie and Gerald Williams were involved in trade talks for four different players in the span of two weeks. Both were almost sent to the Pittsburgh Pirates for Barry Bonds, which would have likely put in motion an intriguing twist to baseball history.

Then, either Bernie or Gerald was nearly dealt for Baltimore third baseman Craig Worthington, who would end up hitting 729 fewer home runs than Bonds. Next, the Yankees considered sending a Williams to Toronto for catcher Pat Borders (693 few career home runs than Bonds). And finally, both Williamses, plus a couple of other young prospects, were almost packaged for California Angels pitcher Chuck Finley (200 more career victories than Bonds).

But no major trades were made, and the Yankees instead began the season trying to prove they were no longer one of the worst teams in the major leagues. It was a tough sell.

Twelve games into the season, the Yankees had rapidly eased back into last place with a 4-8 record. The pitching rotation was erratic and flimsy. Andy Hawkins had been pounded in his first three starts. His tortured Yankees odyssey was about the end. He was released on May 9 with a 0-2 record and a 9.95 ERA. The Yankees still owed him more than $1 million, which was a lot of money in 1991 dollars.

The rest of the rotation was only marginally better. Scott Sanderson, acquired from the Athletics, was the ace and pitched like one. But he had no backup: Tim Leary, whose 19 losses in 1990 led the major leagues, was on his way to a 4-10 season; Wade Taylor and Jeff Johnson would be a combined 13-23; and Pascual Pérez's season ended in injury again after six decisions. He would never return to pitch in the major leagues.

The batting order mostly lacked consistent punch. The best hitter was the new catcher Matt Nokes, who had 24 homers. Mattingly, whose balky back continued to sap his power, hit a humbling nine homers. Outfielder Mel Hall contributed 19 homers and 80 RBI but made few friends in the clubhouse, most especially Bernie Williams, who was called up to the big league club for 85 games. Hall, several Yankees said, believed in rookie hazing. Williams did not respond well, batting .238.

Although Steinbrenner was not seen around the club, there continued to be distractions from his misbegotten personal feud with Winfield. Howie Spira's extortion trial was playing out in Manhattan, and on April 23, Steinbrenner took the stand. He was asked to read the names of family members targeted for harassment on telephone lists confiscated from Spira's apartment. The list included Steinbrenner's eighty-four-year-old mother, Rita.

Steinbrenner, in tears, broke down on the witness stand, his voice quivering. It was a scene, in retrospect, that probably helped to soften Steinbrenner's image. It humanized the Yankees' boss-in-exile, who was left weeping on a witness stand because his misguided actions had brought some measure of threat to his widowed mother. Already there had been talk among other baseball owners that Steinbrenner's punishment had been too harsh. Fay Vincent, of course, had never intended to impose a lifetime ban.

Spira was convicted of five counts of extortion and would serve 22 months in prison.

By early May, the Yankees once again had the worst record in baseball. Merrill's job seemed threatened, at least in the newspapers. Attendance at Yankee Stadium was spiraling downward.

But far from the Bronx, in Baton Rouge, Louisiana, and in San Juan, Puerto Rico, there was considerable good news for the Yankees. It went unnoticed, because the transactions executed in those two distant locales generated not a single story or news item from any media outlet at the time. But on the business transactions wire that connected every major league club, it was recorded that on May 24 and May 25, the Yankees completed two player deals that would reshape the history of the franchise. A team of Yankees scouts and Bill Livesey, the personnel director, successfully negotiated — with deft, experienced skill — the signing of Jorge Posada and Andy Pettitte. Both players had been Yankees picks from a year before, but had the team waited even a few hours or a day longer, it would have lost the rights to the two of them.

And especially in the case of Pettitte, the Yankees very nearly did lose a pitcher they had been watching faithfully for a year.

From the summer of 1990 until the spring of 1991, Pettitte had indeed flourished at San Jacinto Junior College, as the Yankees hoped. His coach, Wayne Graham, had put him on a diet of mostly tuna sandwiches and orange juice, which trimmed the pitcher's lumpy physique by sixteen pounds. Graham started Pettitte on a weight-training regimen at the San Jacinto gym. He also helped hone Pettitte's pickoff move to first base, which became a prized weapon. Finally, the coach put Pettitte's famed competitiveness and temper to good use by teaching him to channel fiery emotions into a cool but fierce comportment in pressure situations.

The remade Pettitte went 8-2 for Graham's 1991 team, and his fastball had jumped from the 87–89-mile-an-hour range to the 91–93-mile-an-hour range.

"Joe Robison calls me and says, 'Pettitte has grown into a man — some games, I've had his fastball at 94,'" Livesey said. "Robison was now insisting that we have to sign him."

But Pettitte, who did not have an agent, was beginning to think he might do better waiting for the 1991 amateur draft in June. He might be a first-round pick. "I was torn and coach Graham told me that another pitcher in the Houston area was likely to be picked in the first round," Pettitte recalled many years later. "Coach Graham thought I was throwing as hard as that pitcher. Back then, a first-round pick was going to get at least $100,000."

In 1990, the Yankees had dangled a contract worth $40,000.

"So, as I said, I was of two minds," Pettitte said. "But I also knew that Mr. Robison had been the first to scout me, and he had stayed with me. He had gone to dozens of my games."

With the May 25 signing deadline approaching, Pettitte and his father, Tom, decided to go to his grandmother's house in Baton Rouge. As it happened, Robison was already in the area, scouting a tournament at Louisiana State in Baton Rouge.

"We had upped our contract offer to Andy from $40,000 to $55,000, and Joe Robison was trying to convince Andy to take it," Livesey said.

It was early in the afternoon of May 25. Pettitte was holding out for at least $80,000, close to first-round money.

Said Livesey: "Joe calls me again and says, 'Boy, this kid is stubborn.' And I said, 'Isn't that what you want? When he has to pitch in front of fifty thousand people at Yankee Stadium, don't you want somebody who is stubborn and won't give in?'"

Pettitte got his $80,000 contract and signed it. It turned out to be a steal. Pettitte, like many others in baseball, spent years wondering if he might have gotten three times as much if he had waited for June and become a first-round pick.

"You never know," said Livesey. "But I'd rather think of it as a great scouting story. Here was a scout who saw something in a raw kid and stuck with him when no other scout was even looking at him. Joe Robison saw the moth that would turn into a butterfly."

The negotiations in Puerto Rico for Jorge Posada took place one day before Pettitte's meeting in Louisiana. They were not as tense, although it was not a certainty that Posada would sign either.

As a scout, Jorge Sr. knew the reputation of the Yankees organization under Steinbrenner. Throughout the eighties, so many minor league prospects had been traded away for big league talent. Even if Steinbrenner was banished, Jorge Sr. did not want a similar fate for his son, and he counseled Jorge Jr. to be wary of the Yankees' contract offers.

Jorge Sr. also knew that baseball prospects from Spanish-speaking countries, perhaps because few had been away from home before, tended to develop later than American prospects, who had often played for youth travel teams or major colleges. Jorge Sr. wanted the Yankees to guarantee in writing that his son could not be traded for at least three years.

Leon Wurth, the Yankees' scout who had first discovered Jorge at Calhoun Community College in Alabama, had been handling the contact with the Posadas. In his 2015 autobiography, Posada wrote that he and his father liked dealing with Wurth because they could discuss their negotiating strategies in front of him in Spanish, which Wurth did not speak.

But in late May of 1991, the Yankees sent several representatives to the Posada home, including Roberto Rivera, the scout who had found and signed seventeen-year-old Bernie Williams six years earlier. "Seeing that group of Yankees employees proved to me that the Yankees were serious —they were here to talk to me directly," Posada said in a 2017 interview.

Still, the Yankees had been offering just $20,000, in part because they were not sold on Posada's middle-infielder skills. Muddling the negotiations, in the spring of 1991 Posada had agreed to accept a full athletic scholarship to play baseball for the University of Alabama. He could develop at a high-level college program and probably at some point be drafted in the top ten rounds, although the contract amount for a future tenth-round pick was hard to predict. And Posada, who was only nineteen years old that May, would be older as well.

He also knew that teams liked to get their prospects into the minor league system as soon as possible, especially if they came from Spanish-speaking countries.

Because Posada came from a family with ties to professional baseball, the Yankees did not think Posada truly preferred to attend the University of Alabama. And, as Wurth and Rivera had suggested, Posada might someday be converted to catcher. The Yankees raised their offer to $30,000 but declined to offer any no-trade guarantees. Posada would be Yankees property, just like the other three hundred minor leaguers in the organization.

Posada signed on May 24. "It seemed like a lot of money to me," he said. "I mean, I was nineteen. Yeah, I could have waited and maybe gotten twice as much, but I always wanted to be a major league player. The best way to do that was to start playing professionally.

"I'd be in the minor leagues competing with other guys trying to get to the majors. And on those teams, how much we had signed for wouldn't matter as much as what we did as batters and fielders for that team in that season. I figured that those numbers would count more than the salary numbers. And I wanted to get started."

In his autobiography, *The Journey Home,* Posada said there was no household celebration of his 1991 contract. "We were a baseball family," he wrote. "Think about it this way: If you were raised in a family where everyone had advanced degrees and worked as doctors, lawyers and professors, no one would go nuts when you graduated from high school."

But in the Yankees' minor league and scouting operations offices in Tampa, there was a new, cheery bounce in everyone's step.

"You very rarely think you've signed a sure-fire major league star-to-be," Lukevics said. "But you know potential when you see it. So when it came to Pettitte and Posada, we were very high on their potential. And that's all you can seek — great potential.

"I can tell you this — we felt like we were building toward something."

But there was no time to rest on the scouting or negotiating accomplishments of late May. The 1991 amateur draft was approaching on June 3, and within the Yankees organization it was being treated as one of the most pivotal days in the team's recent history. With Steinbrenner holding tightly to the purse strings, free-agent acquisitions had been restricted, and with an inferior major league roster, trades to upgrade the talent level had been a daunting challenge. But the amateur player draft was the one golden opportunity where the woebegone Yankees finally had a substantial edge.

There was going to be some benefit to the disastrous 1990 season. The first overall pick of the upcoming amateur player draft was awarded to the team with the worst record in the major leagues. Unyielding failure had delivered the Yankees their first overall choice since 1973.

Throughout the spring of 1991, deciding whom to pick had been the all-consuming task of Livesey, Michael and a host of scouts. They had narrowed their choices to two players: Mike Kelly, a junior center fielder for Arizona State, and Brien Taylor, a nineteen-year-old high schooler from North Carolina whose fastball had been clocked at 100 miles an hour. At the time, there may not have been anyone in the major leagues who threw that hard.

Kelly was a six-foot-four power hitter (46 home runs and 194 RBI in three college seasons). Taylor was an inch shorter, with a long, sinewy left arm that seemed almost magically blessed. With little outward effort, Taylor hurled blazing fastballs that jumped and dived. The dozens of scouts who flocked to his games began referring to him as a left-handed Dwight Gooden.

Taylor, a soft-spoken wunderkind from the tiny coastal town of Beaufort, North Carolina (population 3,707), lived in a double-wide trailer with no air conditioning. The dwelling's sole source of electricity was a plug in the living room ceiling, from which lightbulbs dangled on a cord strung throughout the trailer. Taylor's father was a bricklayer, and his mother, Bettie, worked six days a week picking and sorting crabmeat at a nearby seafood processing plant.

Taylor threw the baseball so hard that occasionally his high school catcher would miss the ball completely. It would whiz past him to the backstop. The umpire often still called the pitch a strike, because it had passed through the strike zone, even if the catcher wasn't quick enough to get his glove on it.

"Brien's arm slot was the same as Randy Johnson's — not over the top and not sidearm but at three-quarters," Gene Michael said. "And that arm slot made the ball move late, just before it reached home plate. And one other thing I'll tell you about Brien: He threw harder than Randy. Even at nineteen years old, he threw harder."

Livesey, now retired, said that the best amateur position player he had ever scouted was Alex Rodriguez and the best amateur pitcher he ever saw was Brien Taylor. "I don't know that there was anyone else who was even all that close to Brien," Livesey said. "Brien had size, strength, a live, loose arm, athleticism, and he had a pretty good curve ball, too."

But drafting a high school pitcher with the number one pick was exceedingly risky. It had happened only once before, in 1973, when the Texas Rangers selected Texas high schooler David Clyde, whose career proved to be underwhelming. Still, the Yankees' scouts were unanimous in their opinion that Taylor was the best amateur player in the nation, despite his modest roots in a small town where the level of baseball played was not especially high.

To make a final judgment on their scouts' recommendation, Michael, Livesey and Lukevics went to North Carolina to watch the final two starts of Taylor's high school career. It was about two weeks before the draft.

"I'm sitting there with a radar gun, and the first pitch Taylor throws is 94 miles an hour," Lukevics said. "The next pitch was 96, and the next one was 98."

In the early 1990s, the radar guns used by baseball scouts were not always reliable. On the next pitch, when Lukevics's radar gun once again registered 98, he turned to a scout from another team who was seated nearby. "What'd you get on your gun?" Lukevics asked.

Answered the scout: "I've had him at 100 for each of the last two pitches."

In his final high school start, Taylor struck out 17 of the 21 batters he faced in a seven-inning game.

The Yankees were sold. They took Taylor with the first pick. It would be twenty-three years before another high school pitcher went first in the amateur draft. (Mike Kelly, in 1991, was selected by the Atlanta Braves with the second overall pick. He would end up playing six seasons for the team, hitting .241 with 22 homers and 86 career RBI.)

Taylor's agent was Scott Boras, known for contract stalemates and big-money victories. And almost from the beginning, the two sides were at loggerheads. The Yankees were offering $750,000, a total Boras and the Taylors deemed unacceptable. Boras had arranged for Taylor to enroll at a local community college. He made it plain that if Taylor didn't sign with the Yankees, he would play college baseball and reenter the draft in 1992, which was his prerogative.

As the Taylor contract deadlock continued into the summer, Steinbrenner was contacted by a New York reporter. George was not only lonely, he was disgusted. If the people running his Yankees couldn't sign Taylor, Steinbrenner said, "someone should be shot."

Said Michael: "That someone was me. That's what George meant. But all that did was make our negotiating position impossible. It hurt the club."

Boras and Taylor rebuffed the Yankees' contract offers for two months, an acrimonious eight weeks during which Bettie Taylor accused Michael of lowballing her son because he was poor and black. Boras, meanwhile, had his client fully registered at Louisburg Junior College and had told the baseball coach there to expect him at his team's late-summer practices.

On August 26, Boras and Taylor accepted a Yankees offer of $1.55 million. The year before, a college pitcher with considerably more experience, Todd Van Poppel, had been drafted by Oakland and signed for $1.25 million.

At a Yankees press conference to introduce Taylor, broadcaster and former Yankees shortstop Tony Kubek asked Boras how much Steinbrenner's "someone should be shot" statement cost the Yankees.

"Boras said, 'Probably about $750,000,'" according to Michael, who recounted the exchange in 2017. "And Boras was right."

At the next quarterly Yankees ownership meetings, Steinbrenner lambasted Michael, yelling at him for giving Taylor so much money.

"You're the one who jacked up the price by saying I should be shot if I didn't sign him," Michael shouted back.

Some of the other Yankees part owners were impressed. "Gene Michael won over some people that day," said Marvin Goldklang, a longtime minority owner. "He made some allies by standing up for himself."

Brian Cashman, the Yankees' current general manager, was an assistant to Lukevics at the time and soon to be hired as Michael's assistant. "It was classic George," Cashman said in 2017. "He had basically said that we better sign this guy. Then he ripped Stick for signing the guy. It was vintage Boss. He took both sides."

Brien Taylor instantly became *Baseball America*'s number one–rated prospect, something that noticeably improved morale in the team's front office. It was only two years earlier that the Yankees did not have anyone in the top 45.

"I felt sure we were going to be very proud of the Taylor pick," Michael said. "It gave us some hope."

12

Yankee Clipper

HOPE WAS IN short supply for the big league team in the summer of 1991. A couple of weeks before Brien Taylor signed, the Yankees were 51-62 and 10½ games behind the first-place Toronto Blue Jays. A month earlier, they had been at .500. But two losing streaks — of six games and seven games — dropped them back into an irrelevant fifth place.

As if things weren't already bleak enough, the wheels fell off completely on August 15. The roster was never whole again.

"Stump lost the team that day," said Buck Showalter.

And the impetus for the implosion was a few locks of hair that somewhat obscured Don Mattingly's collar.

Since 1973, Steinbrenner imposed a policy prohibiting any Yankee player from having facial hair other than a neatly trimmed mustache. The players also could not have long hair, although what constituted "long" was inexact. If a player's hair drooped too far over his collar, it was likely that someone in the organization would suggest a judicious trim.

And usually, that's what the players did. They might cut it one-half inch, an almost imperceptible trim, but the report would get back to Steinbrenner that the offending player had consented to the grooming protocols, and that appeased the owner.

Before a game on August 15, Stump Merrill called Mattingly into his office and told him management was ordering him to cut his hair. He would not play until he did. It would not be hard to comply, since the Yankees' bullpen catcher spent off-seasons as a barber. He cut hair in the clubhouse all the time.

But given his status as the heart and soul of the team, and given the way the policy was being presented, with an on-the-spot ultimatum — his hair had not grown to that length overnight — Mattingly was incensed and chose to sit out the game. Later, he revealed to reporters why he wasn't in the lineup and was no less infuriated.

He also asked to be traded. He had been named the tenth captain in Yankees history earlier in the season, and now he wanted that rescinded, too.

"It doesn't mean anything," Mattingly said of the captaincy. "Maybe I don't belong in the franchise anymore. I've been impeached. I'm just overwhelmed by the pettiness of all of this."

No one in the Yankees' clubhouse disagreed. "It's nickel-and-dime bullshit," said Steve Sax. "Somebody's hair is a ridiculous way to tear down a team."

Three other Yankees were asked to cut their hair. Matt Nokes did so. Reliever Steve Farr did not cut his hair until the next day but was not needed in the August 15 game. The directive also went out to Pascual Pérez, but he was injured and not easy to find.

But Nokes, Farr and Pérez became footnotes to history.

That the team's best and most beloved player — one of the most popular Yankees of the previous twenty-five years — was being persecuted for slightly long hair set off a media firestorm. Newspaper columnists nationwide used the Mattingly incident as proof of the comical, pathetic depths that the once great Yankees had now reached. Headline writers had a field day, with many playing off "the Yankee Clipper," which was Joe DiMaggio's nickname.

Recognizing just how buffoonish the Yankees had become, two *New York Post* sportswriters had the pictures above their columns altered to make them appear bald and wondered if the Yankees might ask all their players to shave their heads. Dozens of fans showed up the following day at Yankee Stadium wearing Mattingly's number 23 jersey and wigs of long, flowing hair.

But when the derisive laughter subsided, a darker mood pervaded. The nation of Yankees fans had had enough. They were embarrassed and disgusted. For the second consecutive season, the team on the field was clownish. Now the Yankees were a joke off the field, too.

Throughout the Yankees organization, it was understood that Steinbrenner — exiled but not entirely silenced — had surreptitiously sent a message through the chain of command that he wanted Mattingly's hair cut. It was one of Steinbrenner's best-known rules, the one he instituted during his first days as Yankees owner in 1973. Gene Michael, who told Merrill to give Mattingly the ultimatum, never admitted that Steinbrenner gave the order, and he wouldn't revisit the subject when asked to in 2017. But from time to time in 1990 and 1991, Yankee employees confided to reporters covering the team that Steinbrenner would sometimes furtively communicate his wishes to the front office through a family member or one of his allies in the ownership group. It usually concerned something trivial.

But if it was Steinbrenner who stealthily pushed the haircut issue, the fallout and the bulk of the searing ridicule for the fiasco fell on Merrill, who has always said that he assumed the haircut directive came at Steinbrenner's urging. Michael took some blame, though not most of it, because he was one person removed. As for Steinbrenner, he was already in baseball jail. Out of sight, out of mind.

Unmistakably, a majority of players turned their back on Merrill forevermore. Fans began to boo him when he went to the mound to remove a pitcher. Players argued with him behind closed doors and criticized him to reporters.

Mattingly, Michael and Merrill each got haircuts on August 16, and Mattingly was back in the Yankees lineup, but the episode was never forgotten.

In an interview twenty-seven years later, Stump Merrill conceded that the Mattingly hair flap eventually led to his dismissal. "A fucking haircut cost me my fucking job," he said, sitting in the lobby of a Tampa hotel. "That's fine; that's the way I look at it. It was certainly the start of the downfall. I lost the respect of some of the players. I don't think there is any question about that. But would I do it again? You're damned right I would."

Buck Showalter, Merrill's third-base coach, felt badly for Stump and also thought it might have been a chance to stand up to Steinbrenner, who was clearly still watching closely. "I wanted to say, 'Stump, this is important to Donnie, and if you do this to him, the rest of the players are going to go apeshit,'" Showalter said in 2017. "Which is what happened."

Showalter filed it away as a lesson — a Yankees manager has to be careful how he chooses sides in a snit initiated by George Steinbrenner.

"What people missed was that you're going to lose in the long run with Steinbrenner if you don't stand up to the things you thought he might be wrong about," Showalter said. "You couldn't fight him on every little thing because that became a distraction, but when you were certain he was doing the wrong thing, you had to stand up and fight back. And the interesting thing is that when you did stand up to him, he had some respect for that. He might listen. But if you didn't, you had no chance with him."

As for Mattingly, many years later he was asked to reminisce about the day he was benched for not cutting his hair. He compared it to a nightmare that one tries to recount the morning after. "You do ask, 'Did that really happen?'" he said, laughing, adding that he would have cut his hair had he been warned ahead of time.

"I was told, 'If you don't get your haircut today, you don't play,'" Mattingly said. "Well, they could have told me two days earlier and I would have got it cut."

But an ultimatum at the ballpark hours before a game made Mattingly bristle, and he pushed back.

He also began a seven-game hitting streak on August 16, a stretch when he hit .357 (10-for-28) with three doubles.

"Yeah," Mattingly said. "I was mad."

He also came back to earth and fell into a mini-slump at the plate. But he wasn't the only one staggering to the finish.

After the Mattingly hair fiasco, the Yankees lost 29 of their remaining 49 games, including one August–September period when they lost 20 of 27 games. The final record was 71-91 and 20 games out of first place. It was a very slight improvement over the disaster of 1990.

"It wasn't Stump's fault; it just didn't work out," said Michael more than twenty-five years later. "We weren't good enough and a change had to be made."

About an hour after the final game of the season, Michael met with Merrill in his mezzanine-level office. "Stick asked me if I was going to be around for a few days," Merrill said. "And I said, 'No, I'm going to Maine today. Tell me now. Skip to the meat.'"

The meat of the conversation was that Stump was relieved of his managerial duties. His wife and family were waiting downstairs when he left the general manager's office. Wordlessly, he grabbed a packed bag and got in his Mercedes, along with his family, for the seven-hour trip to Maine.

About five minutes into the drive, Stump broke his silence: "I want you to know that I just got fired."

And that's how he began the rest of his life.

"My permanent title became 'the ex-manager of the Yankees,'" he said, knowing it was both a compliment and a snub.

For Merrill, a dream job too good to even consider five years earlier had turned out to be, for the most part, a humbling and disquieting experience.

In 2017, retired and living in a beautiful oceanfront home in the coastal Maine town of his boyhood, Merrill, who typically laughs easily, still could not bring himself to smile when discussing the Yankees of 1990–91. "I was the manager of nine teams that won minor league championships before I got the call to come to the major leagues," he said. "That was my big chance. And I'm appreciative of it — even if it wasn't much of a chance. But that's life."

Merrill's record as a minor league manager across 21 seasons was 1,745-1,474, for a winning percentage of .542. In 1990–91, he was 120-155 (.436 winning percentage).

Looking back, Stump said: "We didn't have a third baseman. You've got Álvaro Espinoza at shortstop. At second base you've got Sax, who can't throw the ball to first base. You got Mattingly on the downside of his career. And a pitching staff that was . . . whatever. It wasn't real pretty.

"I mean, I don't know how we won 71 games. I wish George had been there. He wouldn't have allowed that. Maybe my ass would have been fired, but George would have done something to help the roster, and whoever replaced me would have benefited."

The end of the 1991 season was the first time Merrill had been fired from a job. And he took it hard. "I almost went off the deep end," he said in 2017. "It was bad."

Like many baseball lifers whose formative years in the major leagues were in the fifties or sixties, Stump drank plenty of beers after games. It was perhaps not the healthiest habit, and he was hardly alone in choosing that postgame routine. But after his 1991 firing, it became something more dangerous.

Merrill went back to work as a manager in the Yankees minor leagues for another ten seasons, and in fact was an influential presence in the minor league careers of about two-thirds of the young, developing players who would go on to win four Yankees World Series championships from 1996 to 2000. That included Jeter, Rivera, Pettitte, Posada and Bernie and Gerald Williams, all of whom played for Merrill.

But Stump's failure to win during his one shot at the big time continued to haunt him. And a drink, or hundreds of drinks, did not erase the letdown he felt.

"I had never failed at anything in my life, but when I went home to

Maine in 1991, I knew I had failed," he said. "I went through a divorce, which was the biggest mistake I ever made. It was my own fault.

"And so I'm living by myself and the easiest thing to do was drink a couple of beers, and then you're in a deflated mood every fucking day. I'd start thinking about my stint with the Yankees: What could I have done differently? Why did I fail? Why didn't I do this or do that? Why did it happen? Then I'd say, 'Oh, fuck this,' and I'd have another drink. And another. One day I said, 'Hey, you stupid fuck — you're gonna kill yourself.'"

His last drink was in 2002.

Now Stump is remarried and in his seventies, and the biggest decision of his daily life might be when to take an excursion on his boat, based on the tides and Maine's changeable weather.

"I am a firm believer that everything happens for a reason," Merrill said. "I look back and think that not everybody in the world can say they managed the New York Yankees. Some people in Maine will tell me I'm a legend. But I didn't do well enough to be a legend.

"I did go back to do my job, which was working with all those guys who helped revive the big club. And now I have a home on the water, a boat and a beautiful wife who supports everything I do. I'm happy."

If the unpopular Stump Merrill era ended abruptly, it did not in any way portend a new period of prosperity for the Yankees franchise. If anything, for a few weeks, there was more chaos.

From the outside at least, the Yankees appeared more adrift than ever.

The day after Merrill was fired, Gene Michael called Buck Showalter at his home in Pace, Florida. Buck was happy to hear the general manager's voice. There had been rumors in the newspapers that Showalter was a leading candidate to replace Merrill. "Stick mentioned the rumors, then said, 'I want you to know that we're starting over and redoing the whole coaching staff,'" Showalter said years later, recalling the conversation. "He said, 'You're not going to be considered for the managing job as much as people may be telling you that. I know you have a family, and I want you to start looking around for work elsewhere.'"

Angela Showalter was in the room when her husband hung up the phone. She thought he looked scared. "Buck said, 'I don't have a job anymore,'" she said. "I was almost eight months pregnant. We were young. We had never been fired. We didn't know anything about COBRA health insurance coverage that people get when you lose a job. We thought I was pregnant with no health insurance.

"Buck was quite panicked. It was a rather numbing part of life. We were like, 'What do we do now?'"

All of Merrill's coaches were fired but one. Showalter remembers thinking he would have been better off remaining a minor league manager in a little town in upstate New York, where the skipper gets a free leased car and a break on his local rent.

"I wanted to get to the big leagues, but be careful what you wish for, right?" he said. "If I was still in the minors this wouldn't be happening. But it was another lesson, too. Regardless how well you may be doing your job, if the team doesn't win, you get fired. Still, I was just thirty-five years old. It was very sobering, and very unnerving for your family, who you're supposed to be protecting and providing for."

Showalter's angst did not last long. His exit from the Yankees came as a stunning development in the greater baseball community. Soon, the Seattle Mariners called about their vacant manager's position. Six other teams called, offering top coaching positions.

"There was a lot of interest and I went to Seattle," Showalter said. "I was starting to figure out my post-Yankee life after fifteen seasons in the organization."

At the time, and decades later, Gene Michael said his first goal had been to find a manager with major league experience. "I liked Buck, and once I got to know him, later, I liked him a whole lot more," Michael said. "But at first I wanted an experienced manager. The minor league people were telling me about Buck's qualities, although some of them didn't like him. Everybody didn't like Buck.

"Firing managers is awful, and hiring a new one is really tough. I don't like talking about that period. Even now."

In the fall of 1991, Michael had narrowed his choices to two candidates, Doug Rader, who had been the manager of the Texas Rangers for three years and was recently dismissed after three seasons at the helm of the California Angels, and Hal Lanier, who had spent three largely successful years as the manager of the Houston Astros, from 1986 to 1988. Interestingly, Rader and Lanier had both had lengthy careers as players in the major leagues, at the same time Michael had played for the Yankees. Lanier had even been Michael's teammate for two years in New York.

A frequently cited Showalter shortcoming at the time was his lack of experience as a major league player. It had been said about Merrill, too. Michael was wary of the Yankees making the same mistake twice.

A week passed, with Michael weighing the candidacies of Rader and

Lanier. The former Yankee Don Baylor, who was a hitting coach in Milwaukee, asked to be interviewed. Because Lou Piniella's Cincinnati Reds had slumped to a fifth-place finish in 1991, there was talk that Piniella might return for a third stint as Yankees manager.

Michael was being patient, and holding his cards close to his vest.

Then, on October 18, George Steinbrenner, still the Yankees' principal owner, convened a quarterly meeting of the team's partners, or limited owners, in Cleveland. Steinbrenner was allowed to fully participate in such meetings. Michael told the roomful of owners that he was deciding between Rader and Lanier for the manager's job. Michael was then excused from the meeting.

A couple of hours later, Robert Nederlander, the new managing general partner, informed Michael that the new and top candidate for the managerial job was to be Buck Showalter.

"I don't know what changed. I just know what Nederlander told me," Michael said. "They wanted Buck. I mean, George was there. George never told me anything about what he felt about Buck, but he could tell the other owners."

In an interview at his Tampa hotel in 1994, Steinbrenner acknowledged that he wanted Showalter all along. "Billy Martin had told me several years earlier not to let Buck out of the organization — that he was my future manager," Steinbrenner said. "And Billy was right."

Another voice influenced the decision: Hank Steinbrenner. He had traveled throughout the Yankees minors from 1985 to 1987 and watched Showalter closely. He had also been one of the few in the organization to read Showalter's elaborate, detailed reports as the team's eye-in-the-sky coach. And he had observed him as a third-base coach. In October 1991, Hank lobbied his father to overrule Michael and bring Showalter back into the Yankees fold.

On October 20, Showalter was summoned to Yankee Stadium and offered the job, which he accepted. It would be officially announced after the World Series ended later in the month.

In roughly two weeks, Showalter had gone from being expendable to being the thirtieth manager in Yankees history.

"I know that initially Stick didn't think I was ready, and rightfully so, because I would have felt the same way," Showalter said in 2016, sitting in the office of his Texas home, where plaques commemorating his three American League Manager of the Year awards hang from the walls. "Obviously, Billy's input from a couple years earlier probably moved George to do something. But I also think it helped that I would come cheap. Mr. Steinbrenner wasn't exactly throwing gold coins around at that point."

Showalter got a one-year contract worth $225,000 — or $700,000 less than Piniella would have cost the Yankees. "And most veteran managers wouldn't have come for a one-year deal," Showalter said. "But I didn't care. I had already had fifteen one-year contracts with the Yankees."

On October 29, at a news conference inside Yankee Stadium's lavish Diamond Club, Showalter, alongside Angela and his daughter Allie, was introduced as the new manager.

"There were so many cameras and spotlights pointed at us and a roomful of reporters shouting questions," Angela Showalter recalled. "We had never been in the limelight like that. I remember leaning over and whispering in Allie's ear, 'Now you know what Mickey Mouse feels like.'

"Then Buck got up and started speaking and handled the throng like he had done it twenty times before. And I was like, 'Oh, my goodness, where did this come from?' I knew that Buck and all of his family were well educated, but he was so eloquent. So poised. I also remember thinking how many ups and downs and twists and turns our lives had taken in just a few years."

Angela paused, then added, "I should have known it was only the beginning."

The floundering Yankees, who had not been to the playoffs in a decade, and whose record in the last three seasons was 212-273, had a new, altogether different leader. Showalter was the youngest manager in the major leagues and the youngest for the Yankees since 1914, when twenty-three-year-old Roger Peckinpaugh was a player-manager for 20 meaningless games at the end of a dreadful season.

But for Yankees fans, Showalter's hiring was met with a collective yawn. Here was another guy they had barely heard of.

Stump, Buck . . . Who are these guys?

And everyone knew that Showalter wasn't on the team's original list of candidates.

At the news conference announcing Showalter's ascension to one of the most prominent jobs in sports, Gene Michael was asked if Showalter was his first choice. He chirped, "He is now."

Part Two

Planting the Seeds

13

Band of Brothers

SINCE THE END of the 1991 season, Buck Showalter had been fired, rehired, witnessed the birth of his second child and lost his father, who died while undergoing open-heart surgery nineteen days after Showalter was handed the Yankees managerial job.

Continuing family tradition, Buck named his son William Nathaniel Showalter IV.

Two months later, sitting in his office the day before the Yankees would open their 1992 spring training camp, Showalter vowed to carry on the teachings of his father. "My dad was determined. He studied so that he was always prepared, and he paid attention to every detail," Showalter, forever the principal's son, said. "He also thought it was imperative to believe in people."

Showalter paused, then said: "It helps, however, if they are the right people. You have to trust who you're going into battle with."

If it sounded like a summary of his plans to rebuild the Yankees, that's because it was.

Showalter, thirty-five, was almost a generation younger than his dugout peers (the average age of a major league manager in 1992 was forty-seven). Perhaps not surprisingly, he immediately introduced to major league baseball some of the unconventional methods he had been contemplating for years. They were the tactics, ideas and procedures he had been jotting in his journal for decades. In many ways, he had been prepping for the Yankees job since his father took him as a boy to Alabama football games to scrutinize Bear Bryant. It was the reason he had been an ever-inquisitive minor league player. It was why he tested out his own theories on certain canons of baseball ideology, like the notion that things "even out" during the course of a baseball season.

Nothing the new Yankees manager did occurred without considered forethought. Absolutely nothing.

Take, for example, filling out a lineup card, a daily duty for a manager, who must make out a batting order, listing the starting hitters and their positions from 1 to 9. The manager also had to name the starting pitcher. Then, after that, the other 15 eligible reserve players and pitchers on the team had to be listed on the same sheet of paper, below the starters.

Managers customarily wrote down the nonstarting players in no particular order. But Showalter would not do something so haphazard. He always insisted on listing the remaining 15 names in alphabetical order. If a new player was acquired or called up from the minors, one of the first things Showalter would do is figure out where the player fit alphabetically on the roster.

Why go to all that trouble? And what did it have to do with helping a team win?

"Every player looks at the lineup card closely," Showalter explained. "When I was playing, if I wasn't starting, I'd look at the list of reserves. If my name was listed at the bottom, I'd say to myself, 'I'm the last person on the manager's mind. He's writing down names as they come to him, and my name pops into his head last.' That was demoralizing."

So Buck Showalter made a note to himself that when he was a manager, he would never dishearten any player if he could avoid it. He would list every reserve player alphabetically so no one would feel slighted.

"And believe me, the players notice," he said. "Even big leaguers who have been in the majors for ten years notice. They don't perceive an obvious pecking order, which is good for camaraderie. They also now realize that everything is done for a reason — nothing happens by happenstance.

"It's a small thing, but getting a team of 25 guys to strive together for a long season sometimes is about small things."

In the end, to Showalter, it was about changing the culture of the Yankees' clubhouse, which was his foremost and most meaningful goal. And he had a multifaceted plan for that, too.

"When Showalter took over there was definitely a transformation and we all saw it," said Brian Cashman, who had been promoted to assistant general manager in 1992. "I think there was a period of time in the 1980s and early 1990s when there was constant change in the organization. We lacked cohesion.

"The idea that the devil was in the details stopped mattering until Gene Michael hired Buck Showalter and put him in play. And then, next thing you know, Buck went out of his way to find little things that added up to big things."

Cashman recalled that Showalter was "obsessed" with making every part of the team's facility first rate. "And not for show or vanity," Cashman said. "He was testing a theory of his."

Showalter believed it would lead to a closer, more connected team. A team that was better than the sum of its parts.

"So Buck had us completely renovate the Yankee Stadium home clubhouse — new sound system, new TVs and couches," Cashman said. "We fixed up the players' lounge. We upgraded the batting cage under the grandstand. We improved the players' parking lot. We focused on the best food for the players."

Showalter's goal was to have the players eager to come to work. "Buck wanted to create an atmosphere where the players would come to the ballpark earlier than normal," Cashman said. "He said, 'Instead of having lunch away from the park and eating before they get here, maybe they'll get here, have lunch in the clubhouse and eventually get here even earlier.'

"Buck thought that having the guys spend more time together would improve team chemistry. Everyone always says that winning teams have great chemistry. Well, how does that happen? Buck had developed philosophies on how to build team chemistry, and we tried them all."

Another Showalter initiative, one spawned by a conversation with Angela: "Buck said that if you make each player's wife, significant other or family members happy, you will make the player happy," Cashman said. "He wanted to have a deluxe family room so that the wives were taken care of, and therefore the kids were taken care of. And he thought that would be a huge attraction.

"Some managers think the families are a distraction. Buck wanted them here at the ballpark. He'd say, 'Let's make the families welcome.' I don't recall, until then, any other manager caring about stuff like that.

"And it wasn't just about making the current players happy. It was about attracting free agents. Buck would talk about how free agents are making decisions about where to sign — to choose us over somebody else. Buck would say, 'How can we differentiate ourselves? Let's pay more attention to the off-the-field things.'"

Showalter's push for a greater sense of camaraderie on his team was in lockstep with an overarching philosophy of his about the importance of a baseball roster being a tight band of brothers. (And Showalter had read *Band of Brothers,* the book about an especially unified World War II infantry company, when it came out in 1992. Years later, the book became a popular HBO television series.)

In Showalter's perfect baseball world, his players would not choose to fraternize on the field with opposing players before games — something that was becoming more common in baseball in the early nineties. "I don't like to see it," Showalter said at the time. "There are 24 other guys on your team. Something is wrong with you if you have to go to the other side of the field to find a friend to talk to before the game."

Glenn Sherlock, the Yankees' major league catching instructor in 1992, recalled that Showalter believed a team was only as strong as the relationships developed across a season. "Buck spent a lot of time with the players, and he encouraged the coaches to as well," said Sherlock, who, like Showalter, was young enough to be a player. "Trying to have a tight-knit group was Buck's goal."

Showalter found myriad ways to build the bond. To keep his players from feeling singled out for a miscue or embarrassed, he forbade the operators of Yankee Stadium's video scoreboard to show replays of Yankee errors or bad plays during home games. "It should be about the team," Showalter said, "not about any one player's missteps. All teams make missteps."

Cashman was the general manager who presided over four of the five Yankees world championships from 1998 to 2009 and a total of 18 postseason appearances. Interviewed in 2018, he was asked if Showalter's methods in 1992 were successful. "Culturally, it was a turning point," he answered. "We're still doing them to this day."

Looking back with the perspective of more than twenty-five years, Showalter said he felt the Yankees had been so browbeaten and cowed, making changes wasn't much of a gamble. "I felt like I was playing house money, you know what I mean?" he said. "I wasn't going to be timid about it. I felt just the opposite — I'm going to bring everything I've got. I'd been thinking about this stuff for years — why wouldn't I do what I wanted?"

He also felt he owed it to the organization, which was the only employer he had known in his adult life. "Yes, I was getting this window of opportunity personally," Showalter said. "But the window of opportunity was not just for me, it was for the organization. I was tired of getting our ass beat, too."

Gene Michael was Showalter's willing partner in the minor revolution taking place behind the scenes. "Buck and I had a lot of meetings and conversations in early 1992 and I started to see how his mind worked," Michael said. "I understood how he had thought about all these things for years. And I knew we could make it work."

Said Showalter: "I had my input at the clubhouse and field level, but let's not underestimate Stick's impact, which was, in my opinion, bigger than my impact. He had to find the players and navigate all those changes with the owners."

Told of Showalter's comment in 2017, Michael guffawed. "The owner was in exile!" he said. "That's why we could do whatever we wanted. That's what made it work."

But changing the clubhouse culture also meant changing the players in that clubhouse, and that's where Stick Michael did some of his best work for the next four years.

In 1992, the Yankees were not overhauled in one fell swoop, but there were significant roster changes between the 1991 and 1992 seasons. Michael, for example, worked quickly to acquire a quality cleanup hitter to give some needed muscle to the lineup, and he cleverly upgraded the team in other ways — without trading away the best prospects on the farm.

"Stick used to call it bottom-feeding," Showalter said. "He'd want to snatch away some players from other teams he considered underrated and trade away some of our guys in the minors that he thought were overrated."

Michael's first major purchase was free agent Danny Tartabull, who was coming off an All-Star season when he had driven in 100 runs for the Kansas City Royals and led the majors in slugging percentage.

Tartabull, twenty-nine, was an outfielder who had already produced three 100-RBI seasons. Mercurial and moody, Tartabull had squabbled with management in Kansas City, but with Mattingly's declining power-hitting numbers, the Yankees desperately needed a bona fide home run threat.

Next, Michael traded second baseman Steve Sax to the Chicago White Sox for talented starting pitcher Mélido Pérez — brother of Pascual but with a much better off-the-field reputation — and two White Sox minor league pitchers, Bob Wickman and Domingo Jean.

The acquisition of Pérez, who had a 45-46 record, got most of the media attention, but Michael knew the jewels of the deal were the two pitchers who came with him. Wickman had compiled a 20-14 record with a 2.64 ERA in two minor league seasons, but Michael was most intrigued by a quirk buried in a Yankee scout's report on Wickman. "Lost half his right index finger in a farm accident when he was young, which might explain why hitters have so much trouble with his sinker/slider," the scout wrote. "The pitch dips and dives near the plate. Probably the four and one-half finger grip . . ."

Michael called the scout himself.

"He said that Wickman didn't look special, but he *was* special," Michael said.

And while Pérez would give the Yankees valuable innings in 1992, it was Wickman who would prove invaluable for many seasons to come. As proof that all prospects don't pan out, Jean also was highly regarded but never blossomed at the major league level.

As for Sax, 1992 was his last full season in the majors. He hit .237 with only five home runs for the rest of his career. To replace Sax at second base, Michael planned to use touted rookie Pat Kelly, along with Mike Gallego, another free agent the Yankees signed from Oakland. With the Athletics, Gallego had hardly been a feared hitter, batting in the .230s with only 11 home runs and 111 RBI in his first six major league seasons.

But in 1991, Michael noticed that Gallego's power statistics had suddenly jumped: 12 homers and 49 RBI. His OPS (a combination of on-base percentage and slugging percentage) had risen to .712, a leap of 163 points from the previous season. The OPS statistic had not been officially or regularly tabulated in 1992, but Michael had already begun to use the rubric.

Showalter was skeptical that the five-foot-eight Gallego could play shortstop and second base, since the Yankees might need him at both positions. Michael, once a Gold Glove–level shortstop, assured his manager that he would come to love Gallego's infield skills.

"Stick was right," Showalter said of Gallego, who would go on to belt 19 home runs, drive in 109 runs and bat .262 with the Yankees from 1992 to 1994.

Next, Michael turned his attention to the gaping hole at third base. The Yankees had a revolving door at the position in 1991, with third basemen producing just six home runs and 38 RBI in 162 games, by far the worst production at the position of any major league team.

Michael had his eye on the Philadelphia Phillies' third baseman Charlie Hayes, a four-year veteran with power whom the Phillies were planning to bench for Dave Hollins, a rising, switch-hitting prospect with substantial upside.

Michael acquired Hayes by sending Darrin Chapin, a minor league starting pitcher who was 10-3 with 1.95 ERA at Columbus in 1991, to Philadelphia. The Yankees had taken Chapin in the sixth round of the 1986 amateur draft, and the team knew him well. He had pitched for five Yankees minor league clubs. But the scouting department believed that Chapin's standout 1991 season at Columbus was something of an illusion.

Chapin ended up pitching just one game for the Phillies in 1992, then spent the rest of his career in the minors.

The remake of the Yankees was taking shape bit by bit. The team resigned free-agent catcher Matt Nokes, a lefty hitter who had led the team in home runs in 1991. But it was another free-agent catcher, twenty-eight-year-old Mike Stanley, who was the Yankees' biggest steal of the free-agent market.

Michael had been watching Stanley closely in his six previous seasons with the Texas Rangers, even though Stanley averaged only about 160 at-bats a year and rarely hit higher than .249. Michael signed Stanley, who had 16 career home runs, to a meager contract worth $175,000 annually and told him he would be the right-handed-hitting part of a platoon at catcher with Nokes.

But secretly, Michael thought Stanley could be the full-time catcher, and maybe even an All-Star. "Whenever I watched Stanley hit, he almost always had a quality at-bat," Michael later said. "He would take the measure of the pitcher and battled him mentally, pitch for pitch. He was clearly studying the pitchers."

Stanley, in fact, was making the most of all the time he spent on the bench. He sidled up to the pitching coach and listened as the coach assessed the strengths and weaknesses of each opposing pitcher and hitter.

"Early in my career, there were times I played so little, I thought about going home to Florida and opening a tackle shop because I love to fish," Stanley recalled decades later. "But while I was there in Texas, I was determined to learn as much about being a major league catcher and a bona fide major league hitter as I could. I took every day seriously."

That made Stanley a good fit in Showalter's clubhouse. "We needed guys like Nokes and Stanley because they were dirt-tough, hard-nosed guys who would hold teammates accountable," Showalter said. "It's all about being accountable, and I was going to hold our team to standards when it came to playing hard and being prepared.

"But you need the players to hold each other accountable, too. Someone like Nokes or Stanley would do that and finally give Don Mattingly some backup in that way. Now there were a few guys of stature who had Donnie's back. And Nokes and Stanley wouldn't let any of the bullshit hazing of the young guys continue either. If you're trying to promote a youth movement, you can't have some veteran guys jumping all over the rookies."

Outfielder Mel Hall was a case in point. He had relentlessly badgered the reserved Bernie Williams in 1991, making fun of his thick eyeglasses and his guitar playing and nicknaming him "Zero" for his lack of production.

"We had to do something about that," Showalter said.

The Yankees hadn't given up on Williams. Michael had once again rebuffed multiple trade offers for him. The Milwaukee Brewers dangled starting pitcher Chris Bosio, who had won 14 games in 1991. Stick Michael demurred.

Off the field, the operation of the Yankees was less tumultuous. Robert Nederlander had resigned, saying that running the team took up too much of his time. He also intimated that answering to George Steinbrenner, even though he was in exile, was another full-time job.

Joe Molloy, the husband of George's daughter Jessica, was named the new managing general partner. It wasn't hard for Steinbrenner to make his wishes known to his son-in-law, but years later, Molloy, who divorced Jessica in 1998, said Steinbrenner had not imposed his will in 1992. "He was too busy trying to get Fay Vincent to reinstate him — that was his focus then," Molloy said evenly.

Increasingly, Vincent gave indications he was willing to amend his lifetime ban at some point. Steinbrenner, to no one's surprise, was doing everything he could to lobby for a reprieve.

On March 22, he bought a $7 ticket to watch a Yankees exhibition game in Clearwater, Florida, against the Phillies. It was the first game he had attended since his banishment. Seated behind the first-base dugout, Steinbrenner was asked to name the one thing the 1992 Yankees needed most.

George answered, "Me."

Three days later, Steinbrenner dispatched a strangely emotional letter to the other 25 major league owners in which he begged for their help in his crusade to be reinstated.

A handful did petition the commissioner on Steinbrenner's behalf. It was the first signal that Vincent did not have the unanimous support of baseball's owners. It was a trickle in the tidal wave to come.

The Yankees' 1992 regular season almost started without the team's new manager. The Showalters' five-month-old son, whom the family called Nathan, was rushed to a New Jersey hospital with spinal meningitis thirty-six hours before opening day at Yankee Stadium.

Nathan's fever broke and he improved in time for his father to make his managerial debut in the season's first game, which the Yankees won, defeating Roger Clemens and the Red Sox, 4–3.

The Yankees also won their next five games and were alone in first place in the American League East. By May 17, they were only one game over .500, but the day was symbolically important because the Yankees, a laughingstock for three years, gained a measure of respect.

The opponent that day at Yankee Stadium was the Oakland Athletics, who were still a powerhouse and just two seasons removed from their three consecutive World Series appearances. Oakland had also won 31 of their previous 42 games against the Yankees, including 16 in a row at one point. More conspicuous, the Athletics and their manager, Tony La Russa, often seemed to delight in tormenting the Yankees. Oakland had a big and intimidating team, with brawny sluggers like Mark McGwire and José Canseco and a growling ace pitcher, Dave Stewart, who wasn't averse to throwing at hitters (nine hit batsmen in 1991).

In the fourth inning of the May 17 game, Mélido Pérez threw an inside pitch to Oakland's Scott Brosius. La Russa and Athletics outfielder Willie Wilson began shouting at Pérez.

There was some recent bad blood between the teams. The previous week, the Yankees' rookie second baseman Pat Kelly had been hit twice by pitches in a three-game series in Oakland. It would be like the Athletics to try to unsettle or frighten a first-year phenom.

But on May 17, after the inside pitch to Brosius, La Russa turned his ire toward catcher Matt Nokes, yelling, "We'll show you what an inside pitch is."

At that moment, Showalter stomped to the top step of the dugout and bellowed at La Russa, tapping his chest with a finger. Said Showalter: "If you've got a problem, you can come to me."

La Russa, a future Hall of Famer, was considered the game's genius manager at the time. He responded to a rookie manager's insolence by charging at him from the Oakland dugout.

Showalter met the challenge with a sprint from his dugout as well. The two managers looked willing to fight and were hastily separated by home plate umpire Al Clark. But Clark was outnumbered and the tussle continued. At one point, Showalter and La Russa each cocked their fists. Neither actually threw a punch, but they kept jabbering and had to be restrained by several players. The benches and bullpens emptied. It took a few minutes to get La Russa and Showalter apart.

Showalter was particularly enraged. Mattingly was jawing at La Russa as well. When the game resumed, the Yankees won, 11–2.

Afterward, Showalter, who kept a picture of Billy Martin on his office wall, said the incident was payback for years of Oakland's bullying. "We're not going to back off from anybody," Showalter said. "We're not going to let people do some of the things that were done here. I'm not going to sit there and allow anyone from another team to yell at our players."

In the clubhouse, the Yankees were energized. "I like what Buck did," said reliever Steve Farr. "We needed that."

The 1992 Yankees had something that had not been seen at Yankee Stadium for some time: a fire in their eyes. At the same time, there was a newfound sense that the franchise could see the light at the end of a very dark tunnel. "Throughout the organization, there was relief, even an optimism — like maybe some good things are going to fall our way for a change," Cashman said.

At roughly the time that Buck Showalter was challenging Tony La Russa to a fistfight, Bill Livesey, the Yankees' director of scouting, called his top Midwest scout, Dick Groch. Livesey knew that Groch was planning a trip to watch a prospect in Ohio.

"Don't you know that Jeter's team is playing?" Livesey asked Groch.

Jeter had recently sprained his ankle, and Groch said he wasn't expected to play for another week.

"Well, that's our kid, so you'd better go over and sit on him anyway," said Livesey, who had recently become Jeter's biggest fan.

Livesey had made the protracted trek to Kalamazoo, weaving through the tractor-trailers barreling toward Chicago on Interstate 94, then pulling off the highway and driving the ten miles to Jeter's high school. He watched Jeter play in the rain and cold, a day when it was hard to assess any player's talents, and then, two days later, after a trip to watch a prospect at Michigan State, Livesey circled back to watch Jeter in better weather.

"That's when I saw why Dick Groch's reports were so glowing," he said.

Still, Livesey knew that Jeter had also agreed to play for the University of Michigan. The commitment was not binding, but still, he wondered.

"Isn't this kid going to Michigan?" Livesey asked Groch.

"The only place this kid is going is Cooperstown," Groch shot back.

As directed by his boss in mid-May, Groch went back to Kalamazoo to watch another game, "even though none of us ever thought we'd get our chance to draft him," Groch said, cognizant that the Yankees had the sixth overall pick on June 1. "But the draft is a funny thing. You never give up, especially on that kind of prospect."

Groch stood in the trees beyond the outfield fence again, the only scout at the game and out of sight, too. He wanted to see if Jeter played hard even when he was not being watched by scouts.

He did, despite his aching ankle. He batted .508 as a senior. Those were not the only numbers that impressed the Yankees. Although Jeter was clearly on his way to college or professional baseball and could have shirked his schoolwork in the final months of his senior year, he instead finished with a 3.8 grade point average.

"We spent the week before the draft tearing up our board of prospects, with all the scouts and personnel people in a conference room at Mr. Steinbrenner's Tampa hotel," Livesey said.

No matter how they shook the board, no matter how much they argued, Jeter was everyone's top pick.

On June 1, the Houston Astros had the first overall pick. They had narrowed their choices to Jeter and Phil Nevin, a power-hitting corner infielder and outfielder at Cal State–Fullerton. Houston had drafted two shortstops with their first-round draft picks in 1990 and 1991. So they took Nevin.

"We thought Nevin was a solid third baseman, nothing more," Livesey said. Nevin would play twelve years in the major leagues and have a worthy career (.270 batting average, 208 homers), but he was a vagabond. And he played only 18 games for the Astros.

The Midwest scout for Houston was Hal Newhouser, a Hall of Fame pitcher in the 1940s for his hometown Detroit Tigers. When he had retired as a player in 1955, Newhouser had gone into scouting. He strongly advised the Astros to take Jeter, saying Jeter was as good a player as he had ever seen. When the Astros took Nevin instead, a disgusted New-houser quit and never worked in baseball again.

The Cleveland Indians had the next pick. They wanted pitching and selected Paul Shuey, a right-hander from the University of North Carolina. "Shuey had a really big leg kick. He was going to have trouble holding runners on," Livesey said. "We liked him, but not at that pick." Shuey became a middle reliever and pitched 11 seasons, most of them for Cleveland, retiring with a 45-28 record and 3.87 ERA.

Up next was the Montreal Expos. They also sought pitching, taking B. J. Wallace, a lefty from Mississippi State.

Livesey: "Wallace? We didn't like him up that high."

Wallace never got out of the minors, cresting at the AA level.

Baltimore had the fourth pick. Jeter did not fit the Orioles' plans, since they had Cal Ripken Jr. at shortstop. They went with Jeffrey Hammonds, an outfielder from Stanford. "Hammonds was a good outfielder, but we already had a bunch of outfielders: Bernie and Gerald Williams, Roberto Kelly and Carl Everett," Livesey said. Hammonds had a solid thirteen-year career (.272 average, 110 homers, 423 RBI), although he made the All-Star team only once, in 2000, with the Colorado Rockies.

The fifth choice belonged to the Cincinnati Reds, who had a history of drafting high schoolers. Most everyone figured the Reds would snatch Jeter, though they already had Barry Larkin, who at twenty-eight years old was coming off his fourth successive season as an All-Star shortstop.

At home in Kalamazoo, Jeter was lamenting an ominous, and increasingly obvious, fate. "I was thinking I'd be sitting behind Larkin for years," he said in a 2017 interview.

But the Reds did not have the deepest pockets. Thinking that Jeter would not last until the fifth pick, they had been in contact with Chad Mottola, a six-foot-three, 215-pound outfielder from central Florida who hit such towering homers even the Astros considered him with the first pick.

Mottola had told the Reds that he was looking for a contract of about $400,000. The Reds convinced themselves that Jeter, who would not turn eighteen until June 26, would enroll at Michigan. Plus, Mottola might come at half the price that Jeter would fetch.

The Yankees' scouting and player personnel executives were assembled in a large meeting room at Steinbrenner's Tampa hotel as the draft played out. The picks were being delivered via conference call, with each team announcing its pick into a speakerphone connected to 25 other speakerphones around the country.

There was silence in the Yankees' meeting room as the Reds deliberated. But when Cincinnati announced Mottola's name, someone in the room hit the mute button so the rest of major league baseball did not hear the cheering that had erupted in Tampa. "We were going pretty crazy — we couldn't believe what had happened," Lukevics, the farm director, said. "I mean, we would have taken Jeter if we had the first pick."

The Yankees' view of Mottola?

"Not to degrade any of these guys, but we didn't have Chad up that high," Livesey said. Mottola became a terrific minor league hitter — he played 16 minor league seasons — but in the majors he would play a total of 59 games and hit four homers and bat .200.

Once Cincinnati had made their selection, there was no hesitation in Tampa. Kevin Elfering, the assistant scouting director, unmuted the phone and spoke into it. "Derek Jeter of Kalamazoo Central," he said. "Maybe the most famous words I've ever spoken."

Jack Curry, an intrepid sports reporter for the *New York Times*, reached Jeter by telephone from Texas, where the Yankees defeated the Rangers, 7–1, to go five games over .500. They were within four games of first-place Toronto. Curry, who would be writing a book with Jeter in a few years, was struck by the poise of the teenager on the other end of the line. Jeter said it was "50-50" whether he would go to college or sign with the Yankees. "We'll make a decision as a family," Jeter told Curry.

But Gene Michael knew the Jeter contract negotiations would be nothing like what he went through a year earlier with Brien Taylor. "Derek grew up a Yankee fan in New Jersey," he said, smiling. "We knew he had been telling people he was going to play for the Yankees since he was a little boy. We were going to give him a good contract, and we did — $800,000 — and he was going to begin his lifelong dream."

Standing in a corridor beneath the grandstand at the Yankees' spring training complex twenty-five years later, Michael laughed. "When Jeter fell to us with the sixth pick," he said with a wide smile, "we felt like maybe, as a franchise, we were on a little roll. I mean, that was a good day.

"It worked out pretty well, right?"

14

The Yankee Way

THE MINOR LEAGUE system that Derek Jeter would be joining was different from any other in professional baseball. By design, the Yankees farm clubs stood apart because of the amount of money invested, because of what was emphasized and because of a meticulous, ultraorganized structure.

The leaders of the Yankees minor league system were outliers. While other teams considered the catcher to be the most important position player, the Yankees put catcher at the bottom of their priorities in the amateur draft. They would find other skilled position players and turn them into catchers.

While other teams shied away from players from the Dominican Republic or Puerto Rico because they typically took longer to develop, the Yankees doubled the scouting staff in those countries and encouraged them to find younger players, to leave more time for development.

And most prominently, while other clubs looked at their farm teams primarily as incubators of individual talent and did not put a premium on developing winning teams, the Yankees stressed that the goal of each of the minor league teams was to win a championship. "Winning is a teaching tool," said Bill Livesey, the scouting director.

It was more than a theoretical goal. It was pragmatic, too.

"In the minors, you're trying to see your guys play as much as possible, to evaluate them and to help them develop," said Brian Sabean, a Yankees scouting and player personnel vice president in the late eighties and early nineties who would go on to mold three World Series winners as general manager of the San Francisco Giants. "If they're in the postseason, contending for a championship every year, they're going to have to play another 15 or 20 playoff games — that's another month of baseball, which is good for them and good for us as evaluators. Plus, we get to watch how they perform under the pressure of the postseason. Why would you want to wait until they get to the major leagues to find out whether they can perform under pressure?"

Everything that was done in the Yankees minor leagues was part of a master plan, for which there was even a written manual, penned by Livesey and Mark Newman, the coordinator of minor league instruction, who also had a law degree. Officially, it was called "The Yankee System Developmental Manual," but to players, coaches and executives, the tome of more than five hundred pages was "the Yankee Way."

It included things as simple as how the home and road uniforms were supposed to be worn — the famed home pinstripes had to align vertically from the jersey top to the pants, for example, and four inches of the blue stirrup sock was supposed to be visible between the bottom of the pant leg and the top of the shoes. But the Yankee Way was complex, too. There was a chart for the model height and weight of players by position, and scouts memorized it. First basemen and third basemen were ideally expected to be six-foot-one or taller and at least 190 pounds. Outfielders could be smaller if their time in a 30-yard dash (the distance between the bases) was fast enough.

The chart was extremely detailed and it prioritized by position the five elemental baseball skills of hitting, power hitting, fielding, running ability and arm strength. For example, in the Yankee Way, the most important skill listed for a center fielder was fielding ability, followed by running ability, then hitting, arm strength and power hitting. At third base, it was hitting ability, power hitting, fielding, arm strength and then running ability. For first basemen and right fielders, it was primarily about power hitting. Running ability came last.

"The Yankee Way manual was an unbelievably meticulous, valuable tool," said Glenn Sherlock, who before joining Showalter's staff in 1992 was a Yankees minor league manager and coach. Sherlock went on to spend more than twenty years as a major league coach in Arizona and with the New York Mets.

"I still have that Yankee manual and I still refer to it," Sherlock said in 2018 when he was the Mets' third-base coach. "They used it to train all the Yankee coaches on how to coach. It would tell you not only how to teach an outfielder to catch a fly ball, it would also tell you how the outfielder should move his feet before he caught the ball and after he caught the ball. Everything Mark Newman and Bill Livesey did was a baseball education."

The Yankee Way emphasized some other details, like instructing players to get to the ballpark at 1 p.m. for a 7:30 game. Why so early?

The Yankees employed a cadre of roving infield, outfield, catching and hitting instructors — coaches who rotated through the nine minor league teams for one-week stints — and they conducted drills and worked with the Yankees' farmhands from 2 to 4 p.m. every day. There would be a 45-minute break and then the team's regular coaches would put the players through more practice to prepare for that night's game.

And every Yankees minor league team had more coaches on staff than teams from other major league organizations. While the typical team usually had a manager who doubled as a third-base coach, that was unacceptable to the Yankees. They had at least two coaches, and often three. That way the manager could remain in the dugout throughout the game. There was frequently a pitching coach as well.

"First of all, we wanted the manager in the dugout where he could coach and instruct his team as the game is going on instead of being 120 feet away in the third-base box," said Mitch Lukevics, the director of minor league operations. "You can't explain tactics or explain what went right or did not go right from the third-base coaching box. And having a pitching coach was just common sense. Everyone says that developing enough good, young pitching is the hardest thing. Well, young pitchers need a lot of attention to develop. They might need a pitching coach more in their first year of pro baseball than they do in their tenth year of pro baseball."

The salary of the Yankees' minor league players was about 10 to 15 percent higher than the salaries of other teams. The managers and coaches were also paid more handsomely. The equipment was of major league quality. There were full-time athletic trainers assigned to every team.

"On some teams, the bus driver was the trainer," said Elfering, the assistant scouting director.

The coaches were instructed to keep track of unusual statistics, ones not found in a traditional box score. The Yankees brain trust wanted to know how many times each player got a bunt down successfully (or failed to do so), or how many times a hit-and-run was performed properly, or how many times a player lofted a run-scoring sacrifice fly. They wanted to know how many times a batter hit behind a base runner to advance him. And they kept a log for each player of something called "hard-hit balls," which were well-struck balls that were nonetheless outs. (Buck Showalter had wondered why this stat wasn't kept when he was a Yankees farmhand.)

The Yankees' scouts were reimbursed for their travel expenses promptly. The clubhouse food was constantly evaluated, and upgraded if need be. The team had started to videotape every batter and pitcher weekly, if possible. The videos were cataloged and stored. If a player was promoted to a higher level, his videotape — a clunky VHS tape back then — went with him, so his new manager could become familiar with his new player before seeing him play.

And, of course, no player or coach was allowed to have facial hair or hair drooping over his collar.

"We were instituting a system in every sense of the word," Livesey said of the Yankee Way. "Some of it involved spending more money, and Mr. Steinbrenner was great with that — he never rejected spending anything on the minor leagues if we made the case for why it was important.

"He had a football background and went to a military prep school. Mr. Steinbrenner believed in structure and organizational methods and tactics.

"And he certainly liked to win, and knew why it was important."

The Yankee Way was an outlier in some ways compared to other organizations. Every team knew that the major league club would need one or two quality catchers. But in general, the Yankees did not target catchers in the amateur draft, at least not with their top picks. "A lot of high school and college coaches use players where they need them, or because it's the only position they can play, not because they're perfect for that position," Livesey said. "So you have a lot of burly, more physically mature kids playing catcher. Athletically, they may have topped out. And often they weren't all that quick. But in the minors, you want a quick, nimble catcher who is still getting better athletically. We started looking at kids we thought we could switch to catcher."

A case in point: Jim Leyritz, an undrafted infielder and outfielder from the University of Kentucky who also had some experience behind the plate. Leyritz would end up catching 2,348 major league innings and play nine seasons for the Yankees.

The Yankee Way also favored size. Yankees minor league teams sometimes resembled a basketball roster. Or as Livesey put it, "All things being equal, a five-foot-eight guy and a six-foot-two guy are not equal."

The system worked, and Yankees minor leaguers won dozens of championships in the 1980s.

"The problem was that George Steinbrenner was so competitive and that made him impatient," Livesey said. "If the big league club was not winning enough, he wanted to change that immediately. And if that meant trading a top prospect, you couldn't talk him out of it by saying that the prospect would be a perennial All-Star in four years. He didn't care about four years from now."

But starting in 1990 and on into 1992, Steinbrenner was no longer actively making the trades that robbed the team's stable of minor league talent. "We had time for the crops to ripen," Livesey said. "And it was a really good harvest."

Early in 1992, the Yankee major league and minor league coaches and managers got their first look at Brien Taylor, who threw from a bullpen mound at the team's Fort Lauderdale spring training complex.

"I was Brien's catcher in that first bullpen session with everyone watching," Sherlock said. "Frankly, it was hard at first just to catch the ball. He had one fastball that broke to the right and another fastball that broke to the left. He also had two different curve balls. It was an unbelievable show — such an electric arm. And everyone watching was kind of covering their face, trying not to act too impressed, because he was just a young kid and raw. But he had so much energy and you could see the confidence."

When spring training ended in 1992, Taylor made his debut in the Florida State League for the Fort Lauderdale Yankees, where he struck out 187 batters in $161^1/_3$ innings and had a 2.57 ERA.

"And that's coming out of a low-level high school without any real experience pitching against top hitters," said Lukevics. "One of his coaches at Fort Lauderdale said to me, 'Brien has no idea how to hold a runner on first base.' And I said, 'That's because nobody has ever gotten to first base on him before.'"

Taylor developed a cult following. His picture graced the cover of the Fort Lauderdale game program, and his face was splashed across billboards near the team's stadium. His number 19 jersey was stolen from the home clubhouse. An opposing manager compared Taylor to Mozart. Mike Wallace of 60 Minutes wanted an interview.

"He was like the Elvis of the minor leagues," Lukevics said. "Those Florida State League games would usually draw 500 fans. When Brien pitched, there would 2,500 people there. He would walk to his car and

20 people would be pulling on his sleeve for an autograph. I'd never seen anything like it. Everyone knew he was going to be a big star. He already was."

Bobby Valentine, the Texas Rangers' manager, saw Taylor pitch that season in Florida. "That kid looked like the kind of talent you only see once every fifty years," he said. "Dynamic stuff. Just wow."

Mariano Rivera was Taylor's teammate and friend at Fort Lauderdale. Rivera had a good season, too (5-3 record, 2.28 ERA). "But I was nothing like Brien," Rivera said. "He was *the* prospect. He threw the most effortless 98 miles an hour I ever saw. Pure gas. We all knew we were watching greatness."

Taylor struck out 14 batters in his last start of 1992. Rivera's season did not go out on the same high. He had been experiencing pain in his right elbow, and during one start, he felt a pop.

Rivera visited Dr. Frank Jobe, the inventor of ulnar collateral ligament reconstruction, which came to be known as Tommy John surgery. Dr. Jobe wanted to remove some of the loose bodies in Rivera's elbow, but Rivera would avoid a reconstruction. Tommy John surgery usually requires a year of recovery. Dr. Jobe thought Rivera could resume throwing in four or five months.

But that was not the word that went forth throughout the minor league baseball world. What people knew was that Rivera's 1992 season ended abruptly, and that Dr. Jobe had performed surgery on his elbow. The understanding was that he had reconstructive surgery — Tommy John surgery. The Yankees did not dissuade such talk. It was to their advantage for the rest of the baseball community to be misinformed, since there was an expansion draft coming late that year, when two new teams, the Florida Marlins and Colorado Rockies, would be cherry-picking players from the major and minor league rosters of the 26 established teams.

Meanwhile, another Yankees pitcher, Andy Pettitte, was in his second season of professional baseball in 1992. He had won six of nine decisions with a stellar 1.55 ERA in 1991, most of them for the Oneonta Yankees, where he was teammates with Jorge Posada, the starting second baseman.

Posada hit only .235 in 1991, but he also had four homers and 33 RBI. And most significantly, he began the transition from infielder to catcher. He caught only 11 games that season but then spent much of the winter of 1991–92 in Tampa, playing instructional league games at catcher.

"He had a lot of the natural skills you need — good feet, good hands, strong arm," said Sherlock, one of the organization's top catching instructors. "He asked a lot of questions, which is something you want, because a good catcher has to be a thinker."

Posada was also being schooled in the many facets of the position with an endless succession of grueling catching drills. No one enjoys flinging himself in the dirt to block pitches fired at 90 miles an hour, but the Yankees had ways to keep Posada motivated for the task. They told him that there were several middle infielders ahead of him on the franchise depth chart.

They did not, however, have a switch-hitting catcher. That would be a truly valuable asset.

What was that Yankees saying? "If you can't get to the ball, we have a place where the ball comes to you."

Though resistant at first, Posada got the message. By 1992, when he was at a higher level of Class A in Greensboro, North Carolina, Posada spent 90 percent of his time on the field as the team's catcher. And his hitting improved — .277, 12 homers, 58 RBI.

Pettitte was on the Greensboro team, too. Posada caught Pettitte one night when he pitched a complete-game one-hitter without a walk and threw only 90 pitches. After the game, Posada called his father. "I know what a major league pitcher looks like now," Posada said to him. "Because I just caught one."

Late in the Greensboro season, Derek Jeter, skinny and unseasoned, joined the team. He would play 11 games and make nine errors. At the plate, he was a sucker for a breaking ball and hit .243.

Said an incredulous Pettitte: "This is our top pick? This is our best prospect?"

It had actually been worse for Jeter earlier in the year when he played for the Tampa Gulf Coast League Yankees. In 47 games, he had hit .202.

And he might have hit under .200 if a friendly official scorer hadn't mercifully given Jeter a hit on a bobbled ground ball in his last game, just to get him over .200.

"Everyone in the organization noticed that batting average," said Lukevics. "I saw Mr. Steinbrenner in the hallway of his Tampa hotel, which is where Jeter and all those rookies were staying, and he said something to me like, 'How's your top pick, the .200 hitter?'"

Normally, Lukevics only heard from Steinbrenner about the newest and youngest Yankees minor leaguers because one of them had left his swimming trunks hanging on a balcony outside his hotel room. That was a major no-no at Steinbrenner's hotel, and Lukevics and the player would be called into the Boss's office for the offense.

Jeter may have been hitting poorly, but he was not violating hotel protocol. Indeed, it seemed he never left his room. It was where, Jeter confided years later, he was constantly on the phone, calling his home in Michigan. He'd sometimes cry to his mother, asking if he could go back to Kalamazoo, wondering why he hadn't just gone to the University of Michigan.

"That first year away from home was a hard lesson for Derek," Lukevics said. "He struck out seven times in his first doubleheader and booted a couple of ground balls. He was the ugly duckling out there. His feet weren't under him fielding ground balls, and he was off-balance when he threw, so he was airmailing throws. He had great range and got to so many balls, but that gave him more chances to make errors.

"We saw potential not performance, but the failing was still there."

At the Yankees' expense, Jeter's parents flew to Tampa, as did his high school girlfriend. They stayed for a weekend and buoyed his spirits.

"I talked to Derek every day in Tampa," Livesey said. "He was struggling but he never showed self-doubt. I'm sure that he did, in fact, have self-doubt. Baseball is a game of failure. But it's how these high school kids respond that matters.

"Derek would go 0-for-4, and the next morning he would be there bright and early — earlier than he had to be. He would be ready to work; he was determined. "People in the organization asked me a lot of questions about Derek. What's going on? Are you worried? And I would answer, 'I'll be worried when he looks worried.'"

Late in 1992, Jeter was in Greensboro because the team's starting shortstop had been injured. For weeks, Posada had heard his Greensboro teammates talk about the organization's top draft pick. It was always "Jeter this and Jeter that," said Posada, who was still grasping the nuances of the English language, wondering what all the fuss was about.

Then Posada watched as Jeter ran onto the diamond to warm up before his first game. He was gangly and no more than 160 pounds, with long spindly legs that sprouted from high-top shoes and ankle braces, which Jeter wore to protect against the bad ankle sprain he had sustained that spring in high school. His cap was tilted backward, as if it didn't fit his head.

Said Posada: "That's a Jeter?"

Posada was more impressed when Jeter hit a long home run in his first Greensboro game. He also made two spectacular fielding plays — one to his left and one to his right. Jeter was soon returned to the lower rung of the Yankees minors.

"I hadn't said a word to the kid," Posada said. "But I knew what they were talking about now. That's Derek Jeter."

That year, *Baseball America* ranked the talent in the Yankees minor league system 4th among all franchises. Brien Taylor was the top-rated prospect and Jeter was ranked 44th. Four other Yankees, Gerald Williams (52nd), third baseman Russ Davis (60th), reliever Bob Wickman (75th) and starting pitcher Sterling Hitchcock (90th), made the top 100. Bernie Williams, who spent much of 1992 at AAA Columbus, was not on the list because he had by then played 147 major league games. *Baseball America* had yet to size up Rivera, Pettitte and Posada.

Much of what was going on in the Yankee minors went unobserved. The franchise was less than two years removed from its laughingstock season of 1990. The high-flying Toronto Blue Jays, led by the ex–Yankees star Winfield, were the talk of baseball. The Atlanta Braves, whose sterling center fielder Otis Nixon was a former Yankees farmhand, were on their way to 98 wins. Oakland, behind another sparkling season by ex-Yankee Rickey Henderson, would make the playoffs for the fourth time in the past five years.

The Yankees? No, nobody in baseball was talking about the Yankees, or paying much attention to what the team's executives were plotting in Oneonta, Greensboro or Fort Lauderdale.

"It was a great blessing to be under the radar," said Livesey. "We knew what we had and we knew our system — the Yankee Way — was working. And it helped an awful lot that people weren't really looking at us, at least not on the big league level. There was already a lot going on with George Steinbrenner's suspension and Buck and Stick starting over up there.

"In the minors, we were just determined to keep our heads down, stay the course and keep the young talent under wraps a little longer. If we could do that and get a little lucky, we thought we could be sitting on something special."

15

Culture Creators

MIDWAY THROUGH 1992, the Yankees' fast start to the season, halcyon days for a franchise desperate for something uplifting, became a distant memory.

"We don't win as much as we used to, do we, Daddy?" Allie Showalter, the manager's five-year-old, asked.

"No, honey, we don't," her father replied.

"When do you think that will change?" Allie inquired.

"Go brush your teeth," Buck Showalter said.

But Showalter was not as downtrodden as he might have seemed (for starters, with a laugh, he told the story to reporters the day it happened). The Yankees had descended to the middle of the pack in the American League East, but Showalter knew that his Yankees, one game under .500 at the time, were still a work in progress.

While the Yankees minor league operation was shaping the future of the franchise in outposts far from New York, the renovation of the big league club continued in the Bronx. Showalter and Michael were tinkering with the team, though not necessarily making more immediate roster changes. What they were doing was watching, assessing and scheming about significant alterations in the off-season. Showalter was definitely making mental notes.

On July 11, the Yankees hosted their annual Old-Timers' Day, a tradition dating back to the 1940s. Showalter, a baseball historian, revered the Yankee elders and considered Old-Timers' Day one of the most valuable days on the calendar. He wanted his players to soak up all the wisdom from the Yankees who had played for the franchise's many championship teams. With a wide smile, he would walk around the clubhouse, where for a day the old-timers dressed in the same stalls as the current players — all the while hoping the gilded touch of the elders would, like osmosis, pervade his young charges.

The old-timers would also take informal batting and fielding practice before their exhibition game. On this sunny day in 1992 they were doing just that, with Showalter watching from the dugout, when left fielder Mel Hall walked up the ramp to the field.

Hall, who that year was leading the team in home runs and RBI, looked onto the field and said, "Who are these old fucking guys?"

Showalter did not react. But he had a thought.

"I knew right then we had to get rid of Mel Hall," Showalter said years later. "That was it."

Hall had a career high 81 RBI in 1992, but when he became a free agent after the season, the Yankees ignored him. So did every other major league team. He spent the next three years playing in Japan and retired in 1996. In 2009, he was sentenced to forty-five years in prison after being convicted of two counts of sexual assault with minors.

As the 1992 season wound from spring to summer, the Yankees had become Showalter's team, and a sense of stability emanated from the manager's office. In July, he agreed to a $1 million, three-year contract extension, a deal that did not expire until after the 1995 season.

That same month, a tremor shook the measured equilibrium Showalter and Michael had sought to instill. Fay Vincent announced that Steinbrenner's lifetime ban had been commuted to roughly a two-year suspension. Steinbrenner could return to run the Yankees on March 1, 1993.

"It gave everyone a little pause, but it was still off in the distance," Showalter said.

Or, as Michael said: "We knew we still had time to make some more big moves. We couldn't finish what we started, but we could take a few more steps. And who knew what George would say or do when he did return. I didn't know if I'd even still have a job."

Years later, Vincent explained his reasoning for reinstating Steinbrenner. "Two years of suspension was what I wanted to impose in the first place," he said. "Some people told me I wimped out. I didn't look at it that way. He was the one that chose to go on the permanently ineligible list.

"But he didn't understand the terms or the fairly ruthless contract that he signed in 1990. And since then, he had called me several times to talk about how he could get back into baseball. He missed it. He admitted he made a mistake. I waited two years and let him back in."

Until March 1, 1993, Steinbrenner was still prohibited from engaging in day-to-day activities with the team, and that included participating in the decisions about trades or free-agent transactions. Steinbrenner did not overtly breach those prohibitions, although over the next several months he would skirt around them from time to time.

The Yankees fan base reacted to the news of Steinbrenner's impending return with a mix of wariness and forgiveness. That was something of a substantive turnaround from the response when he was banished. Back then, there was cheering in the Yankee Stadium grandstands. But by 1992, the fans were well aware that the team had been penny pinchers during the past two years, at least when it came to prominent big league acquisitions. There was hope that with Steinbrenner's return, the Yankees could once again chase the highest-profile free agents. And there was a feeling Steinbrenner might now appreciate the steadiness and consistency that had grown up around the team's management in his absence.

Or, as Fran Shipley, a Yankees fan from Ridgewood, New Jersey, told the *New York Daily News:* "I hope George has learned his lesson. I hope he has the smarts to realize he doesn't have to run everything. He has to figure that out sooner or later. Now is a good time."

Mattingly had a similar warning from the players' locker room. "George should leave the manager and general manager alone," he said. "In some ways, maybe we do need him back as the owner. But not in all the old ways. Some of the things he did in the past hurt the team, year after year. Some of that stuff should stay banned."

In a sign that he may have been listening, at least on some level, Steinbrenner said almost nothing about his reinstatement. He would wait for March 1, 1993, when he would be four months shy of his sixty-third birthday.

At lunch in Manhattan that summer, Steinbrenner did say that Yankees fans had once again begun to stop him on the street for pictures. "It's a warmer greeting," he said, adding with a smile, "I guess they've never been around a man who was thrown out of baseball before."

But Steinbrenner was also pensive and contemplative. In the previous eighteen months or so, he said, he had spent many hours alone, playing the piano, a little-known pastime of his. He had reflected on the purpose or meaning of his exile. At one point in the conversation, he mentioned a favorite painting by Monet.

The painting was cleverly composed so that different elements of the image became apparent only as a viewer stepped farther back from the canvas.

In a soft voice, which was extremely rare for him, Steinbrenner said, "I've had a chance to step back."

He had also taken his lumps outside of baseball. His company — his father's once proud company, American Ship Building — was sinking and would soon file for bankruptcy. Steinbrenner would sell the company in 1995. The Steinbrenner family's net worth would be wrapped mostly around the Yankees, who were valued at more than $400 million.

Meanwhile, the Yankees had sunk to last place by early August. In another sign of how much things had changed in Yankeeland, Steinbrenner remained silent. But Gene Michael's response was telling.

First the Yankees recalled Bernie Williams from AAA Columbus and installed him as the starting center fielder. In doing so, they shifted the gifted, lissome Roberto Kelly, who many believed was the team's center fielder of the future, to left field. Mel Hall went to right field, and then, a week later, was benched for Gerald Williams, who was also promoted from Columbus.

Hall was not happy and said so. Neither was Kelly, an All-Star in 1992, who also expressed his dismay at the switch. Showalter declined to comment.

In his first game, Bernie Williams made a spectacular over-the-shoulder catch against the Milwaukee Brewers. And he also continued to display the quizzical decision-making that still made him something of an enigma.

In a crucial situation with a teammate on second base, Williams was instructed to swing away if the Brewers' infielders charged to defend a bunt just before the pitch. He was told to bunt if they did not shift and remained back on the infield dirt.

On the first two pitches, the Brewers charged and Williams squared to bunt. On the next pitch, when the Brewers stayed back, he swung away.

When Williams was told after the game that he had made the wrong choice three straight times, he seemed surprised. "I thought I did what I was supposed to do," he said.

Showalter, in his office, remained calm. "There's a learning curve at work here," he said.

Many years later, Showalter said of Williams: "What can you say? Bernie is a unique guy and we all had to accept that. You can teach him something, but that doesn't mean he has learned it. He was on his own timetable in terms of learning. But I know Stick and I were not planning on giving up on him. Athletically, there were times when he could just overpower the game. Everyone knew that. You had to just give him time."

As for Kelly, he continued to seem demoralized by playing left field. Showalter made another mental note one day when Kelly seemed to jog after a double in the left-center-field gap, which allowed a runner on first base to score.

Michael, meanwhile, made other moves to double down on the youth movement. From Columbus, he recalled Bob Wickman, the pitcher with the mangled index finger whom he acquired in the trade for Steve Sax. The Yankees would win Wickman's first three starts, and he finished the season with a 7-1 record. Sterling Hitchcock, the crafty lefty, was also promoted to the big team, and although he lost his two starts, it was a valuable experience for a twenty-one-year-old who in 83 minor league starts at three levels had compiled an ERA of 2.56.

The Yankees surged dramatically in September to climb into fifth place. Their final record (76-86) was only a five-victory improvement over 1991, but playing the final month with a .500 record seemed important to many on the team.

"At the end of this season, we showed the exact opposite of what happened last year when we were a team going nowhere with no hope and no future," Mattingly said. "This year, we've kept playing hard. Hopefully, we can make another move next year."

There was other major news late in the 1992 season. A faction of baseball owners, convinced that Vincent was too amenable to the demands of the players' union, united to oust the commissioner. Eighteen owners endorsed a vote of no confidence in Vincent, who soon after resigned.

With their eyes on another divisive labor fight looming in 1993–94, the owners decided to reduce the powers of Vincent's replacement. The owners would operate more like a board of directors, and the commissioner would act mostly as a chairman of that board. But he would be one of their own in every way, which proved to be manifestly true when Bud Selig, the owner of the Milwaukee Brewers, became the next commissioner.

While the Blue Jays were on their way to a World Series victory in October, Gene Michael was busy negotiating with several big-time free agents. Over and over, he was rebuffed. Some of the big-name players only talked to the Yankees to be courteous. Steinbrenner might have loosened the purse strings, and the Yankees might have seemed on the cusp of a turnaround, but they were still a team coming off four consecutive losing seasons. They had not been to the postseason in eleven years. The team's reputation was still besmirched. "It was an uphill battle — really uphill — when it came to the really spotlighted, premier free agents," Michael conceded.

The Yankees offered Barry Bonds several contracts to come play left field in Yankee Stadium, where he could swing for an inviting, short right-field porch. They dangled a deal that would have made Bonds the highest-paid player in baseball by several million dollars.

"He said no thanks," Michael said.

Bonds instead signed a six-year deal, worth $44 million, with San Francisco.

The Yankees also whiffed on signing top free-agent pitchers like Greg Maddux, David Cone and Doug Drabek, their former farmhand. That trio went to Atlanta, Kansas City and Houston, respectively. Maddux took $6 million less than the Yankees offered to play for the Braves.

"I started to think we had to do something more basic like a trade," Michael said. "At least for a big first move."

Michael, a scout at heart, had not stopped scouring the major leagues in search of talent. Throughout the 1992 season, he had attended the games of nearly every other team, looking for players who might resolve some of the Yankees' deficiencies and who were a good fit with the home ballpark and the strengths of their minor league talent.

He needed starting pitching and he needed a left-swinging outfielder, because the Yankees lineup had only one middle-of-the-order left-handed hitter — and that was Mattingly, who was no longer driving in 100-plus runs per season. Michael also wanted to add a veteran who might help Mattingly set the tone of personal accountability that Showalter was seeking for the clubhouse.

"I started thinking about the Yankees championship teams in the 1970s and what made them successful," Michael said. "It was a bunch of guys who hated to fail. I wanted the fire and tenacity of Thurman Munson, Graig Nettles, Lou Piniella and guys like that.

"When you make a trade, it's not all about the stats — home runs, runs produced, runs scored. Sometimes you're trading for an attitude."

But the trade Michael engineered on November 3 had Yankees fans scratching their heads. Throughout the baseball community, most thought the Yankees had been fleeced. A recent search of newspaper stories written about the trade did not turn up a single article from November 1993 in which the author wrote that the deal would make the Yankees better.

"Was it a ballsy trade?" Showalter said. "You bet. Shit, people thought we were panicking. But Stick had done his homework."

The trade sent twenty-seven-year-old, right-hand-hitting Roberto Kelly, who was considered the Yankees' number one big league commodity, to Cincinnati for thirty-year-old lefty Paul O'Neill, a player perhaps better known for his temper than for his hitting or fielding.

Kelly, even if he had been switched to left field, was coming off an All-Star season. When he signed with the Yankees as a seventeen-year-old in 1982, the team thought so much of him he was called "a Panamanian Mickey Mantle."

O'Neill had slumped in 1992, when he had bristled under his demanding manager, Lou Piniella. At that point, O'Neill was a lifetime .191 hitter against left-handed pitchers. He was a right fielder, and the Yankees were already paying Danny Tartabull $5 million a year to play right field. And even if they were going to move Tartabull to designated hitter, wasn't that to make room in right field for Gerald Williams?

If the Yankees' primary need was starting pitching, why would Michael instead choose to crowd the outfield? As best as anyone could figure, O'Neill would platoon in right field with Williams or Tartabull.

And, more perplexing, the Yankees had given up one of their best young players for a part-time player prone to tantrums.

"I had watched O'Neill play a lot, and to me, I felt sure he was coming into his prime," Michael said. "I liked that he got riled up about making outs. I liked the passion. It could have been a mistake, but I was no longer sure that Roberto was going to blossom the way we had envisioned."

It was a deal in lockstep with one of Michael's oft-stated tenets: Trade a talented young player whom others value before everyone else finds out what you already know — that the player may be overrated.

"It's often a key to a good trade," Showalter said. "I'm not disparaging Roberto; he had a good career. But we saw some faults that others didn't because they were viewing him from afar. But in the end, it was more about what we received. As it turned out, getting Paul O'Neill was hugely instrumental to our success going forward.

"We had to get more left-handed, and Paul was that piece. He was a good defender and had a good arm. He would get along with Donnie and the other veterans, which was important. And he understood the New York media — that wouldn't be a problem."

O'Neill's older sister, Molly, was a writer for the *New York Times*. He knew the landscape.

At the time, a case could be made that both Kelly and O'Neill were coming off poor years. Although Kelly had surged at the beginning of the year to make his first All-Star team, his offensive numbers lagged as the season went on, and he finished with only 10 home runs after hitting 20 in 1991. His batting average was .272. Worse, as Michael noticed, Kelly's on-base percentage was a paltry .322. Kelly was explosive but impatient at the plate. And Gene Michael knew he already had enough speed in the outfield. What he needed was prudence in the batter's box.

O'Neill had indeed had a lousy year in 1992. Piniella had badgered him about pulling the ball more often in an effort to make him more of a power hitter. But that approach failed, and O'Neill's power numbers actually went down, from 28 homers and 91 RBI in 1991 to 14 home runs and 66 RBI.

That falloff grated on O'Neill, especially since he grew up a Reds fan in Columbus, Ohio. Of course, all failure grated on O'Neill, whose temper was already legendary. He had destroyed dugout water coolers and batting helmets with his bat in outbursts after strikeouts. Any kind of failure might cause O'Neill to erupt, even failing to advance a runner on the basepaths with a well-placed out.

"He tormented himself," said Piniella, who had a similar reputation for hotheadedness. "I know how he felt. It's a good thing, because it means you have high standards. But it's sometimes a bad thing. And you can look pretty foolish."

O'Neill had famously bobbled a ground ball in the outfield and then drop-kicked it into the infield.

"None of that bothered me," said Michael, who saw O'Neill's reasonably good .346 on-base percentage and thought it could be closer to .400 with the right tutelage. "He tried so hard at everything, but that made him a little overaggressive at the plate. He lunged a lot. We corrected that."

Brian Cashman recalled that the Yankees brain trust was meeting at Steinbrenner's Tampa hotel on the eve of the O'Neill trade. "It was far from unanimous about what to do, because there were people who still thought of Roberto as the All-Star center fielder he had been," Cashman said. "Gene Michael made his arguments for the trade and then he asked for everyone else's opinions. And Gene wanted to hear them.

"But he was also his own man. Gene would do what he thought, regardless. Even if everybody said no, he was going to do that deal, regardless. He believed in it."

But trading Kelly meant the Yankees were committing to Bernie Williams as their center fielder of the future. They had no one else to play the position. It had been seven years since Williams was hidden away in Connecticut, then signed as a seventeen-year-old. In that time, no top prospect had flummoxed the Yankees as routinely as Bernie had.

Although he had almost been traded multiple times, the Yankees had stuck with Williams as he grew from a teenager in braces to a twenty-four-year-old about to be handed one of the most celebrated jobs in baseball: center fielder for the Yankees.

"It takes a leap of faith to think that Bernie Williams is going to be the guy," Cashman, Michael's assistant in 1992, said. "For several years before that, there was a certain amount of indecision about exactly what he was going to become. It took him a while, and some guys will take longer. But his physical attributes were not in question — a switch-hitter who was tremendous defensively. A power hitter.

"Yes, he was quiet and you wondered how he would do in the pressure cooker of New York. But he deserved the chance to succeed, and Gene was going to give him the chance to succeed."

Showalter considers the O'Neill trade, and the decision to make Williams the everyday center fielder, one of the pivotal moments in the somewhat silent resurrection of the Yankees that was taking place in the winter of 1992–93.

"Sometimes you have to force yourself to have faith in a guy," Showalter said at his Dallas home in 2017. "And with Bernie we talked about that in 1992: Hey, we've got to stop wondering whether he's our center fielder and make a decision whether he is or isn't. Because it was time.

"It meant that the franchise had to accept that there will be growing pains. And while some people, especially ownership, might continue to question our faith in the player, the rest of us had to keep the faith. Although I'll admit, even for me, there were some nights when if someone had told me that this guy was going to be a batting champion, a postseason MVP, an All-Star five or six times, I'm not sure I would have believed it. But there were many other nights — many more nights back then — when I saw all those attributes in Bernie and did actually see the future."

But Showalter knew that twenty-four-year-old Bernie Williams could not shoulder the Yankees spotlight alone. O'Neill was one way to deflect attention from the new center fielder. "And we needed some more vets, a surrounding cast that put the right kind of peer pressure on the young guys," Showalter said. "It wasn't Mel Hall's kind of peer pressure. It was confident guys like Mattingly, O'Neill and Mike Stanley. We called them clubhouse culture creators."

The Yankees had also recently re-signed Stanley as a free agent.

"And there were more to come," Showalter said. "That was a very busy winter. Culture creators. You know, you can talk all about stats and analytics, and I get that. But you can't measure how to build the most productive team culture. And that gets lost. Or it can. We tried to make sure it didn't."

But before the Yankees could resume reshaping their roster, they were going to lose some players in the expansion draft on November 17, 1992.

For weeks preceding the draft to stock the lineups of the embryonic Colorado Rockies and Florida Marlins, the Yankee leaders had been in countless meetings to try to figure out which players to protect from the draft.

The Yankees could list only 15 players from their major league or minor league rosters as unavailable in the first round of the draft. They could protect four more players after the first of three rounds. Not everyone in the Yankees organization was eligible to be drafted—players selected in the 1991 or 1992 drafts and players signed in those years could not be drafted. That meant that Jeter, Pettitte and Posada were safe. Nonetheless, another 109 Yankees players were available, including Mariano Rivera —unless the team chose to make him one of the 15 untouchable players.

Michael and Showalter agreed not to put Rivera on that list.

"It was a gamble—all of that draft was a gamble," Michael said. "And I was worried about Mariano, but I also knew that everybody thought he was coming off Tommy John surgery."

The Yankees protected Bernie and Gerald Williams, Sterling Hitchcock, second baseman Pat Kelly, Wickman and some other jewels of the system. They did not protect Danny Tartabull, hoping he and his $5 million contract would be scooped up by either the Rockies or the Marlins.

But with the third pick of the expansion draft, the Rockies instead chose Yankees third baseman Charlie Hayes, who had hit 18 home runs with 66 RBI for Showalter's 1992 Yankees, when he earned about $850,000.

"We thought the Rockies and Marlins would mostly take prospects in the first round, so we were trying to sneak Charlie through and then protect him after the first round," Michael said. "It didn't work, and that hurt."

The Yankees also lost Carl Everett, their first-round pick in the 1990 amateur draft, and in a surprise, the Rockies took minor league catcher Brad Ausmus. Everett became a two-time All-Star, but he had a turbulent career, frequently clashing with umpires, teammates, managers, reporters and opponents. He played on eight teams in 14 major league seasons. Ausmus, a former shortstop, would play nearly 2,000 major league games at catcher, drive in 607 runs and eventually become a major league manager.

"The day of that draft, we felt like maybe we had made only one mistake," Michael said. "We weren't sure what we'd do without Charlie Hayes at third base. Yes, Everett and Ausmus were prospects that you hated to lose, but we were going to lose somebody. Carl was an outfielder and we thought we had enough young outfielders. Brad turned out to have a long career but we had some other catchers.

"The farm system was deep. You had to trust it."

The real news was that neither the Rockies nor the Marlins even considered taking a chance on Rivera, who would set the record for career saves.

With the expansion draft behind them, the Yankees went to the winter meetings in Louisville knowing they had to bolster their starting pitching. The record of Yankees starters in 1992 had been 47-60. They were in hot pursuit of several top pitchers, all of whom would be signed or traded for in a span of a few days. Tensions were high.

Twenty-five years later, Showalter still vividly recalled the charged winter meetings atmosphere: "We had been in Joe Molloy's suite for something like two days straight — visiting with other teams and having these tense meetings amongst ourselves to consider all the options."

At baseball's winter meetings, which take place at a large hotel, each team books a phalanx of rooms for its front-office employees and manager. And the team rents one large suite with a bedroom and something akin to a conference room for the general manager or chief executive where the bulk of the negotiations with other teams or players' agents occur. In the Yankees' case, the gathering spot was the suite assigned to Molloy, the team's general partner and the son-in-law of the principal owner.

"So it's getting late one night and everyone wants to go out to dinner," Showalter said. "I volunteered to stay in Joe Molloy's suite to man the phone in case there was an important call, because we were weighing a couple of big moves. This was before cell phones. I had the phone number of the restaurant where everyone was eating.

"So I'm sitting there in the suite all by myself and back in Joe Molloy's bedroom the phone rings. Well, it's not the conference room phone we had been using, but I am there to answer the phone, so I go into the bedroom to get it. I figured it was his wife or something."

Buck picked up the receiver and said hello.

"And all I hear is 'Who the fuck is this?'" Showalter said. "And, you know, I'm sitting there by myself not getting to eat dinner. So I yelled back, 'Who the fuck is *this*?'

"And the voice at the other end says, 'This is Mr. Steinbrenner.' And I said, 'Oh, hi, Mr. Steinbrenner, this is Buck Showalter.' I was thinking to myself, 'I'm not supposed to be answering this phone because he's on probation or whatever.'

"And he just said, 'Tell Joe to call me when he gets back.'"

There was nothing in Fay Vincent's banishment of Steinbrenner that prohibited the Yankees' owner from talking to his son-in-law. And it was probably a coincidence that the phone call came during winter meetings as the franchise — Steinbrenner's principal investment — pondered whether to make a crucial trade or to pay tens of millions of dollars for several free agents.

Truth be told, Steinbrenner's occasional, covert involvement in team activities, which probably violated the terms of his exile, had been a not-so-hidden secret around the Yankees for months. And that was sometimes a problem, since Vincent's office — before he resigned — not only made team employees sign affidavits vowing they had no contact with Steinbrenner, but also made employees submit to random lie detector tests. But those could be a bit of a ruse, too.

Showalter recalled the one time he took the lie detector test. "The guy giving the test considered it a pain in the ass as much as I considered it a pain in the ass," he said in 2017. "I told the guy giving me the test, 'I'm not going to lie.' And he said, 'You won't have to lie. Just trust me.'

"So I get hooked up to the thing and he asks me, 'Have you had face-to-face contact with Mr. Steinbrenner?' And I say, 'No.' And he asks if Mr. Steinbrenner has visited my house at any point and talked to me. I say, 'No.' He never asked me a single question like, 'Has he called you on the phone or anything?' And then after a few questions, he said, 'OK, that's it.'"

After he was fired in 1991, Stump Merrill had been subjected to questioning by Vincent's office as well. He was required to fly from Maine to New York City, where he insisted he'd had no face-to-face contact with Steinbrenner. "I was interrogated for four hours by four different people," Merrill recalled. "And I must have said twenty-five times, 'What part of fucking NO don't you understand?'"

Merrill was then asked if he knew which Yankees employees had been in touch with Steinbrenner. "And I told them, 'I have no idea, but if I did, I wouldn't tell you. That's your job, not mine.' It was a waste of my time, the whole fucking nine yards."

The Steinbrenner banishment, even while his family still ran the team, caused a variety of peculiar, even comical, situations for team employees. Once, Molloy and Showalter decided to meet at the Steinbrenner horse farm in Ocala, Florida. As they gathered in a small cottage on the property, they looked out the window and saw Steinbrenner walking the grounds. The duo spent the rest of the day hiding from him — then left early.

The Yankees were soon very busy at the 1992 Louisville winter meetings. On December 5, they acquired starting pitcher Jim Abbott for three prospects, including first baseman J. T. Snow, who would end up playing 16 major league seasons and drive in 877 runs.

Since Abbott pitched only two Yankees seasons and compiled a 20-22 record, it could be argued that the trade was a bust, given Snow's production, which included four seasons when he drove in 95 or more runs.

But to the Yankees, Abbott was another "culture creator."

Born without a right hand, Abbott was one of the most admired athletes in the country from 1988 to the early 1990s, because he had learned to pitch with his left hand and arm while resting his glove on the end of his right forearm. After delivering a pitch, he would switch the glove to his left hand. Abbott was tall, blond and always seemed to be smiling, and he became one of the feel-good stories of the era. Raised in Flint, Michigan, he pitched three years for the University of Michigan and led the victorious US baseball team at the 1988 Summer Olympics.

The California Angels made Abbott the eighth overall pick in the 1988 draft, and he moved into the Angels' starting rotation the next season without having to pitch a single game in the minor leagues. He won 40 games in his first three seasons, including an 18-11 season in 1991, when he finished third in the Cy Young Award balloting. But his record slumped to 7-15 in 1992, although he did have a sparkling ERA of 2.77.

The Yankees liked that they were getting a quietly confident twenty-five-year-old who already had four years of major league experience, and they believed Abbott would be another good fit with Mattingly. They were correct about that assumption, as the two became close friends who frequently socialized off the field.

"Jim was another guy who hated to lose, and he cared about all the things that mattered," Mattingly said of his friend. "He wanted things done the right way."

Five days after the Abbott trade, the Yankees acquired another dynamic left-handed starter with a venerable track record who was known for his understated leadership.

Jimmy Key, who in nine seasons with the Toronto Blue Jays had a 116-81 record, signed a four-year, $17 million free-agent contract with the Yankees. Key, who had just won two games in the 1992 World Series for the world champion Blue Jays, was known as a soft-spoken assassin, and he pitched that way. He did not throw especially hard, but he had precise control of his pitches and could pinpoint a fastball that nonetheless overpowered many a hitter. He had cunning and an array of breaking pitches, most notably a backdoor slider. He was the only pitcher in the major leagues at the time who had won at least 12 games in each of the last eight seasons. He had a career record of 8-1 in Yankee Stadium and was 3-1 in five postseason starts.

Key was raised in Alabama but expressed no reservations about playing in New York. He even gave the city a backhanded compliment of sorts. "My wife says I'm lifeless inside on game days — things don't bother me," said the thirty-two-year-old Key, who was considered a no-nonsense leader on a Toronto team that had won its division in four of the previous five seasons. With a quizzical smile, Key added, "I guess that means I'm a good fit for New York."

The Yankees had found themselves another culture creator.

In another coincidence (there would continue to be a series of them involving the Yankees' owner and his son-in-law), George Steinbrenner had publicly lobbied for Key to be signed. Joe Molloy, by himself, had been dispatched to negotiate with Key's wife, Cindy, who acted as her husband's agent. Molloy, it turned out, somehow knew exactly how much money his father-in-law was willing to spend on Key.

"He's the guy we wanted as much as anybody," Steinbrenner told reporters in telephone interviews from Tampa.

The Yankees roster was undeniably improving, even if Barry Bonds, Greg Maddux and other top stars wanted no part of the Bronx, where the last World Series championship trophy was raised fourteen years earlier. "We're not dwelling on who doesn't want to come here," Showalter said at the time. "If one part of the equation doesn't work out, then you move on to the next part. And we're not through yet."

Since the expansion draft, the Yankees had been without a third baseman. The onetime blue-chip prospect at the position, Hensley Meulens, who was signed alongside Bernie Williams in 1985, was trying to sign a contract to play in Japan, and the Yankees were not yet standing in his way. Meulens was not in the team's plans. Not all Yankees prospects blossomed.

"You have to give up on some young players, too," Michael said. "It's painful, but you have to be able to admit you were wrong."

That winter, the most prominent free-agent third baseman available was Wade Boggs, the eight-time Boston All-Star. But Boggs's batting average in 1992 had plummeted to .259, the first time in his career he had not batted over .300. He had endured back spasms and blamed blurry vision for his hitting woes since he was adjusting to new contact lenses.

Gene Michael and Buck Showalter each had reservations about signing Boggs, at least initially. Again, it was all about the clubhouse culture.

Boggs was an odd personality. He was perceived as egocentric, which made him fit in perfectly with the Red Sox of the late eighties, a team slapped with the enduring label "25 players, 25 cabs." The term summed up a complete lack of unity, based on an anecdotal scene outside a Red Sox hotel after a road game when players going out to dinner each called separate cabs.

Whether Boggs deserved to be denigrated by association, he was undisputedly a bit of a mysterious loner with quirky superstitions. Most important to Showalter, Boggs and Mattingly were far from friendly. The two had vied for the American League batting title several times between 1983 and 1988. Boggs had won every year except 1984, when Mattingly did instead. But famously, in 1986, Boggs had sat out the final four games of the season, coasting to the title over Mattingly with a .357 batting average.

The Red Sox hosted the Yankees in those final four games that year.

With Boggs resting in the dugout, Mattingly hit .422 in the series and fell five points short of catching Boggs. In the visiting clubhouse afterward, Mattingly, who had played 162 games that season, barely concealed his ire toward Boggs, who under baseball's unwritten rules of conduct had committed an act of cowardice.

Boggs's nickname was "Chicken Man," because one of his superstitions was that he had to eat chicken before every game.

"Chickenshit Man," many Yankees grumbled that weekend at Fenway.

Six years later, things may have calmed down, but Showalter was worried nonetheless. Besides, Boggs was thirty-four years old and coming off his worst season. And he was a Red Sox, Yankees archrivals since the middle of the century. What would that do to the clubhouse culture?

But George Steinbrenner was having none of it. Once again, Molloy was put in charge of wooing Boggs and his agent, Alan Nero. Molloy had lunch with Nero to begin the negotiations at Steinbrenner's Tampa hotel. Seated across the lunchroom, in plain sight of Nero, was George Steinbrenner. He was joined by *New York Daily News* sportswriter Bill Madden, a mainstay on the Yankees beat since the 1970s.

Madden said Steinbrenner was endorsing the Boggs deal throughout lunch, predicting it would get done. In his 2010 book, *Steinbrenner,* Madden wrote that George called Nero in his hotel room after Nero's lunch with Molloy ended.

"I just want to tell you — be patient," Steinbrenner said.

Madden wrote that Steinbrenner added, "You'll get what you want."

The Yankees were the only team to offer Boggs a three-year contract. Nero and Boggs leaped at the offer.

At breakfast the next morning in his Tampa hotel, not long after Boggs's signing had been announced, Steinbrenner insisted he had not known about the negotiations: "I swear my daughter called me and said, 'We just traded for that Red Sox third baseman.' That's the way she phrased it. Of course, we signed him, not traded for him."

He was asked, "Which of your daughters called you?"

"Jessica."

"So, Joe's wife, then?"

"Yeah," George said. "I mean, I'm allowed to call my daughter's house."

Steinbrenner paused and stammered. "I mean, ah, I can take calls from her," he said.

By then, in northern Florida near the Alabama line, where Showalter lived in the off-season, there was not much alarm about the Boggs signing. Showalter had already consulted Mattingly, his former minor league teammate.

"I told Buck it would be fine," Mattingly said. "We now had a bunch of guys who would set the tone. I figured Wade would be a pro about it and go along. And he did."

Michael was happy to hear about Mattingly's acquiescence. Privately, Michael knew there was much to like about Boggs. He thought the Chicken Man might have been dragged down by a horrific 1992 season in Boston when the Red Sox finished in last place. Boggs had also lobbied for a new contract during spring training and complained when he did not get one. The response of Fenway Park fans was to boo him after every out he made.

"And, let's face it, if we wanted guys who had high on-base percentages, you couldn't do better than Boggs in his prime," Michael said. Boggs had led the major leagues in on-base percentage six times. In 1988, his OBP was 24 points shy of .500.

"Boggs may not have been my idea from the start, but when we did get him I was thinking that if we got Boggs at 85 or 90 percent of what he was in his prime, he would still help us," Michael said in 2017.

During the first week of January 1993, the Yankees held a news conference to introduce all their new players. As if schooled earlier — the players did have dinner with Showalter the night before — Key, O'Neill and Boggs each used the words "attitude, intensity and character," attributes important for both a player and the team as a whole.

Showalter used the occasion to unveil a new word for what he wanted in a player. "I've been saying I want integrity, but it's really sincerity that I want," he said. "A player has to be sincere about wanting to win and wanting to be a good teammate. And other players know who the sincere players are."

The setting for the news conference was the same Yankee Stadium luxury ballroom where a host of Yankees managers had been hired and fired. Whether it was Billy Martin, Dick Howser, Bucky Dent or Stump Merrill, it sometimes felt as if their pinstriped ghosts haunted the room. But in 1993, the ballroom had been renovated. Walls had been removed, the lighting had been redone, and new windows brightened the space.

On that day, the facelift seemed symbolic. There was a sense that the franchise's dark days were in the rearview mirror. The roster had been gutted. Just four players — and only one starter — on the 1993 roster had been with the team in 1990.

At Showalter's request — remember, every little detail had a themed message in Showalter's world — the aging black-and-white photos of Yankees stars from the 1950s and 1970s had been replaced by vibrant color photos of the team's current players: Mattingly, Stanley, Wickman.

Showalter loved tradition, but he wanted to turn the page, too. Scores of photographs from around the stadium had been updated similarly. Out went the fading shots of the old Yankee Stadium, the one of Babe Ruth and Lou Gehrig. In their place were photos of a refurbished, sold-out Yankee Stadium (captured on the rare recent occasion when that occurred).

The embarrassing memories of the 1990 and 1991 seasons were being whitewashed. George Steinbrenner's humiliating exile was soon to end. Reinforcements for the beleaguered Mattingly, still by far the team's most popular player, were on the way.

"I felt rejuvenated," Mattingly said in an interview twenty-five years later.

Showalter told Angela that he felt a new Yankee spirit imbuing the team.

"Buck really thought the franchise was getting a transfusion," Angela Showalter said in 2017. "Life was being breathed into the place.

"Buck almost always tried to go to work with a smile, but he has always said that the beginning of the 1993 season was when he finally felt confident he might come home from work with a smile."

1990 NEW YORK YANKEES

Back Row—JIMMY JONES, MARK LEITER, STEVE BALBONI, MIKE WITT, LEE GUETTERMAN, CHUCK CARY, DAVE LaPOINT, PASCUAL PEREZ, ANDY HAWKINS, DAVE RIGHETTI, ERIC PLUNK, MELL HALL.
Third Row—CARL TAYLOR (Batting Practice Pitcher), ALVARO ESPINOZA, KEVIN MAAS, ROBERTO KELLY, JIM LEYRITZ, STEVE SAX, JESSE BARFIELD, BRIAN DORSETT, JEFF ROBINSON, ALAN MILLS.
Second Row—DR. STUART HERSHON (Team Physician), GENE MONAHAN (Trainer), OSCAR AZOCAR, MATT NOKES, GREG CADARET, BOB GEREN, TIM LEARY, BRAD HOWLAND (Video Coordinator), JOHN DUFFY (Batting Practice Pitcher), JOHN RODRIGUEZ (Batting Practice Pitcher), GARY WEIL (Strength and Conditioning Coach), BOB FLEMING (Equipment Manager), STEVE DONOHUE (Trainer).
Front Row—BUCK SHOWALTER (Coach), MARK CONNOR (Coach), BILLY CONNORS (Coach), MIKE FERRARO (Coach), STUMP MERRILL (Manager), MARC HILL (Bullpen Catcher), DARRELL EVANS (Coach), RANDY VELARDE, RICK CERONE, WAYNE TOLLESON.
Seated—(Batboys) WILLIAM WOODS, ROBERT DICHIARO, ALIATU BURKE, JOHN BLUNDELL.

The 1990 Yankees. Their 67–95 record was the team's worst since 1913.
Photo courtesy of National Baseball Hall of Fame and Museum, Cooperstown, N.Y.

Bill Livesey, longtime scouting director, at an amateur draft meeting in the 1980s. Livesey was a pivotal figure in rebuilding the Yankees' mid-1990s roster. *Photo courtesy of Bill Livesey*

Yankee Stadium attendance plummeted in the early nineties. Some games drew only a few hundred fans. *AP Photo/Susan Ragan*

George Steinbrenner and his star slugger Dave Winfield in better days. The two feuded for decades. *Barton Silverman/New York Times/Redux*

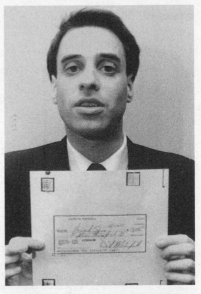

Howie Spira cashed a check for $40,000 from George Steinbrenner, allegedly for supplying "dirt" on Dave Winfield, a transaction that led to Steinbrenner's banishment from baseball. *Getty Images/New York Daily News Archive*

Baseball commissioner Fay Vincent, left, banished Steinbrenner from baseball. Bud Selig, right, Vincent's eventual successor, presided over the 1994 strike that canceled the World Series. *AP Photo / Frankie Ziths*

In 1990, fans at Yankee Stadium blamed Steinbrenner for the team's woes. *AP Photo / Ron Frehn*

Reinstated in 1993, Steinbrenner at first rarely interfered with manager Buck Showalter. *Larry C. Morris / New York Times / Redux*

Gene "Stick" Michael as a Yankee infielder in the 1960s. *Photo courtesy of National Baseball Hall of Fame and Museum, Cooperstown, N.Y.*

Michael as the Yankees' general manager, outside Yankee Stadium in the early 1990s. *John Sotomayor/New York Times/Redux*

Don Mattingly and manager Stump Merrill clashed in 1991 when Mattingly's hair grew over his collar. *Getty Images/Focus on Sport*

Third-base coach Willie Randolph, left, catcher/left fielder Jim Leyritz, middle, and Don Mattingly in 1994 when the Yankees had the best record in the American League. *Getty Images/New York Post Archives*

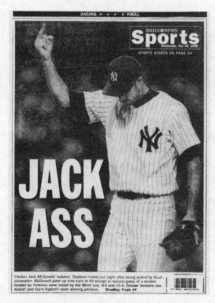

Jack McDowell's famous 1995 salute to the home fans. Another headline read, "The Yankee Flipper." *Getty Images/New York Daily News Archive*

In an overhaul of the Yankees culture, Buck Showalter, here with son Nathan, insisted that the families of players be welcomed behind the scenes at Yankee Stadium. *Photo courtesy of Angela Showalter*

Michael and Showalter remained close friends until Michael's death in 2017. *Photo courtesy of Angela Showalter*

Bernie Williams expected to pursue a career in music or medicine. Instead, he signed with the Yankees on his eighteenth birthday in 1985. *Getty Images / Sporting News*

Mariano Rivera as a 1995 Yankee rookie. Five years earlier, he was signed for $2,000. *Photo courtesy of National Baseball Hall of Fame and Museum, Cooperstown, N.Y.*

Jorge Posada as a rookie in 1995. Posada came to the team as a second baseman, but like other infielders the Yankees converted him to a catcher. *Photo courtesy of National Baseball Hall of Fame and Museum, Cooperstown, N.Y.*

Andy Pettitte's rookie photo in 1995. An intrepid Yankees scout took a chance on Pettitte when few others would. *Photo courtesy of National Baseball Hall of Fame and Museum, Cooperstown, N.Y.*

Derek Jeter as a rookie in 1996. Four years earlier, the Yankees were shocked that Jeter was still available when they picked sixth in the amateur draft. *Photo courtesy of National Baseball Hall of Fame and Museum, Cooperstown, N.Y.*

The view from just beyond Derek Jeter's backyard onto his high school diamond in Kalamazoo, Michigan. From this vantage point, scouts could observe the young Jeter without being noticed. *Photo courtesy of Joyce Pennington*

Pettitte won 149 regular-season games, and 13 in the post-season, for the Yankees from 1995 to 2003. *Photo courtesy of National Baseball Hall of Fame and Museum, Cooperstown, N.Y.*

The 1996 Yankees celebrate the team's first World Series championship in fifteen years. *Getty Images / Timothy A. Clary / Stringer*

16

An Ugly Duckling No More

THE ORIGINAL PLAN for George Steinbrenner's triumphant return to the Yankees on March 1, 1993, was richly choreographed and full of twists and turns.

A helicopter was supposed to land in the outfield of the team's main spring training diamond in Fort Lauderdale, and then a Marilyn Monroe look-alike was supposed to hop out waving a *Welcome Back, George* sign.

Then the plan called for a line of long black limousines with a police escort to arrive at the field. From the back of the motorcade, a President George H. W. Bush look-alike would leap onto the field, asking reporters: "Where's the man of the hour? Where's George?"

There were other distractions planned — skydivers and trained dogs jumping through hoops — each one aimed at turning the field into a cir-cuslike spectacle. Hundreds of media members had been credentialed for the event, including dozens of TV camera crews and photographers.

The idea was for the media to be so focused on the show they would not notice a solitary bearded figure sitting in the front row of the stands, a man wearing a denim jacket and a floppy hat that barely covered long, flowing shoulder-length hair.

At just the right moment, George Steinbrenner would jump onto the top of the home dugout roof and pull off his disguise, throwing down the floppy hat, wig and fake beard. He'd shout, "The Boss is back!"

That was the plan. Steinbrenner had already been on the cover of *Sports Illustrated* dressed as Napoleon as he sat on a white horse. He had made appearances on *The Larry King Show* and the *Today* show and taken calls from fans for two hours on WFAN, the influential sports-talk radio station in New York.

But on February 28, the day before Steinbrenner's exile from the day-to-day operation of the Yankees was to conclude, there was a deadly shootout between federal agents and an extremist religious sect in Waco, Texas. Two days before that, a truck bomb had exploded beneath the north tower of the World Trade Center in lower Manhattan. The terrorist attack was meant to topple the north tower into the south tower. The structures remained intact, but six people died.

The tragedies saddened Steinbrenner, who for all his bluster and exasperating excesses was staunchly patriotic.

"I decided it wasn't the right time to make a big, frivolous display calling attention to my return to baseball," he said. "It would be selfish and it wouldn't be respectful to the rest of America."

So George, wearing a white-collared shirt, tan slacks and a blue V-neck sweater with *GMS* inscribed on the left breast, toned down the act and walked onto the Fort Lauderdale field instead.

There were still plenty of *The Boss Is Back* signs and placards. Steinbrenner also met with reporters and did not make any news.

"I will be different," he vowed. "You'll see. Wait and see . . . a different George Steinbrenner."

Few reporters were convinced. The newspaper columnists in the group mocked the notion that Steinbrenner could turn over a new leaf.

But he was not seen much that spring. And he granted no more prominent interviews for months.

Three days later, there was another unveiling on the main spring training field when Brien Taylor pitched two shutout innings during an intrasquad game against big league hitters. The stands were packed, as were both dugouts. Everyone in camp wanted a glimpse of the Yankees' most famous minor leaguer.

Before the game, Showalter asked Taylor if he was nervous.

Replied Taylor: "Why should I be? They should be nervous."

Showalter liked that reaction. "If I had that fastball," the manager said, "I'd probably feel the same way."

Taylor gave up one single and routinely threw his fastball in the mid-90s (again, in the early nineties maybe two or three major league pitchers in total threw that hard). He showed command of a two-seam slider or cutter that catcher Mike Stanley struggled to catch cleanly because it broke so much at high speed. Taylor also displayed his newly learned pickoff move at first base.

Bernie Williams faced Taylor in the game and hit a fly ball to left field for an out. "Dominant fastball," Williams said later. "Impressive stuff. I was struck by how poised he was. Very calm on the mound."

Derek Jeter, Jorge Posada, Mariano Rivera and Andy Pettitte were in the big league camp that spring and made sure to witness Taylor's outing. They had been Taylor's teammates in the minors the previous year. "Brien was a good dude," Jeter said years later. "Everyone liked Brien."

On March 14, Taylor, Jeter, Posada, Pettitte and Rivera were all demoted to the Yankees' minor league camp in Tampa. About a month later, they would be sent to their minor league outposts — Taylor to Class AA Albany, Jeter and Rivera to Class A Greensboro, and Pettitte and Posada to a team in Prince William, Virginia, which played in a higher-level Class A.

Each of the players improved his standing with the franchise that season, although in Jeter's case, his play in 1993 launched a considerable debate about whether he was playing out of position. "There were factions that wondered if he shouldn't be switched to center field," Michael said.

The jumping-off point for the discussion was simple: Jeter made 56 errors in 126 games for the Greensboro Hornets. It was a record for the South Atlantic League, which had been founded in 1904.

"He was the ugly duckling out there," said Mitch Lukevics, the team's minor league director. "He had the long legs and arms, but little of him was centered. He'd bobble a ball for an error, grab it and hurry an off-balance throw for another error."

Said Livesey: "It was a choppy, bad field with poor lighting, and his first baseman (the team's top slugger, Nick Delvecchio) didn't help either — he could have saved Derek from a lot of errors."

But the Yankees top minor league executives never lost faith. "First of all, he had such great range, he continued to get to all these balls that no one else would have gotten to," Lukevics said. "He was hitting well and with power."

Jeter finished the year with a .295 batting average, with 11 triples and five home runs. He was fourth on the Hornets in RBI with 71. But he was the team's best hitter with runners on base. Those in the organization who preached the Yankee Way also noticed that when Greensboro made the postseason, it was Jeter who led the Hornets in RBI and had a late-inning, run-scoring double that nearly won the final game of the South Atlantic League championship series.

Jeter, once homesick and trying to find himself, had begun to settle into a role as a team leader. He fostered unity whenever he could, whether it was inviting teammates over to his apartment to watch and compete in *Jeopardy!* or organizing brief, competitive baseball skills contests hours before games.

And once every other day or so, Jeter would do something in a game that stunned his teammates. Like the time he charged past his third baseman to backhand a slow-rolling ground ball next to the pitcher's mound. As he was gloving the ball he yelled for the pitcher to duck, then flung the ball in an underhand motion across his body on a line to first base, to get the runner by a step.

In the dugout, R. D. Long, Jeter's friend and roommate, turned to the coaches and other players and said, "This dude is no joke, yo."

Yankees executives felt similarly. "He made unbelievably acrobatic plays in the field and hit rockets into the outfield," Lukevics said. "And he was the fastest guy on that team when we timed the players from the batter's box to first base — and that was from the right-handed batter's box.

"You have to keep reminding people that the minor leagues is all about potential, not necessarily performance in every facet of the game. That will come."

Still, while everyone loved Jeter's overall upside, some people in the Yankees brain trust saw the airmailed throws on routine grounders and the dribblers that scooted through Jeter's legs and wondered aloud if the franchise's prized number one pick wouldn't cause less damage in the outfield. Perhaps the gangly, six-foot-three, long-striding Jeter would be more comfortable where he had more space to roam.

"It came up a lot in 1993," said Michael, who as a rail-thin, lanky shortstop had made 56 errors in his first full minor league season in 1959. "Derek in the outfield was a frequent discussion. George had people talking in his ear, and George would bring it up to me. And I said, 'George, he's a shortstop. He's *our* shortstop. Get used to it.'"

Livesey and Lukevics never wavered in defending Jeter. "The talk about moving him to center field was always from people outside of the player development department," Lukevics said. "I assure you that no one in player development thought he should go to center field.

"Now, could he have played center field? Yes, of course. Derek could have done it stone drunk in a snowstorm. But that wasn't his best position. He was a shortstop, and finding a shortstop with major league ability in the minor leagues is hard. We were lucky to have the best one. He just hadn't found himself yet."

Said Livesey: "I'm sure it bothered Derek to make all those errors. He was a number one pick with a bull's-eye on his back. But externally, he never showed that the pressure was getting to him."

Looking back more than a decade later, Jeter had a different perspective on what was going on with his career at that time. He had never considered playing anywhere other than shortstop.

Why? He was too busy absorbing every facet and feature of the Yankee Way. "In the Yankee minors, certain principles were instilled in us — just drilled into us — and the most important thing was accountability and responsibility," Jeter said in a 2017 interview, just weeks after he headed a group that purchased the Florida Marlins.

"I wasn't worried about making errors or anything else," he said. "I wasn't worried about what position I would play. I was just going to be accountable for those mistakes, take responsibility for them and seek the help I needed to eradicate them. I would simply work harder and overcome it."

So it's as simple as that?

Jeter did not smile. If anything, he glared his response. "There was nothing simple about it," he said. "It's just what I was going to do, and the Yankees were going to help me."

It was this resolve that had Livesey telling his Yankees front-office colleagues to calm down when it came to Jeter. Livesey reprised one of his favorite maxims about the then young Derek Jeter: "I'll stop thinking of him as a shortstop when he stops thinking of himself as a shortstop."

And Jeter had been saying he was going to be the shortstop of the New York Yankees since he was a child.

Jeter, at age nineteen, had also adjusted to life away from Michigan. He had bulked up a bit with an off-season lifting regimen, and he had friends on the Hornets, including Rivera.

In fact, it was Jeter, aware that Rivera was coming off elbow surgery, who helped Rivera count his pitches during his 1993 starts. Jeter would visit the mound and the two would talk about his pitch count. "It'd be something encouraging but helpful," Rivera said. "He'd say, 'Hey, forty pitches, time to sit this batter down, Mo. This is probably your last inning. Let's get out of here.'"

The Yankees had been cautious with Rivera. He made only 12 starts in 1993, and usually those appearances lasted no more than three or four innings. And the surgery had not much changed Rivera's strengths: precise control, a decent fastball with movement.

Rivera's ERA was 2.08, and he had 38 strikeouts and only 16 walks in 43⅓ innings pitched.

"We still didn't know exactly where Mariano was going to fit in," said Livesey. "But we knew he was healthy. We knew he still had that loose, live arm. You never give up on guys with a fluid motion like that."

In Prince William, Pettitte was padding his already impressive minor league résumé, winning 11 of 20 decisions. His ERA was 3.04 with a WHIP (walks and hits per inning) of 1.209. Pettitte was working on a cutter, a hard breaking ball that would eventually confound major league hitters.

"He wasn't there yet with the cutter," Posada said. "But he was on his way."

Pettitte's favorite two-strike pitch had once been a knuckleball that he threw as hard as he could. It approached the plate like a dancing fastball. But like most knuckleballs, the pitch was hard to predict. Catchers, including Posada, who was still new to the position, tended to miss it.

The Yankee coaches told Pettitte to abandon his knuckleball. It struck out some batters but it led to many walks. Pettitte was told he could resurrect the pitch if he was an established major league pitcher. But by the time that happened, he couldn't remember how he threw the knuckleball.

Pettitte made one 1993 start at Class AA in Albany and won the game. He was delighted to hear that Albany would be his destination in 1994. But it grated on him that Sterling Hitchcock, the other promising lefty starter in the organization who had already made his debut in New York, was still ranked ahead of him on the franchise's depth chart. Pettitte was a year younger than Hitchcock and seemed to have the backing of more Yankees coaches and scouts than any other left-handed pitcher in the team's minor league system. And that bugged Pettitte to no end.

"Andy took the competition with Hitchcock very personally," Gene Michael said. "He really wanted to prove to everyone that he was the better pitcher. Or would be. I didn't have a problem with that. I took it as an indication of how competitive he was and how much drive he had.

"But it was a different kind of thing. They eventually were teammates, but man, Andy always wanted to do better than Sterling."

Unbeknownst to Pettitte, when the Yankees executives gathered they were constantly comparing the notes of scouts and coaches about both pitchers. Because they knew that at some point they might have to include one or the other in a trade to upgrade the team in some manner.

"There might have been five hundred conversations about who was going to be better, Pettitte or Hitchcock," said Lukevics. "It was like the Bernie and Gerald Williams debate. By 1993, everyone had pretty much elevated Bernie to number one. But the Pettitte-Hitchcock conversations continued all the way until the end of 1995."

Posada, meanwhile, was still struggling to adjust to his new position. Two stints in the winter instructional league had made Posada a full-time catcher, but it didn't make him a good catcher. In 107 games at Prince William in 1993, he led the Carolina League in passed balls with 38, and he made 15 errors, but he also slugged 17 homers and drove in 61 runs — good production from a position that the Yankees organization normally did not rely on for offense.

"I was encouraged by my hitting, but I had no clue behind the plate," Posada said many years later. "I was still guessing about some things. I mean, 38 passed balls? In my major league career I averaged about eight per year."

Nevertheless, Posada was also promised a spot at Albany in 1994.

Brien Taylor had spent the season in Albany, and while he was strangely wild (102 walks in 163 innings), he had also struck out 150 batters. He had a 13-7 record with a 3.48 ERA and 1.405 WHIP.

"But Brien was still the man, still the brightest prospect," Lukevics said. "Yes, he was not yet polished, but his stuff was already of major league quality. Actually, he threw a higher percentage of fastballs over 95 miles an hour than anyone in the major leagues at the time. And his velocity didn't diminish usually. He'd still be throwing really hard in the eighth inning.

"It was an amazing thing to watch. His autograph was already prized and collected."

Taylor's breaking ball, however, was still not as reliable as the Yankees wanted. It led to many walks. And he was only a so-so fielder. The Yankees asked Taylor to go to a winter instructional league that began in the fall to work on pitching and fielding mechanics. Taylor declined, saying he wanted to go home to North Carolina.

The Yankees could not compel their twenty-one-year-old top prospect to participate in the instructional league. They told him the plan was to have him pitch at Class AAA Columbus in 1994, and maybe later that season he would be promoted to the big league club.

Jeter, however, was going to the instructional league. He had been hit on the left wrist by a pitch late in the 1993 season, and while he played through the injury, it still bothered him to swing a bat. The Yankees' medical team recommended that Jeter not swing a bat for a couple of months. But since it did not hurt his wrist to field ground balls, he could go to the instructional league for hours of tutelage in how to play shortstop.

Because he could certainly use it.

Brian Butterfield was the man waiting for Jeter at the instructional league in Tampa. Butterfield's father, Jack, was the Yankees' top player development and scouting executive who died in a 1979 New Jersey traffic accident.

The summer before his father's death, Brian had spent his first year as a professional with the Yankees farm club in Oneonta. It was the first of five seasons in the minors, a time when the switch-hitting Butterfield played shortstop, third base and second base. When his playing career ended in 1983, he became a roving infield instructor in the Yankees farm system and later a minor league manager for the organization.

By 1993, Butterfield was considered the Yankees' top infield guru. In the fall of that year, he was assigned to lead a five-week infield technique and skills clinic. Jeter was his only student. "You cannot explain Derek Jeter's development as a shortstop and not talk about the weeks that Brian Butterfield spent with him," Lukevics said. "It was the time when Brian broke things down in Derek's technique. He kind of reversed some bad tendencies and elevated the things Derek Jeter did well. It was exhausting — just to watch — but it was critical."

At no time did Jeter pick up a baseball bat. But early every morning, Butterfield and Jeter were on a diamond somewhere in the Yankees' vast minor league training complex.

"Brian hit ground balls at Jeter in an endless succession," Lukevics said. "To his right and to his left, high bouncers and slow rollers. He changed how Derek turned double plays, making him more aggressive in receiving the ball from the second baseman so he could make the throw to first base quicker and get out of the way sooner, for his own safety and longevity. Brian even changed something as simple as how Derek held his glove on his hand. He wanted it more relaxed, more open and welcoming to the ball. It was all advanced, expert instruction."

The morning sessions, which were videotaped, would last an hour and a half. Then Jeter and Butterfield would watch the videotape to assess what Jeter did well and what he could do better. That afternoon, Jeter would either have another infield workout or play shortstop in an instructional league game — but not bat.

"Derek came to work every day ready to learn more," said Butterfield, who from 1997 to 2018 taught infielders as a coach for five major league teams. "He'd take it all in, make it his own and ask for more."

Jeter was also gifted enough that he could be tutored in a particular fielding lesson and then have the ability to swiftly and smoothly assimilate it into his quiver of skills.

"There was a lot of progress being made, and we started to see groups of young Yankee players maturing at the same pace," Livesey recalled. "We didn't know who was going to be matched together exactly. But players like Pettitte and Posada, Rivera and Jeter, were coming along at the same time and they were on a lot of the same teams. They were developing alongside each other.

"That's never a bad thing."

17

Gamers

WHILE THE YANKEES' prospects were getting familiar with each other in the minors, the players on the big club were hastily trying to adjust to the newness all around them. Compared to the 1992 season opening lineup, there were new starters in center and left field, at third base, shortstop and second base, behind the plate and on the pitching mound. There was a different principal owner, if not a new one, overseeing the whole operation.

The manager in the dugout was not new, but he had something new in his pocket. It was a cell phone, Showalter's first. It did not ring that often. But George Steinbrenner insisted that Buck Showalter keep it with him at all times nonetheless.

The new-look 1993 Yankees won their home opener against the Kansas City Royals, 4–1, behind a complete-game eight-hitter by Jim Abbott. Paul O'Neill had four hits and made a diving stab of a sinking line drive in left field that prevented two runs from scoring. After O'Neill's grab, which ended the inning, Abbott walked halfway to left field to congratulate his teammate. The two then jogged to the dugout together with the crowd of 56,704 on its feet cheering.

Bernie Williams caught the final out of the game and jumped in the air with both arms raised over his head. Then, when Williams left the field, he went directly to the training room, lay down on a table with a towel for a pillow and prepared to nap. Despite the blare of loud music from the adjacent locker room, Williams was sound asleep within 90 seconds and awoke without an alarm in exactly 20 minutes.

It was, as his teammates would grow accustomed to saying, "just Bernie being Bernie." It happened often.

George Steinbrenner had strolled into the bleachers early in the game to greet fans and shake hands. He did the same thing in the players' locker room after the victory. "The stadium was alive — I haven't heard electricity like that in years," Steinbrenner told reporters.

He was reminded that he wasn't allowed in the building for almost a year and a half.

"Well, even before that," George said.

He was asked how his time went in the bleachers.

"Terrific," he said. "It was fun."

Asked why he had not taken a bow before the entire stadium before the game — it was, after all, his first game back in the Bronx — George answered: "Because I feared for my safety. I don't know if I'm popular enough to try that. Nobody likes being booed."

O'Neill enjoyed the stadium atmosphere with a childlike glee. "This place is so cool," he said. "I was looking around during the whole game. The fans, the fights, the beer throwing. Man, just awesome."

In the next six weeks, O'Neill became a fan favorite, hitting well and keeping up a running chatter with people in the stands. He also was benched against left-handed pitchers, a managerial choice he hated. He talked to one and all about wanting to be an everyday player. Showalter tried to stay out of the debate.

The manager would post a lineup without O'Neill in it and then jog into the outfield for batting practice, trying to blend in with the rest of the players and team personnel. "I was trying to hide from Paul," he said.

But eventually O'Neill would emerge from the dugout and search for his manager. "I'd be running from left field to right field and then to the infield just trying to get away from O'Neill," Showalter said. "But Paul would always find me. He was never nasty; he just wanted to plead and make his case. In essence, he was pissed at me.

"At the time, Paul was a .191 hitter versus left-handed pitching. I knew I was going to have to start off platooning him. It wasn't a permanent thing. But as I tried to explain to Paul, it's really important — really big — that a new Yankee player gets off to a good start. The fans and media will eat you alive if you start the season with a bunch of hitless games. I was trying to protect him from that. I told him he'd be an everyday player eventually. 'Just trust me.'"

O'Neill was only slightly appeased, and decades later his recollection of how Showalter would deliver the news of a benching differed as well. O'Neill said he would be standing in the outfield with first-base coach Brian Butterfield before a game and see Showalter coming toward him.

"I found out later that Paul would tell Butterfield, 'Here comes that stumpy little fuck to give me his bullshit on why I'm not playing,'" Showalter said in 2017, laughing.

Or, as O'Neill, with a smirk, said many years later, "I might have said something like that."

But a sense of détente nonetheless continued between Showalter and O'Neill. Winning helped.

By mid-May, the Yankees were six games over .500 and two games behind the first-place Detroit Tigers in the American League East. Starter Bob Wickman was 4-0 and Jimmy Key was 3-0. Danny Tartabull was leading the team in home runs, just ahead of catcher Mike Stanley. Boggs was hitting .310 and minding his own business, usually with a smile on his face. New second baseman Pat Kelly was flirting with .300.

Bernie was being Bernie, and playing stellar defense. Gerald Williams, after an early-season demotion to Columbus, was filling a variety of roles. In one game with Chicago, after Showalter shrewdly detected a defect in the delivery of White Sox pitcher Wilson Álvarez, Williams stole home, breaking from third base as soon as Álvarez came to the set position.

"Buck explained to me how Álvarez had a routine that he had to follow after the set position, and it was slow," said Williams.

It was one run in an 8–2 Yankee win, a game that saw Abbott take a no-hitter into the eighth inning. Bo Jackson hit a broken-bat single with one out in the eighth, then tipped his cap at Abbott, who saluted back.

"I'd love to throw a no-hitter one day," Abbott said. "Maybe my day will come."

Overall, the Yankees' attendance and TV ratings were up. The owner was startlingly quiet, and the Yankees had somehow become New York's only feel-good baseball story of the summer.

The crosstown Mets had reached the dismal depths that the Yankees had found themselves in three seasons earlier. On the field, the Mets were putrid and would lose more than a hundred games for the first time since 1967. Off the field, the players on the last-place team were caught up in a series of repugnant episodes.

Early in the season, Bobby Bonilla, the Mets' major off-season acquisition, tried to pick a fight in the locker room with *New York Daily News* sportswriter Bob Klapisch. Bonilla, who was brought to the Mets to provide veteran stewardship and leadership, didn't like something Klapisch had written. It was an ugly, public scene that dominated the back pages of the New York tabloids for a week. In the same room in June, pitcher Bret Saberhagen filled a large water pistol with bleach and shot it at reporters, staining their clothing.

Later, outfielder Vince Coleman injured teammate Dwight Gooden with a wild swing of a golf club in the clubhouse. Gooden would go on to have the worst season of his career. Coleman wasn't done. He also lit a firecracker and flung it out the window of a car toward a crowd of autograph seekers outside a stadium, burning three of them.

The Mets were in the midst of a long, rough stretch. It would be four years before they had another winning team, and thirteen years before they won their division.

In this climate, the Yankees were once again the favored team of the Manhattan glitterati, admired if not yet beloved because they were a team of fresh faces, and because they had an enigmatic, thirty-six-year-old manager who answered reporters' questions with quizzical homespun proverbs, spoken in a drawl honed on the Alabama-Florida state line.

Even Jerry Seinfeld, the comedian raised on Long Island to be a Mets fan, chose instead to feature the Yankees on his top-rated television show by 1993.

The Yankees were woven into a *Seinfeld* episode a year earlier, but in 1993, the new stars of the team were well enough known that *Seinfeld's* producers approached the Yankees to see if Showalter, Steinbrenner, O'Neill, Tartabull and other players would be willing to appear with the show's cast. It was the beginning of a long run for the Yankees on *Seinfeld*, with the show shooting scenes in the locker room, at spring training and in other locales.

O'Neill made an early appearance, arguing with Seinfeld's neighbor Kramer because Kramer promised a hospitalized boy — without the player's permission — that O'Neill would hit two home runs in a game for him.

"Two? Where'd you get that?" O'Neill yelped. "That's terrible."

Kramer countered that Babe Ruth had done it, which O'Neill disputed.

"You're calling Babe Ruth a liar?" Kramer retorted.

"I'm not calling him a liar, but he wasn't stupid enough to promise two," O'Neill said.

In another episode, Jerry's friend George Costanza decides to do the opposite of every normal instinct he has. The tactic leads to great success, and Costanza even lands a job interview with George Steinbrenner. Walking into Steinbrenner's office, Costanza greets the Yankees' owner with a diatribe:

"In the past twenty years, you have caused myself and the city of New York a good deal of distress, as we have watched you take our beloved Yankees and reduce them to a laughingstock, all for the glorification of your massive ego."

Steinbrenner answers, "Hire this man."

Costanza becomes the team's assistant traveling secretary, which in another episode permits him to corner Showalter in the Yankees' clubhouse and propose that the team should be wearing cotton uniforms, not polyester ones.

"Cotton?" Showalter said. "I think you've got something there, George."

The team switches to cotton, which works for a while. Until the uniforms are washed and shrink dramatically.

Near the end of the episode, a Yankees game is on the television in a New York bar and a broadcaster is heard yelling, "Oh my God, Mattingly just split his pants."

More than two decades later, Showalter said people still stop him and recite his *Seinfeld* lines back to him. "I didn't realize it at the time because I didn't have time to watch the show back then," Showalter said, "but that show was wildly popular. So it was really a big deal for us and all of the team. I guess we had arrived."

Showalter has a quibble, though. To appear on the show, he had to join the Screen Actors Guild. And somehow, all these years later, he is still paying dues, or taxes, on the residuals when the show airs in reruns. As Showalter explained: "When people walk up to me and say, 'Hey, Buck, I saw you on that *Seinfeld* show,' I say back to them, 'Nineteen dollars and twenty-seven cents.' Because every time they play that show, it costs me $19.27. It really does.

"The Actors Guild, the taxes they pay every time there's a residual on the episode . . . when you figure all this stuff in, it costs me money. I'm not kidding. It was great for us then — a nice step up from where we had been — but I've been paying for it ever since."

The Yankees were clinging to second place, even as the Toronto Blue Jays vaulted into first. But the Yankees remained in sight of a division crown, which disrupted the reasoned thinking of some.

As the July trading deadline neared, George Steinbrenner was getting antsy. He loved the idea that the Yankees' long playoff drought — no full-season division crown since 1980 — could end in the same year that he had returned from baseball exile. The pressure was on Gene Michael to make a deal that might put the Yankees over the top in a stretch run.

As he often had, Steinbrenner zeroed in on Bernie Williams, whose batting average had dropped to around .240. Williams continued to play a superior center field and it was just his first full season in the major leagues. Michael and Showalter were determined to be patient. Williams was too good a talent to abandon, they said.

Yes, the Yankees had been nurturing Williams for eight years now, which was a long time to wait. That did not mean it was time to quit on the seventeen-year-old they had sequestered in Connecticut in 1985.

But Steinbrenner felt differently. He was tired of hearing about what Bernie Williams could become. The Yankees were only two games out of first place, and Steinbrenner wanted a playoff berth and the postseason games (and revenue) that would come with it. So ordered Michael to call every team in the majors to gauge their interest in Williams.

"We were in a meeting and George told Stick that it was time to move Bernie," Showalter said. "He said, 'You guys messed up and he's not what you think he's going to be.' Then George got up and left."

Showalter looked at Michael worriedly, asking: "What are we going to do? You're not going to move this guy, are you?"

Michael shook his head. "No, I'm not doing that."

What Michael did do the next day was call the general manager of every other major league team and have a conversation. Then he went to Steinbrenner and informed him that he had talked to every team and nobody expressed an interest in Bernie.

"Of course," Showalter said with a laugh, "what Stick didn't say was that he never brought Bernie's name up. And neither did any other team.

"But George's reaction was 'See, I told you nobody likes him. Now we're stuck with him.'

"And I remember that Bernie got three hits that night. Then two hits in the next game and three hits in the one after that. He kinda took off from there."

By August, the Yankees were in a tie for first place and Williams had a 21-game hitting streak. O'Neill, who had been playing against most left-handed starters since the All-Star break, had at least one hit in 25 of his last 26 games. His .324 batting average was fourth in the American

League. Boggs and Stanley were both over .300, too. Stanley was on his way to a career-high 84 RBI. Jimmy Key was having an All-Star season and would win 18 games, the most of his 15 years in the majors.

Nearly all of the Yankees' recent transactions were paying dividends.

In one series with the Chicago White Sox, the trade that had sent second baseman Steve Sax to Chicago could not have looked more lopsided in the Yankees' favor. Mélido Pérez, acquired from the White Sox for Sax, won the opening game of the series. Domingo Jean, also part of the trade, won the second game with relief help from Bob Wickman, who was the third player picked up from Chicago.

"We got lucky on some trades," Michael said of the deal many years later. "We got the right guys and got rid of the right guys."

And some trades were sort of a win-win, as both teams benefited. Well, almost. Roberto Kelly hit .319 for the Reds in 1993, although injuries limited him to 78 games. The following May, the Reds traded him to Atlanta for the former Yankees farmhand Deion Sanders, who soon became more of a full-time NFL football player.

But O'Neill proved to be just what the Yankees needed. He was productive, and perhaps just as important, he brought with him an unbridled passion during games that heightened the focus of his teammates and kept them giggling, too.

Everyone knew about O'Neill's tantrums in Cincinnati, but in New York, the media capital of the world, they were appreciated as a form of performance art. An O'Neill strikeout could mean a helmet would go flying across the diamond. A ground out might send a shin guard skittering across the dugout, with O'Neill stomping his feet and shouting at himself. Most of all, the Yankees got used to the sight of O'Neill sitting in the dugout mumbling to himself after some at-bat did not go exactly as planned.

"It's really pretty funny and we kid him about it," Pat Kelly said. "Although we don't do it right in the moment. But what makes it funny is that Paul will smack a line drive single and later he'll end up muttering his disgust about the hit because he didn't hit the ball out of the park.

"The pursuit of a kind of perfection is so all-consuming to him. It inspires the other guys on the team for sure. But still, sometimes it's a little light comedy for us."

Or as Showalter said: "One day, he hit a homer into the upper deck and it bounced onto the field. He was mad because it didn't stay in the seats. Now that's being demanding of yourself."

When asked about his high standards, O'Neill answered, "There's no reason to not expect to go up to the plate and hit the ball hard every time."

He knew his teammates sometimes snickered behind his back. "There is some fun and games to it," he conceded. "But this is my job. The problem is that baseball is more frustrating than most jobs, more frustrating than being an accountant or a banker. We fail all the time and frankly it can get to you. Some people keep it locked inside. I guess I don't."

Mattingly, who had bonded with O'Neill as Showalter and Michael had hoped, felt O'Neill was imbuing the Yankees with much-needed intensity. "I always liked that he cared that much," Mattingly said years later. "And it wasn't about his personal goals, which is an important thing to recognize. He would get upset because he hadn't done something to help the team.

"The truth is, we hadn't had enough of that attitude in the past. We needed more people like him."

Culture creators.

"You can't be a sustained winner in baseball unless you have a lot of guys on your team who care about pleasing their teammates," Showalter said in 2017. "It can't be about pleasing the manager. Or pleasing themselves. They have to be playing for each other.

"And the opposite is true. You can have a lot of talent on the roster, but if you've got a bunch of guys who don't give a shit about what their teammates think, then you're dead. But we had found guys who did not want to let their teammates down. And it showed."

On July 30, Mike Stanley's three-run, game-tying home run led to the Yankees' 23rd win in their last 28 home games. The victory lifted the Yankees into a tie for first place with Toronto. The team had not been in first place in July since 1987.

Six days later, the largest crowd since opening day came out to Yankee Stadium. More than 52,000 fans watched the Yankees remain in first place with another victory.

Steinbrenner was pleased with the crowd, but he was still negotiating with New York State and New York City for a new stadium. The latest proposal had the Yankees moving to a site on the West Side of midtown Manhattan. Steinbrenner's talks with officials from New Jersey, where the biggest bloc of Yankees fans lived, had not abated either.

Other off-the-field issues posed possible distractions to the first-place Yankees. The collective bargaining agreement between the players' union

and baseball's owners was set to expire at the end of 1993. There had been
no substantive talks between the two sides, just perfunctory meetings.

Fearful that the owners would lock them out of spring training camps
next year or impose new rules on salary arbitration over the winter, the
players had been weighing a strike in late August or September. They felt
it was the only leverage they had.

The owners, who were seeking a salary cap system, pledged not to lock
out the players in the spring. Nor would they alter the salary arbitration
guidelines. Those assurances caused the players to call off their plans for
a strike.

But it was still understood that the two sides were far apart. Compromise was not being valued either. Since the ouster of Fay Vincent as commissioner in 1992, a powerful, antagonistic cadre of owners — a group
that excluded George Steinbrenner — had taken control of the labor negotiations. They seemed determined to teach the players' union, which
had gotten its way in previous negotiations, a brutal lesson at any cost.

Steinbrenner did not appear engrossed by the labor strife. When he
attended an owners' meeting in Wisconsin on August 12, he emerged
afterward and was quickly surrounded by reporters. Steinbrenner's first
words were "What was the final score?"

The still-in-first-place Yankees were playing an afternoon game in
Boston. While some businessmen carried cell phones in 1993, it was
many years before the smartphone era of texting, web surfing and news
alerts. (The Yankees won again.)

In ways that were different from the past, Steinbrenner was captivated
by his surprisingly competitive 1993 squad. Aside from his brief fixa-
tion with trading Bernie Williams earlier in the season, Steinbrenner was
more of a hands-off owner in 1993.

To be sure, Showalter's cell phone still rang.

"Mr. Steinbrenner would never start a conversation by saying 'Hello'
or by identifying himself in any way," Showalter said. "I would say 'Hello,'
and then he would just start barking questions."

But at least they were questions instead of orders. Or mostly questions.
As his son Hal said, Steinbrenner was never a touchy-feely person. But
when Steinbrenner returned from his banishment, those around him noticed changes.

"When George came back from the sabbatical," Gene Michael said,
smiling at his choice of words — sabbatical, not suspension or exile — "a
funny thing happened. He was actually pretty good to work for. He was

the same pushy guy but he was different in other ways. I had convinced him that we had to stay with the young players and not trade them away. And he listened. That might have been the biggest thing. You could get him to listen. He would consider opinions other than his own."

Cashman, then Michael's assistant, saw the same changes. He believed that Steinbrenner's time away from baseball had made the man deeply reflective. "After his banishment, when he came back, my own personal opinion is that he had started assessing his legacy," Cashman said. "And he thought about how he could change the narrative.

"He wasn't the same. He was still fire and brimstone, but he did kind of allow a lot of baseball decisions to be made instead of making them himself. Not all of them. But a lot more than he did previously. He came back with more patience.

"He was more apt to rely on his baseball people. In the past, it was more his decision-making. He'd say, 'This is what we're going to do.'"

It was that kind of management style that had once held the Yankees back. Cashman was doubtful, for example, that the team's later successes would have occurred had Steinbrenner not been exiled. "I don't believe that we would have been able to accomplish some of the stuff that we did," he said in 2017.

And, just as important, Steinbrenner's absence gave him a chance to gain an appreciation for the good work being done without his input. In most cases, he continued to let others have robust roles in the Yankees' rebuild.

"There was no question that after George's time away there was more consensus-building," Cashman said. "He would gather his knights of the round table and be convinced of the right direction or decision."

Of course, Steinbrenner still had his unreasonable moments. During one game, the Yankees' owner called the dugout to complain about the opposing pitcher. "Their pitcher is cheating," Steinbrenner bellowed. "He's scuffing the ball. Go tell the umpire."

Answered Showalter: "I know that, but our pitcher is scuffing the ball, too. And he's cheating better than their guy."

Another time, Steinbrenner was upset that Showalter had altered the pitching rotation by moving Jimmy Key's start back a day. Steinbrenner thought Jimmy Key was being unnecessarily delayed.

Showalter explained that he always studied the rotating umpires' schedule, as he had since he was in the minors. He wanted Key to pitch one day later to match him up with a certain umpire who would be working behind home plate that day. That umpire called a lot of low strikes, which was usually a good thing for Key's devastating sinker/slider/low fastball combination of pitches.

Steinbrenner acceded. "OK, just checking," he told his manager.

In general, there wasn't much for Steinbrenner to criticize about any of the recent decision-making by his executives and field staff. Mike Stanley, the bargain-basement acquisition in the off-season, was a glaringly obvious case in point.

By early August, Stanley, the thirty-year-old who had never been a starter, had wrestled the full-time catcher's job away from Matt Nokes. He had done it with timely hitting and surprisingly resourceful catching acumen. "One of the biggest things going right for us in 1993 was Mike Stanley's contribution," Gene Michael said years later. "He really took charge of the pitching staff and we needed that. He had a lot of big hits, but you need an on-field leader of the pitchers."

The ace of the staff recognized Stanley's value early in 1993, and typical of the resurgent Yankees, it was a little thing that made a big difference. "What I like about throwing to Mike," Key said in the midst of the season, "is that he doesn't move too early for a pitch. Some guys move too soon when they set up to catch the pitch, and a base runner can signal the batter with a hand or body motion about where the pitch is going to be, inside or outside. Mike sets up at the last possible moment. He doesn't give the pitch away."

Stanley had learned the technique during his years sitting on the bench. "You see base runners tipping batters off and you see the results," he said. "For most batters, location is more important to know than the pitch itself. Why give the batter that information?"

Stanley also boosted his pitchers' confidence in their breaking pitches, encouraging them to throw them regardless of whether there were runners on base. "Mike would say, 'Throw that curve as deep and as nasty as you want, because I'm going to block it,'" said Jim Abbott.

Stanley again credited his apprenticeship in Texas. "I came to realize that the key to blocking a pitch was anticipating that it might be in the dirt," he said. "Some guys call a breaking pitch and think it will be over the plate, because most of the time it is. Then they're almost shocked when it isn't.

"I would expect a pitch in the dirt. I'd be a half second faster to get down that way. And a half second is a lot on that play."

Stanley was also on his way to slugging 26 home runs — two more than he had in his seven-year career before 1993 — and hitting .305 with a .389 on-base percentage, which was startlingly high for a catcher.

But like Michael, Showalter appreciated that Stanley still knew his first job was managing the pitching staff and being dependable behind the plate. "What you want in a catcher," Showalter said, "is a guy who, even if he's gone 0-for-4 as a hitter, he's still a part of a winning game. And he understands the value of that."

Years later, Showalter still recalled a situation when Stanley was catching a game with Abbott on the mound. "Abbott threw a curve ball that fooled Chili Davis," Showalter said of the former Angels cleanup hitter. "So on the next pitch, Mike puts down one finger for a fastball. But Abbott shook it off.

"Mike put one finger down again. Abbott shook it off because he wanted to throw another curve like the one that had just worked. In the end, the pitcher has to throw what he wants to throw. So Abbott threw another curveball and Davis whistled a single right past Boggs at third base. It almost took Wade's ear off.

"After the inning, Mike came back to the dugout and he was steaming mad. He was mad at the lack of communication. But a lot of catchers just wouldn't have cared. They'd say they tried and got shook off. Not their problem. But to Mike, he becomes like a part of the pitcher. He felt like they failed together.

"That's the kind of bonds we were developing in 1993. In a lot of ways, it exemplified the kind of team we were becoming. We had a bunch of gamers out there."

But in late August that season, the Yankees began to fade in the AL East standings. On Saturday, September 4, with the Yankees now behind Toronto by two games, Abbott took the mound at Yankee Stadium. He had lost four of his previous six starts. His last start might have been his worst, when he gave up ten hits, three walks and seven earned runs in only 3⅔ innings.

Abbott began that Saturday game against the Cleveland Indians by walking the first batter he faced. But he induced the next batter to bounce into a double play. The third hitter, Carlos Baerga, flied out.

Abbott walked another batter in the second inning but struck out Cleveland's cleanup hitter, Albert Belle, and got the equally dangerous Manny Ramirez to fly out.

By the end of the fifth inning, Abbott had gotten ten outs on ground balls and not given up a hit. The Yankees led, 4–0. Jim Thome, another

Indians power hitter, smashed a hard liner in the sixth inning, but Yankees shortstop Randy Velarde moved to his right and stabbed it for another out.

Abbott got six more ground outs and took a no-hitter into the ninth inning. Cleveland's first batter in the inning was the speedy Kenny Lofton, who slapped a hard ground ball up the middle. Yankees second baseman Mike Gallego covered a lot of ground to get to the ball, planted his right foot and made a strong throw to get Lofton at first base by a half step.

The Indians' shortstop Felix Fermin was next, and after two hard foul balls, he laced a long drive into the left-center-field gap. Bernie Williams gave chase, using the long strides that had made him a champion sprinter, to pull even with the fly ball as it descended. Williams stuck out his glove about head high and made the catch, two steps from the outfield wall in front of the Yankee bullpen.

With Abbott one out from a no-hitter, Mattingly began jumping up and down on his toes at first base, a gesture that was a mix of anxiety and amped-up preparation. Gallego was doing the same. At shortstop, Velarde later said he saw his teammates bopping up and down. He tried to imitate them but said he was too nervous to feel his feet.

Gene Michael, who had acquired Abbott, was pacing in a private team box. Normally dapper, at this moment Michael had disheveled hair and his tie was loosened and crooked.

Carlos Baerga rapped a slow roller at Velarde, who scooped the ball and fired to Mattingly for the final out. Abbott was quickly engulfed by teammates at the center of the diamond. Michael smiled, watched the scene for a minute, then walked up a short flight of stairs, out of sight on the way to his mezzanine-level office.

Showalter, as he always did after Yankees victories, kept his seat in the dugout.

"That is the players' moment," he said. "They played the game."

Abbott high-fived each teammate. When it was Williams's turn, Abbott instead hugged his center fielder.

As Showalter and Michael both noted after the game, it was nice to see another Yankee pitch a no-hitter.

"And win," Showalter added.

It was the first Yankees no-hitter since July 1, 1990, when the ill-fated Andy Hawkins was immortalized by three ninth-inning errors and lost the game.

The last Yankees no-hitter in a victory was on July 4, 1983 — Steinbrenner's fifty-third birthday — when Dave Righetti held the Red Sox hitless. Righetti struck out Wade Boggs for the final out that day. For Abbott, Boggs had made a diving stop at third base on a blistering ground ball off the bat of Belle in Cleveland's seventh inning.

"I liked the end of this game a lot better than the end of the other no-hitter I've played at Yankee Stadium," Boggs said. "This is going to give us a big lift."

The next day, with Wickman improving his record to 11-4 and Stanley hitting his twenty-fifth homer, the Yankees were back in a tie for first place.

18

A Buzz

TWO DAYS AFTER the Yankees had climbed back into a tie for first place with the Toronto Blue Jays, they traveled Texas to face the Rangers. With the Yankees leading by a run in the seventh inning, Bernie Williams broke in quickly on a fly ball hit by Julio Franco.

On the swing, Franco had broken his bat, and the sound of splintering wood had fooled Williams, who suspected a bloop fly to shallow center field. But as Williams raced forward, Franco's drive instead carried over his head. As the ball rolled to the wall with Williams chasing after it, the tying and winning runs came across the plate in a 5–4 Texas victory.

It was the second consecutive Yankees loss. When reporters entered the visiting clubhouse after the game, they saw George Steinbrenner consoling Williams at his locker.

"He's a young player and he's got a lot ahead of him," Steinbrenner said. "If we're going to be there, he's going to be there with us."

The endorsement was appreciated; the Yankees still lost their next two games as well.

The team made a brief rally with two wins in the next three games, but a disastrous Abbott outing led to a 15–5 drubbing that stifled whatever momentum the Yankees had been building. It was only eleven days since Abbott's no-hitter, a blissful, sunny day in the Bronx. On the road in Milwaukee and playing in a spitting rain, the Yankees had fallen three games behind Toronto.

Then came a four-game losing streak. Starting pitchers Mélido Pérez and Scott Kamieniecki were also forced to miss starts because of injuries.

Their rookie replacements were not up to the pressure of a pennant chase. O'Neill had badly bruised his left elbow after crashing into an outfield wall in pursuit of a line drive and would miss several games. Mattingly was batting .221 since August, and the bullpen had blown three saves.

In mid-September, a story surfaced in the *New York Post* that Steinbrenner had been badgering Showalter with second-guessing phone calls throughout the Yankees' recent slide in the standings. The next day, other New York newspapers confirmed Steinbrenner's meddling and added another thunderbolt to fuel the news cycle: Showalter was so annoyed by the owner's harangues he might resign at the end of the season.

"I don't know where these things come from," Showalter said, "but they are totally untrue and unfounded."

Nonetheless, the Yankees kept sinking in the standings. By late September, they could only catch the Blue Jays if they won their last nine games. It didn't happen.

When the Yankees were eliminated from the pennant chase on September 27 — Toronto won its third successive AL East — Showalter refused to discuss whether the season had been a success overall, despite the fact that the team was on its way to a second-place finish. "I know what the goals are in this organization," he said. "Success? I'm not going to use that word."

But others were doing it for him. With an 88-74 record, the Yankees had their best results in six seasons. If baseball's wild-card playoff system, established in 1994, had been in place that year, the Yankees would have been the first wild-card qualifier.

The 1993 Yankees had also drawn more than 2.4 million spectators, which was an increase of about 700,000 fans from the previous year. The team's television ratings had risen to heights not seen since 1985, a jump that had the MSG Network and New York's WPIX battling bitterly over broadcast rights for the 1994 season.

The Yankees, seemingly in a death spiral just two years earlier, were relevant again, even if they had fallen short of a division title.

Mike Stanley made note of the difference from year to year. "In September last year, there were foul balls into the upper deck and they would clatter and bounce around and set off a mad scramble for the baseball," he said. "This year, people were catching the ball on the fly because the upper deck was filled.

"There was a buzz in the stadium again. There was a buzz in the city about the Yankees when you walked the streets."

Stanley was one of the big surprises, batting .305 with a .389 on-base percentage, an impressive number for a slow-footed catcher. Stanley led all the starters with a .923 OPS. An even bigger surprise was left-handed outfielder Dion James, whom Michael signed on the cheap as a free agent for less than $400,000. James was meant to be a steady reserve and insurance against injury, but he ended up playing in 115 games and batted .332 with a .390 on-base percentage.

Boggs proved that 1992 was the fluke he said it was and again batted over .300 while driving in 59 runs. O'Neill, playing every day by season's end, hit .311 and had 75 RBI.

Other Michael and Showalter experiments with the lineup paid dividends, too. Danny Tartabull complained about being relegated to the role of everyday designated hitter, but he thrived at the plate with 31 homers and 102 RBI. Mostly as a backup, Mike Gallego batted .283 with 10 home runs and 54 runs batted in. Another bench player, the longtime Yankees farmhand Jim Leyritz, hit .309 with 14 homers and 53 RBI.

The Yankees brain trust also guessed right about which of the "Williams brothers" to promote to a starter in 1993. Gerald Williams hit just .149 in 42 games. Bernie Williams slumped badly in the last month of the season when he hit under .240, but for the season overall he was a .268 hitter with 12 homers and 68 RBI.

"My stats were OK but they didn't reveal how much growth there had been as a player," Williams said, looking back at 1993 more than twenty years later. "That was my first full season in the majors, and that's a big adjustment — at least it was for me. It's the moment when you stop wondering if you belong at that level and become convinced you belong at that level. But there's still a long progression. It takes time. I improved in incremental steps."

Mattingly had a reasonably healthy season, driving in 84 runs with 17 homers and a .291 batting average. "But the biggest thing was, it was fun to come to the ballpark every day," he recalled. "We had reversed so many of the things that had brought us down in 1990 or 1991. Yeah, we fell short in '93. But so what? We were getting better and better and we knew it.

"Most of all, other teams knew it."

On the mound in 1993, Abbott's record was disappointing (11-14), but he remained injury-free and started 32 games, two fewer than the Yankees ace, Jimmy Key, who had a sparkling 18-6 record with an ERA of 3.00. As both a starter and a reliever, Bob Wickman appeared in 41 games and won 14 of 18 decisions. The thirty-six-year-old closer Steve Farr saved 25 games despite a series of arm troubles.

"What I liked about the 1993 team was how gritty and defiant they were," Showalter remembered many years later. "We were neck and neck with the Blue Jays for about two months and they would win their second straight World Series that year. People kept expecting us to collapse because we didn't have the deepest pitching and we were playing plenty of inexperienced kids. But we hung in there. And you know why? Because we had guys who stuck together and fought for each other. It was a different feel — different than even one year earlier. I felt like the plan was working."

Michael, too, was convinced it was working. "Just look up the 1993 team's on-base percentage," he said with a grin in 2017. "I won't tell you; just go look it up. And when you do, remember how important I said on-base percentage would be to our production."

As a team, the on-base percentage that year was .353, the second best in the majors. Just three years earlier, when Michael was named the new general manager, the team's on-base percentage had been .300, the worst in the major leagues.

After the 1993 season, Showalter narrowly missed winning the American League Manager of the Year award, which went to Gene Lamont of the White Sox, who won the AL West. Steinbrenner said his manager — "Bucky," he called him — should have won the award. He also agreed to sign Gene Michael to a new general manager's contract.

"We knew we had more work to do, but we knew things had turned around and everyone could see that," Michael said. "The big league club was a good team. And the minor leagues were still stocked." *Baseball America* ranked the Yankees' farm system fourth.

"People throughout our organization felt pretty good," said Bill Livesey. "Things were looking up."

In early October, Livesey and Lukevics made another plea to Brien Taylor, trying to convince him that he would benefit from one more off-season instructional camp in Tampa. "We said, 'Brien, you don't even have to pitch, just go there to work on fielding fundamentals and your pickoff move to first base,'" Livesey said. "And frankly, all our minor league guys usually benefited from staying a little busy in the off-season. Although Brien was not someone we ever worried about off the field. Quiet as a mouse. But young. Still young."

Taylor once again refused to visit the instructional camp. "I want to rest and take it easy," he told the Yankees.

19

Lost Promise

THE ASSOCIATED PRESS reporter called Bill Livesey at his Florida home on Sunday, December 19. "The guy from the AP wanted my reaction to Brien Taylor's shoulder injury," Livesey said. "My first reaction was that this is a gag, because guys in the business would do that — make gag phone calls to be funny. To make a joke."

When Livesey recalled the moment nearly twenty-five years later, his voice grew quiet and melancholy. "But it wasn't a gag. It was a tragedy."

The previous night, eight days before his twenty-second birthday, Taylor got in a fight defending his older brother, Brenden. The initial details were hazy, but something had happened to Brien's shoulder.

His agent, Scott Boras, told the Yankees it was a bruise. "Boras called me and said Brien would be fine — he'd come back 100 percent," Gene Michael said. "I didn't believe him."

The Yankees immediately called the Carteret County Sheriff's Office in North Carolina, because several men had been charged, including Brien, who was unquestionably the area's most prominent citizen at the time. Police had not witnessed the altercation, but a sheriff told the Yankees that Brien left the scene in an ambulance and in great pain, his right hand grasping his $1.55 million left shoulder.

"No one knew what was certain," said Lukevics. "But the first report was that it was probably really bad. And your heart just sank. Yes, I felt bad for the organization, but I felt worse for the human being."

Even after a quarter century, facts about the fight are hard to come by. The criminal charges were eventually dropped or pled down to minor misdemeanors, so there was never any court testimony or depositions taken about the incident.

Taylor has never given an interview about the precise details of what happened. He answered phone calls to his Beaufort home in 2017, but hung up whenever he learned that it was a reporter calling to ask about his days as the greatest pitching prospect in Yankees history. Others involved in the fracas gave interviews in 1993 and for years afterward, but their versions have always differed in small but meaningful ways.

Everyone agreed that on December 18, 1993, Brien was at home in the brick and frame house he had built for himself and his parents on the plot of land where the family trailer had been when he was drafted by the Yankees. It was Saturday night and after 11 p.m. Although many reports later described the incident as a bar fight, Brien had been at home for several hours, perhaps even all night.

But earlier that evening, in a town twelve miles away, one of Brien's friends, Ron Wilson, had been in a heated argument with Brenden Taylor. The dispute escalated to pushing and shoving and then Wilson twice punched Brenden, knocking him down.

Brenden called Brien about the confrontation. Over the years, Brien's friends revealed to reporters that Brenden told his brother that he had been jumped from behind. Incensed, Brien drove to Wilson's home with a cousin, Donnell Johnson. It was past 11:30 p.m.

In an interview with Wayne Coffey of the *New York Daily News* in 2004, Wilson said he was shocked when Brien began pounding on the door of his trailer home demanding that Wilson come out and fight. Wilson, who considered Brien "practically family," told his friend that they had no beef to settle. "I don't want to fight you, Brien," Wilson shouted through the door. "But it was like he couldn't even think."

Another man, Jamie Morris, who was Wilson's cousin, appeared on the scene and started grappling with Johnson. Brien leaped into the struggle. He later told friends that he fell hard on his left shoulder. But Wilson said Brien threw a wild haymaker of a punch at Morris, and when he missed, Brien yelped in pain and reached for his shoulder.

"I asked everyone I could, but I never got a full story about what happened," said Gene Michael. "You know how late-night fights are — everyone has a story."

Livesey said Brien had told him he was just trying to help his brother.

"But if you don't want to slip," Livesey added, "don't go into slippery places."

The Yankees soon sent Taylor to Dr. Frank Jobe, the California orthopedic surgeon who had operated on the arms of several major league pitchers, most notably Tommy John.

As Brien was flying across the country with his left arm in a sling, his mother, Bettie, told Jack Curry of the *New York Times*: "Brien hasn't done anything wrong. I don't know what all the hoopla is about. I know he's a ballplayer with the New York Yankees, but he was reacting to what happened to his brother. I think any family member would have done the same thing.

"Maybe the only thing he did was act quickly. Brien reacted with his heart, not his head."

On December 27, the day after Brien Taylor turned twenty-two, the Yankees announced that Dr. Jobe would operate on Taylor's pitching shoulder, where both the capsule and the labrum were torn.

Dr. Jobe, who years later called Taylor's injury one of the worst he had seen, recommended that Taylor not pitch again until 1995.

Taylor had been slated to be in the starting rotation for the Yankees' top farm team in Columbus in 1994 — one phone call away from the major leagues. Instead, he would spend that season slowly and carefully rehabilitating his shoulder at the Tampa minor league complex, where he had been asked to attend the 1993–94 off-season instructional camp.

He would have plenty of time to work on his fielding.

"We remained hopeful of Brien's future," Michael said in 2017. "But frankly, it made me sick to my stomach to think about it."

The rest of the Brien Taylor story was no more uplifting.

He did spend almost all of 1994 at Tampa, with occasional visits to Dr. Jobe for checkups and a week at Columbus to familiarize himself with his expected place of business in 1995. Except when Taylor was finally allowed to pitch during spring training in 1995, Yankees officials were aghast at what they saw.

"He was a shell of what he had been," Michael said. "His entire pitching motion was different."

Standing beneath the grandstand at the Yankees' spring training complex in 2017, Michael imitated where Taylor's arm was positioned as he delivered the baseball before his injury. "He had that high arm slot, a little more than three-quarters, with his hand high above his head, exactly like Randy Johnson," Michael said. "After he got hurt, it was here." Michael held his arm almost sidearm, no more than a couple of inches above his shoulder. "It was real low. Because of the injury or the surgery or both,

Brien couldn't extend his arm. He just couldn't get his arm back to the same arm slot position. And that made all the difference."

At the start of 1995, his fastball did not break 90 miles an hour. His curveball was so erratic it was a nonfactor.

There was no way that Taylor could take that pitching arsenal to Class AAA Columbus. Instead, the Yankees sent him back to the rookie Gulf Coast League and winced as he gave up 37 runs in 40 innings pitched and lost five of seven decisions against kids fresh out of high school and college.

The Yankees thought that maybe Taylor's arm just needed a year to heal. He was sent back to North Carolina, made four visits a week to a physical therapist and told not to pick up a baseball.

In 1996, at Class A Greensboro, Taylor made only nine starts and gave up 40 runs. When his record fell to 0-5 with an 18.73 ERA, he was shut down again. More rest followed, along with a stay in the instructional league, where pitching coaches tried to reteach twenty-four-year-old Brien Taylor how to hurl a baseball like the nineteen-year-old Brien Taylor had.

The goal, along with more intense physical therapy, was to get him back to his original arm angle. He did get his fastball up to 91 or 92 miles an hour. But he had no command on the mound, averaging more than two walks per inning.

In spring training in 1997, Taylor was hoping to get back to Class AA Albany, where in 1993 he had been an Eastern League All-Star and had struck out nearly one batter per inning.

In an interview that March in the home dugout, a reporter asked him a question that began, "Do you dwell on—"

And Taylor interrupted to complete the thought: "What I could have been?"

He continued: "Sure, I think, barring injuries, you have to think back to what kind of numbers I could have put up. How devastating I could have been. How dominant I could have been. What could have happened."

Taylor stared out at the empty diamond of the Yankees' spring training complex. "For a year, I felt real terrible," he said. "But after a while, I decided I really had to put it behind me. It's happened, and it's done. I can't live like that: 'I should have done this or I could have done this.' Or, 'I might have been the man. I would have been a twenty-game winner.'

"Because it didn't happen. It's over with."

Taylor looked at his questioner. "I know it's not the story everyone wanted, me included," he said. "I can only look at it as something that was meant to be. It's too bad, but there are guys out there who every day do things worse than I did."

Taylor did not go to Albany that year. He went back to Greensboro. In 1998, he was there again when the Yankees tried to convert him to a reliever. The experiment failed; he gave up 76 runs in a little more than 52 innings pitched.

At the end of the 1998 season, the Yankees released their former number one pick. He had at least earned all of his $1.55 million.

In the four seasons after that chaotic fray outside Ron Wilson's trailer late on a Saturday night, Taylor struck out just 66 batters and walked 175 batters in 108⅔ innings. His ERA in that period was 10.85.

He did not pitch in 1999, and the Cleveland Indians gave him a look at Class A ball in 2000, but he lasted less than three innings in five relief outings and gave up 11 runs. It was his last time on a professional mound. He was twenty-eight.

Taylor went back to Beaufort and lived on Brien Taylor Lane, the bumpy road to his house that had been renamed for him. After a year, he moved to the Raleigh area and worked as a truck driver and at a beer distributorship.

He moved from town to town for a few years and was involved in a series of relationships that produced five children. By 2006, he had moved back to Beaufort, where his father helped him get a job as a bricklayer, earning about $900 a month. He was often seen downtown playing pool at the Royal James Café.

He kept to himself, and when newspaper reporters periodically made the sojourn to Beaufort to revive the story of the baseball phenom who wrecked his magic arm in a clumsy, inconsequential fistfight, Taylor would not talk to them. "We're private people now," his mother, Bettie, said. "Brien is minding his own business."

But in March 2012, police arrived at the home on Brien Taylor Lane and took him away in handcuffs. He was indicted on trafficking charges after undercover agents had purchased a large quantity of cocaine and crack cocaine over several months. Taylor pled guilty.

At his sentencing, he said: "I made poor decisions. I just want to say I'm sorry for all the harm I caused to individuals and their families. I'm sorry to my children for letting them down."

US District Judge Louise Flanagan, who presided over the case, remarked in court that Taylor "seemed completely unprepared for a life after baseball."

In sentencing Taylor to thirty-eight months in federal prison, Flanagan also admonished him: "You were viewed by many in your community as a hero because of your baseball career. A hero dealing drugs is a very dangerous person."

He served roughly two years in jail in Grantsboro, North Carolina.

The news of Taylor's fate filtered back to the Yankees executives who had made him the top pick of the 1991 draft and rewarded him with a record contract for a high school baseball player. More than a quarter century later, they still seem shaken by the turn of events.

"So sad," Michael said. "And Brien was a good kid."

Said Lukevics: "I remember watching him in Beaufort. It's still the most phenomenal performance I've seen by a high school pitcher."

Even Derek Jeter, Taylor's old minor league teammate, dropped his head to his chest when asked about Taylor in 2013. "Brien was a shy, happy-go-lucky country boy," Jeter said. "It just shows how one little decision in life . . ."

Jeter paused.

"Sometimes one thing goes right, one thing goes wrong, and it can change the course of a career," he said. "Unfortunately, for him — and for us."

Jeter, along with Andy Pettitte, Mariano Rivera and Jorge Posada, will forever be known as the Yankees' Core Four, players acquired by the team from 1990 to 1992 who led the franchise to four World Series championships from 1996 to 2000. But the plan was for Brien Taylor, drafted in 1991, to join them. It might have been called baseball's Fab Five.

Bill Livesey feels bad not just for Taylor and the Yankees. "I think the game of baseball got cheated," he said. "He was that special."

Reminded of Brien Taylor's drug offenses, Livesey had another thought: "Sometimes unfulfilled potential might be the greatest burden."

Part Three

Rebirth

20

A Spark

A DAY BEFORE the 1994 season was to begin, George Steinbrenner praised Buck Showalter: "He's done the finest job I've seen in my twenty years in baseball."

Then Steinbrenner added an important caveat: "Of course, now Showalter has a team with the highest payroll in baseball, and there's more pressure on the manager than before. He's done a great job but he can't fall back.

"He's in a tough spot. It's harder to do something well two seasons in a row."

Twelve games into the season, the Yankees had won only half of their games. Some of the team's biggest hitting threats, like Mattingly, Bernie Williams and Mike Stanley, were batting about .200 or less. The eight beat writers traveling with the team, representing newspapers from Newark to Hartford, began leaving daily messages with Steinbrenner's Tampa office. The writers were waiting for the Yankees' mercurial owner to return their calls, fuming with concerns and condemnations.

It was a newspaper writer's ploy that had worked since 1976. Among the writers, it was likened to putting quarters into a jukebox, where once you push the buttons, a voice will likely sing. In this case, the voice would be that of George M. Steinbrenner, whom the Yankees writers in the 1980s began calling "Mr. Tunes."

But this time Steinbrenner did not take the bait. Since his return from baseball exile, Gene Michael had been begging him to only make his complaints directly to the general manager. "The more he left the press out of it, the better," Michael said.

He added with a snicker: "It certainly wasn't better for me. But it was better for the team."

In 1994, Steinbrenner was not playing Mr. Tunes.

Michael, who earlier that year had received a new contract that doubled his salary, had succeeded — for the most part — in diffusing a dangerous triangle of power and influence that had distracted many of the Yankees teams since the 1970s. It worked like this:

There was Steinbrenner, there were the newspaper reporters, and there were the team's players, manager and/or general manager.

If Steinbrenner was unhappy with a player's performance, or if he was flummoxed by a game strategy or a managerial decision — he was particularly obsessed with the batting order — he was more than proficient at letting the manager and general manager know of his displeasure. But he was so persistent in making his views known that virtually every Yankees manager or general manager would regularly ignore Steinbrenner's rants. It was the only way to maintain any equilibrium.

But when Steinbrenner's complaints to his manager or general manager did not effect the change he sought, eventually Steinbrenner would grow frustrated enough to go to the press, speaking either on or off the record, so long as his message still got into print. Steinbrenner seemed to enjoy these phone calls to reporters, because they never argued or disagreed with him. They only took notes.

And those calls would produce a story or stories, which would mean that the manager, general manager or a player — or all three — would end up being grilled before a game about the stinging criticism levied by the Yankees' owner. Sometimes the player, manager or general manager — or all three — would fire back at the noisy owner. And then Steinbrenner might return the fire, usually through the press (although by 1994, New York had a 24-hour sports-talk radio station as well).

Obviously, it was a destructive cycle. Hence Steinbrenner's 19 managerial changes before the hiring of Showalter.

But by 1994, things had changed. Showalter, for instance, was closing in on the record for most consecutive days as a Yankees manager under Steinbrenner. It helped that Steinbrenner had been banished, but after his return, Showalter gave Gene Michael most of the credit for keeping a semblance of normalcy.

"Stick took a lot of the heat and he was great about that," Showalter said. "Most of the time, he'd never even tell me about it. George would say this or that and Stick would just listen. When he was in New York,

George also liked to have meetings in his stadium office hours before a home game. He'd tell Stick he wanted me up there, and Stick would say I wasn't available. Actually, I'd never even know George wanted a meeting.

"Sometimes Stick would call me and say, 'OK, George wants a meeting with you and the coaches. So this time you have to come up here to his office. But don't bring the coaches.' And I would do that, keeping the coaches out of the fire. And then, rarely, he'd say, 'OK, this time you do have to bring the coaches.' But for the most part, he tried to shield as many people as he could."

Michael adopted this approach after decades as a player, scout, adviser, general manager and manager for Steinbrenner. "Most of all, I had been a manager for many years, for George and elsewhere," said Michael, who was the Chicago Cubs' skipper in 1986–87. "You're pretty damned busy. You're trying to win games and trying to juggle a lineup. You're worrying about your starting rotation and the scouting reports on the opposing teams. You've got to talk to the press before the game.

"You don't have time to defend every move you make to the owner. And even if you do have to do that, it causes so much stress the players see it in your eyes or in your mood around them. And that affects team morale — it puts everyone on edge. It can ruin the flow of a season. So I worked as hard as I could to be the buffer. And frankly, George trusted me on baseball matters."

Michael also believed that Steinbrenner's time away from the game, and the gains the franchise made in his absence, had altered the dynamic between the owner and his chief baseball executives. "We had credibility by 1994," Michael said. "We had rebuilt things. I remember, after he came back from his sabbatical, he said to me, 'While I was away, you guys have messed things up.' And I said, 'Oh, really, so things were going well when you left in 1990?'

"And he said, 'Yeah, for the most part.' And I said, 'Let me ask you something, George. If things were going so well in 1990, how come we had the number one pick in the amateur draft the next year? Because that goes to the team with the worst record in all of baseball.'

"He laughed and said, 'Oh, you're a wise guy.' But he got the point. He backed off."

Showalter and Michael had developed a close partnership, a tandem of astute, incisive baseball minds. Both had been good, productive players but not stars, and both had been studying the game faithfully since they were teenagers.

"Stick was not only smart, he was as good an ally as a manager could have," Showalter said. "I would be stewing in my office ninety minutes after a tough loss, rewatching a tape of the game, and Stick would come down and try to push me out of the building. He'd say, 'Get in the car and drive home.'"

The Showalter family was then living in the leafy suburb of Rye, New York, north of the Bronx.

"So then I'd be driving up I-95, and he'd call again and say, 'How's the traffic?'" Showalter said. "And we'd talk about traffic or something to get my mind off the game. And finally he'd say, 'You can't win every game, Buck. If you win 60 percent in baseball you're considered a fucking genius. Now go home and kiss your wife and kids goodnight.'"

Angela Showalter saw the pressure building on her husband — it was in his eyes, she said — although she insisted he spent the hours at their home happily playing with the couple's children. "Buck was always totally devoted to his job — that was a given," she said. "But he could see the big picture. And in 1994, I really think he knew the Yankees were about to get pretty good."

After a 6-6 start to the 1994 season, the Yankees won 27 of their next 37 games. They moved into first place on May 7 and never left. By mid-June, they had the best record in the American League, which was newly realigned into three divisions. Their record was 38-25, a winning percentage of more than 60 percent. Managerial-genius territory.

The new third-base coach, Willie Randolph, had been skeptical in spring training of what the 1994 team could accomplish. He was largely an outsider to the coaching staff and wasn't versed in their methods.

"I figured we'd be competitive, but I didn't really get a feel for the team until the season started and we started to jell," Randolph said. "Then I said to myself, 'Wow, we've got an actual squad here, man.' We've got some guys that are stepping up and doing some nice things. Everyone seemed to have a nice feel for each other. The young players on the team seemed to understand the Yankee Way. It was the way we played. And they were tough enough to understand their responsibilities."

There was little going wrong for the Yankees. Paul O'Neill was batting an astounding .462. Boggs was hovering around .350 and had shown surprising power, having clubbed eight home runs. Mattingly, who was hitting .184 in mid-April, had raised his batting average to .323. Backup catcher and sometime outfielder/designated hitter Jim Leyritz already had 30 RBI and 10 homers.

In the starting rotation, Jimmy Key was 9-1, Scott Kamieniecki was 5-1 and Jim Abbott was 6-2. The trio of Bob Wickman, Steve Howe and Xavier Hernandez, an off-season acquisition, handled the late-inning bullpen situations.

Most notably, the Yankees enjoyed playing with each other. The culture creators had infused the team with a harmony of effort, purpose, fun and accomplishment. The clubhouse was alive and exuberant.

Luis Polonia, the disgraced outfielder discarded by the 1990 Yankees, returned to the team in 1994 as a pesky leadoff hitter (and was hitting .310 in mid-June). Polonia saw stark differences from his last time in Yankee pinstripes. "There's no comparison to what it was like when I was here before," he said. "That wasn't even a team then. It was a bunch of guys worried about numbers and trying to get their money. Guys rooted for their teammates to screw up so they'd get a chance to play."

Mattingly had seen the best Yankees teams of the eighties and the worst ones of the nineties. Looking back, 1994 still stands out. "That was one of my favorite teams because we had guys in sync and pulling together," he said. "Buck and Gene had done a great job with their plan. It had worked. That was probably the most fun team I played on."

Mattingly remained the cynosure of the team, but he had morphed into something more. He was now both a chief motivator and the team's principal motivation. Mattingly had been the Yankees' foremost star for 11 successive seasons, all of them without a single playoff game. At the start of the 1994 season, no other active player had been in as many games as Mattingly (1,560) without a postseason appearance.

Getting the popular Mattingly into the playoffs drove his teammates, especially since he was so dedicated to the cause himself.

"I've never seen anyone push his teammates the way he does," said Polonia, who was an eight-year veteran in 1994. "He spends nine innings doing it. It's amazing how he never lets up. He wasn't that way when I was here the last time. Now he constantly gets everyone going. I know guys say, 'God, look at this guy. Let's do it for him.' He wants this team to win more than anybody."

O'Neill, who to this day still calls Mattingly "Cap," in a reference to Mattingly's five years as the team captain, believes the overarching theme of the 1994 season was a quest to get Mattingly into the postseason. "He commanded such respect in the clubhouse," O'Neill said. "You didn't want to let him down. You knew that he wouldn't fail you, so you didn't want to fail him. It was like our duty to help him get to the playoffs. Because you knew how much he wanted it."

O'Neill was certainly doing his part — in his own manic way. In one Yankee win, when O'Neill hit his twelfth home run and had three hits, he was almost despondent afterward.

Why? "I struck out with the bases loaded today and had no hits in last night's game," he said. "I'm making too many outs."

O'Neill's drive, and even his temper, endeared him to Yankees fans, and they rallied around him. O'Neill was left off the 1994 All-Star Game ballot because the Yankees had four primary outfielders and were permitted to list only three on the ballot. (In the preseason, Showalter had his outfield quartet draw straws to see who the odd man out would be.)

So O'Neill was not among the 42 outfielders on the ballot, but when the first wave of voting results was announced in June, O'Neill had received the second-most votes of any American Leaguer — all of them from fans who had written his name on the ballot.

Like a write-in candidate making the All-Star Game, nothing seemed impossible for the 1994 Yankees. At the end of June, they won eight straight games to increase their AL East lead to five games. They were 20 games over .500.

It had already been an enchanted year for New York sports fans. The Rangers ended a 54-year drought, winning their first Stanley Cup since 1940. Their cohabitants in Madison Square Garden, the Knicks, had played a thrilling seven-game series in the NBA Finals, ultimately losing to the Houston Rockets. Soccer's World Cup came to the United States for the first time, with nearby Giants Stadium in New Jersey hosting seven games in June and July, including several played by the Irish and Italian national teams, which had fanatical followings in the area.

Around the country, as in New York, the news was most often positive and uplifting. It was almost the midpoint of the nineties, the longest sustained period of economic growth in American history. The internet was slowly beginning to change the nation. In 1994, Amazon.com made its debut. So did three distinct but unforgettably influential films: *Forrest Gump, The Lion King,* and *Speed.*

There was much to smile about, especially if you were a long-suffering Yankees fan.

Only one disquieting issue loomed, a blight threatening to ruin the best Yankees season in a dozen years or more. The tone of the negotiations between baseball's owners and the players' union had gotten thorny and vindictive. Neither side had yielded an inch. If anything, the owners had grown more entrenched and combative.

There was a feeling on the players' side that ownership's true goal was to smash the union rather than come to a new collective bargaining agreement. It was a perilous tactic. The baseball players' union was the strongest in American sports, and had survived — indeed had won — a string of showdowns with the owners dating back to 1972.

But it was those defeats to the players in past years that caused the owners to dig in their heels and fight so stubbornly in 1994. At seemingly any cost, they wanted a salary cap that they hoped would curb the free spending of bigger-market teams in free agency. And there was no longer a baseball commissioner to intercede or try to soften the owners' stance. Bud Selig, the acting commissioner, was the Milwaukee Brewers' owner and in lockstep with his brethren. Besides, the owners had recently voted to dramatically limit the baseball commissioner's powers.

In June, the owners grew more bold, withholding $7.8 million that they were expected to pay, according to the collective bargaining agreement, to the players' pension and benefit plans.

Steinbrenner read the handwriting on the wall — he had his best team in nearly a generation but knew it could all be taken away — and he was desperate to change his fellow owners' hard-line negotiating strategy. "I didn't fear a salary cap or the free-agency status quo," he said years later. "I thought we as owners were playing with fire. The union was not going to cave or disintegrate. I did my best to barter, cajole or be diplomatic with the other owners."

But Steinbrenner, owner of the richest baseball franchise, had few allies in ownership. He had friends but little power. The owners were preparing to stand their ground. The tension mounted, along with the anxiety of Yankees fans and others in certain cities, like Montreal, where the Expos were having their best season ever.

Frustrated but powerless, Steinbrenner instead turned his attention to a new Yankee Stadium. New Jersey still courted the Yankees and would for a couple more years, but the state now had a fierce opponent across the Hudson River. He was Rudy Giuliani, the newly elected mayor of New York City.

Giuliani was a die-hard Yankees fan, and he vowed that the team would never leave the city on his watch. Steinbrenner suddenly had several sites to choose from for his new stadium — from Staten Island to the North Bronx to midtown and uptown Manhattan.

Funding the new Yankee Stadium would be no problem, Giuliani said. The city owned the current stadium and would likely own, or finance, its replacement. Giuliani made that implicit. In his mind, it's possible that all he wanted in return was a front-row seat to any and all Yankees games. He got that and more: his own set of box seats next to the Yankees' dugout for his family and friends for many years to come.

While the wrangling over a new stadium took more than a decade to resolve completely, in 1994 Steinbrenner knew that he would eventually get his new palace with all the revenue-boosting luxury suites, pricey restaurants, team stores and elite, private clubs he sought. It was just a matter of bargaining. In time, the city did subsidize the construction of the new stadium with $1.8 billion in taxpayer funds, an outlay that would have been unthinkable and immensely controversial in 1990. But that was when the Yankees were a laughingstock, not a team with the best record in the American League.

So it was evident in every way that the Yankees had not just been revived on the field. The Yankees empire — fresh, flourishing and trendy — had been restored as well. Yankees caps once again were omnipresent on New York's streets and in its bars and subway cars. (It did not hurt that the 1994 Mets were again a flop.)

"In 1994 around the Yankees, without question, there was a spirit and a new young spark just taking over the team — the whole franchise really," said Hal Steinbrenner, who earned his graduate degree from the University of Florida that spring and immediately began working in an office adjacent to his father's.

"Having the office right next to George's office wasn't always the best place to be," Hal said with a laugh in 2017. "You're right in the line of fire. And years later, I was happy when I got my office moved down to the other end of the hall.

"But I recall the energy of '94. You couldn't help but feel it. Everything was just clicking on all cylinders. It was July and people were already talking about the World Series. Nothing seemed farfetched. My father was ebullient."

21

The Jewels

WHEN HE WAS fired as Yankees manager, Stump Merrill loved being home for the length and breadth of a beautiful Maine summer, something he had not been able to enjoy since he was in college. But as much as he loved his native state, after about ten months he needed to get out.

"I wanted a job," he said. "Not just a check."

Merrill returned to the Yankees as a special adviser in the minor leagues, and by 1994, Merrill was back as the manager of the Columbus Clippers, the franchise's flagship minor league team. His roster included all of the farm systems' jewels: Jeter, Posada, Pettitte and Rivera. But he did not coddle the most prized prospects, especially Posada, now the organization's top farm system catcher.

"I can remember we flew back from Ottawa after a game and then we had to fly to Rochester, and after that, we would bus back to Columbus," Merrill said. "So near the end of that long trip I posted the lineup, and Jorge, who was in the lineup, comes into my office and says he can't play that night.

"I asked why, and he said, 'I'm tired.'"

Merrill stood up from behind his office desk and bellowed: "What the fuck do you mean? I'm fucking fifty years old and I have to memorize every fucking pitch in every game. I have to worry about twenty-five guys every day and every night. You've got nine innings and four at-bats to worry about and you're telling me you're tired? Let me ask you something: Are we training a front-line major league catcher or are we training a backup?"

Posada said he wanted to be a major league starter.

Merrill roared, "Then get your fucking ass out there and play, and I'll tell you when you're tired. You understand?"

"Yes, sir."

Posada never asked for another day off.

"He never bitched about it again — to his credit," Merrill said. "He wasn't a soft player, but I think he wanted that discipline. The good ones realize they're going to be challenged and pushed. And after that, it's how they respond.

"I played Jorge on days when I could see he was tired. But I wanted him to understand what would be expected of him. If he was a big league starter, his teammates would want that of him."

Posada's defensive work as a catcher continued to improve, thanks to another perk of the bountiful Yankees minor league system. The franchise employed a coach, Gary Tuck, whose specific assignment was to tutor the team's minor league catchers in all the intricacies of baseball's most demanding field position.

"Gary Tuck just kept instructing me on all the things you need to do to be a top catcher," Posada said in 2017. "You have to learn and understand all the personalities on your pitching staff. You had to memorize the scouting reports of the opposing hitters. You had to work on your mechanics constantly. You had to develop your relationships with the umpires in the league and learn their tendencies as home plate umpires, like who favored the low strike or who favored the high strike. Everything mattered.

"I was overwhelmed at times but I kept at it, and Gary stayed with me. I was polished, but he kept getting a little shine out of me day after day."

Posada took the weight of his responsibilities seriously — and took them home with him after games. He would rehash pitch sequences, even in bed. His future wife, Laura, recounted years later that her husband, while sound asleep, would sometimes shout, "Why didn't I call a fastball there?"

"After a Yankees loss, that might go on all night," Laura said.

In 1994, Posada's determination and resolve were being rewarded. By midseason, he was second on the Clippers in home runs and RBI. A year earlier, his 38 passed balls had led the Carolina League, but now he had just eight passed balls. He was throwing out almost 30 percent of base runners who attempted to steal, which was far above the Class AAA average.

In the pages of the organization's bible, the Yankee Way, a catcher's defense mattered far more than his offense. The Yankees, from the big league club to the lowest minors, wanted durability and dependability when it came to blocking pitches and calling a good game.

Merrill saw Posada evolving into a Yankees prototype for the position. "On the few days when we sat him down, that's when I knew what we had with Jorge," Merrill said. "Because that's when the pitchers would come to me and complain that Jorge wasn't behind the plate. His teammates knew he made them better. He had become that kind of leader on the field.

"And he was smart. We had to do very little with him in terms of setting up hitters and the scouting reports before the game. He knew all the stats and strategies. And if we had a pitcher carrying good stuff into the game, Jorge made sure that pitcher went seven or eight innings.

"He had improved in all phases. I think he had a chance to make the 1995 big league team, until that one play at the plate."

In the summer of 1994, in a game against the Norfolk Tides, which was the Mets top minor league affiliate, a journeyman but speedy outfielder named Pat Howell raced around third base, trying to score on a slow-rolling infield ground ball. Posada saw Howell coming and used his left foot to block home plate as he awaited the throw from first base. The ball and Howell arrived at the same time, with Howell sliding into Posada's lower leg.

"I can still hear his leg bone snapping," Merrill said. "I heard it from the dugout. Just awful."

Posada's fibula was broken and his left ankle was dislocated. Several tendons were torn.

Carried by stretcher into the Clippers' locker room, Posada was placed on a table where athletic trainers took off his chest protector and shin guards and dropped them to the floor.

Posada looked down at the gear and said: "I'm not ever putting that stuff on again. Never. I'm done."

Said Stump Merrill, who was standing over the table: "You're going to be OK. Relax."

As Posada wrote in his 2015 autobiography: "I think Stump thought I was talking about the injury ending my career. I was trying to say I didn't want to catch again. I'd gone along with everything everyone had told me to do. I had improved, and this was how the baseball gods rewarded me? Work your ass off for what?"

Posada was not permitted to put weight on his left leg for the next six weeks. A lengthy rehab would follow. But he did return to catch again.

"The injury didn't change the organization's position about Jorge," said Brian Cashman. "We were still very high on him. And we weren't the only ones. A bunch of teams brought up his name in trade talks. It was right about that time that all of the guys who came to be known as the Core Four were regularly coming up in trade talks.

"Gene Michael was still wearing himself out saying no to every team. That was especially true when it came to Jeter. The answer was always an emphatic no when the topic was Jeter."

Derek Jeter made the rarest of developmental leaps in 1994. Coming off his left-wrist injury at the end of 1993 — and Brian Butterfield's expert tutelage — Jeter began the season with Tampa of the Class A Florida State League. Then he went to Class AA Albany of the Eastern League and finished the season with Columbus in the International League, the highest level of minor league baseball in the eastern United States. It was a meteoric ascent.

"We had never had a position player do that," Livesey said.

On his 1994 journey, Jeter hit .329 in Tampa, .377 in Albany and .349 in Columbus. For the year, he hit .344 with 43 extra-base hits and 50 stolen bases in 58 attempts.

Gene Michael surely smiled when he noticed Jeter's on-base percentage for the year. Despite jumping from league to league — and having to adapt to new and different pitchers at each stop — Jeter had a .410 on-base percentage and an OPS of .873.

Somewhere, Butterfield must have been beaming, too. Jeter made 25 errors in 138 games in 1994, even as he adjusted to about twenty new infields in the Eastern and International leagues. He still needed to improve, but the internal organizational argument about whether he should be a center fielder had come to an end. In 1993, he had made an error once in every 2.25 games. In 1994, he averaged an error every 5.52 games. He had 506 fielding chances in 1993, which equates to one error every 9.03 chances. The next year, Jeter had 616 fielding chances for an average of one error every 24.64 chances.

"That gangly ugly duckling had become a swan," said Livesey.

Added Mitch Lukevics: "And he still had that incredible range. He was getting to everything."

Jeter's fielding assists rose from 292 in 126 games in 1993 to 402 in 138 games in 1994. Butterfield's double-play drills worked as well. Jeter turned 16 more double plays in '94 than he had in '93.

"The Derek Jeter I saw in 1994 was a man compared to the boy I had seen the year before," Mariano Rivera said. "He always had confidence, but now he had acquired the skills to turn that confidence into success on the field."

It was a potent, heady mix: talent, confidence and know-how.

"A natural progression," he said with almost a shrug in an interview more than twenty years later. "I was growing into things and I had a lot of help."

In 1994, Jeter was named the Minor League Player of the Year by *Baseball America*, *Baseball Weekly*, and the *Sporting News*.

In a meeting of the Yankees front-office executives that summer, Merrill was asked if twenty-year-old Jeter was ready for the big leagues. "I said he was by far the best shortstop I ever had," Merrill said. "Bring him up and see what happens." The consensus was that Jeter would be called up to New York in late August, or September at the latest.

Buck Showalter did not need to be convinced. He had been watching and dissecting videotape of Jeter since 1992, which was Showalter's first season as Yankees manager and the year Jeter was drafted.

Showalter, in fact, had saved the tapes. The collection went all the way back to Jeter's senior year in high school. At his home in Dallas during the winter of 2017, Showalter quickly summoned the Jeter high school tape on his office laptop. He watched the skinny kid in high-top shoes chase down ground balls behind second base at Kalamazoo Central High School and then toggled on his laptop to another tape of Jeter, at Columbus in 1994.

"Do you see that?" Showalter asked, his eyes wide. "You know what he has in both tapes?"

Showalter answered his own question. "He has a grace," he said. "There's a grace to his game that goes with the obvious flow of athleticism."

As manager of the Orioles, Showalter routinely shows the tape to young, developing scouts in the Baltimore organization. "People think someone like Derek Jeter must have been an obvious first-round pick," he said. "And I show them this tape, where Derek is only 165 pounds and is bouncing all over the infield — he's all arms and legs. And I ask these young guys: Would you have projected this kid to be a major league All-Star over and over?"

But when analyzed properly, Showalter emphatically believes Jeter's high school tape has all the answers. "You have to perceive the tempo and rhythm to Derek's game," he said. "A common attribute of quality major league players is that they have a great internal clock. Those players know when to hurry and when to slow down, which is a really important thing to know.

"In our instructional league every winter, we had a lot of Latin shortstops who tended to rush every ground ball. I was trying to figure out how to slow them down, and one day I was flipping through the TV channels and I ended up watching a water polo game for a few minutes. And they had a shot clock at the top of the goal net.

"So, long story short, I got one of those clocks and put it behind first base. The average major leaguer runs to first base between 4.2 and 4.4 seconds. So I set the clock for 4.35 seconds and started hitting ground balls to the shortstops. And they're charging the ball and gunning it over at like 3.1 seconds. I'd stop the clock and say, 'Look how much more time you have. What are you rushing for? Learn to sense how much time you have.'

"But here's the thing about Derek. He came with that clock. He had it in high school. And that's very unusual. That was the thing about evaluating him. He had that 'it' factor. What is 'it'? Well, it is hard to define. But Derek had it."

The former Yankees second baseman Willie Randolph had left the team's front office to become Showalter's third-base coach in 1994. A six-time All-Star, he was also a fielding instructor during spring training that year, when Jeter was in the big league camp. "I worked with all the infielders and Derek was still a little raw, but had a certain swagger," Randolph said. "You could see he wasn't scared. Don Mattingly had that. There are certain players that are comfortable in their skin around veterans.

"Derek knew he belonged. The moment was not too big. It was in his posture. Yeah, he played the rookie role respectfully, but he wasn't intimidated. I remember saying to myself, 'This kid's gonna be all right.' So I wasn't real surprised when I heard he might be joining us later in the year."

There was less certainty about the future of Rivera.

In 1994, Rivera had also made the jump from Class A Tampa to AA Albany and then to the Columbus Clippers. It was a climb that was a little more common for a pitcher, and since Rivera was twenty-four years old, the Yankees were under pressure to more quickly figure out whether he was going to be a major league contributor.

Rivera, still a starter, was dominant in Tampa and Albany, with a combined 6-0 record in those two stops, an ERA under 3.00 and a WHIP (walks and hits per inning) below 1.1, which is stellar.

But when Rivera got to Columbus, he seemed overmatched. He had a 4-2 record in six starts but gave up 20 earned runs, 34 hits and 10 walks in 31 innings pitched. His ERA was 5.81, and he was still throwing his fastball at about 91 miles an hour — pedestrian for a Class AAA pitcher without a superior breaking ball that kept hitters off-balance.

"Mariano could be impressive, and he was an ice man on the mound," Merrill said. "Terrific poise, great control, and he threw so effortlessly. But you had to ask yourself: Is that going to be enough?

"The biggest leap in professional sports is from AAA ball to the major leagues. There is nothing like it in any other sport. There are guys who will light it up — just crush it — at the AAA level for two or three years straight. And yet, when you send them to the majors, they get their ass handed to them. It happens all the time. So it's hard to tell sometimes.

"At that point, we weren't sure what would happen when Mariano made the leap. But he was only in Columbus for a little while in '94. It was a small sample. You wanted to see more the next year."

If Rivera made it to 1995 as a Yankee.

Rivera was a frequently mentioned name in trade talks in 1994, and for a year thereafter. And unlike Jeter, Michael did not immediately take Rivera off the table during trade negotiations. "We were trying to be patient with him, but you know you can't keep them all," he said. "You're going to have to give up some prospects. And at the time, there's no question Mariano was not projected as high as other minor league pitchers we had. That's just a fact.

"But I held off with dealing Mariano."

As for Andy Pettitte, he continued to impress despite being overlooked in favor of the other top left-handed pitching prospect, Sterling Hitchcock, who in 1994 was pitching in the Bronx for a third successive season (with some success).

Pettitte, then twenty-two years old, began 1994 in Albany, where he won seven of his 11 starts with a sparkling 2.71 ERA. He was promoted to Columbus and became the Clippers' best starter, winning another seven games with a 2.98 ERA and a WHIP of 1.262.

"That year, I felt I showed at Columbus that I was ready for the big leagues," Pettitte said when asked to recall his 1994 season two decades later. "I think I expected a call-up later that year. In retrospect, I probably needed another off-season of development, of weight training and conditioning. But I was pretty pleased with my growth as a pitcher."

Pettitte's fastball still was no more than 91 miles an hour, but his breaking pitches had become sharper and more reliable. "Andy had total command of a game even at that age," said Brian Cashman. "He was very assured on the mound. He was six-foot-five and getting pretty muscular. He just stared down hitters. The will to succeed was evident."

And still, Pettitte had not overcome the comparisons to Hitchcock, who had compiled a 4-1 record in 23 games as a starter and reliever for Showalter's Yankees in 1994. But Hitchcock was more erratic and walked a lot of batters, which elevated his pitch count and got him into long innings.

The Pettitte-Hitchcock debate raged on in countless front-office meetings, especially since most everyone felt one of the two would eventually be traded. But which one?

Merrill was often asked his opinion, since he had managed both in the minors. "The thing is, neither Pettitte or Hitchcock were flamethrowers," he said. "And baseball people always say the most important pitch is the fastball. And it is. But only if that fastball is well located. Speed is not the only factor. So, to me, Pettitte had better command. And that mattered.

"Which one would I have traded? It wouldn't have been Pettitte. The secret to good major league pitching is screwing up the hitter's timing. And that's what Pettitte was able to do.

"But you had to see him over and over to appreciate all his attributes. He had intense concentration, the ability to locate the baseball, and he could change speeds. And he hated to get beat—his dark eyes would narrow like he was going to explode. It was almost scary.

"Looking back, in 1994 I didn't know he was going to be as good as he was, and anybody who says they did is probably misremembering—or full of shit. But Andy did have a look. And the look was a mix of 'Don't count me out' and 'Don't mess with me.'"

22

The Best Laid Plans Ruined

IN THEIR FIRST matchup after the 1994 All-Star Game, the Yankees swept four games against the Seattle Mariners, whose young, promising hitters were easily manhandled by the Yankees' wily, veteran pitching staff.

The Yankees did get another look at Seattle's newly improved six-foot-ten left-handed pitcher, Randy Johnson. In seven major league seasons, Johnson had always thrown about 100 miles an hour, in an era when no one threw that hard. But he had also led the league in walks three times. In 1994, Johnson had learned to get his breaking ball over, and his walks were down.

The Yankees still found a way to beat him this time, peppering Johnson for eight runs in barely more than six innings. But Johnson made an impression, one that lingered. "If Randy keeps fine-tuning that breaking ball, he's going to become a nightmare," Mattingly said.

In the meantime, for the Yankees, the dreamlike 1994 season continued. They won 10 of 11 games on a sojourn through Seattle, Anaheim and Oakland, a grueling excursion that usually tests and grates on East Coast–based teams. But the Yankees treated their West Coast swing like a blissful retreat, scoring 90 runs, smacking 19 home runs and batting .315 on the trip. The Yankees record was 60-36, the best in baseball, and they had been in first place for 78 consecutive days.

"The plan was working perfectly," Willie Randolph, the third-base coach, recalled years later. "Stick had said the goal in '94 was to have a mature professionalism in the clubhouse and on the field. As he said, 'Guys more in line with how Mattingly played the game.' And you could really see that. We now had players who were grinders. Guys who would work an at-bat and take a pitch. They were playing unselfish, team-based ball.

"All teams have their own style — a certain way they play. But Stick and Buck and the other leaders of the team knew they wanted high on-base-percentage guys, and you hadn't heard too much of that before '93 or '94. They did a great job of going out and finding guys who fit into that philosophy.

"And as guys saw the results, they understood what was going on and really bought into the plan. I keep saying it was the Yankee Way like it's some kind of magic formula, but we did have a certain approach that was a little bit different than other clubs. We were able to grind, to beat people up and to wear people out. We got into other teams' bullpens and won a lot of games. It was all working."

No other American League team was seriously threatening the Yankees' incandescence. The top team in the AL West, the Texas Rangers, were five games under .500. Baltimore trailed the Yankees by six games in the AL East. The Chicago White Sox were on top of the AL Central, but they had been plagued by inconsistencies. The White Sox had just one feared hitter in their lineup, the future Hall of Famer Frank Thomas. The pitching staff was suspect, with a team ERA over 4.00.

The startling Yankees were the class of the league. "We just had every part of our act together — I don't know if I'd ever been on a team that hummed along like that," Jimmy Key said many years later. And remember, in his career, Key was on two World Series winning teams and four other playoff teams.

"The '94 team had a potent combination of talent," Key continued. "There was timely hitting, versatile starting staff and a very good bullpen. We had tough guys and we had a couple of young rising stars like Bernie Williams who mixed in well with the older vets like Boggs, Mattingly and Stanley. Paul O'Neill was really finding his groove. The coaching staff had a lot of experience — Randolph, Clete Boyer and young guys like Butterfield and Glenn Sherlock.

"And Buck? Buck was a mastermind, up until the wee hours plotting for each game."

In the middle of the Yankees' West Coast swing in 1994, the *New York Times* beat writer Jack Curry published an absorbing account that took the reader into the complex baseball strategies and tactics that Showalter pondered every day. The piece covered a single game against the Oakland

Athletics and their gifted manager, Tony La Russa, who was regarded as baseball's resident genius — and with whom Showalter had tangled in a near brawl on the field during the 1992 season, Showalter's rookie year as manager.

Curry, a future Yankees broadcaster, wasn't in the dugout with Showalter, but he met with Showalter at length before or after the game, going over the manager's scouting, scheming and in-game machinations.

An early revelation in the story has Showalter studying videotape of Oakland's starting pitcher Todd Van Poppel the night before the game. Showalter noticed a pattern to how and when Van Poppel threw a fastball. On the mound and staring at the catcher's signals, Van Poppel usually nodded his head once, then shook his head once, then nodded affirmatively again.

Showalter surmised that Van Poppel was saying yes to the call of a fastball, no to a specific location and yes to the next location.

Over and over, Van Poppel repeated the sequence, almost always unhappy with the first location when his catcher called for the fastball. Showalter also noticed that Van Poppel started nearly every batter off with a fastball.

The next day, Showalter communicated his intel to the Yankees hitters — if they saw the yes-no-yes sequence, expect a fastball. Van Poppel did go through that progression on the mound in the first inning of the game while pitching to Bernie Williams, who crushed a Van Poppel fastball for a deep drive that was caught at the center-field wall.

In the third inning, Van Poppel did it again, and Yankees designated hitter Danny Tartabull jumped on the fastball to slam a three-run homer to give the Yankees a 3–1 lead.

An inning earlier, Showalter's advance prep might have saved the Yankees a run. Watching video of the previous Yankees-Athletics game, he saw that Oakland base runners attempted to steal second base after Yankees pitchers threw to first base twice.

When starter Sterling Hitchcock walked Oakland's Scott Brosius, Showalter instructed Hitchcock to throw to first base three times. On the third throw over, Brosius had already begun his break for second, but Mattingly relayed the throw and Brosius was tagged out at second base. It turned out to be a big out when Hitchcock walked two more batters in the inning.

By the fourth inning, the Yankees led 5–2 and had Williams at first base and Tartabull on third. Showalter noticed that Oakland middle infielders were playing deep and not doing something customary when there's a runner on first base. Normally, the shortstop would hold his glove in front of his face to exchange a covert signal that indicated who would cover second base on a steal.

But if they weren't bothering to signal, Showalter knew the infielders were instead planning to play so deep that neither would cover second base. With a Yankee runner on third base, La Russa might also have decided not to risk a Yankee double steal.

La Russa's motivation didn't matter to Showalter; all that mattered was his suspicion that the Yankees were being given a free base. Williams broke from first on the next pitch and cruised into second base standing up, since no Athletics infielder moved from his position and there was no throw from the catcher.

A single promptly extended the Yankees lead by two more runs. They romped to an easy victory.

Three days later, on July 28, the 31 players on the players' union executive board voted unanimously to go on strike if the terms of a new collective bargaining agreement could not be reached with the owners by August 12.

The players' decision cast an ominous cloud on all future games, because everyone knew the talks between representatives of the owners and players had been at a stalemate for months. There weren't even any new negotiating meetings scheduled before August 12.

The chief issue remained a per-team cap on player salaries, a system already adopted by the NBA and the NFL.

The players felt a strike was the only bargaining leverage they had against the owners, who could wait for the existing labor agreement to expire at the end of 1994 and then unilaterally impose new work rules, including a salary cap.

By striking in August, the players imperiled the 1994 postseason, which, not insignificantly, put in jeopardy the $140 million to $170 million in revenue those postseason games would make for baseball's owners. But collectively, players would lose more — as much as $180 million in unpaid salary. The players, however, had a large strike fund to reimburse the rank and file.

Thirteen years earlier, there had been similar labor strife in the middle of a season, and the issue then had also been a salary cap that the owners wanted to impose. In 1981, a fifty-day strike interrupted the season, and when it was settled (without a salary cap), the postseason was held, albeit with an extra playoff round to account for first-half division champions and second-half division winners.

With good reason, the players in 1994 may have expected an outcome comparable to 1981. But that would prove to be a serious miscalculation.

Unlike 1981, when the owners had only a meager amount of strike insurance, baseball's ownership in 1994 came to the bargaining table well prepared financially. Intent on a long fight for a salary cap, the owners had for years been funding a plentiful strike insurance policy.

In 1981, the labor impasse ended when the owners ran out of strike insurance. In 1994, when it came to contingency plans, the sides were more evenly matched.

In the Yankees' clubhouse the day the strike date was set, the mood was unusually glum. "I've lived through a bunch of these strikes and lockouts," Mattingly said. "But this one feels different. It feels worse."

The team was tense and tempers flared in that night's game as pitcher Jim Abbott, normally poised on the field, jawed at the home plate umpire over balls and strikes. Shortstop Randy Velarde slammed his glove to the infield dirt after an error. Paul O'Neill, who never needed an excuse to throw a tantrum, went hitless and stormed into the clubhouse, where he destroyed a wooden chair with his bat.

"We better settle this strike," Showalter said later. "I don't know if we'll have any furniture left with Paul O'Neill in that mood."

But the Yankees did not let up, extending their lead in the AL East. On August 3, they won their sixth straight game, which assured them the first-place spot in the division on August 12.

The team did not pop any champagne afterward.

"It's not a celebratory occasion at all," Mattingly said. "We all want a settlement. We all want a 162-game season. I don't think anyone in this clubhouse wants an asterisk beside this season."

Though not pleased, George Steinbrenner was at least impressed. He had been pleading with Showalter and Gene Michael to do whatever they could to get the Yankees into first place on August 12. Steinbrenner remembered 1981 when a first-place finish on the day of the strike meant an automatic berth in the postseason.

Steinbrenner, like most at the time, felt sure that even if there was a strike, it would be settled in time to continue with the baseball playoffs and World Series, which had been held every year since 1905. Even two world wars had not disrupted the playing of the World Series. "Our game has some serious issues right now," Steinbrenner said. "But none of them will be made better by depriving baseball and baseball fans of October playoff baseball."

Michael had been the Yankees' manager in 1981. More than thirty-five years later, he said he approached 1994 just as he had 1981. In both cases, he expected the season would eventually be finished with a World Series champion. "To me, '81 and '94 felt the same," he said. "I kept telling Showalter: 'Don't think about the strike. Don't think about the "what ifs" that other people are throwing out there. Just keep winning. Just pile up the victories, because we'll need them when we resume the season.'

"I was convinced and I think Buck was convinced. No World Series? It was inconceivable."

On August 11, the day before the strike deadline, Mattingly brought his two sons — Preston, who was six years old, and Taylor, nine — to Yankee Stadium five hours before the scheduled game that night against Toronto.

Mattingly hit grounders to his kids in the outfield and played catch with them. He wanted them to play on that field at least one more time.

"This could be my last game," Mattingly said.

He did not mean his last game in 1994.

"Who knows what's going to happen?" he said. "I may never play again. You never know what's going to happen."

Seated at his locker, Mattingly, whose 6,540 at-bats without a postseason appearance were a franchise record, packed a cardboard box with belongings before the game.

"Maybe I never play in the World Series or the playoffs," he said. "If that's my fate, then so be it. But as much as it makes me sick right now, I don't think we're doing the wrong thing by striking. I know it's not popular with the fans, and it shouldn't be. But at the same time, fans don't understand the issues.

"It's not about how much money any of us are making. It's about protecting the future players. Guys older than me went on strike to ensure the generation of players in this clubhouse now — my generation — would have some kind of free agency available to us. I have to do the same thing for the guys coming after us. We have to do what's right for all the players even if it's hard right now, since we're in first place."

Mattingly was right that the baseball strike was not popular with fans. The *New York Post* sent a reporter into the bleachers for that night's game and heard an earful of animus directed at the players and owners. "These players are very selfish," said Adam Droz, a twenty-one-year-old college student whose bleacher ticket cost $6.50. "I've got no pity for them or the owners."

The scene in the Yankee clubhouse before the game looked familiar, except it usually happened in October. Players were exchanging off-season telephone numbers and baggage was being packed. Lockers were emptied and baseballs were being autographed, an end-of-season ritual when each player would customarily take a box of signed baseballs home to donate to charitable causes.

There were conversations about what to do next. Some players were considering the rarest of things: a midsummer vacation with the family. Danny Tartabull was heading to a beach resort, but would not divulge which one. "I don't need ESPN following me there to talk about the strike," he said.

Wade Boggs wanted to go fishing. Jim Leyritz would return to Florida to finalize divorce proceedings. Showalter also planned to be in Florida. He had promised his daughter Allie that he would drive her to her first day of second grade. "There's one positive about all of this," he said.

The Yankees lost that night's game to the Blue Jays, their fifth defeat in the last six games. Their record was 70-43. The Yankee Stadium public address system had played several songs that spoke to the mood of the 37,333 in attendance: the Beatles' "We Can Work It Out," Elton John's "Don't Go Breakin' My Heart" and finally REM's "The End of the World as We Know It."

Lawyers for the owners and representatives of the players' union did not meet on August 11. Their positions unchanged, they had little to discuss. The strike, the fifth in baseball, began as soon as the last game of the night, Seattle at Oakland, concluded. Ken Griffey Jr. hit his fortieth home run in that game. Earlier, San Diego's Tony Gwynn had two hits to raise his batting average to .394. San Francisco's Matt Williams had smacked 43 homers.

Paul O'Neill's .359 batting average was the highest in the American League. The first-place teams were the Yankees, Chicago White Sox, Texas Rangers, Montreal Expos, Cincinnati Reds and Los Angeles Dodgers. Montreal had the best record, 74-40.

George Steinbrenner had the most to lose of any owner, since postseason games in New York generated the largest revenues available in baseball, as well as the most bountiful sponsorship dollars in the next season. He held a small meeting with reporters outside his Yankee Stadium office after the August 11 game.

He began by insisting he was in solidarity with the owners. He then spent a fair amount of time disagreeing with many of the stances taken by the owners' chief negotiator, Richard Ravitch, especially the notion that the owners needed a salary cap to restore competitive balance to the game. Ravitch had repeatedly informed the players that without a salary cap, teams from large markets with higher payrolls would dominate smaller-market teams with lesser payrolls. But, Steinbrenner said, "it's very difficult for Ravitch to argue competitive balance when Montreal, with the second-lowest payroll, has baseball's best record. I don't know how that helps the case for a salary cap."

A handful of owners sided with Steinbrenner, but the majority did not. A hard-line, influential coalition of owners had drawn a line in the sand. They were tired of giving in and tired of losing at the end of every labor impasse. To them, 1994 would be the year that the owners finally stood together and won meaningful concessions from the players.

At any cost.

As Steinbrenner said in a 1998 interview at lunch in his Tampa hotel: "There was a bitterness and a resentment boiling within some owners in 1994. You could not, and would not, change their minds."

Showalter was the last player or coach in the Yankee clubhouse on the night of August 11. "I am in a stage of denial right now," he said as he waited to leave. "Every time I think about closing that door behind me and what might happen after that, I get a lump in my throat."

Twenty-four years later, Showalter had no trouble recalling the moment.

"You know when you think something isn't real, like you're having a nightmare?" he asked. "That's what it was like. I was almost dazed. I walked to my car in the parking lot, and I sat in it for like fifteen minutes. I really thought someone, a security guard or a clubhouse guy, was going to come running out to tell me that there was a settlement and the strike was off. I didn't want to leave.

"Eventually, I started the car and headed home. The next thing I remember is waking up in the middle of the night. I still thought I was having a nightmare."

23

Like a Dagger

FOR THE NEXT three weeks, the United States Congress, a gaggle of veteran National Labor Relations Board mediators and finally President Bill Clinton each took a crack at trying to facilitate a strike settlement.

They failed. A year earlier, Clinton had turned the country's chronic succession of annual federal government budget deficits into a surplus, but ending baseball's labor strife was too big a task to ask of the president. He threw up his hands and walked away. "I can't make them agree," Clinton said.

In early September, Commissioner Bud Selig announced that the strike would have to be settled by mid-September in order for the season to continue. Selig reasoned that baseball needed at least two more weeks of regular-season games for the division races to be considered credible and worthy of a postseason.

On September 8, the players' union suggested the owners try a revenue-sharing plan they had devised. The teams with the highest payrolls would be hit with a 2 percent payroll tax, with the money going to the teams with the lowest payrolls.

It was a version of a system that Major League Baseball would adopt in 1996 and has kept in place ever since. There is a payroll threshold based on the average payroll of all teams. If a team exceeds the threshold, it pays a penalty.

In the 1994 players' union proposal, a portion of all gate receipts would also be shared by every team, leveling some of the revenue imbalances between the haves (Yankees, Dodgers, Rockies) and the have-nots (Brewers, Twins, Expos).

The owners rejected both pieces of the players' proposal outright. They had deliberated on it for just a few hours.

Six days later, on September 14, at a news conference in Milwaukee, Selig announced that the owners had voted, 26–2, to cancel the remainder of the regular season, the two rounds of playoffs and the World Series. "There is a failure of so much," he said. "And an incredible amount of sadness. Lest anybody not understand, there can't be any joy on any side."

Peter Angelos of the Orioles and Marge Schott of Cincinnati were the two dissenting votes among ownership. Angelos criticized Selig for blaming the players.

At home in Cincinnati, Paul O'Neill felt disbelief. "Deep down, I never wanted to believe it could happen," he said in 2017. "Sometimes I still can't believe it."

Michael recalled kicking chairs and tossing a few things around his Yankee Stadium office when he got the news. "I was so hot because I knew one thing right then," he said in 2017. "I knew that the '94 Yankees would never be remembered for having won anything. And I was right. But at that moment, it just bothered me so much because that was a special group. It was like raising a family, you know? We had put together a tight unit and watched as they helped each other day after day.

"It had been only a few years since those embarrassing, losing years, and now we had a team that really should have gone to the World Series. I mean, Jesus, it was a team that was good enough to win the World Series.

"And then what do we get? Nothing, that's what."

Sitting in a meeting room at the Yankees' Tampa complex all these years later, Michael still looked wounded as he relived his reaction to Selig's 1994 news conference. "Like a dagger," he said.

Michael had been a scout for the 1977 Yankees and a coach on the 1978 team, both world champions. He was a special adviser for five championship Yankees teams, from 1996 to 2009. Throughout that time, he was known for his even temper, for an easy-smiling countenance.

Surely, he was asked, all that winning has assuaged his discontent over the cancellation of the 1994 postseason? "Yeah, it helps," he answered. "But it doesn't erase it. The '94 team deserved better."

Jim Leyritz would also become a part of two Yankees World Series champions. But looking back, he still feels the ache of what was not accomplished in 1994. "You know how they say you're only young once?" he said. "A lot of us were young guys who had been through some mighty tough times."

Leyritz, after all, had made the outfield error that most directly led to Andy Hawkins's 1990 no-hitter that ended in a loss. "To us, '94 was like a payback, and it felt great to be on top," Leyritz said. "There was a contagious spirit. It was a collection of hungry guys reaching for that brass ring. Not many of us had been able to grab it yet. And that same group, we were never together like that again. We'll always wonder what we might have accomplished — and how that would have felt."

Most Yankees took the cancellation as a personal affront to Don Mattingly. "Knowing that Donnie was on his way to a first postseason game — and to have that stolen from him — that just tore at the rest of us," Bernie Williams said. "How unfair can something be?" George Steinbrenner said his heart "ached for Mattingly."

Mattingly, who had escaped to his hometown of Evansville, Indiana, issued a statement. He conceded the decision was "very difficult for me to accept."

Mattingly added: "It is in many ways embarrassing to me that the owners and players are responsible for shutting down an industry that even the act of World War I and World War II couldn't do. We have failed the fans."

Nearly twenty-five years later, Showalter's recollection of September 14, 1994, is clear. It was nothing like the nightmare he felt he was experiencing about a month earlier. "No, it's a very real, permanent memory," he said, sitting in his office at the Orioles' spring training home.

In 1994, he had been a thirty-eight-year-old manager, one with blond hair and a youthful, wrinkle-free face. In 2017, his hair was nearly all gray. Wincing, squinting and worrying his way through nearly 2,800 games as a major league manager had carved crow's-feet at the corners of his eyes.

Showalter watched Selig announce the cancellation of the 1994 season on television. "It's not at the same level, but it's like you remember where you were when you heard that President Kennedy or Martin Luther King had been shot," he said. "I remember sitting at home and listening to Selig. And I was like, 'My God, this is gonna happen. This is actually gonna happen.'

"I knew we had a team that could have gone deep in the playoffs. Deep into the postseason. We had the pitching. We had the defense. We had everything you need. It was all set up. So when it all went away, that was devastating. For the fans. For the players. For all the tough times we had gone through. For everybody. Forever."

Willie Randolph, who came into the major leagues in 1975, had been

through a number of work stoppages. He recalled that two days before Selig's announcement, a handful of Yankees players had gathered
at Hackensack High School in northern New Jersey to work out. "I saw
them — running, taking ground balls — that kind of thing," Randolph
said in 2017. "So when Selig canceled everything, I was stunned. To this
day I still can't believe it happened. The strikes, the lockouts, they were
always volatile, and I thought I had seen it all. But the game always went
on and we got to the World Series.

"But this time? I'm mean, you can't cancel the World Series, right?
That is a national fixture, part of the American fabric. We were on a nice
run. We had a good rhythm as a team and the guys were believing in the
process. To have the rug pulled out from us . . ."

Sitting on a bench next to a practice diamond at the Yankees' spring
training complex, Randolph paused and shook his head. "That 1994
thing still bothers me."

Randolph played on two Yankees championship teams and was a
coach for four more Yankees teams that won the World Series. "Doesn't
matter, 1994 still stings," he said. "I was so angry with the whole system
and how things went down."

Hal Steinbrenner recalled the atmosphere in the Yankees front office. "There wasn't a smile on anyone's face for maybe a month," he said.
"There had been so many years that weren't too exciting at all, and then
all of a sudden we could see a glimpse of what could be. And to have that
snatched away from you over something that had nothing to do with
balls and strikes. That was really a hard one to take."

Steinbrenner could have added that the team offices in the last months
of 1994 were missing the forty full-time employees and nearly four hundred part-time stadium workers laid off during the strike. The City of
New York estimated it would lose about $100 million from taxes gener-
ated and economic impacts from ticket sales, concessions, hotels, restaurants, taxis, parking, luxury boxes and subway fares. The sale of baseball
paraphernalia around the country ground to a halt. The Baseball Network, a pioneering joint broadcasting venture of ABC, NBC and Major
League Baseball, launched in 1994, all but dissolved. The Baseball Network, the first television network owned by a professional sports league,
officially folded in 1995. It took fifteen years for Major League Baseball to
reenter the lucrative television market with the MLB Network.

The strike and cancellation of the playoffs and World Series had left
the institution of baseball in America broken. The game's fans were not

so much bereft and grieving as they were inflamed and offended. Baseball's biggest problem was its own rancorous, divided house, and fans blamed both sides with equal vitriol.

All the fans in New York knew was that the Yankees' first shot at the playoffs in thirteen years had disappeared. To the fans in Montreal, where the Expos desperately needed something special to happen to keep the franchise viable, the cancellation of the postseason was like a cruel, callous joke. The Expos, chasing their first World Series appearance, had also not been to the postseason since 1981.

All around the country, in different but nonetheless painful ways, fans were absorbing a coldhearted punch in the gut. The 1994 season was meant to be the first with one wild-card team from each league qualifying for the playoffs. When the strike started, the team in place to earn the American League wild card was the Cleveland Indians, who had not played a postseason game in forty years. As the leaders of their division, the Texas Rangers were in position to advance to the franchise's first playoff appearance.

Also lost when baseball did not finish the 1994 season was the stirring opportunity to see whether Ken Griffey Jr. or Matt Williams could surpass Roger Maris's season record of 61 home runs. Tony Gwynn's batting average was forever stuck at .394, robbed of the chance to become the first .400 hitter since Ted Williams in 1941.

The 1994 season could have been one of the most distinctive, thrilling seasons in the final flourishing years of baseball's prosperous twentieth century. Instead, it nearly ruined the game. It created a cloud of resentment that hung over every baseball constituency for years. It left baseball wounded and lurching toward an uncertain future.

Staggering more than most were the revived New York Yankees, who spent the next several months trying to convince themselves that 1994 had been a success when it had ended in such utter disappointment.

24

Really Bad Hangover

THE BAD NEWS kept coming for baseball when team owners implemented a cap on players' salaries on December 22, 1994. The new system was meant to curb the spending of teams with the highest revenues by imposing a limit on their player payroll. That would, in theory at least, level the playing field for smaller-market teams with more meager earnings and TV contract income.

The players' union filed a protest with the National Labor Relations Board, citing unfair labor practices.

By January, with nothing resolved in the strike and no meaningful negotiations scheduled, the owners also announced that they would open spring training camps in a month using replacement players in exhibition games. If needed, these baseball substitutes would open the regular season on April 2.

That did not improve the players' mood. For those who had remained in New York, neither did a rough, snowy and cold winter in the region.

"Depressing," recalled Yankees outfielder Paul O'Neill. "As if I needed to be any more depressed."

To raise his spirits one day in late January, O'Neill drove from his suburban home north of the Bronx to visit Yankee Stadium. "I felt worse," O'Neill said. "The stadium was cold, barren, lifeless."

Don Mattingly had dropped by to see his normal place of work that winter. "I swung by Yankee Stadium and hated being reminded that there was no World Series and that we didn't know when we'd play again," said Mattingly, who was in New York to watch his wife, Kim, run in the New York City Marathon.

Buck Showalter had also been in the Bronx. After he had been named the 1994 AL Manager of the Year, the Yankees had feted him in a stadium news conference. He was the first Yankee manager to win the award since one of his mentors, Billy Martin, won in 1976.

When the strike began in August, Showalter had requested that clubhouse manager Nick Priore leave his office as it was when he left after the last game of the 1994 season. It made him feel like he might be gone only a short time. That did not prove to be true, and when Showalter returned to New York to receive his award, he descended the single flight of stairs to enter the Yankees' clubhouse under the first-base stands.

In his office, he found the tentative lineup card he had filled out for the next day's game on August 12, a contest never played. He found injury updates and advance scouting reports. Everything was in exactly the same place and undisturbed, except for a layer of dust.

"I felt like I was in the Twilight Zone," Showalter said. "I started packing some things up, but I stopped. It felt too much like packing up someone's belongings after they had died."

Spring training in 1995 opened with a hodgepodge of ex–college players and castoffs from the minor leagues, who were paid $5,000 for reporting and were offered another $5,000 if they made an opening-day roster.

"It was not real baseball, but if you were part of management, it was what the owners ordered," Gene Michael recalled. "It was a shame but it was part of the bargaining. The owners didn't want to say they had no plan come April."

Baltimore owner Peter Angelos, who had made a career as a lawyer for union causes, vehemently insisted that his Orioles would never use replacement players and eventually canceled the entire spring training schedule. Detroit manager Sparky Anderson refused to manage the substitute players and was put on an involuntary leave of absence. Toronto manager Cito Gaston found himself in a similar limbo.

The players' union announced it would refuse to settle the strike if replacements were to play regular-season games. In Canada, various labor boards ruled that according to existing labor laws, replacements would be prohibited on baseball diamonds in Toronto and Montreal.

At the Yankees' spring training complex in Fort Lauderdale, the scene was chaotic and acrimonious. To buttress their numbers in camp, the Yankees summoned dozens of minor league players to the big league camp. Normally, they would have remained at the team's minor league spring training headquarters in Tampa. But early on, three of the minor leaguers refused to take the field for drills with the replacement players. The Yankees sent the trio home and suggested they were violating their contracts because they were not yet part of the players' union, which was reserved for major league players.

Interestingly, the Yankees' best and most promising minor leaguer, Derek Jeter, was not invited to the big league camp. The Yankees clearly did not want Jeter anywhere near the replacements. The strike, the team knew, would end eventually. They didn't want their top prospect smeared or sullied by any inference that he had crossed a picket line (even if the players were not actually walking a picket line outside the spring training complexes).

As it turned out, Jeter wouldn't have shown up in the big league camp under any circumstances. It was part of Jeter's aura, as well as a telling measure of his unshakable belief that he would soon be a major league player, that he viewed the existing strike as his struggle, too.

Approached by reporters at the Tampa minor league spring training facility, Jeter said: "I wouldn't go [to Fort Lauderdale] no matter what. That's an easy question, easy answer. If someone is out there striking for me, it would be like stabbing them in the back if I played. I wouldn't do that.

"I didn't consult anybody; I'm just not going to do it."

In retrospect, it is easy to understand Jeter's confidence. But at the time, there were still lingering doubts about him in some quarters of the Yankee hierarchy. Just a month earlier, the team had signed the veteran, former Toronto shortstop Tony Fernández to a two-year contract.

Jeter's response? "They had to sign somebody," he said with no edge to his voice. "I don't mean that with disrespect. But to cover themselves they had to sign someone with major league experience. I don't look at it as, 'Oh, my God, Tony Fernández is here.'"

It was suggested to Jeter that perhaps Fernández might impede his path to Yankee Stadium.

"You mean, like a two-year roadblock?" Jeter asked.

Yeah, or something like that.

"I don't think so," he said. "They're going to play whoever can help them win a championship."

Jeter was twenty years old.

By early March, there was some movement in the strike negotiations. The owners were willing to consider the payroll tax proposal the players had put on the table in August of the previous summer. Except the owners wanted the penalty — now being called a luxury tax — to be greater on high-revenue teams, perhaps as much as 30 percent.

The players' union balked but agreed to compromise. The door to a settlement was at least open.

The owners were also facing even more devastating losses if the 1995 season did not begin in April. Baseball's fan base, already fed up, was turning from sullen to mutinous, a perilous tipping point.

About a week before the regular season was to begin, the players agreed to return to work if their unfair labor practices complaint was upheld by a judge of the District Court for the Southern District of New York.

That judge turned out to be Sonia Sotomayor, the future Supreme Court justice. On March 31, Sotomayor issued a preliminary injunction against the owners, siding with the players. Two days later, Sotomayor's decision received the support of a key appeals court panel. The ruling gave the players important leverage, which made a return to work less risky.

It also led the players to make a new offer: They would end the strike if they could come back under the terms of the old collective bargaining agreement that had been in place during the 1994 season. It meant that there would be no new accord between the players and owners, but the games would go on while negotiations continued.

The owners were expected to agree, though it would be a punishing setback for them. They would reap none of the financial gains they had sought throughout the impasse. A salary cap, the hot-button issue that had caused the 234-day strike, would not be part of baseball's future.

Nonetheless, on April 2, the day before the season was set to start with replacement players, the owners surrendered.

The players did not celebrate. Everyone knew there had been no winners. The sense of loss spread evenly throughout the baseball community. "The fans especially were bitter — pissed off might be a better way to phrase it," Hal Steinbrenner said decades later. "I think there was some of that everywhere. It lingered; it was there."

Buck Showalter welcomed many of his former players in Fort Lauderdale, but there were new faces, too. The Montreal Expos had barely survived the strike financially, and with the strike over, they commenced a fire sale, auctioning off all of their best players.

The Yankees acquired the Expos bullpen closer John Wetteland, who had saved 25 games during the previous, shortened season with a 2.83 ERA. Wetteland came to New York primarily for cash — and one low-level minor league prospect.

Montreal general manager Kevin Malone said his team couldn't afford to keep Wetteland, whom he praised effusively. "John is the best closer in the business," he said. "People on the Yankees and in the city of New York will fall in love with him. The Yankees will feel they've won any game he comes into. I mean that."

The team's starting rotation also had the former Cy Young Award winner Jack McDowell, whom the Chicago White Sox sent to the Yankees for minor leaguer Lyle Mouton, a decent outfielder who had no future in a Yankees organization already crowded with top young outfielders. "McDowell is the kind of experienced pitcher who helps keep things calm," Gene Michael said. "When things get tight in big games — and hopefully we'll have a bunch of them — he'll be a steadying force. You trade for him for the now, and for the late-season games we need to win, too."

In the Yankees' spring camp, there was almost no competition for starting jobs. The lone exception was in the starting rotation, where Showalter had officially not settled on a fifth starter, even if the consensus was that Sterling Hitchcock was the most obvious, tested choice.

Not surprisingly, Andy Pettitte did not agree with that sentiment. "I felt like I had shown enough to get my shot," he recalled years later. "I was like, 'Come on, give me a chance. You'll see.' Besides, I now had a wife and a five-month-old son. I needed that big league money."

Pettitte's pleading — and conspicuous poise on the mound — earned him a roster spot, though not initially in the starting rotation. He began the year in the bullpen. Still, the baseball journey of the pudgy prospect from outside Houston — a player whom the determined scout Joe Robison had to beg Yankees executive Bill Livesey to watch six years earlier — had passed a pivotal milepost. Pettitte would pitch only two more minor league games in his career (not counting a few injury rehabilitation assignments much later in his career).

He was a big leaguer now.

His former minor league teammates — Jeter, Posada and Rivera — each began 1995 back in AAA Columbus. And they belonged there.

Posada was struggling to come back from his badly broken left leg and ankle, which throughout the spring and summer of 1995 remained stiff and limited his mobility. Posada was again the Columbus starting catcher but struggled to find his old form.

Rivera, meanwhile, was expected to be a stalwart of the Columbus starting rotation. He had put on a few pounds, and since his English had improved dramatically, his calm, confident countenance had made him a quiet leader of the Columbus team. He was also now among Jeter's best friends.

Jeter was biding his time in the Class AAA International League. He was a consistent, graceful fielding machine in the middle of the infield, a shortstop who made the spectacular play and the routine one with equal aplomb. In the batter's box he was feared by opposing pitchers, a hitter who would turn on an inside pitch to rip doubles down the left-field line. But he was cagey, too, and even more likely to use his inside-out swing to scorch a rope into right field — and occasionally over the right-field fence.

At the start of the Columbus season, Jeter had a 17-game hitting streak, a period in which he batted .440. "By 1995, if we didn't know before, we knew for sure that at least one of our number one picks was going to make it big," Michael recalled. "Jeter definitely helped make up for the bad feelings we were all still feeling about what happened to Brien Taylor."

The 1995 major league season was set to begin on April 26. Two days earlier, George Steinbrenner was asked about the contracts of Gene Michael and Buck Showalter, both of which were set to expire at the end of the season.

"No, I'm not expecting to extend either of their contracts," Steinbrenner said. "That's not necessary. They each know what I think of them. They did great work last season."

The Yankees' owner was asked why he wouldn't prolong the two contracts if Michael and Showalter had performed so well. Why risk losing either at the end of the season?

"Gene and I have been through this before — many times, in fact — so I'm not going to change that dynamic," Steinbrenner answered of Michael's status.

And what about the thirty-eight-year-old Showalter?

"Pressure is part of this game and Buck understands that," Steinbrenner said. "He'll be more of a man as he gets older because he's able to understand pressure and knows how to operate under it."

The comment irked Showalter. But he didn't bite. Steinbrenner's words were an example of the kind of pressure the owner believed he needed to exert on his charges. He wanted to see how Showalter would react.

Showalter did not respond. Yes, he knew a manager with the benefit of an extended contract held more sway in the clubhouse. He knew that if the team had a loss of confidence — from a long losing streak or a spate of injuries — players would begin to look inward and feel even less secure because the manager might be gone soon. A manager without a contract for the next season could have trouble wielding his authority. It could be a dangerous brew in the quirky cauldron of a major league clubhouse.

If it spelled trouble, Showalter chose to feign contentment. At times, it wasn't even a ploy.

"I had already been through about eight years of one-year contracts as a nobody minor league manager and coach," Showalter said twenty years later. "Sure, a contract extension would have been nice. But, you know, I wasn't owed anything. My father always told me that you can be fired any day if you haven't done the job."

Showalter added: "It was always Mr. Steinbrenner's way to keep you on edge."

As for Michael, he said in 2017 that he was not fixated on a new contract in 1995. "Nah, I was too preoccupied with making sure we showed everyone that our success in 1994 was the real thing — something we earned and deserved," he said. "I had the attitude that we had to defend the title, even if we never actually won it."

The first game of the 1995 season was held in Miami, where the Marlins hosted the Los Angeles Dodgers. The opening-day custom then, as it is now, was for the uniformed members of both teams to be introduced on the infield foul lines before the first pitch.

The majority of the 42,125 fans at Miami's Joe Robbie Stadium responded to the sight of the players with robust, sustained and enthusiastic booing.

Around the country, the reaction was much the same, and in some cases far more antagonistic.

At the New York Mets home opener at Shea Stadium, three fans wearing T-shirts inscribed *Greed* dashed onto the field and confronted the infielders, tossing more than a hundred $1 bills at their feet. The crowd erupted in cheers.

In Detroit, near the start of a game, fans booed and hurled beer bottles and cans and other debris, including a car's hubcap, at the players on the Tiger Stadium field, causing a twelve-minute delay. There was a similar demonstration in Pittsburgh, where fans littered the field with trash, food and large plastic containers of beer that were still full. In Cincinnati, someone paid for an airplane to fly over Riverfront Stadium dragging a banner that read, *Owners & Players: To hell with all of you!*

The atmosphere was toxic in myriad ways. The major league umpires were without a labor contract and on strike. Groups of them picketed outside major league stadiums, even as the games went on with minor league umpires as substitutes.

In an oddity of allegiance, many fans resented the replacement umpires as well. Players and managers complained about their competence.

"The whole mood during that early part of the 1995 season was sour," said Yankees infielder Pat Kelly. "We were happy to be back, but all around us, people weren't happy."

The Yankees home opener was attended by 50,245 people, but that was about 8,000 short of a sellout. Fans along the third-base line held aloft two signs. One read, *R.I.P. Baseball 1869–1994.* Another read, *You owe ME money.*

Robert Liebowitz, thirty-five, a Brooklyn playwright, stood outside Yankee Stadium on the home plate side, next to the eight-story replica of a baseball bat that graced the plaza adjacent to the ballpark. He held a placard: *There are times in one's life to draw a line in the sand.* Approached by a reporter, Liebowitz said: "I've been a Yankees fan since the days of Jake Gibbs (a 1960s Yankees catcher). But I'm not going in there, inside the stadium, today. As soon as I hear them make the first pitch, I'm getting on the subway and going home."

Nearby, Mayor Rudy Giuliani was trying to preach conciliation. "The strike was sort of like a lovers' feud," he said. "It's all over now."

Maybe. It seemed like the fans, and by association, even the players, were still holding a grudge.

"It was a strange situation," Mattingly said. "I'm not sure anyone knew what to make of what was going on."

The Yankees won the opener behind Jimmy Key, whose surgically repaired arm had been a concern. Wetteland saved the game, and Bernie Williams and Danny Tartabull hit home runs.

McDowell won his inaugural Yankees start two days later (with Wetteland getting a second save).

The same day, the Yankees' number one pick from 1994, outfielder/first baseman Brian Buchanan, who was considered the premier power hitter of that year's draft, tore two ligaments in his left ankle at Class A

Greensboro when his foot slipped as he stepped on first base running out a ground ball.

Buchanan was finished for the season and never played for the Yankees.

On May 5, in the top of the second inning of a game against Milwaukee, Showalter's team lost its number four starter, Scott Kamieniecki, who felt something come loose in his elbow. In the bottom of the inning, Don Mattingly pulled up lame with a hamstring injury as he ran out a double.

One day later, Paul O'Neill, who was hitting .413, sprained his right thumb diving for a fly ball in the outfield. The same day, Wade Boggs left the lineup with a sore back after an awkward play at third base. A few days later, Yankees doctors discovered that Jack McDowell might have strained the latissimus dorsi muscle — a lat, for short — in his rib cage.

"We were all paying the price for a shortened spring training, which was almost like no spring training at all for a pitcher," McDowell said in an interview more than twenty years later. "All the starting pitchers especially, who need time to develop the muscle strength to last a hundred or more pitches, were in a precarious position."

On May 20, Key was placed on the 15-day disabled list with inflammation in the rotator cuff of his left shoulder. That same day, Mattingly returned from his hamstring injury but then sustained back spasms so debilitating, he left the field gingerly after a mighty swing and miss at a hanging curve ball. He was placed on the disabled list as well. Team doctors advised him that he had to be cautious with his balky back.

Mattingly had been trying to avoid violently pulling pitches toward right field for several seasons — the torque was too much for the worsening back disk problem that had first flared in the late eighties. But occasionally, he could not help himself. "I was batting in the middle of the order," he said years later. "I was trying to drive in runs."

But a new reality was setting in one month into the truncated 1995 season. Mattingly's days as a power hitter, which had been a distant image in the rearview mirror for about five years, were now officially, emphatically, all but over. If Mattingly wanted to stay an active player, he had to be content to slice base hits to left and center field and pull pitches to right field only occasionally. And it was downright dangerous to his health to go to home plate thinking about a home run.

The Yankees left New York on May 22 for an eleven-day, nine-game West Coast swing through Anaheim, Oakland and Seattle — in that order. It would prove to be an action-packed trip that included the major league debuts of Jeter and Rivera and Pettitte's first major league start. Along the way, the Yankees were nearly no-hit twice, almost won a game on a no-hitter, were embroiled in a ten-minute near brawl and watched as one of their catchers was beaned by a 98-mile-an-hour fastball.

They also lost eight of the nine games. By the time they returned to Yankee Stadium, the feel-good karma of the magical 1994 season had been extinguished. Doused was the soul and spirit of that journey, and in its place was something new and wholly dispiriting.

For starters, the 1995 Yankees were a last-place team and seven games out of first place.

What had happened?

"When you look back at it, I think there was still a lot of hidden, unconscious anger about how the 1994 season had ended," Willie Randolph, the third-base coach, said. "It was like a really bad hangover. We hadn't put away 1994 yet and it really knocked us off our axis.

"It's harder than you might think when you get that close to winning a pennant or a World Series — so close that you can taste it — and then someone takes it away from you. And you worked so hard to get there and then you don't even get to play for it. You don't win it or lose it. You slink away in shock and then you take seven or eight months off, and when you come back they say to you, 'OK, just do it again.'

"Well, it's not that easy. We had to start over and get that feel back from 1994. We had to find the old rhythm. But there was resentment still there. There was a malaise. And it was just going bad for us. Really bad."

25

Limbo

ON MAY 23, 1995, against the California Angels, the inaugural day of the Yankees' first major road trip of the season, Mariano Rivera walked to the pitcher's mound of a big league park for the first time. It was only his second time inside any major league stadium. The first was two days earlier, when he sat on the bench at Yankee Stadium.

Rivera had been having a good year at Columbus, although his right shoulder had been aching for more than a month. It was diagnosed as normal soreness, the kind of thing that pitchers must endure. But Rivera felt the discomfort was inhibiting his fastball and cutter and limiting the velocity on those pitches to 87 or 88 miles an hour when he had been used to throwing about two or three miles an hour faster.

Rivera had been given Yankees jersey number 42, something he considered a step up, since he had worn 58 in spring training. Rivera started the game with a largely uneventful first two innings. He did give up two hits but managed to escape without the Angels scoring a run.

In the third inning, California scratched out two runs on three hits, and in the bottom of the fourth, Rivera quickly gave up back-to-back singles. California center fielder Jim Edmonds then swatted at a so-so fastball that hung over the middle of the plate, launching it over the right-field fence.

Rivera exited with an ignominious pitching line: 3⅓ innings pitched, 8 hits, 5 earned runs, 3 walks and 5 strikeouts. His record fell to 0-1 when the Yankees lost, 10–0. California starter Chuck Finley didn't give up a hit until the sixth inning and yielded just one single and a triple in nine innings. "I wished I had done better," Rivera said when asked to recall his first outing years later. "But I felt like I got some batters out with good pitches. I wasn't overly discouraged."

The next night, the Yankees' Jack McDowell took a no-hitter and a 1–0 lead into the eighth inning. California's Chili Davis broke up the no-hitter and soon after scored to tie the game. Another hit put the Angels ahead, and an error by Bernie Williams helped make the game 3–1, which became the final score.

"Yeah, I pitched well for most of the game but that's not what I'm paid for, am I?" McDowell said afterward. "I'm paid to win games."

The Angels completed the three-game sweep with a 15–2 thrashing the next day. The Yankees moved up the coast to Oakland, where their losing streak continued when Sterling Hitchcock lost a 3–2 lead in the seventh inning on a two-run homer by Athletics catcher Terry Steinbach.

The next game was Andy Pettitte's chance to show, for the first time in the big leagues, what he could do as a starter.

Pettitte had good command of all his pitches but trailed 2–0 after two innings, with both runs unearned because of an error by shortstop Randy Velarde. When Oakland's Rubén Sierra, who would be a Yankee in another few weeks, homered in the sixth inning for a 3–0 lead, Pettitte's night was over.

Meanwhile, the Yankees were being held hitless again. Finally, in the sixth inning, there was a solitary single for the visiting team, and the Athletics starter Steve Ontiveros closed a one-hit, 3–0 shutout. Pettitte's line was reasonable if uneven: 5⅓ innings pitched, 7 hits, 1 earned run, 2 walks and 3 strikeouts.

"Not bad, not good enough" is how Pettitte evaluated the start more than twenty years later.

Rivera earned his first victory the next afternoon, on Memorial Day, protecting a 4–1 lead into the sixth inning after home runs by O'Neill and Williams.

Earlier that day, the Columbus manager, Bill Evers, woke Derek Jeter with a 6 a.m. phone call. Evers told Jeter to get out of bed, because he would be at Jeter's hotel room in ten minutes.

Gene Michael might have spent the last few years insisting that the Yankees would keep their homegrown talent in the team's system, but the Yankees' long-standing reputation for impatient and impulsive moves lingered. It still had legs. The evidence?

Jeter was scared. He figured he had been traded.

"I thought I was done," he said.

Evers instead told him that Tony Fernández had pulled a muscle in his rib cage. Fernández's replacement, Kevin Elster, was hitting just .118, and the team's executives knew that Jeter was batting .354 at Columbus.

Jeter was ordered to meet the Yankees in Seattle, where they would begin a three-game series the next night.

The news spread to 2415 Cumberland Street in Kalamazoo, where Jeter's father, Charles, left his home the next morning at 3 a.m. and arrived in Seattle in time to see his twenty-year-old son go 0-for-5. With two outs in the eleventh inning, Jeter struck out with his former minor league buddy Gerald Williams on third base as the go-ahead run. Seattle's Rich Amaral led off the twelfth inning with a walk-off homer.

In his second at-bat of the next night's game, Jeter rapped a single to left for his first major league hit in yet another Yankees defeat.

The Yankees couldn't wait to get home and end their nightmare along the Pacific Ocean. But there was still one game left.

Showalter decided to alter his personal routine in hopes of shaking his team out of its torpor. Instead of taking a taxi to the Kingdome, he walked the two miles from the team's hotel to the stadium. Along the way, Showalter, though not impetuous by nature, unexpectedly walked into a barbershop. He had not planned to get a haircut. "I walked past it and after about ten yards decided to go back and open the door," he said. "It looked like a nice place."

He struck up a conversation with the barber, who wanted to know if Showalter was in town for business.

"Yeah, and it's not going too well," Showalter answered. "It's driving me crazy, in fact."

The barber changed the subject to talk about the weather.

His haircut finished, Showalter was leaving a tip on the way out the door when the barber said he hoped to see him on his next business trip to Seattle.

Showalter chirped, "By the time I come back, I might not have any hair."

Seattle's pitcher for that night's game was Randy Johnson. It was the first start for the six-foot-ten Johnson against the 1995 Yankees, to whom he'd lost two of three games he started in 1994. His last appearance against the Yankees was a 9–3 thrashing inside the Seattle Kingdome.

In addition to Johnson's pursuit of redemption — as if the game needed any more weight for the Yankees — there was recent bad blood between the teams. The Yankees' Steve Howe, a brash, trash-talking reliever who was unpopular with many opponents, had nailed Mariners shortstop Felix Fermin with a fastball in the elbow the previous night. The Yankees were so sure there would be retaliation, Paul O'Neill went to the plate the next inning of the game and told Seattle catcher Chad Kreuter, "Get it over with now; hit me in the leg and let's be done with it."

But no Yankee was plunked. Some in the visiting clubhouse afterward thought the Mariners were taking it easy on an opponent they had already beaten twice. But Showalter was convinced otherwise. He predicted that Johnson, who had already led the major leagues in hit batsmen in two previous seasons, would throw at some Yankee in the series finale.

With two outs in the sixth inning and the Yankees leading 5–3, Johnson came inside with a high fastball against Leyritz, whose batting stance had him leaning toward home plate as he began his swing.

Leyritz threw up his left arm to deflect the thunderbolt hurtling toward him. The pitch ricocheted off his elbow and careened into his left cheek, just below the eye.

As Leyritz lay on the ground, with trainers trying to get him to recite the alphabet or spell his name, the Yankees' dugout emptied. Seattle manager Lou Piniella and his reserves charged from their bench to keep it an even fight. There were no punches thrown, but for several minutes there was plenty of pushing, shoving and cursing.

Showalter was livid with home plate umpire Tim Tschida, whom he had warned about Johnson before the game. He forecast a high, inside pitch to a Yankee, and now that it had happened, he wanted Johnson ejected. Showalter stuck a finger in Tschida's face to emphasize that point of view. Tschida didn't throw Johnson out of the game, but he did give Showalter the thumb.

That brought on a new level of histrionics by a slew of Yankees. When order was finally restored, Leyritz stayed in the game. Hitchcock, the Yankees' starter, quickly gave up a host of hits, and suddenly Seattle was leading 7–5. The Yankees charged back in the seventh inning to take a 9–7 lead, but gave up that advantage as well on a long home run by Seattle first baseman Tino Martinez, who was becoming something of a Yankee killer.

After the game, yet another heartbreaking loss, the Yankees vowed that their dispute with Randy Johnson was not over. "He better hope he doesn't see me out anywhere," Leyritz, sporting a golf-ball-size welt under his left eye, said as he packed for the red-eye flight home.

Piniella, the former Yankees player and manager who was a veteran of many years of open feuding and fisticuffs between the Yankees and Boston Red Sox, seemed to relish the budding, hostile rivalry between his old team and the up-and-coming Mariners. "You can tell the Yankees that we're not going anywhere," he said.

Piniella, whose team was beginning to take on his pugnacious approach to the game, added, "We've got some feisty guys, too."

The Yankees took their browbeaten, wounded team back east. And the hits to their psyche and lineup kept coming. After the game, the team announced that second baseman Pat Kelly would need arthroscopic surgery to repair torn ligaments in his left wrist. Kelly would become the sixth Yankee on the disabled list in a season that was not much more than a month old.

Said Wade Boggs: "It's MRI heaven around this place. MRI, surgery, rehab, ice, rehab — that's us."

If the Yankees were physically ailing, when they returned home there was news that jabbed at their psyches as well. It was, in a way, the resurrection of the 1991 Mattingly haircut flap. Except this time it was about facial hair. And the timing couldn't have been worse. The Yankees responded by losing the first two games of their ten-game homestand to fall into last place, nine games behind first-place Boston.

George Steinbrenner's policy about longish hair and facial hair had been in place since the mid-seventies. Hair could only tickle the collar, not obscure it, and the Yankees were expected to be clean-shaven (or close to it) except for mustaches.

But then Jack McDowell came to the Yankees. Nicknamed "Black Jack," McDowell was a six-foot-five, intimidating presence on the mound. Throughout his seven years with the White Sox, when he won a Cy Young and more than 61 percent of his decisions, he sported a full goatee that was almost like a Fu Manchu mustache.

During one of his earliest days as a Yankee in spring training, McDowell asked to meet with Steinbrenner, and when he was summoned to the owner's office, McDowell explained that part of the "Black Jack McDowell" persona was his goatee. He told Steinbrenner that he thought it added to his aura as a tall, hard-throwing pitcher. It was a psychological advantage he held over hitters and part of why he had averaged almost seven strikeouts per nine innings for most of his career.

"I'm a better pitcher with the goatee," McDowell said.

And Steinbrenner, softened by his banishment, agreed to let McDowell wear a goatee. "I figured that everyone would know it was just a one-time thing," Steinbrenner later said.

Except it wasn't.

By June and the Yankees' disastrous West Coast road trip, Mattingly, Pat Kelly and John Wetteland had grown goatees. When the Yankees got back to New York, Showalter and Michael — who were close witnesses to the calamitous 1991 Mattingly haircut dustup — informed the players that the old facial hair policy had been reinstated.

McDowell, Mattingly, Wetteland and anyone else halfway to a goatee or Fu Manchu had to shave.

Times had changed. Steinbrenner's dictum did not fracture the clubhouse or prompt the insubordination it did previously. Back in 1991, significantly, the order had not come directly from Steinbrenner, because officially he was forbidden from communicating with his players and manager. In 1995, there was no mistaking the origin of the newly reenforced facial hair policy.

The players shaved. But they weren't happy about it. "Slap-on-the-wrist bullshit," Mattingly said. "They shouldn't have relaxed it in the first place if they were going to take it away."

Steinbrenner, meanwhile, sounded like a school principal who had finally put his foot down after he realized the bad kids were leading the good kids astray. "I didn't figure it would be player see, player do," he said. "I thought they would understand what I was doing for Jack and realize it was a way to make him feel at home as a Yankee. But pretty soon all of them had one. I just got tired of it.

"They're all such good-looking guys, and the beards were making them start to look like not such good-looking guys."

McDowell was annoyed but sardonic. "I guess I wouldn't get the full flavor of what the New York Yankees are without something like this coming up during the summer," he said. "It's great for the New York tabloids."

McDowell's goatee was not as big a deal as Mattingly's clipped locks four years earlier. It did not make for screaming headlines because McDowell simply didn't move the needle that much.

At least not yet. His tabloid prime time was coming.

But McDowell's clean-shaven face soon went 0-2, dropping his record to 1-4. McDowell had not won a game since his Yankee debut in late April — eight successive starts without a victory.

In the midst of the persistent losing — the Yankees had one victory in their last 13 games — there was a career milestone to mark. Showalter surpassed Billy Martin's record for most consecutive games managed under Steinbrenner's Yankees. From 1975 to 1978, Martin had survived for 470 days.

As reporters quizzed Showalter about the signal achievement for a Yankees manager in the Steinbrenner era, he all but squirmed in his office desk chair. Perhaps it was because Martin's framed 1976 jersey hung on the wall behind his desk. Or maybe it was the painting of Martin that graced another wall in the office. Showalter knew how tenuous praise for longevity under Steinbrenner could be. He had personally witnessed the 1988 season, when Steinbrenner dismissed Martin even though the Yankees were 12 games over .500 and had been in first place for most of the season. It turned out to be Martin's last season as a manager.

"I knew Billy had been fired five times," Showalter said, recalling the moment many years later. "It felt a little weird to be talking about how long I had lasted in the job, especially with Billy as the reference point. I knew the history."

He was also practical, a trait he highly valued.

Showalter, for example, had rented an apartment or home since he had begun working in New York. Once, Steinbrenner asked him why he didn't buy a house.

"Because I work for you," Showalter answered.

Still, Steinbrenner used the occasion of Showalter's consecutive-games-managed record to offer praise for his manager's detailed pregame preparation. Steinbrenner added that it was "something more like what a football coach does."

It was the ultimate compliment from the former assistant on the Northwestern and Purdue University football staffs.

Showalter remained cautious. "It's flattering, but at the same time it doesn't change anything. There's a boss and we're employees working under him, and you have to understand that arrangement. I had respect for the ground rules from the first day I took the job, and I'll have it until the day I leave."

Murray Chass, the New York Times's national baseball writer, called Lou Piniella on the occasion of Showalter's milestone. Piniella, twice fired by Steinbrenner, congratulated Showalter on his record. Then Piniella, who is more of a serious baseball scholar than his regular-guy demeanor lets on, chuckled and said, "It's certainly not going to be a threat to Connie Mack's record."

Mack managed the Philadelphia Athletics for 7,396 successive games from 1901 to 1950.

But Showalter had far bigger problems than trailing Connie Mack's record by nearly 7,000 games. His team continued to flag, sinking deeper in the cellar of the AL East. The Yankees seemed to be more than sleepwalking. It was as if there remained a mental barrier to the team's success.

"It was a team that wanted to have the mentality of a defending champion after 1994," he said in 2017. "But everywhere we went, we were told that 1994 didn't matter. We were told that we hadn't won anything. Or we were reminded that we hadn't won anything.

"So it was like we were asking ourselves: What was it that happened in 1994, then? It left everyone out of sorts. It took a long time to get the right feel back. We were just kind of wandering in limbo."

Since so many Yankees still had a foot in the 1994 season, the 1995 Yankees needed a jolt from someone unconnected to the previous season. And on June 7, Andy Pettitte successfully stanched some of the bleeding by winning his first major league game. He gave up just four hits and one run in seven innings.

But the boost that Pettitte provided was short-lived. Some of his rookie brethren were not making contributions of equal value.

Four days after Pettitte's debut victory, Mariano Rivera gave up seven hits and five runs in a little more than two innings against Seattle. In his previous start, he had been bashed for two homers and seven runs, including a monstrous grand slam.

Most disturbing to the Yankees brain trust, Rivera's velocity was down. He had not struck out a single batter in the outing against the Mariners, who had also rocketed several Rivera pitches deep into the vast expanse of left-center field at Yankee Stadium. Rivera's ERA was 10.20.

Derek Jeter had played shortstop in the Seattle game on June 11, going 1-for-4. As Tony Fernández's replacement for 13 games, Jeter had hit .234. But Jeter was never meant to be the everyday shortstop in 1995, and Gene Michael had little interest in exposing the franchise's best prospect to the rocky tumult of an uneven, confounding season. Especially since George Steinbrenner was already grousing about Michael having wasted far too much money on an underachieving, last-place team. Michael wanted Jeter out of the spotlight for now. That is why he had paid

Fernández, a thirteen-year veteran and four-time All-Star, $1.6 million to come to the Yankees. Let him take the heat. Let the thirty-three-year-old Fernández weather the pennant chase pressure and ever-increasing scrutiny of an exasperated Steinbrenner. Fernández could handle it. It was time to let Jeter, who would turn twenty-one in a couple of weeks, return to the shadows just outside the New York spotlight.

The Yankees were about to begin a road trip with four games in Detroit. Before departing Yankee Stadium, Rivera and Jeter, one by one, were summoned into Showalter's office, where they learned that they would not be on the team's charter flight to Detroit. The two players were instead handed tickets for their flight the following day from Newark to Charlotte, where the Columbus Clippers were continuing their road trip.

"Maybe, in the back of my head, I didn't expect to stay in the majors," Jeter said. "But it didn't make me feel any better at the time."

The Yankees' traveling secretary had arranged for a cab to take Rivera and Jeter to a hotel that the team had reserved for the players in New Jersey. They would fly out first thing in the morning so they could resume their Class AAA minor league careers in a game the next night.

Rivera recalled that the cab ride to New Jersey was silent. He and Jeter walked across the street from their hotel to a Bennigan's, an Irish pub–themed casual-dining chain that was popular in the New York area in the mid-nineties. It was the kind of place that would have likely been filled with Yankees fans in the summer of 1995. But no one recognized the two players who had just been dispatched from the big league club. They sat in a booth facing each other.

Rivera apologized to Jeter, suggesting that had he pitched better, maybe the two of them wouldn't have been sent down.

Jeter dismissed that idea. "I just said that we would have to prove ourselves again," he recalled. "It was the only way to get back up there. And I said so — once or twice." Jeter smiled, adding, "Maybe I said it more than that."

Rivera quietly nodded in agreement. He also said he was going to confess to the Columbus coaches how much his shoulder was bothering him, something he was reluctant to do during his past two starts with the Yankees.

Arriving in Charlotte the next day, Jeter started at shortstop.

"Derek had a walk and two hits that night — a double and a triple," said Stump Merrill, who was a Yankees roving minor league adviser in

1995. "I think he stole two bases, too. I thought to myself, 'So much for the kid reacting badly to the letdown of a demotion.'"

Rivera, meanwhile, was placed on the 15-day disabled list. The hope was that some rest would do Rivera's usually resilient arm some good. If that didn't work, the Yankees front office was already discussing another plan. They would trade Rivera while he still had some worth. They would do it, as Michael liked to say, before the rest of baseball discovered what the Yankees already knew about the struggling pitching prospect, who had cost the team $2,000 in 1990.

26

Jedi Powers

IN 2013, A study of fossil remains by Harvard University scientists determined that humans acquired the ability to throw an object overhand at high speed about two million years ago. Some humans, the scientists said, probably threw an object harder than others.

But understanding why some people throw harder than others — and the shadowy steps to developing that skill — has, for the two million years since, largely remained a mystery.

Harvard's scientists revealed new evidence proving that the act of a powerful overhand throw was an evolutionary anatomical adaptation that humans developed to hunt big game. It was necessary because the best hunting method in earlier ages was throwing sharp objects at great speed. But over time, the structural makeup of humans had to change to allow for the cocked arm technique that is the key to a modern, high-speed throw by humans.

Using motion-capture video to analyze throwing motions of top baseball pitchers, Harvard's scientists determined that it was a human's ability to store energy in the shoulder and elbow as the arm is raised behind the head — much like an elastic band — that resulted in 90- or 100-mile-an-hour fastballs. It was not simply musculature; it was the slingshot action of a pitcher's windup, something made possible by highly supple shoulder and elbow ligaments.

Also, humans, over time, evolved in a way that they could twist their waist to increase the rotational forces that amplified the stored energy. A pliable shoulder joint helped considerably, too.

The first species with some of these capabilities, *Homo erectus,* used objects like rocks in hunting small game. *Homo sapiens,* who appeared on earth about 200,000 years ago, used sharp projectiles, like spears, which they could throw for greater distances and at higher speeds that felled larger prey.

It was this same motion — the cocked arm behind the head, the twisted waist that builds torque and an elastic shoulder capable of storing and then unleashing the energy at precisely the right time — that eventually led to fastballs hurled at eye-popping speeds approaching 100 miles an hour.

It was a function of one's arm anatomy, not one's size. A beefy, powerful 230-pound man or woman did not necessarily throw a baseball harder than a rail-thin, wiry 180-pound man or woman. What mattered was a hard-to-define combination of genetics, mechanics and practice.

"Some people throw harder than others not because of their muscles or how strong they are, but because of things like fast-twitch or slow-twitch fibers in their physiology," Dr. Glenn Fleisig, a foremost expert in baseball biomechanics and the research director of the American Sports Medicine Institute, explained in a 2018 interview. "So the first step to throwing a baseball very fast is that you must pick your parents carefully. The maximum window for how hard you might throw is set by the anatomy you were born with.

"But you can maximize whether you will throw to the top or the bottom of that maximum window by learning good pitching mechanics, by working out and by following the right nutritional diet.

"So it is a combination of things," concluded Fleisig, who is also the chairman of USA Baseball's medical and safety committee. "Not one magical thing."

As Mariano Rivera rested his shoulder on the bench of the Columbus Clippers in June 1995, Gene Michael was in New York preparing to trade him to the Detroit Tigers for left-handed starter David Wells.

Joe Klein, the Detroit general manager, had an extensive background as a minor league scout and manager. Though he had also been the general manager of the Cleveland Indians and the Texas Rangers, Klein happily continued to roam the back roads of the rookie-level leagues in Florida and the Carolinas. He was a fixture at Class AA Eastern League games, where he had once been a player and manager.

Klein had seen Rivera pitch dozens of times, as early as 1990, when he first made notes about Rivera's fluid delivery and mound poise for the

Gulf Coast League Yankees. He saw Rivera the next season in Greensboro, and again in 1994 with the Albany Yankees.

"It's easy to say this now, but back in the mid-nineties I believed he was
miscast as a starter and would make a better reliever," Klein said in 2017.
"I'm not saying I knew he would be as good as he became — I'm pretty
confident that no one did. But I thought he had a big upside as a guy who
pitched in limited outings rather than someone who a batting order saw
two or three times in one start."

Wells, who was thirty-two at the time, was having a good year for the
Tigers. In late June, he had a 5-3 record with a 3.11 ERA. But Wells was
making more than $2.3 million, then a princely sum, and the Tigers were
a .500 team gasping to keep up with the surging Boston Red Sox in the
AL East.

Wells was going to be traded that summer to some team and for some
prospect, and Klein's first choice of compensation was Rivera. Klein, like
every general manager, watched the waiver wire and saw that Rivera had
been sent back to the minors. And like all baseball executives at the time,
Klein also knew that Gene Michael was under unending pressure from
his owner to make a move that might turn around the waning Yankees.

At that moment, Klein ramped up his pleas for a Wells-for-Rivera
trade.

"You're often discussing various trades, but I think Gene and I both
thought that Wells might thrive in New York," Klein said. "And that
proved to be true eventually, when David went there later. But in '95, it
was about whether they were willing to part with Rivera. The way he had
been pitching, I was very sure they were going to make that trade."

But Michael stalled. And Klein, understandably, wanted to wait until
Rivera returned from the disabled list. He had to know that any injury
was not serious. Wells had a 68-56 record in nine major league seasons,
and the Tigers weren't going to trade him for a sore-armed minor leaguer,
no matter how good Klein's scouting report might have been.

"I had not agreed to trade Mariano," Michael recalled. "But we were
certainly leaning that way. At that juncture of the season, we certainly
needed a proven starter."

On June 26, Jeter's birthday, Rivera returned to the mound against the
Rochester Red Wings. He was pain-free, and his shoulder felt strong and
loose.

In the second game of a twilight doubleheader at Columbus, Rivera mowed down the Red Wings in the first inning, striking out two of three batters. The third batter was retired on a weak grounder to Rivera.

Behind the plate for the Clippers, Jorge Posada was stunned by the velocity of Rivera's pitches. "His fastball was exploding out of his hand," Posada said many years later. "He was hitting my glove with that loud smacking sound. The hitters had no chance."

Posada approached Rivera in the dugout and jokingly asked him if he had eaten something different that day.

"He told me to just keep doing whatever I was doing," Rivera said.

A rainstorm shortened the game after five innings. Rivera had not given up a hit and faced only 15 batters, the minimum for five innings.

The next morning, in his Yankee Stadium office, Michael received the minor league reports from the day before, as he always did. He saw that Rivera's pitching line had zero hits, but the numbers that jumped off the page were the radar-gun readings on Rivera's fastball. Most were at 95 and 96 miles an hour.

Rivera had never consistently thrown that hard in any start. Michael doubted that Rivera had ever been clocked at more than 91 miles an hour.

He called Columbus to verify that the report wasn't a mistake and was assured that everyone in Columbus was as flabbergasted as Michael by Rivera's newfound velocity. "They said the ball was flying out of Mariano's hands," Michael said, retelling the story. "But, you know, this was 1995. The radar guns weren't as sophisticated. They could be wrong. Or something odd might have happened. I said to myself, 'It's one reading. I need another reading from that game.'"

Michael had the phone numbers of a vast network of scouts and player personnel directors who worked for a variety of major league teams. As a group, they were a close-knit tribe, a collection of baseball lifers united by their nomadic lifestyles and the tedium of sitting in the creaky seats of broken-down minor league parks night after night. Since they tended to stay in the same midlevel hotels and eat and drink in the same sports bars on the road, they became friends and communicated regularly, not to give away team secrets or fess up about a top prospect they might have uncovered, but to kibitz and convey basic, relevant data — like the news that a new, pristine Holiday Inn had opened in Wheeling, West Virginia.

Since he had been a scout for decades, Michael was treated like a charter member of the group, and within it he had a friend, Jerry Walker, the St. Louis Cardinals' director of player personnel. Michael had known

Walker since the 1960s, when each played in the American League. Walker became a pitching coach when his playing career ended, then moved into a series of front-office jobs. Two years earlier, Walker had been the Detroit Tigers' general manager.

Michael knew that Walker was likely a witness to Rivera's June 26 five-inning no-hitter, because St. Louis was interested in Rivera as well. The Cardinals were hoping the Yankees-Tigers trade fell through.

Michael dialed Walker's phone number and confirmed that Walker had been in Columbus the evening before. As he usually did, Michael asked Walker generally about a variety of players. It was all a pretense, but it wasn't out of the ordinary. Everyone did the same kind of casual nosing around. Then, in an off-the-cuff sort of way, Michael asked Walker if he had gotten a radar-gun reading on Rivera.

Walker gave him the number.

Michael engaged in small talk for a few minutes longer, then hung up.

"The next person I called was Showalter," Michael said. "I told him, 'We're recalling Rivera to New York right now. I don't know how he did it, but he's throwing 95 in Columbus.' Then I called Joe Klein and told him the deal was off."

Returned to Showalter's Yankees, who had been on a mini–winning streak, Rivera started a game on July 4 at Chicago's Comiskey Park, where five years and three days earlier Andy Hawkins had pitched his fateful no-hitter in a loss.

But on this day, the Yankees' starter struck out 11 batters in eight shut-out innings. Rivera gave up just two hits in a victory that moved the Yankees into third place. More importantly, the team was within four games of something new in baseball that season: a wild-card playoff berth.

For most of the rest of his nineteen-year career, Rivera threw fastballs in the mid-90s. Accentuating that ability, he also learned to throw a distinctive and sometimes virtually unhittable breaking ball, a cut fastball — or cutter for short. But the success of each of those pitches was dependent on the existence of the other. Neither works without the threat of a baseball arriving at home plate around 95 miles an hour.

But how does a twenty-five-year-old in his sixth year of pitching professionally suddenly increase his velocity from a norm of 90 miles an hour to 95 or higher? And how does he do it in two weeks?

The deeply religious Rivera has always called the transformation an act of God. Michael and Showalter, much less inclined to ascribe developmental baseball skills to spiritual intervention, were dumbfounded at the time. "I questioned if he had somehow been throwing harder before but I never noticed," Showalter said. "But we had radar-gun readings from hundreds of days. The fact is, it didn't really make sense. And it still doesn't make sense."

Said Michael: "I've never seen it happen to anyone else. I've seen it happen to a really young pitcher over the course of a couple years. But that wasn't the case here."

Fleisig, the sports-medicine researcher who has been studying biomechanics in athletics since he was an engineering major at MIT in the early 1980s, has no explanation for Rivera's jump in velocity. "I don't know of any situation where a pitcher went from 90 to 95 in two weeks," he said. "I have no idea how that could happen. There have been pitchers who change their mechanics and then also undergo a vigorous strength and conditioning program. After six weeks, although probably more, they'll have some gain in velocity, which over time and with more work, they can continue to build on."

But Rivera did not change his pitching mechanics. He did not alter his diet or anything else about his routine. He rarely lifted weights throughout his life, unless you count the arduous labor of six days a week at sea as a fisherman.

"But to go from 90 to 95 in two weeks?" Fleisig said. "Two weeks? That's phenomenal. That's extraordinary. Maybe Rivera's right. Maybe God did something."

There were other unconventional theories. Jorge Posada, who along with Jeter was one of the first to witness Rivera's sudden jump in velocity, offered an uncommon hypothesis: "Jeter always used to say that Mariano had Jedi powers."

Seated in a lounge at the Yankees' spring training complex in 2017, Gene Michael stifled a giggle when he remembered how close he came to trading the greatest relief pitcher of all time. "As they say, sometimes the best trades are the ones you don't make," he said.

Then Michael laughed heartily. "Who knows how Mariano found that extra five miles an hour." He shifted in his chair and added: "But I'll tell you what. At the time, we didn't give a shit about how it happened. We were just going to get him out on that mound as often as we could."

27

Yankee Flipper

IT TOOK A month for Michael, Showalter and the franchise's many pitching gurus to realize that the best way to get Rivera on the mound as often as possible was to turn him into a reliever. When his velocity was topping out at 90, the Yankees didn't think Rivera could be counted on to enter a game with runners in scoring position and get a big strikeout.

But if he was throwing 95? That sounds like a reliever. And in retrospect, it might seem like converting Rivera into a reliever was a no-brainer. Yet it did not immediately occur to the Yankees.

History is a good editor, and over time the established narrative of Rivera's career has him transferred to the bullpen as soon as his velocity jumped. But those aren't the facts. The Yankees brain trust was indecisive about what to do with Rivera. Throughout July 1995 and into August, he was still a fixture in the starting rotation, where he had good but not overpowering results.

One reason Rivera was starting was the ongoing spate of injuries to Yankee starters that season. But there were other factors.

"Hey, we didn't know what we had with Mariano — not yet," Showalter said. "Nobody knew what was to come. At least no one that was in our dugout, bullpen or front office at the time."

When asked whether he wanted to be a starter or a reliever, the affable, incisive Rivera answered that he "wanted to be a big leaguer." To him, it didn't matter when he got to pitch as long as it was in the major leagues, and as he wisely added, "On a winning team."

Meanwhile, as June ended, Andy Pettitte won consecutive starts, and the second of those victories was a harbinger. In seven innings pitched against Detroit, Pettitte gave up five hits and walked two, but with runners on base, he found a resolve to shut down every scoring threat. No runs scored. Since he was still relatively new to the major leagues, opposing teams also had not yet learned of another Pettitte weapon — the nasty pick-off move he learned from Wayne Graham, his coach at San Jacinto.

In the late-June game against Detroit, two Tigers were embarrassingly caught off first base because of Pettitte's deception. "I've always felt like I could win up here," Pettitte said after the game. "I've got a lot of confidence."

The Yankees had won five straight games, although they were still six and one-half games behind division-leading Boston and five games back in the chase for the single AL wild-card berth. "A little energy from the young guys might be good for us," Showalter said. "It gives you a little boost."

If the Yankees' spirits had been lifted, they were dampened yet again when Jimmy Key walked off what was supposed to be a three-inning re habilitation assignment in Tampa after throwing only 10 pitches. The left-shoulder inflammation hobbling Key since May was not recovering sufficiently. Key, who had a 35-10 record for the Yankees in 1993 and 1994, was done for the season with a 1-2 record.

The day after Key's setback, another Yankees starter, Mélido Pérez, was routed by the Milwaukee Brewers. He complained of stiffness in his right shoulder. He would take the next six weeks off, and when he returned, he threw one inning before walking off the field holding his right arm. Pérez never pitched in the major leagues again.

"We were in trouble at that point, no doubt," said Willie Randolph. "When people look back at the '95 season, they don't necessarily remember how bad things were at times. Most of the news wasn't good at all."

The bad tidings spread throughout baseball. The poststrike malaise was real. "Attendance was down, merchandise was down, and fans were still mad," said Hal Steinbrenner. "And I understood that. But it was amazing; it took a long time — maybe longer than other sports — to gain the fans' trust back. They were still pissed, and in our case, that anger extended to how we were playing."

Hal said his father talked about it in the team offices. To George Steinbrenner's mind, the summer of 1995 was the worst possible time for the Yankees to be an unreliable baseball team. The fans had had enough of unreliable baseball teams.

Nonetheless, the fourth-place Yankees entered the midseason All-Star break reeling. O'Neill, who was hitting .344 with 11 homers, and bullpen closer John Wetteland, who had 12 saves and a 2.51 earned-run average, were the only players having superior seasons. Mattingly had one home run and just 22 RBI and was batting .207 with runners in scoring position. The weakened, tattered pitching staff was particularly unproductive.

When the team returned from the All-Star break, it had a new pitching coach. At the time, it did not seem like a big change, but ultimately many saw the move as significant. The displaced pitching coach was Billy Connors, who had been recruited to the job by Steinbrenner himself in 1993. Connors, the Yankees' pitching coach in 1989 and 1990, had also been a good friend of Showalter's since their days as coaches under Stump Merrill.

But those alliances had grown more strained and convoluted by 1995. It wasn't unusual that Steinbrenner wanted to fire Connors; it was a classic knee-jerk reaction by the owner and not aimed at Connors personally. But what did stand out was Showalter's reaction to Connors's demotion.

A month earlier, Showalter had vehemently resisted Steinbrenner's order to replace two of his hand-picked assistants, first-base coach Brian Butterfield and hitting instructor Rick Down. But Showalter could not — or would not — spare Connors.

Speaking with reporters, Showalter endorsed the change, which installed minor league pitching coach Nardi Contreras as the new Yankees pitching coach. Connors never forgot Showalter's reaction. "Buck said he'd stand behind his coaches — that he'd quit for them," Connors told the *New York Daily News*. "He didn't quit for me."

In another typical Steinbrenner maneuver, Connors remained with the Yankees. In fact, he would be working out of the Tampa minor league complex, a reassignment that kept him in regular contact with the owner.

Connors had been a Steinbrenner confidant before. Now he was free to rekindle that relationship, which would not benefit Showalter. Connors's anger with Showalter would not dissipate as the season continued. Reporters who called him in Tampa would get an earful about the shortcomings of Showalter, whom Connors demeaned as someone the media had made into "the boy wonder Yankee manager." Connors also believed that Showalter thought he had been a spy for Steinbrenner, something Connors, who died in 2018, denied. (Steinbrenner almost always had someone on the clubhouse level of Yankee Stadium who acted as his ears and eyes.)

But Connors's ire at Showalter overflowed. In the *Daily News,* he called

Showalter "paranoid and insecure." He said that the atmosphere around the manager had become too tense, serious and ultrafocused on painstaking details. No one smiles anymore, Connors lamented.

Whatever the truth, Connors was unquestionably in a position to influence Steinbrenner's opinion of Showalter's handling of the team's struggling pitching staff — not just in the short term but for the rest of the season, and after it ended.

In the meantime, the pitching wasn't getting any better, and the Yankees' record fell to seven games under .500. Jack McDowell said he was called into Showalter's office. "Buck talked about Jimmy Key and Pérez being out, and he said, 'Jack, we're going to have to ride you to soak up innings because we don't have anyone else we can count on to do that,'" McDowell said in 2018. "It may not be fair, but I was just going to have to stay out there. And I was all good with that.

"That '95 team was full of gamers. We all knew that Donnie was playing in pain and so was Wade Boggs, and they were two of the best players of that generation. I had never played with so many guys giving up themselves for the team. So I would do the same — I didn't care about my ERA."

On July 18, with the Yankees seven and one-half games back in both the division and wild-card races, McDowell took the mound for the second game of a doubleheader at Yankee Stadium with the Chicago White Sox, his employer for the previous eight years. The home team had already been blown out in a 9–4 loss in the opening game.

By the third inning of the nightcap, the Yankees were trailing 7–0. McDowell had given up ten hits and three home runs. "I didn't have it that night," McDowell said two decades later. "But I couldn't come out."

By the fifth inning, the Yankees were losing 9–4 when Showalter called for a new pitcher. When he was pulled from the game, the crowd of 21,118 rose to its feet to jeer McDowell, the highest-paid Yankee, whose record was about to slump to 7-6.

The booing was loud and sustained. About five steps after he left the mound, the six-foot-five McDowell raised his right middle finger over his head in an unmistakable reply to the crowd. If his message was not clear at first, McDowell also waved his middle finger in the air in a circular motion.

The picture of McDowell's salute to the crowd filled the back pages of the New York tabloids. One had the headline "Jack Ass!" But the best one belonged to the *New York Post*: "Yankee Flipper!"

In better times, McDowell was an amiable and popular teammate and media favorite. In college, he had led Stanford to the 1987 College World Series championship. The same year, he made his debut with the Chicago White Sox and soon became an All-Star. He won the Cy Young Award in 1993.

McDowell, twenty-nine years old in 1995, played guitar in a rock band and hung out with famous musicians from the alternative music/grunge band scene. His band was good enough to be the opening act for some of those top performers, and he was a drinking buddy of Pearl Jam's Eddie Vedder. He lived in Manhattan, was often seen on the streets with his wife and young child and had been treated well by Yankees fans and the local gossip press.

That was before the night of July 18. No one could recall any other Yankee who had given the bird to a booing Yankee Stadium crowd.

Gene Michael met McDowell in the Yankee clubhouse minutes after he left the game and yelled in his face, "You've embarrassed the Yankee franchise, which is not just any franchise." Michael also fined McDowell $5,000. Major League Baseball did the same a day later.

McDowell almost immediately tried to take back his gesture, although he did not apologize. He never apologized; he only offered explanations. "You're supposed to be stoic in a moment like that and hold your emotions in — but it's tough sometimes," he said. "It was something where right away I knew it and said to myself: 'Stupid.'"

Interviewed in 2018, McDowell, who was then a college coach in North Carolina, offered a new perspective. "Under normal circumstances, I'm out of that game, but they needed a couple more innings for the long-term good of the team," he said. "So I'm walking off the mound getting booed and I'm thinking, 'You should be cheering me for what I'm doing for the Yankees.'

"And let's face it, I was pretty frustrated to have pitched so miserable against my old team who had traded me. It was just a two-second reaction. But it was kind of a big thing for a day or two."

Years later, Showalter said that he wondered what else was going to go wrong to sabotage the season. He had few healthy starting pitchers left. And now his best remaining starter appeared to have made himself public enemy number one for an already annoyed Yankees fan base.

But looking back, Showalter could not stifle a laugh. He said, "'The Yankee Flipper' has to be an all-time headline, don't you think?"

McDowell, who said he has autographed a picture of that moment hundreds of times, now feels the same way about what he called his "incident." "The fans got over it; in a weird way, I think it put me on their good side," said McDowell, who, when given the chance in 1995, declined to postpone his normal place in the starting rotation so that his next start would be on the road instead of at Yankee Stadium. "I was ready to go out there and be amongst the fans. I think they knew I was as unhappy as they were. I don't think I had to do anything to win them back other than pitch better. And I did."

Indeed, the Yankee Flipper may have sparked something in the dormant Yankees. McDowell pitched well in his next six outings, winning four of them. He would make four starts in September and win each one. Three of those victories happened at home, where he often received a standing ovation when he left the game. In the end, McDowell, whose record had improved to 15-10, led the Yankees pitchers in victories, shutouts (2), complete games (8), strikeouts (157) and innings pitched (217).

"A lot of people think I didn't like New York or it was too tough because of that one incident, which didn't go over too well," he said. "But that's not true. It was one of the most fun years I ever had. I loved that team."

McDowell also praised Steinbrenner, because he would never stop trying to reinvent the roster. McDowell's chief case in point: the acquisition of David Cone, the savior who seemed to have rescued the 1995 season when he arrived in New York, ten days after the Yankee Flipper episode.

Since June, the Yankees had been pursuing Cone, who was having another excellent season in Toronto, where he had won the 1994 Cy Young Award. But Cone was in the last year of his Toronto contract, and the Blue Jays, who were on their way to a fifth-place finish, had decided not to re-sign their pitching ace over the winter. Toronto had already paid Cone, who was months away from his thirty-third birthday, $3 million of his $5 million 1995 salary.

Before the trading deadline in August, the Blue Jays were trying to find a team willing to pay the remainder of Cone's salary. They also hoped to receive several young pitchers in return for Cone. Many contending teams were in the Cone sweepstakes, including the division-leading Los Angeles Dodgers, the Boston Red Sox and the team the Yankees were chasing for the AL wild-card berth, the Texas Rangers.

Toronto had their eyes on Andy Pettitte or Rivera for Cone. They also wanted two other Yankees minor league pitchers.

"It was touch-and-go for a while with Pettitte," Michael said, recalling the Blue Jays negotiations. "But we were lucky to have a lot of highly ranked prospects, and I was pretty determined to entice the Blue Jays with other players in our minors. We had already been through the trade talk about Rivera, so we didn't let them bring up Rivera for too long."

Instead, Toronto zeroed in on Pettitte. Michael countered with other names, most especially Marty Janzen, a six-foot-three right-handed pitcher the Yankees had signed as an eighteen-year-old undrafted free agent in 1991. Since then, Janzen had compiled a 21-15 record for four Yankee minor league teams. He had a lustrous 2.70 ERA. Best of all, Janzen was 11-5 while pitching for two Yankee minor league teams in 1995. He was seen as one of the team's best pitching prospects.

"Janzen was a good strikeout pitcher who had good control," Michael said. "But he wasn't left-handed and he didn't, in my mind or in the opinion of our scouts, have Pettitte's upside. Pettitte was winning games in the major leagues at that point."

As the trade talks continued, privately, the Yankees' minor league chiefs raised one stat of significance about Janzen. It was a small sample size — just three games — but it was Janzen's pitching line in his first three games at Class AA Norwich that summer: 20 innings pitched, 17 hits, 11 earned runs and a 1-2 record. It was the first time that Janzen had pitched at the AA level, two notches below the big leagues.

"We stayed firm that Janzen would be the guy, not Pettitte," Michael said. "Pettitte came off the table."

The Yankees included two other pitchers with Janzen when the trade for Cone was consummated. One was Mike Gordon, who had compiled middling minor league statistics since he was selected in the eleventh round of the amateur draft in 1992. The other pitcher was Jason Jarvis, a thirteenth-round choice in 1994 with a 13-9 minor league record.

Gordon and Jarvis never made it out of the minor leagues. Janzen won five of his six starts in the Class AA Blue Jays minors after the Cone trade. That promising record got Janzen promoted directly to the Toronto roster during spring training in 1996, but in the two seasons that followed, he had a 6-7 record, mostly as a starter for the Blue Jays. Janzen then drifted off the Toronto roster. He spent the next eight years playing for minor league teams in the United States and around the world — from Korea to Mexico to Canada — but Janzen never returned to the majors.

Cone, meanwhile, had an immediate impact on the Yankees. He brought a crafty repertoire of pitches — forkball, fastball, slider and curve — that he threw from various arm angles, confounding hitters. As important, Cone had the calm and poise of a seasoned veteran, something the Yankees missed with Jimmy Key sidelined. Cone had been through multiple pennant races and had pitched in seven postseason games. He won a World Series with the Blue Jays in 1992.

Cone won his first four starts for the Yankees, giving up a total of eight earned runs in those games. The rudderless Yankees seemed to have found a new on-the-field helmsman. But their erratic 1995 season would not be fixed that easily. Another fork in the road lay ahead.

The last of Cone's four consecutive victories came on Sunday, August 13, in the midst of a bright, sunny afternoon at Yankee Stadium. Cone's six-hit, complete-game shutout — he threw 130 pitches — pushed the Yankees three games over .500, and pulled them within a game of Texas in the wild-card race. More than 45,000 fans cheered on the home team, but the mood was bittersweet.

On that Sunday, Yankee Stadium, the hulking gray edifice at the crossroads of 161st Street and River Avenue that had been the South Bronx home to the Yankees since 1923, was turned into more than a baseball cathedral. At two o'clock that morning, Mickey Mantle had died of liver cancer in a Texas hospital.

Cone did not know of Mantle's death until he arrived at the stadium and saw the marquee atop the building, which read, *Mickey Mantle, No. 7, A Yankee Forever.*

When Cone left his car, he went directly onto the field, walking across the grass and beyond the outfield wall into the stadium's Monument Park, a shrinelike oasis near the bullpens. Cone found the plaque dedicated to Mantle's storied Yankees career. "I just read about everything Mickey Mantle meant to this franchise — to all of baseball," Cone, who was raised in the Kansas City area, said after the game. "It wasn't new to me, but it made me realize what a privilege it was to pitch here today.

"Baseball as we know it today in America might not be the same without Mickey Mantle."

In the stands during the game, hundreds of fans held up homemade placards and signs saluting Mantle. The scoreboard in center field played a three-minute video tribute to Mantle's career. Standing on the top step of the dugout, Mattingly, several of his teammates and a handful of coaches wiped away tears as they watched.

Showalter grew up idolizing Mantle, like so many other sixties-era Little Leaguers. "Everyone always wanted the jersey with number 7," he said. "We won the game today, but it's still a very sad day. Many a kid played this game because he wanted to be like Mickey Mantle."

Days later, another legend was gone from the team. Phil Rizzuto, the former Yankees shortstop and Baseball Hall of Fame inductee who became a quirky, charismatic and beloved Yankees broadcaster, announced he was retiring and would no longer work the team's games.

Rizzuto had missed Mantle's funeral on August 15 to be in the broadcast booth for that day's Yankees game. Later, Rizzuto said he felt so guilty about that decision, it made him rethink how much of his life he still spent at ballparks. Rizzuto, seventy-eight, now wanted more time with his family. He had been a player or broadcaster for the Yankees for fifty-four years.

"Missing Mickey's funeral just made me understand how much else I was missing," said Rizzuto, a fixture around the stadium who traveled with the team and was popular with players. "I just have to walk away."

Mattingly summed up the Yankees' reaction. "It's been a tough week around here," the team captain said. "I think everyone is a little out of sorts, frankly."

It was not an idle notion. Embarking on a lengthy road trip to Boston and then the West Coast, the Yankees promptly lost eight of their next ten games. On the final stop, in Seattle, Yankees closer John Wetteland gave up three ninth-inning runs to squander a Yankees lead. The game ended on a soaring two-run, two-out home run by Ken Griffey Jr.

Griffey would not have come to the plate if Yankees shortstop Tony Fernández had caught a soft liner hit directly at him one batter earlier. "It's a ball even my eight-year-old son could catch," Fernández said of his misplay after the Mariners' 9–7 victory.

The Yankees lost the next two games inside Seattle's cavernous Kingdome, which was fast becoming the team's house of horrors. The final, ignominious defeat of the Yankees' long late-August journey saw Mariners starter Randy Johnson yield just three singles while his teammates knocked three visiting pitchers around for 12 hits in a 7–0 thrashing. It was the Yankees' eighth successive loss, the longest losing streak for the team since the dismal, humiliating 1991 season.

The Yankees, now four games under .500, were 15½ games behind Boston in the AL East. Five games separated them from the top of the standings for the league's lone wild-card berth — and they would have to climb over four teams to earn that last playoff spot.

As the Yankees flew home from Seattle, it was only twelve months since the magical, dominant 1994 season, when a trip to the World Series seemed assured. That was now a faraway, almost mocking memory.

There was roughly one month left in the 1995 season.

28

Last Stand

GEORGE STEINBRENNER ACCOMPANIED the Yankees during parts of their disastrous West Coast road trip. He was a regular presence in the clubhouse, where he routinely spoke with reporters.

The message was always the same, or nearly so. "I've given my full support to the manager and the players," Steinbrenner said. "We also have the highest payroll in baseball. I hate to keep saying that, but for that kind of money, an owner should expect excellence. Is this excellence?

"But I'm not running things. The manager, the coaches and the players — they're the ones who will decide the team's fate right now."

Steinbrenner's public stance was an admirable improvement on his destructive, bombastic public outbursts whenever his Yankees were struggling in the 1970s and 1980s.

But anyone who had spent even a few days in Steinbrenner's presence knew that, behind the scenes, he was not being as hands-off as he made it sound. His banishment from the game had indeed taught him a modicum of forbearance. He had not aggressively thrust himself into the on-field management of the team for most of the season. But with a place in the playoffs still a remote possibility for his Yankees, and a month left in the season, a switch was flipped and Steinbrenner returned to his roots.

"When the playoffs were right around the corner, when he could almost see and feel the postseason, that's when George became the most worked up," Lou Piniella, who played, coached or managed for Steinbrenner for 15 seasons, said in a 2017 interview. "He always wanted to win so much. He just had trouble containing all that emotion."

And so, as summer turned to fall in 1995, Steinbrenner's phone calls to his general manager and manager took on new urgency. They had a frantic quality that veteran members of the staff, like Piniella's former Yankees ally Gene Michael, recognized immediately. There was no discernible pattern to the calls — Steinbrenner might not reach out for a few days, or he might call several times in one day.

But he would keep calling. Everyone who had been in Steinbrenner's employ knew how persistent and unrelenting the owner could be.

Harvey Greene was the team's media chief in the mid- to late eighties, before the advent of cell phones. "On the road in those days," he said, "if you got back to your hotel room late at night and the hotel phone message light was blinking, you knew either there had been a death in the family or George was looking for you."

Greene added: "After a while, you started to hope that there had been a death in the family."

Greene's successor with the Yankees, Jeff Idelson, who went on to become the president of the Baseball Hall of Fame, was making one of his first trips with the Yankees in 1989. He noticed that his hotel room in Minneapolis had a phone in the bathroom, something Idelson had never seen before.

He was taking a shower before heading to the ballpark one afternoon when the bathroom phone rang. Idelson knew that Steinbrenner had ordered him to always answer his phone.

"I picked up the telephone, and of course it was Mr. Steinbrenner, and he immediately started dictating a press release that he wanted to issue," Idelson said. "I couldn't say, 'Let me wash off the soap and go get a pencil.' I knew this was a guy with not a lot of patience.

"I stepped out of the shower and started writing with my finger on the steamed mirror, taking dictation furiously with my index finger. He was going on and on, and the steam was starting to evaporate. I turned the hot water on full blast to make more steam for the mirror. Mr. Steinbrenner said, 'Now read that back to me.'

"Luckily, I was still able to make it out. But once he hung up, I had to run to get my glasses so I could get it on paper before it disappeared."

In September 1995, this was the world Buck Showalter now inhabited.

Yes, Steinbrenner had been personally involved with the many details of the Yankees' on-the-field operation in past years. But the pressure had been muted. The 1993 team, which produced the first winning Yankees season in five years, had been a pleasant surprise. The 1994 Yankees were a juggernaut. What could Steinbrenner have complained about?

But the 1995 team was a consensus favorite for the American League pennant and was supposed to hit the ground running and coast to the postseason. Instead, several chaotic months of fits and spurts had followed. And yet, the Yankees still had a whiff of a playoff chance and Steinbrenner could certainly smell it. It put his dictatorial tendencies into overdrive. He also had complete control of Showalter's Yankees future. The manager still had no contract for next season.

"Back then with the boss, any Yankees manager in that situation was basically under siege," Brian Cashman, then the assistant general manager, said. "That changed later, but in 1995, with our playoff chances seeming to slip away, that was a tough environment." Or as Gene Michael put it, "George smothered the manager when it got close to the end like that."

Showalter has no trouble recalling Steinbrenner's meddling, mostly in a playful way. Decades later, some of it seems funny. At the time, though, it was more serious, with a host of suggested lineup changes raining down on the manager's office. Among them was Steinbrenner's urging that Showalter make more use of Darryl Strawberry, a free agent whom the Yankees signed that summer when Steinbrenner made it an imperative. The thirty-three-year-old Strawberry, who had played only 61 games in the two previous seasons and was suspended at the start of the 1995 season for cocaine use, had no suitors other than the Yankees.

But Steinbrenner loved giving celebrated players second chances (he also thought it was good marketing and sold tickets). And in retrospect, given Strawberry's impressive postseason record before he became a Yankee and in the years to come, Showalter may have underused Strawberry.

But Showalter, like his mentor Billy Martin, was resolutely loyal. He valued the core of the team; he would stick with his culture creators. "If you believe that certain guys were brought here to be your leaders," he said, "how can you deprive them the chance to lead late in the year when you need it most?"

On August 29, Cone gave up only five hits in a 12–4 Yankees win at home. The next day, Pettitte pitched a complete-game five-hitter in another victory. On August 31, O'Neill hit three home runs in a third successive Yankees win.

"We had gone into emergency mode," O'Neill said in a 2018 interview. "It had become like a last stand. We had squandered enough of the season assuming we'd refind our old selves. There was no more time left. Were we good enough to recover right then?"

On the same day that O'Neill smacked three home runs, Posada and Jeter were recalled from Columbus. It was the first time the quartet that came to be known as the Core Four were together on the Yankees' active roster. They would remain fixtures with the team until 2004 when Pettitte left as a free agent (only to return in 2007 for six more years). The Yankees that day also promoted outfielder Rubén Rivera, a slugging outfielder the team had signed as an amateur free agent in 1990 along with his cousin Mariano.

One day later, with Rubén on the bench, a brilliant middle-relief performance by Mariano contributed significantly to a fourth consecutive Yankees win. Rivera trotted into the game in the fifth inning after the Oakland Athletics had rallied for four runs to erase a three-run Yankees lead. Rivera shut down Oakland without a hit for the next three and two-thirds innings. He was credited with the win when the Yankees came back for an 8–7 victory.

It was Rivera's second straight exceptional relief appearance. Four days later, Rivera started a game against Seattle and lost badly. At the time, that appearance was not recorded as a milestone, but it most certainly was. Rivera went to the pitcher's mound 1,102 more times in his nineteen-year career, all of them in relief.

The 1995 Yankees had finally agreed on what Rivera's role should be. He became the bullpen setup man for closer John Wetteland, and he showed promise when he gave up just one hit in six relief stints to close out the regular season. But Rivera was not yet the dominating pitcher he became in subsequent seasons.

In the six innings of those six relief appearances, Rivera gave up three earned runs, with three walks and only one strikeout. Not overpowering numbers. The Yankees had found the right spot for the quiet, poised son of a Panamanian fisherman, but at the time, no one was surprised when Showalter and his staff continued to guardedly nurture the twenty-five-year-old Rivera.

"I was still learning," conceded Rivera, who finished 1995 with a 5-3 record and 5.51 ERA.

On September 11, the Yankees won for the twelfth time in their last 15 games behind a complete-game shutout by McDowell in Cleveland. "Jack is a warrior, and that's what you need at this time of the season," Showalter said of McDowell, who had given up just three runs combined in his last three starts.

The Yankees also surged into a half-game lead in the wild-card race.

In the next game, O'Neill hit his twentieth homer of the season in a 9–2 rout of the Indians, who were winning nearly 70 percent of their games and had an almost unfathomable 25-game lead in the American League Central Division.

"Once we got on a roll, everything clicked because the team morale was so much better," O'Neill recalled. "The playoffs came into view, and getting there for Donnie was the overriding goal of everyone. Even Mr. Steinbrenner was talking about getting into the postseason for Donnie."

Steinbrenner was also still agitated. With roughly a week left in September, the Yankees were a game behind in the wild-card race. "George was just all over me — all over everyone," Showalter said.

The Yankees had not played in baseball's postseason since 1981, had last won a World Series in 1978 and hadn't been in serious playoff contention in late September for ten seasons.

"George was a relatively young man when we won those 1970s championships," Michael said. "In 1995, he was really wondering if it was ever going to happen again. I would tell him to be calm. But he had seen so many teams fall short for so many years. It had gotten to him."

Steinbrenner appeared irked on several fronts. He had begun to implement cost-cutting measures in various sectors of the franchise. He was exasperated with the City of New York because plans for a new Yankee Stadium continued to drag — the Yankees had recently rejected the city's twelfth proposal for newly improved parking and traffic solutions in the neighborhood near the stadium.

The fans' lingering resentment after the baseball strike was still palpable, and attendance remained down despite the Yankees' presence in a pennant race, which further vexed the owner. The atmosphere in the team's offices in New York, always overwrought because of Steinbrenner's demanding managerial style, was especially tense. So much was at stake on the field, including the substantially added revenue that a long run through the playoffs might provide. In this setting, every facet of the organization was under intense scrutiny — with shocking results in at least one case.

On September 19, in a move that remains something of a confounding mystery more than twenty years later, Steinbrenner abruptly fired three of his most trusted minor league executives. It was a respected trio who had drafted Derek Jeter; signed Pettitte, Rivera and Posada; and helped build the Yankees minor league system into one of the most admired organizations in baseball.

Bill Livesey, the vice president for player development and scouting, Mitch Lukevics, the director of minor league operations, and scouting coordinator Kevin Elfering were unceremoniously dismissed at the annual meetings of Major League Baseball's farm system and scouting directors in Arizona.

"Joe Molloy went with us to those meetings, and we flew out there first class, which was highly unusual to say the least," Lukevics said, recalling the 1995 trip. Molloy, who had run the Yankees during George Steinbrenner's suspension, was still a general partner with the team.

"But it was very strange that Joe was even there," Lukevics said. "And then he suggested that the four of us meet in his hotel room the next morning, before we headed over to the meetings.

"You had a sense something was going on. We got in Joe's hotel room the next morning and he says, 'Your services are no longer needed.'

"There was no explanation. He didn't say, 'You screwed up this,' or 'You guys did this thing wrong.' No one ever said that to us. It was never clear why. It's still not clear.

"We booked a flight back to Tampa that afternoon. We sat there looking at each other and said, 'What just happened?'"

Livesey, who had been with the Yankees since 1979 as a minor league manager, scout or player development chief, did not have an answer to the question then, nor did he have one decades later. "None of us knows the whole story," Livesey, whose tenure with the Yankees was one of the longest of any employee in the Steinbrenner era, said. "I went back and worked for the Yankees in 2008 and never really found out.

"I was told by some really veteran guys at the time that George does this kind of thing every five or six years. And if you study his history, he gives the minor league system guys everything for a while and then he cuts back. He did it in 1982–83 and again in 1987–88. I guess we were caught in a trend."

Asked about the firing of Livesey, Lukevics and Elfering in 2017, Brian Cashman looked down and shook his head. "The boss had some bad advice from people that weren't really baseball people," he said. "And he decided to take a leap of faith and he made some changes and we lost some really high-end baseball people who had contributed very successfully to the franchise."

Asked to elaborate on whom Steinbrenner was consulting at the time, Cashman declined to say more.

There may have been unspoken factors. The Yankees top minor league team in Columbus had missed the playoffs the last three seasons. Only one Yankee minor league team had made the playoffs in 1995. Part of the Yankee Way, the unofficial five-hundred-page manual Livesey helped devise, stressed winning minor league teams.

Joe Molloy, who is still based in the Tampa area, did not respond to multiple attempts to be interviewed for this book.

David Sussman, who was the team's chief operating officer from 1992 to 1996, had no recollection of the firings of Livesey, Lukevics and Elfering twenty-three years later, adding that he would not have been brought into the loop on many baseball-specific decisions.

Gene Michael, meanwhile, did not want to talk in depth about the purge of the three top minor league officials, but he insisted the dismissals weren't his idea. "No way — those guys had helped produce so many players for us," he said. "How much of the 1995 roster was homegrown talent?"

Besides Jeter, Pettitte, Posada and both Rubén and Mariano Rivera, other former Yankee farmhands on the team in September 1995 included Bernie Williams, Don Mattingly, Sterling Hitchcock, Jim Leyritz, Gerald Williams, Pat Kelly, Russ Davis and pitcher Scott Kamieniecki. Many more Yankee farmhands were on the way in succeeding seasons.

In addition, prospects in the Yankee farm system had been used to trade for O'Neill, Cone, McDowell and Wetteland. Importantly, because the Yankees farm system had been rich with high-level talent, those trades could be executed without having to include the most prized prospects, like Jeter, Pettitte, Rivera or Posada.

Less than a week after they were discharged by the Yankees, Livesey, Lukevics and Elfering were hired by the Tampa Bay Devil Rays, who promptly put the trio at or near the top of their minor league and scouting operations.

"It was a shame because we knew the cupboard was stocked for the Yankees," Lukevics said. "We knew the caliber of talent that had been developed and the caliber of the people in that group. Some of them are now headed to the Hall of Fame. They were dependable, reliable guys who had been set up to succeed. And to this day, it's not clear why we didn't get to stick around to see some of that happen."

The sweeping turnover at the top of the Yankees minor league operations did not make much news in the New York press. The team was in the midst of a taut wild-card playoff race with Seattle and the Angels, who were also battling for the AL West title.

The Yankees continued to win at a furious pace, led by Bernie Williams, who was now twenty-seven years old and a feared switch-hitter. Williams was not only on his way to career highs in home runs, RBI and batting average; he was saving his best for the Yankees' surge through September. At one point, Williams, who had also developed into a defensive force in center field, reached base in 20 of 27 plate appearances. A constant of the lineup, he started 195 of the last 196 Yankees games.

The Yankees, winners of 22 of their last 29 games, headed to Toronto for the final three games of the 1995 season with a one-game lead in the chase for the AL wild-card berth. A sweep of the series would clinch a playoff berth.

But there had been much drama behind the scenes before the trip to Toronto. Steinbrenner and Showalter had been arguing for days, a dispute that centered around which pitchers Showalter should start during the final weekend. Steinbrenner insisted that he wanted David Cone, the Yankees ace, to pitch the final game in Toronto.

Showalter wanted to use Cone only if the Yankees faced elimination in the final regular-season game. He was trying to keep Cone as rested as possible in case he was needed for a one-game playoff, should the Yankees end up tied with the Angels or Mariners at the end of the regular season. In the best-case scenario, if the Yankees earned the wild-card spot without a playoff, then Cone would also be ready to pitch the first game of the ensuing AL division series. In the worst case, if the Yankees faltered early in the Toronto series and desperately needed one last regular-season victory to extend their season, he would pitch on three days rest on the final day of the regular season.

"My biggest hope was that we'd have David available to pitch two games in that division series because he was so experienced in the playoffs," Showalter said. "I wasn't sure we could compete in that kind of series without pitching him twice."

There was some risk to Showalter's strategy, especially since he was also giving McDowell ten days off to nurse what was now a torn rib cage muscle, but he thought it was wise to be looking ahead and not just at the three games in Toronto.

"Mr. Steinbrenner thought my strategy was stupid and told me I was going to blow it," Showalter said. "He yelled and called me a stubborn German so-and-so, except he used a stronger word."

Showalter laughed heartily. "I don't even think I'm German," he said. "But, you know, right after that he left the room."

Showalter instead trusted his younger pitchers. Pettitte and Kamieniecki started and won the first two games in Toronto. Sterling Hitchcock won the third and last game, clinching the wild-card berth.

When the final out was registered in the Yankees regular-season finale on October 1, Mattingly dropped to one knee and pounded the turf inside the Toronto SkyDome. After 1,785 regular-season games, he was headed to the postseason.

"Of course, afterward, George didn't tell me, 'Nice going, Buck, our pitching is really set up now,'" Showalter said. "He just moved on."

In fact, several of the Yankees coaches recall that they assembled in Showalter's office after the final game to celebrate when Steinbrenner barged in and shocked the group with a bellowing admonition: "You assholes better get to the World Series."

Outside the locker room, Steinbrenner was far more ebullient. He compared Showalter to Billy Martin, the ultimate compliment in Steinbrenner's world.

Showalter was, the Yankees' owner said, "a genius — every move he made worked out." That prompted a reporter to ask Steinbrenner if he was now ready to extend the expiring contract of his manager.

Steinbrenner, with a look of surprise, smiled and frowned at the same time, then waved off the question.

In the division series, the Yankees would face the Seattle Mariners, who finished the season by winning 25 of their last 36 games. Seattle claimed the AL West title with a one-game playoff victory over the Angels, as Randy Johnson, who won 13 of his last 14 decisions, pitched a complete-game three-hitter and gave up no earned runs.

The Yankees, who would host the first two games of a best-of-five series, had a brief practice at Yankee Stadium while the Mariners were flying to New York.

Mattingly, who hit .321 in September and had been in tears after the playoff-clinching victory in Toronto, was all smiles in the home clubhouse after the Yankees' workout. "We've come back from a lot," he said, opening letters from a knee-high stack of fan mail in his locker. "I mean, we've come back from dark times. That's the big point. It's been a long comeback that was years in the making.

"Now we have a chance to go to the next level."

29

"Did That Just Happen?"

THE FIRST POSTSEASON game at Yankee Stadium in fourteen years was played before a frenzied crowd that was in full throat as soon as the home team's first baseman was introduced in a ceremony before the game.

The unbridled roar that greeted Don Mattingly as he stood beside the other starters along the first-base line seemed like something from another era of Yankees baseball. It was an ovation that shook the franchise from a decade of stagnation, a cheer that both drowned out the painful memories of the early nineties and shouted the franchise's rebirth.

The usually reserved Buck Showalter, the first Yankee to be introduced, had fueled the crowd's passion by waving his cap over his head and pumping a fist as he ran onto the field. Like the nearly 58,000 fans in the grandstand — the largest crowd in the history of the refurbished stadium — Showalter, a Yankee minor leaguer when the team last appeared in the American League playoffs, had been waiting a long time to feel good about something in the Yankee universe.

As fervid as the pregame response was, it was nothing compared to the stadium-shaking, thunderous explosion of noise that filled the building when Mattingly ripped a two-out single in the sixth inning to give the Yankees a 3-2 lead over Seattle. "It was like the whole stadium came to see that moment," David Cone, the winning pitcher in the Yankees 9–6 victory, later said. "I've never heard an outdoor baseball stadium sound that loud."

There were Yankees heroes all over the diamond, as Wade Boggs and Rubén Sierra, who had suffered through a mediocre year as a part-time right fielder, hit home runs.

But the Mariners headliners did not shrink from the spotlight, and it foreshadowed the titanic struggle to come. Ken Griffey Jr. smashed two homers off Cone. Worse for the Yankees, bullpen closer John Wetteland, who had been rocked by Seattle's hitters in the regular season, came in to protect a five-run lead in the ninth and gave up three singles, a walk and two runs.

But the energy and intensity inside Yankee Stadium had been the highlight of the night. The Yankees were more than relevant again. On a crisp, iridescent night in October, they hosted a prescient scene, a window into the franchise's gleaming future.

"It reminded me of why every major leaguer used to want to play here," Mattingly said in the locker room after the series-opening victory. "On a night like this, if you're a ballplayer, I can't imagine a better place in the world to be."

If the crowd for Game 1 of the division series reached rock-concert-like decibel levels, the clamor during the second game, one night later, was a near equivalent, especially in its climactic moment.

Andy Pettitte, who had a 6-1 record and a 3.00 ERA in his final seven regular-season starts, pitched a solid seven innings but left the game with Seattle ahead, 4–3. A solo home run by O'Neill in the bottom of the seventh evened the score, and the game remained tied until the twelfth inning.

That's when Griffey, who ended a dramatic game in Seattle with a ninth-inning homer off Wetteland on August 24, drove another two-out Wetteland fastball into the seats to put the Mariners up by a run. Showalter pulled Wetteland from the game and turned to Rivera, who ended the inning by striking out the dangerous slugger and ex–Yankees farmhand Jay Buhner.

The Yankees tied the game again when Sierra's double brought home pinch runner Jorge Posada from second base. Rivera then pitched the thirteenth, fourteenth and fifteenth innings without yielding a run.

At a little past 1:10 a.m. New York time, the Yankees' Jim Leyritz trudged to the right-handed batter's box in the bottom of the fifteenth.

Five years earlier, in left field on a windy day in Chicago, Leyritz had staggered under a routine fly ball and failed to catch it, a moment in Yankees history that may never be forgotten. It was a three-run error, a misplay that preserved Andy Hawkins's no-hitter, even if it led to an ignominious, humiliating defeat.

Since then, Leyritz had endured a bumpy Yankees career. He became one of the many infielders or outfielders that the team converted into a catcher. In the big leagues, Leyritz played for two of his former minor league managers, Stump Merrill and Showalter, and frustrated each with his quirky and self-aggrandizing ways. He was often benched, reprimanded, or both.

Among his offenses, Leyritz liked to showboat, twirling his bat at the plate like it was a majorette's baton. He talked brashly in the clubhouse and on the field, too, rubbing colleagues the wrong way in each setting. But he also developed a reputation as a dependable clutch hitter, and his teammates came to view him with a certain wonder. He was unfailingly fearless, someone for whom no moment was too big.

"Jimmy is scared of nothing, man," third-base coach Willie Randolph once said of Leyritz, who wore jersey number 13. "Even when he should probably be scared, he isn't."

As Leyritz approached the batter's box in the fifteenth inning, he was 0-for-5 and had been hit by a pitch. It was a warm October night, with temperatures in the high 60s, and Leyritz's Yankee pinstripes were soaked in sweat from a game that was more than five hours old. Teammate Pat Kelly was at first base after a walk.

Leyritz did not swing at the first four pitches from the Mariners' Tim Belcher, three of which were called balls. Leyritz twirled his bat as a light rain began to fall.

Belcher's 3-1 pitch was outside and thigh high, and the right-handed Leyritz rapped it toward the right-center-field alley. But Leyritz had deceptive power, and the drive kept carrying until it sailed over the outfield wall and fell at the feet of a handful of New York policemen stationed in the Yankees' bullpen. Circling the bases, Leyritz was met between second and third base by a middle-aged fan who had dashed onto the field and hastily embraced Leyritz before being apprehended by stadium security.

At home plate, the entire team awaited, and Leyritz leaped into the middle of the celebration. As the jumping pile of players rejoiced mosh-pit style, several Yankees, including Jeter and Posada, toppled to the ground and were nearly trampled before quickly regaining their feet.

In the dugout, Showalter remained seated with one leg crossed over the other. "That's their moment," he later said. "Not mine."

In the seats, fans hugged and cheered. Few retreated to the tunnels and concourses as the rain began to fall more heavily. Since the early eighties, the Yankees had made it a tradition to blare Frank Sinatra's recording of "New York, New York" at the end of every game. But until that night, no Yankee Stadium crowd had ever so enthusiastically sang along to the song as did the fans who remained into the wee hours to watch Jim Leyritz's walk-off home run give the Yankees a 2-0 lead in their first playoff series since 1981.

"That there is a game I'll never forget — Yankee Stadium was crazy," Paul O'Neill said minutes later. "I'm still shaking."

When O'Neill's postgame quote was read back to him twenty-three years later, he laughed. By then, he had won four World Series with the Yankees. "Yeah, I was a little excited, but you know what?" he said. "That was the first big October moment for us. The first one."

Hours after Leyritz's drive cleared the right-field fence, the Yankees took a chartered jet to Seattle, where they would need only one more victory to advance to the American League Championship Series. Three games were scheduled at the Seattle Kingdome, where in 1995 the Yankees had already lost six times in seven tries, including two games that ended with Seattle's final swing of the bat. "By the time that plane touched down in Seattle, no one was celebrating anymore," Randolph recalled. "We were feeling good, but everyone knew what we were going to be up against. No one was fooled."

If any Yankee had dreams of a series sweep, they were soon dashed by Randy Johnson, who turned over a 7–2 lead to the Seattle bullpen in the eighth inning of the third game in the series. Led by Bernie Williams's two home runs, the Yankees cut the deficit, but the Mariners had clearly regained their footing with a solid 7–4 victory. McDowell, pitching for the first time in 17 days, gave up three hits and five runs to the resuscitated Mariners.

It did not hurt the home team that a sold-out crowd of 57,944 was supporting the locals with a cacophony that reverberated around the mostly concrete, barren, unadorned Kingdome. As loud as Yankee Stadium had been, the Kingdome was louder, something the Seattle fans were eager to prove. It was like a competition within the competition, and the Seattle fans had a major advantage: Their passionate cheers were contained by the Kingdome's clamshell-shaped roof.

The domed ballpark was also doomed. Although only nineteen years old, the Kingdome had proved to be a boondoggle. An indoor stadium had seemed a good idea for Seattle's rainy fall and winter seasons, and the NFL's Seattle Seahawks played in the building before sold-out crowds — eight times a year. But in the spring and summer, the weather was usually splendid, even magnificent, and after a winter shuttered indoors, the citizens of the Great Northwest had little desire to spend three hours in a dark, sterile and barnlike atmosphere. Attendance at games was abysmal, abetted by years of inferior Mariners baseball.

By the early nineties, there had been so many dreary baseball seasons inside the Kingdome that the Mariners were determined to leave Seattle. And the city was not begging the Mariners to stay, either. The city council twice rebuffed the Mariners' request for a new, municipally owned outdoor ballpark. It wasn't until Griffey came into his prime, along with Johnson, Alex Rodriguez and another future Hall of Famer, Edgar Martínez, that a new ballpark initiative gained steam.

The Mariners' unexpected, stirring drive to the 1995 playoffs had come along at just the right time as well, rallying the fan base. Eventually, there was sufficient municipal support to fund a new baseball stadium, and that year's team was credited with saving major league baseball in Seattle. The Kingdome hosted its last game in 1999 and was demolished a year later.

But none of that spared the Yankees in 1995. In fact, they were about to play what were considered the two most memorable baseball games in Kingdome history.

The Yankees led the fourth game of the series 5–0 in the third inning, behind the first of Mattingly's four hits and a two-run homer by O'Neill. But the Mariners clawed back to tie the score on a three-run homer by Edgar Martínez and two runs scored on sloppy Yankee fielding gaffes.

The game was tied 6–6 in the eighth when Wetteland came in and promptly loaded the bases on a walk, an infield hit and a hit batsman. Martínez, who hit seven homers off the Yankees in the regular season, then rocketed a 2-2 Wetteland fastball over the center-field fence for a grand slam.

Wetteland unhappily stomped off the mound again. He had pitched four and one-third innings in the series and given up eight hits, two walks and seven earned runs. His series ERA was 14.54.

The 11–8 final score in Game 4 sent the series to a place that might have seemed inconceivable just a few days earlier when Jim Leyritz's home run crashed into the Yankees' bullpen.

"Maybe this is the way it was supposed to be all along," Mattingly said. "We're pretty evenly matched."

Seattle manager Lou Piniella, a popular, valued cog in previous Yankees championship teams, sat in his office after the game smoking a cigarette. "We've already beaten the Yankees three times in a row here this year," he said with a little cackle. "Shit, we've done it twice. I'm not saying we'll do it again, but we have done it in the regular season."

Piniella was asked to compare the Game 5 starting pitchers: Cone and Andy Benes, who was 7-2 for Seattle after a midseason trade from San Diego.

Piniella took a drag on his cigarette. "Let's talk about the bullpens," he said with a sly smile. "They've got their guys. I'm going to have the Big Unit in my bullpen." The six-foot-ten Johnson, the tallest player in the major leagues, was given the nickname "the Big Unit" by teammate Tim Raines during his rookie year in 1988.

The deciding fifth game, as expected, was taut, protracted and gripping. Behind Cone's gritty pitching, a Paul O'Neill home run and a two-run double by Mattingly, the Yankees took a 4–2 lead into the bottom of the eighth.

Griffey's third homer off Cone in the series cut the Mariners' deficit in half. Cone had thrown more than 125 pitches and was clearly laboring, but Showalter did not yet have anyone warming up in his bullpen.

The reason was obvious. He no longer trusted Wetteland, the man whose job it was to rescue the Yankees in these situations. The reliever had been battered throughout the six-day series. The night before in Game 4, Showalter had surely seen enough of Wetteland when he pitched to just four batters and each of them scored.

Showalter could probably have recited, in order, the results of the last six Mariners whom Wetteland faced in the series: home run, single, walk, single, hit batsman, home run. So Wetteland and his 14.54 ERA were probably not going to be stepping on the pitcher's mound unless the game went 20 innings.

But what were Showalter's other bullpen choices?

Steve Howe had pitched one inning in the series and given up four hits and two runs. Bob Wickman had pitched three innings and been knocked around for five hits. Sterling Hitchcock had pitched one and two-thirds innings and yielded two hits, two walks and two runs. No wonder Piniella had been cackling the night before.

There was, of course, the quiet, self-assured Rivera, who had been effective in two previous outings. But at that point in his career, Rivera's experience as a pitcher in the postseason was limited: four and two-thirds innings. Cone had pitched 50 innings in baseball's postseason.

Clearly, as Griffey's eighth-inning home run underscored, Cone was exhausted and no longer had much life on his fastball. Cone was pitching almost entirely on guile. Showalter knew that, but sitting in the dugout, he made a gut-check decision. "I stuck with Cone based on experience and track record," Showalter said twenty years later, sitting in his denlike office just inside the front door of his Dallas home. "David had a track record; Mariano did not."

Rivera would become the greatest relief pitcher in baseball history.

"But at that moment, none of that is a given," Showalter said. "Nor does it necessarily apply to that situation, that night."

Revisiting the subject, Showalter stood up behind his desk, silently paced around his home office for a minute and then plopped back down in a chair. He was transporting himself back inside the Kingdome on October 8, 1995. "It's two entirely different things to sit there then and to sit here now," he said. "You can't travel back in time with the knowledge of the future. And if I had made a different decision, it's not a given that things would have turned out differently." Showalter looked away, gazing out a bay window into his front yard.

Cone stayed in the game, and things went from bad to worse. With two outs, he loaded the bases on two walks and a single.

In the Yankees' bullpen, Glenn Sherlock, the team's catching instructor who was Rivera's first minor league manager in 1990, had placed his hand on the phone that was connected to the dugout. Sherlock was waiting to feel the vibration of the ringing phone, because it would be the only way he would know that Showalter was calling. The roars of the Kingdome crowd would make a ringing phone inaudible.

"Certainly, that's a call you can't afford to miss," Sherlock recalled in 2018.

Asked to describe the mood in the bullpen, Sherlock answered: "Tense. I mean, yeah, real tense. Guys were literally on the edge of their seats. I don't remember anything being said. I don't think there was any conversation at all."

McDowell was one of ten Yankees pitchers or coaches in the bullpen, which was no more than three benches, a tub of Gatorade and a pitcher's mound in foul territory near the right-field stands. "What I remember is that everybody was just silently rooting for the third out," McDowell said. "You're just like, 'Come on, one out.'"

Eventually, Sherlock felt the phone vibrate. Rivera was instructed to begin warming up. And only Rivera.

In a private suite overlooking the field, George Steinbrenner was fuming. Not because he had any particular faith in Rivera. The owner had been peeved for most of the game by dozens of things transpiring on the field. He was joined in his suite by Gene Michael; Brian Cashman, the assistant general manager; the team's chief operating officer, David Sussman; and Frank Dolson, a native New Yorker, Yankees fan and a friend of Steinbrenner's who had recently retired as a sports columnist at the *Philadelphia Inquirer.*

"That box with George was not a place you wanted to be," Cashman said. "Watching a game with him was the worst. Everything was so negative. It was full of stress, tension and sweat. It was horrible."

Cashman called Dolson a sweetheart of a man but a rabid Yankees fan whose brand of rooting would stoke some of Steinbrenner's worst tendencies. "All Frank was doing was making George even more mad," Cashman said. "He'd be like, 'Oh, what's the manager doing? What kind of move is that? That player sucks.' I wanted to choke Frank."

Sussman recalled how Steinbrenner was convinced that Piniella was managing circles around Showalter, and that it was going to cost the Yankees the series. "George was continually berating Buck. He would say things like, 'Our guy is completely outclassed,'" Sussman said. "Or he'd say, 'It's so obvious that Lou is a better manager than this kid.' Or, 'Our guy is just not up to the task; in a key game he's getting his clock cleaned by a more experienced guy.'

"Every move that was made or was not made, George was second-guessing his manager."

Sussman, who had worked for Steinbrenner since 1989, saw something deeper in Steinbrenner's esteem for Piniella and censure for Showalter. "He had a real fondness for Lou, and there's a psychological thread that runs through that," Sussman said. "He was affectionate about his emotional, fiery managers, like Lou or Billy Martin. George's kind of manager was someone who would throw bats out of the dugout or would kick dirt at umpires. George viewed that as standing up for his players or for the owner. He wanted a manager who was demonstrative. That wasn't Buck, who was a very cerebral intellect. You couldn't ask for a more dramatic contrast of styles, and in terms of styles, Buck was not a George guy."

With the bases loaded and the Yankees leading 4–3, Cone had thrown three balls and two strikes to pinch hitter Doug Strange, a switch-hitting middle infielder who was a lifetime .233 hitter.

Again, Cone eschewed a fastball and tried a sinking forkball, hoping to induce a swing and a miss or a weak ground ball as the pitch dropped out of the strike zone.

But Cone's weary arm did not deliver the pitch with enough force. It started losing velocity too soon and bounced in the dirt in front of home plate. Strange did not swing; the game was tied.

Cone had thrown 147 pitches by the time Showalter walked to the mound to replace him with Rivera, who needed just three pitches to end the inning. Seattle's Mike Blowers took one fastball for a strike, fouled back another and watched the third pitch for a called strike on the outside corner.

In the top of the ninth, the Yankees put two runners on with no outs. But the threat was squashed when Piniella did as he promised and summoned Randy Johnson, who retired Wade Boggs, Bernie Williams and Paul O'Neill on just eight pitches.

Showalter called Sherlock again. Pettitte and Jack McDowell, who had pitched five and one-third innings two days earlier, began throwing in the bullpen.

In the bottom of the ninth, Rivera gave up a leadoff single, and the runner was sacrificed to second base with Griffey in the on-deck circle. Again, Showalter had a choice. He decided to intentionally walk Griffey and lifted Rivera for McDowell.

Throughout August and September, when McDowell had won seven of his nine starts, Showalter had repeatedly referred to the 1993 Cy Young Award winner as a "warrior" or a "seasoned warrior."

History, or hindsight, would certainly indicate that it might have been wise to let Rivera face more than a few batters. But that would also be overlooking Rivera's final six relief appearances in the regular season — when he had an ERA of 4.50.

Showalter said he relied on his available pitchers' past body of work and made a judgment. "What if Mariano stays in and loses the game?" Showalter asked in 2017. "Does that change history? Is his career the same after that?"

With two runners on base, McDowell faced Edgar Martínez, who was hitting .579 in the series. McDowell's torn rib cage muscle had swelled to include a golf-ball-size bulge, but McDowell overpowered Martínez with two blazing pitches, then struck him out with an outside breaking ball. McDowell then got twenty-year-old Alex Rodriguez to end the inning with a ground ball to shortstop.

"Adrenaline can mask a lot of discomfort, whether it's your arm or your rib cage or whatever," McDowell said.

The game remained tied until the eleventh, when the Yankees took a 5–4 lead on a walk, a sacrifice and a single. The Yankees had finally gotten to a tiring Johnson. "I think everyone felt pretty good about our chances right then," Bernie Williams recalled. "We bounced out of the dugout. Three outs and we win."

But like the tall and gangly Johnson, the six-foot-five, lanky McDowell was reaching his limit in the first relief appearance of his major league career.

Joey Cora, a speedy, five-foot-seven, 150-pound switch-hitting middle infielder, was the inning's leadoff batter. In the previous day's game, while batting left-handed, Cora dragged a bunt between the pitcher's mound and first base. Mattingly, the nine-time Gold Glove first baseman, fielded the ball and then blundered.

Mattingly had many athletic gifts, but being fleet of foot was not one of them. So it was a mismatch when he tried to pivot and chase Cora, who was streaking down the first-base line. Cora eluded Mattingly. Worse for the Yankees, second baseman Randy Velarde was standing on first base and could have easily received the throw from Mattingly in time for the out.

As Cora dug into the left-handed batter's box, Willie Randolph was standing in the Yankees' dugout screaming at Mattingly, who was just 70 feet away and playing several steps in front of first base. Randolph, a former All-Star second baseman who was in charge of the infield's defensive positioning, wanted Mattingly to take a few more steps toward Cora. "I was yelling as loud as I could, but the crowd was too loud and Donnie never heard me," Randolph said. "I hated that Kingdome."

Cora placed his bunt perfectly, and Mattingly once again grabbed it, wheeled to his left and made a diving attempt to tag Cora, who used every inch of the baseline to avoid the tag. Showalter was on the field an instant later, protesting that Cora had left the baseline. He made an impassioned, face-to-face plea with first-base umpire Dan Morrison, who shook his head side to side and shouted his response. Showalter turned his head so his left ear — his good ear since he was beaned in Oneonta ten years earlier — was inches from Morrison's mouth.

"The umpire had already made his call, and it wasn't like there was instant replay back then," Showalter said. "If I stayed out there any longer, all I would have done is distract my own pitcher."

Griffey, a lifetime .217 hitter against McDowell, was up next and slapped a ground ball to the right of second base, a ground ball that Yankees second baseman Pat Kelly was probably more used to fielding on grass, but the Kingdome's artificial turf was old, worn and rock-hard. The ball bounced just past the diving Kelly into center field, and the Mariners had runners on first and third base with no outs.

Martínez came to the plate and took a well-placed outside fastball for a strike. The next pitch was a split-finger fastball, and catcher Jim Leyritz put his mitt on the outside half of the plate as a target for McDowell. "We called the same pitch that I used to strike out Edgar two innings earlier — a split-finger fastball," McDowell said in 2018. "But I was now going through their lineup a second time."

McDowell's pitch looped and missed its target, hanging inside, about belt high to Martínez. "A horrible hanging split," McDowell said.

Martínez rapped the pitch down the left-field line.

The game was tied as Yankees left fielder Gerald Williams chased down the ball near the outfield wall. Bernie Williams, who first teamed up with Gerald in a Yankees minor league outfield in 1987, sprinted over from center field. He stole a glance toward the infield where he saw that Griffey was almost at third base already.

"Home! Home!" Williams shouted. "He's going home!"

Since he signed with the Yankees as a raw prospect out of the backwoods of Louisiana, Gerald Williams always had the best outfield arm in the Yankees organization. He fielded the ball cleanly and fired a bullet to shortstop Tony Fernández in short left field.

The backup cutoff man behind Fernández was third baseman Randy Velarde, who had an especially strong arm, the best in the Yankees infield. Afterward, several Yankees coaches conceded they were rooting for Williams's throw to float over Fernández so it could have ended up in Velarde's hand.

Fernández, who had an unconventional, almost sidearm throwing motion, inexplicably paused for just an instant as he turned toward home plate. His throw was no match for the streaking Griffey, whose slide into home barely brushed aside the left foot of Leyritz.

A millisecond later, the ball reached Leyritz, who gloved it and then sagged onto his hands and knees as he bowed his head toward the dirt in front of home plate. From Martínez's swing to Griffey's game-winning slide, 9.8 seconds had elapsed.

Across the decades since, Buck Showalter has never purposely watched a videotape of the play that clinched the series for the Mariners and sent the Yankees into an off-season of tumultuous change. He has instead avoided it.

A couple of times, while jogging on a treadmill at home and watching a baseball game or sports show on television, Showalter has seen the highlight clip of Martínez's swing and Griffey's sprint around the bases. He has always turned his head away from the screen before Griffey slides. "I've looked at the tape of the game to review the things I wanted to see and improve on," he said. "But to watch what happened at the end? To dwell on it?"

Standing in the quiet of his backyard in 2017, Showalter looked down at his feet. "No, I haven't. It's painful," he said. "Painful."

Mattingly, in what would be the last few seconds of his career, watched Griffey circle the bases from the middle of the Kingdome diamond. "You see it happening, slowly at first and then faster and faster," he said. "But you're powerless to do anything about it."

Paul O'Neill's view was from right field. "An awful memory," O'Neill said in 2018. "It still makes me sick sometimes."

Randolph looked across the field at Piniella, his former teammate. "Lou had a wide, wide grin on his face," he said. "But I wanted to start crying. Everybody on the bench was looking stunned. Did we just see that? Did that just happen? I closed my eyes and opened them up again, hoping it was just a bad dream."

Slowly, the majority of the Yankees marched back to their clubhouse. The Kingdome was louder than ever as Griffey, who had been tackled at home plate by a mob of celebrating teammates, leaped to his feet and began an abbreviated victory lap around the stadium. He was trailed by dozens of teammates. The Mariners, in their first postseason series, didn't want to leave the field.

Randolph noticed that Jeter, Pettitte and Posada did not leave the Yankees' dugout. "Those guys were sitting there watching the other team jumping up and down," he said. "That showed me something. They weren't lost in the moment. They were soaking it in.

"They hadn't really played much, but you could see they were thinking, 'OK, this is what it feels like to win and what it feels like to lose.' I've never forgotten that."

When reporters were admitted into the Yankee locker room after the game, the scene was disquieting, uncomfortable and poignant.

In the visiting manager's office, Showalter was sobbing face-down at his desk, his head buried in folded arms.

Mattingly, who had batted .417 and had six RBI in the series by swinging with abandon despite the stabbing pain it elicited in his ailing lower back, repeatedly choked back tears as he spoke. But he remained at his locker for nearly half an hour. "I want to remember it all," he said. "Every second."

McDowell recalled that he avoided glancing at Mattingly. "I was in tears and it was just too hard to look over at him," he said. "It was killing me. It took me a long time to compose myself."

The equipment staff was hastily packing bags and lugging them out the door into a waiting truck. A winning locker room is a place of warmth and joy where people want to linger. A losing locker room is stony and cold, a setting that instinctively leads everyone to flee.

Less than an hour after Griffey had blazed around the bases, the Yankees began to file out of the clubhouse. After the second game of the series, as a perk, the Yankees had flown the players' wives from New York to Seattle on the team's chartered jet.

Outside the locker room in Seattle, players and their families were reunited, and in groups of two, four and six, the assembly began walking across the turf field of the now empty Kingdome toward a loading dock beyond the left-field wall. It was there that they would board a bus to the airport.

"Quietest bus I had ever been on," said Sherlock, the bullpen coach.

The flight back to New York was no better.

"It was a flying funeral—people crying, so sad," said Michael Kay, the longtime Yankees broadcaster. "And like a funeral for Mattingly's career. People were overcome with emotion."

McDowell walked to the front of the plane and talked briefly with Showalter. "He told me, 'Jack, I'd do the same thing all over again,'" McDowell said.

Angela Showalter had not flown on the team's chartered flight often, and the scene made a lasting impression. "It was just heartbreaking," she said. "There were so many hopes, so much hard work and so many plans for the future all wrapped up in that one game. I think a lot of the guys knew things would never be the same again."

Gene Michael sat near the front of the plane, a few rows behind George

Steinbrenner. The two had not talked much since Martínez's double and
Griffey's dash.

Michael, the crafty card player who always liked to be two moves ahead
of everyone else and a baseball lifer who saw himself as a farsighted architect, was filled with troubling uncertainty. "As I sat there," Michael
remembered years later, "I knew that if we had beat Seattle, everything
would have been all right. All of us would come back the next year. But
now I didn't know what was going to happen."

30

Purge

GENE MICHAEL LASTED eleven days before he was removed as the Yankees' general manager. Technically, he was reassigned and named the team's director of major league scouting.

But it was not as simple as that, and not the whole truth either. None of the persistent, chaotic upheaval that transpired in the month after the Yankees lost the 1995 division playoff series was simple. And it was almost always shrouded in misinformation and half-truths.

Not long after the charter flight from Seattle landed in New York, Steinbrenner informed Michael that he would have no role in deciding whether Showalter would be retained as manager.

"He told me, 'You stay out of this,'" Michael recalled years later, describing his first weighty conversation with Steinbrenner after the playoff defeat. "He wouldn't listen to me. He didn't want my opinion, although I had already strongly backed Buck's return."

It was the first of several steps taken in the next few days that stripped Michael of his central duties as general manager. Steinbrenner was also pursuing a few free agents without consulting Michael. He was entertaining trade requests. And while Steinbrenner had yet to speak with Showalter about his contract, which would expire on October 31, it had not stopped him from compiling a list of managerial replacements for Showalter, without Michael's input.

Finally, on October 18, Steinbrenner met with Michael and said he could remain as general manager so long as he took a pay cut from $600,000 annually to $400,000, and if he also agreed to cede overarching authority over various baseball matters. As Steinbrenner previously stated, Michael would not pick the next manager.

Michael refused the offer. Steinbrenner and Michael, who was fifty-seven years old at the time, instead agreed on a scouting job at $150,000. "Under those circumstances, I was ready to go back to scouting," Michael said many years later.

But what of the last five years he'd spent restoring the franchise to prominence? He had been named general manager during the team's darkest days, just hours before Steinbrenner was banished from baseball. Surely Michael knew that his shrewd, patient stewardship and the cluster of prized minor league prospects he had helped carefully cultivate had the Yankees on the cusp of a prosperous run?

"Yeah, I expected some of the success that might come to pass," Michael answered. "I knew we were an awful lot better than we had been. And in '95, it was thrilling to see us back in the playoffs with a sold-out stadium and the organization energized again."

Relaxing in the sun and warmth of the Yankees' central Florida spring training complex, Michael took off the baseball cap he was wearing and ran his hand through his gray hair. He smiled. "That was a long time ago — do we have to go back there? It's such a nice day."

But Michael wasn't one to duck a question. Chuckling, he leaned forward in his seat. "OK, look, there was a lot of other stuff going on at the time — changes all around, you know?" he said.

The leadership of the minor league operations had already been gutted.

"It wasn't going to be the same," he said. "That much was obvious."

Michael settled back in his chair and propped his cap on the back of his head with the bill tilted up so the sun bathed his face. He stared at an empty practice infield. "If we had just won in Seattle, I would have stayed as the GM and there would have been no questions about Buck as manager," he said. "But we didn't win that series. George didn't want me to be the GM. He wanted me as an adviser. George liked that."

David Sussman, the Yankees' chief operating officer in 1995, was not involved in the decision to demote Michael. But he had an opinion about what transpired. "My sense was Gene was tired; he was worn down," Sussman said. "He had worked for George for many years. They would scream and curse at each other and slam doors or slam down phones. Regardless, there was a real affection between them. But this time, Gene wanted to step back. He wanted to still be involved but not in the hot seat."

Michael's exit set in motion a series of other departures. Don Mattingly, who was leaning toward retirement, saw Michael's exodus as a sign that a new — or old and familiar — turmoil might soon envelop the team's front office.

Mattingly began to solidify his retirement plans, although he also checked in with his agent, Jim Krivacs, who was Showalter's agent, too. Mattingly wanted to know: Is Buck going to be back?

The removal of Showalter, his former minor league teammate in 1981, would definitely accelerate Mattingly's plans to end his baseball career.

But Krivacs did not know Showalter's fate. No one did, although Steinbrenner's misgivings about Showalter were public knowledge since they had been leaked to the local newspapers.

Most expected a classic Steinbrenner response to the situation: He would offer Showalter a small raise but demand that he fire at least some of his coaches. It was a maneuver Steinbrenner had employed many times before with managers as diverse as Billy Martin and Yogi Berra. As a tactic, Steinbrenner felt it gave him a measure of control. He got to pick some of the voices influencing the manager, who would be knocked down a peg as well. Sometimes Steinbrenner did it as a way to force his manager to quit.

At home in Pensacola, Florida, Showalter was hardly disconnected from what was going on in New York. After nineteen years, he had his confederates in the franchise and he was good at developing sources of information. Always a good student, Showalter grasped the inner workings and politics of an organization that was by its competitive nature partisan and Machiavellian. He was far from a neophyte in that world. He could play the game within the game in major league baseball.

Most of all, he knew that when it came to the Yankees, what mattered most was who had Steinbrenner's ear.

To that end, Showalter understood that Michael's reassignment would have seismic ramifications for him. He and Michael had been close allies, discussing personnel, trades and minor league call-ups sometimes many times a day. Theirs was a unique bond, and they often teamed up to work around Steinbrenner. Most of all, Michael had been the pivotal buffer between the owner's office and the manager's office.

"Stick leaving as general manager was a blow, no doubt," said Showalter, who worried about having to acclimate to a new general manager. When he finally talked with Steinbrenner in late October, he let the owner know that he did not want to discuss a new contract until he knew who Michael's successor would be.

Steinbrenner quickly hired Bob Watson, the Houston Astros' general manager and a 1980s Yankee first baseman, to replace Michael. There hadn't been a lot of competition for the job. A slew of top executives from other teams declined to even interview with the Yankees. They knew the crucible that working under Steinbrenner had become for any general manager.

Showalter did not know Watson well, but he did not view him as an obstacle. Amiable and gentlemanly, Watson was hard to dislike.

But soon there was a major complication. Steinbrenner's initial contract offer was for two years and $850,000, a total that was later raised to slightly more than $1 million. The money, however, wasn't the problem. As expected, Steinbrenner wanted to dismiss Showalter's most trusted coaches: Sherlock, first-base coach Brian Butterfield, hitting coach Rick Down and pitching guru Tony Cloninger. Showalter had worked with the four coaches for at least five seasons. Some considered the quartet a kind of private council crafted in Showalter's image: Only Cloninger had a big league pedigree; the rest, like their boss, had been career minor leaguers.

Showalter rejected Steinbrenner's contract offer during a ten-minute phone call, insisting that he had to have the authority to pick his own coaches. One week remained before Showalter officially left the Yankees' employ.

"I expected a counteroffer," Showalter said in 2017. "It was a negotiation. I had been with the Yankees pretty much my entire working life and I didn't want to leave. I thought we'd talk a little more about what I wanted and what ownership wanted.

"That didn't happen."

For weeks, Steinbrenner had been stewing about what to do with Showalter. The Seattle series had seriously soured him on his young manager. There were also voices in Steinbrenner's inner circle who were anything but complimentary of Showalter, including Billy Connors, whose firing as pitching coach in 1995 Showalter had supported. Another Steinbrenner confidant, Arthur Richman, a former public relations executive who was now a senior adviser, had developed a distaste for Showalter's businesslike approach to his job. Richman, a sportswriter in the 1940s, often traveled with the team and preferred the nightlife habits of old-school managers who regularly took the coaches and team employees out for long, elaborate dinners at pricey restaurants and saloons.

Showalter didn't spend his nights that way and generally distanced himself from Richman, which Richman took personally. In October 1995, Showalter needed allies whispering commendations to Steinbrenner, but few were doing so. Michael had already been pushed aside. Cashman did tell Steinbrenner not to make a change at manager.

"Unfortunately, to no avail," Cashman said.

Richman, meanwhile, went on WFAN, a sports-talk radio station in New York, and disparaged Showalter's record, suggesting that others in the Yankees chain of command deserved more credit for the team's recent turnaround.

Mattingly, reached that day at his Indiana home by Mike Lupica of the *New York Daily News,* stood up for Showalter. "We had lost for five straight years, then we got better and better and this year we went to the playoffs," Mattingly said. "Buck was proud to be a Yankee. He honored the organization. That's the record I'm talking about. That's a record he won't ever have to defend to anybody."

But Mattingly was on his way out of the Yankees sphere of influence. As time passed, Sussman said that most front-office employees who had been in Steinbrenner's presence during and after the Seattle playoff series fully expected Showalter to be dismissed as manager. "In hindsight," Sussman said, "maybe the most shocking thing is that Buck survived that season with George."

Hal Steinbrenner agreed that the team's executives believed Showalter would not be retained. More than twenty years later, he had no trouble remembering how his father's thought process usually worked in such situations. "I mean, that's the way George was," Hal said. "If you failed, somebody was accountable."

On October 26, two days after his last conversation with Showalter and an hour before the fifth game of the 1995 World Series, Steinbrenner issued a statement that Showalter had told the Yankees he would not return to manage in 1996.

That was news to Showalter when a reporter reached him on his way to his Pensacola home after a round of golf. "What I said was that I couldn't accept the stipulations connected to the contract offered," Showalter said, referring to the dismissal of his coaches. "I still hope we can work something out."

But Steinbrenner was steadfast. "I am very upset Buck is leaving and

I wish Buck and his fine little family nothing but the best," he said in the team statement.

The next five days were bizarre, even by the wacky standards set by Steinbrenner's 1980s Yankees, when there were 13 managerial changes in 10 seasons.

Showalter's contract would expire at midnight on Halloween. In the meantime, there was a standoff. Showalter could return to the only adult employer he had known if he let Steinbrenner select the coaches. Or Showalter could take his chances on the open market, where the Oakland Athletics and the Detroit Tigers, two lousy teams, were looking for a new manager.

There were a couple of other remote landing spots for Showalter. In 1998, two expansion teams would join the major leagues: the Arizona Diamondbacks in the National League and the Tampa Bay Devil Rays in the American League. With two and a half years to wait, neither expansion team had named a manager.

A certain amount of back-channel negotiating transpired for a few days. Brian Butterfield ran into Steinbrenner almost by accident at the Tampa instructional league, and after an amiable conversation, Steinbrenner was impressed enough that he removed Butterfield from the list of coaches he wanted to replace. Various newspapers reported that two other coaches, Sherlock and Cloninger, might have been, in effect, pardoned as well. But hitting coach Rick Down remained in Steinbrenner's crosshairs.

Sherlock said the coaches had heard nothing officially. "We were in the dark," he said.

Showalter received unofficial overtures from other major league teams. Contacted at home, he said, "I want to come back. I want to remain a Yankee."

He had rebuffed Steinbrenner's demand to pick at least some of the coaches. Now he waited by the telephone, which did not ring by the midnight deadline on Halloween.

At the time, and in the more than two decades since, much intrigue has grown up around what actually occurred in the final day or days.

In multiple interviews at his Tampa hotel in the late nineties, Steinbrenner refused to go into the details of Showalter's exit. He talked in generalities and occasionally seemed torn by the turn of events.

In late 1996, sitting at a luncheon table, he held both hands about chest high with his palms turned upward. He raised his left hand and said, "On the one hand, let's just say it was unfortunate and might have been averted." He lowered his left hand and raised his right hand. "But on the other hand, it worked out well, maybe for everyone."

Showalter, however, does not understand why there is any mystery about what unfolded. "There is no intrigue at all — it's comical to me when someone tries to say there was," he said in 2017, getting to his feet from behind his home-office desk to enforce the point. "Maybe I didn't say enough at the time to clarify things, but it's really very simple.

"I had two contracts offered to me: In the first one, I would have no say over the coaching staff, and in the second one, I got to bring back Butterfield. But I knew that the continuity of the coaching staff was instrumental to our success. And I also knew that if I gave up my coaches, it would send a clear message to the rest of the clubhouse. It would affect the culture, because everyone would be thinking that as soon as we hit a bump in the road I'm going to give up on them and cover my ass like I did when I gave up on my coaches.

"So it wasn't very complicated. It was about the coaches and the bigger picture. To this day, when I see a manager give up on his trusted lieutenants just to save his butt, I think, 'It's gonna cost you in the long run.' And it does."

While Showalter may not have seen the decision as convoluted, he knew it was life-altering. "Absolutely, I knew right then I was changing the course of my life," he said. "I knew that, and shit, it broke my heart. I didn't want any part of leaving. There were times I'd be saying, 'I can't believe this is happening.'"

As he contemplated what to do, he relied on advice from his late father. "He used to tell me that at some point in your life you're going to have to plant your feet and make a stand," Showalter said. "He said, 'You'll know when it's time. That's when you plant your feet, even if it might be tough and uncomfortable.'"

Two minutes after the contract of the thirtieth manager in Yankees history expired on November 1, 1995, Jerry Colangelo, the owner of the Arizona Diamondbacks, called Showalter's home phone. He wanted Showalter to fly out to Phoenix, where the Diamondbacks had already sold 44,000 season tickets for a 48,000-seat domed stadium that as yet existed only on an architectural drawing. "You can have the chance to help shape an entire major league team from the roots up," Colangelo told him.

Shortly after he hung up with Colangelo, Showalter answered his phone again when a reporter called.

Showalter was struggling to gather his thoughts. He'd just lost his dream job with the Yankees and then suddenly had been offered an opportunity to build a franchise from the ground up.

"But I'll tell you one thing — I'm still a Yankee," Showalter said, talking softly in his kitchen because he didn't want to wake his daughter, Allie, or his son, Nathan, who had finally fallen asleep after a busy night of Halloween trick-or-treating. "I've got all kinds of Yankee stuff in my house. I've got coffee mugs, pictures of my minor league teams, hell, I even have Yankees pajamas on my two kids. What am I supposed to do with all this stuff?

"I'll tell you what: I'm not getting rid of it. I'll always be a Yankee. I just don't work for them anymore."

31

The Living Room Summit

A FEW DAYS later, George Steinbrenner sat in the living room of the Showalters' ranch-style house alongside Escambia Bay in the Florida panhandle, about ten miles from the Alabama border. Steinbrenner had flown there in a private jet from Tampa.

Except Buck was not home to greet Steinbrenner. He was returning from Arizona, where he had spent a few days with Jerry Colangelo.

"I had to go get them at the airport," Angela Showalter said of Steinbrenner and her husband's Tampa-based agent, Jim Krivacs, who accompanied the Yankees' owner on the trip.

That morning, unable to reach Buck, Krivacs surprised Angela with a phone call detailing Steinbrenner's plans to come to Pensacola. Shocked, Angela tried summoning Buck using a beeper, but he was on a flight and unavailable. Thirty minutes later, while he was changing planes in Texas, Buck returned Angela's call.

She posed a question: "Guess who's going to be here at the house in a couple hours?"

Angela answered her own question. Showalter was thunderstruck. "What? What's he want?" he asked.

"I don't know," Angela said. "I just know he's coming here."

Together, they figured Angela would have to entertain Steinbrenner for about an hour before Buck arrived in Pensacola.

"Buck told me to go buy some food to give them," Angela said. "And I said, 'I love to cook, but I'm not making something that might kill him.'"

The compromise choice was a store-made shrimp tray with party dip, which Angela bought on the way to the airport. She located Steinbrenner and Krivacs, then drove the fifteen minutes to her home at 4801 Rose-mont Place, where she parked in the small circular driveway.

Both Showalter children were excited by their unexpected guests, es-pecially the toddler Nathan, who climbed onto Steinbrenner's lap. Plates of shrimp were distributed.

"Well, Nathan tried some shrimp, which he had never eaten before," Angela said. "He made a face, said it was too chewy and spit it out onto George's plate. I'm sitting there staring at George and this half-eaten, gooey pile of shrimp on his plate. I wanted to die."

The group eventually moved to the living room, which is where Buck found them when he walked in the front door.

Steinbrenner had come with a message: He wanted Buck back as man-ager, and he wanted to announce it the next day in New York. Joe Torre had already been named as Showalter's replacement a few days earlier at a Yankee Stadium news conference (which Steinbrenner did not attend).

What exactly did Steinbrenner say that day in the living room?

"He told me, 'I've thought about this — come on back and manage,'" Showalter said, recounting the scene as he sat in his spring training office with the Baltimore Orioles in 2017.

Asked if Steinbrenner wanted him to resume managing the Yankees immediately, Showalter nodded and answered, "Uh-huh."

Dumbfounded, Showalter told Steinbrenner he had already shaken hands with Colangelo and agreed to take over the Diamondbacks.

"Did you sign anything?" Steinbrenner asked.

When Showalter said he had not, Steinbrenner was elated.

"Because I hadn't signed anything, he thought that was good enough, and he said we'd work it all out for me to come back to the Yankees," Showalter said.

Steinbrenner had the same response when asked what would become of Torre: Something would be worked out, with Torre becoming the team president or some other, similar post.

Steinbrenner's attitude was one of acquiescence and compromise. In essence, he wanted to turn back the clock and fix a messy rift. Steinbren-ner had gone all the way to the Florida panhandle to make amends.

And what had motivated him to do such a thing?

"He was getting crucified publicly for the Showalter situation," Gene Michael said. "He was getting killed in the press and the fans were going crazy — just incensed. It was a disaster.

"It really shook George up. It changed him forever."

Brian Cashman, in the days before email, remembered the fax machine in the team's office spitting out page after page of angry missives from fans. "The fax machine was constantly running out of paper, and the phone kept ringing nonstop with angry callers," he said. "We were under siege. I think George was caught off guard by the fallout. He was getting destroyed when Buck wasn't brought back as manager.

"George was definitely impacted by the assault that the franchise was under at that time."

In definable ways, Showalter's exit became more controversial when Joe Torre was named the new manager two days after Showalter was not retained. Torre had been a glaring failure as the New York Mets' manager, and in 14 seasons managing in New York, Atlanta and St. Louis, his teams had just five winning seasons. His overall managerial record was 894-1,003.

The back-page headline in the *New York Daily News* the day after Torre was hired read, "Clueless Joe." A cavalcade of newspaper columnists harangued Steinbrenner for his treatment of the popular Showalter.

But Steinbrenner might have been affected most by the belligerent rebuke he felt from a legion of resurrected but now enraged fans. While scores of Yankees employees — from scouts to minor league directors to the players on the major league roster — contributed to the recent revival of the team, Showalter, who had taken the managerial reins after the franchise's demoralizing season in 1991, was the face of the renaissance. Yankees fans were furious to see him unceremoniously spurned, and the reaction was more heated than it was in the wake of almost any past managerial firing in the Steinbrenner era.

Yes, in the previous twenty years, several respected baseball men under Steinbrenner had been callously terminated as manager, sometimes after only a dozen or so games to start a season. Some of those dismissals provoked spirited protests, but they tended to dissipate in a day or so.

The lone exception was the emotional, forced resignation of Billy Martin in 1978, which was the first time the charismatic Martin was removed as Yankees manager. The outcry then was fierce and impassioned. Steinbrenner received threatening phone calls, and fans burned their Yankees tickets in the plaza outside the team's offices.

How did Steinbrenner respond then? By rehiring Martin six days later. During the announcement of Martin's return at Yankee Stadium, fans cheered and cried tears of joy.

In late 1995, Steinbrenner was going back to a familiar script. It had worked before. Billy Martin had been an influential mentor to Showalter. But the two men were more dissimilar than alike.

In the Showalters' living room, with the shrimp plate all but gone, there was a certain stunned silence after Steinbrenner laid out his plan for Buck's triumphant return to lead the Yankees yet again. Then Buck and Krivacs went into another room to discuss what they had just heard, as well as what had been discussed in Arizona. The Diamondbacks' contract offer was for seven years and $7 million.

Angela remained in the living room with Steinbrenner. "He had a little giddyup — he thought he was going to get Buck back," she said of Steinbrenner. "But I knew Buck had been impressed by his trip to Arizona and by what he had heard there, because he had been calling me to talk about it."

A short while later, Showalter emerged from his conference with Krivacs. Standing inside a house filled with Yankee paraphernalia, Showalter told Steinbrenner he was not returning to the only professional baseball home he had known. He had given Colangelo his word; he was going to honor that commitment.

Steinbrenner, Showalter said, was incredulous. "He couldn't understand what the big deal was — he didn't understand why there was anything to stop me."

As for Showalter's coaches, who were the apparent impetus for the impasse, they had come up briefly. What would be their fate? That, too, was something to be worked out after Showalter agreed to return to the Yankees, Steinbrenner said.

"But I wouldn't consider that anyway, after promising Arizona to come there," Showalter said in 2017. "We had a deal. I had shaken hands. I'm not going to make that phone call."

Showalter had already worked it out to bring his coaches with him to Arizona. Butterfield, Sherlock and one of his former pitching coaches, Mark Connor, would end up with the Diamondbacks for many years. Showalter said that Rick Down, who was about six years older than most of his other coaches, did not want to wait until 1998, when the Diamondbacks debuted, to resume his coaching career. He was instead hired by the Baltimore Orioles and was a finalist for the inaugural Tampa Bay managerial job in 1998.

Steinbrenner remained in the Showalters' home for roughly another half hour. He continued to be surprised at the turn of events.

"But we tried to make some peace," Showalter said. "And I think we did. The man had done a tremendous amount of good for my family, supported us for nineteen years, and I told him that. He recognized that I worked hard for the franchise for all those years.

"I wished him and the Yankees well, and I certainly meant that. Those were still my guys."

Although some of *his* guys were not with the Yankees for long. A few days later, Mattingly announced that he was "trying retirement." Catcher Mike Stanley, a free agent, signed with the Red Sox not long afterward, a move predicated on the Yankees trade for Colorado Rockies catcher Joe Girardi — a deal Torre pushed Bob Watson to make. Infielder Randy Velarde left for the California Angels.

Jack McDowell, another free agent, was not re-signed, making way for Andy Pettitte to be the number three starter behind David Cone and a rejuvenated Jimmy Key. Mariano Rivera would be the primary, late-inning setup reliever in the bullpen.

The Yankees were turning the page. Day by day, the furor over Showalter's exit was diminishing — a seething rage fading into a resigned disgruntlement. There was some chance that Mattingly, the team's most popular player for a decade, might return. But Yankees fans who had watched Mattingly struggle with an ailing back for six years knew in their hearts that he was not coming back.

That became a certainty when Gene Michael was recruited to make one final blockbuster trade, because Watson didn't have much knowledge of the Yankees' personnel in the minor or major leagues. Michael acquired Seattle first baseman Tino Martinez, a left-handed batter who in 1995 had clobbered 31 homers and driven in 111 runs.

Martinez had a hefty contract, and he was available because Seattle was slashing its payroll. But the Mariners nearly quashed the deal several times anyway because Michael refused to include Rivera or Pettitte in the trade. The Yankees were willing to part with Sterling Hitchcock and highly touted third baseman Russ Davis, who had hit 25 home runs for the Yankees' Class AAA team the previous season.

Pushed by Piniella, the Mariners dropped their interest in Rivera, but Piniella had heard about Posada, and he loved the idea of a switch-hitting catcher in his lineup. Would the Yankees include Posada in the deal for Martinez?

Absolutely not, Michael said.

And so the Mariners returned to their demand for Pettitte.

"That trade was touch-and-go for a while, and it came down to the same argument we had been having internally for years," Michael said. "Who do we keep, Pettitte or Hitchcock? I had been on Pettitte's side of the argument all along."

Seattle eventually accepted Hitchcock and Davis for Martinez. Michael also got the Mariners to include reliever Jeff Nelson. Hitchcock pitched only one season in Seattle, then bounced around the National League, finishing his career with a 74-76 record. Davis had three productive years in Seattle but never hit more than 21 home runs in any season. Martinez, meanwhile, would end up hitting 192 homers with 739 RBI in a seven-year Yankee career. Nelson became a key cog in the bullpen for the next five seasons.

"Yeah, that one turned out pretty well," Michael said with a smile twenty years later. "My last trade. A good one."

Showalter was announced as the Arizona Diamondbacks' new manager on November 15. A Phoenix news conference was his first chance to reflect on the previous three weeks, and one of the New York–area reporters in attendance asked the obvious question: Have you had time to figure out what went wrong with the Yankees?

"I'm not going to dwell on that," Showalter replied. "They've made an excellent choice in Joe Torre and Bob Watson. They're in capable hands. I'm moving on to another situation. I'm not going into why and what if. It's not fair to this organization and the one I'm no longer part of."

Notably, throughout his news conference Showalter did not, and would not, say "Yankees." In several subsequent interviews in more private settings, he again did not use the word "Yankees."

Angela Showalter said that at first it was hard for her and Buck to put the Yankees in their past. "You're punched in the gut," she said in 2018. "It hurt."

Her husband did not disagree. "I woke up some days still thinking about the Yankees batting order or some Yankees minor leaguer I wanted to watch film on," Showalter recalled. "I'd have to catch myself. Nineteen years with one team doesn't go away overnight. There were things I wanted to finish." He paused and fiddled with the pens and pencils on his desk. "Life isn't always fair."

He rearranged the pens and pencils some more. "But I do believe things happen for a reason," he continued. "You come to understand that."

Said Angela: "We were in a new place — a really good place. We had far greater stability. Life was pretty good."

In time, Buck said his children got used to drinking their morning orange juice from glasses adorned with the Diamondbacks logo instead of the ones with a Yankees insignia that they had used all of their lives. Slowly, the Yankees trinkets around the house were packed away, replaced by mementos with an Arizona theme.

"I threw myself into my responsibilities with the Diamondbacks, which was easy because we were doing everything from scratch," he said. "There was so much to do. I was very busy — and happy."

But Showalter kept a close eye on the Yankees and always would. He couldn't help himself. "I'm not going to lie to you — I did grow up with them," he said. "Do you ever forget where you went to elementary school or high school? Do you ever want to?"

32

The Pieces All Come Together

DURING THE WINTER leading up to the 1996 season, George Steinbrenner all but went into hiding. But his disappearing act was not, in fact, a magic act. Behind the scenes, he largely left his new manager, Joe Torre, alone.

The unimaginable happened: Steinbrenner changed his meddling ways.

"It was all due to the Showalter thing," Gene Michael said. "He was really stung by the personal attacks he received after Buck didn't come back. The truth is, he never went after anybody in public after that again."

Michael was speaking seven years after Steinbrenner's death in 2010, when the Yankees' inimitable owner died of a heart attack after several years of declining health. Yet Michael still seemed surprised by the turn of events that transpired in early 1996.

"Remember how George used to fire at people in the press?" Michael asked, his eyebrows rising. "And he did it in private, too. He went after all the big honchos. Remember what he would do to Reggie and Billy in the seventies and eighties? He was merciless with every manager. But after 1995, never again. He finally learned.

"That's maybe the last favor Buck Showalter did for the franchise. He helped save George from George."

Cashman saw similar change. "After Showalter, Torre had a honeymoon compared to what the guys before him went through in that job," Cashman said. "Things were different in 1996."

With one exception. And it wasn't new. Steinbrenner wanted to trade young talent for a major league veteran. In this case, he was toying with two crown jewels of the Yankees' meticulous, painstaking early-nineties restoration.

In the last days of spring training in 1996, the overarching question dominating the conversation among team executives was this: Should they trade Mariano Rivera for a veteran shortstop and send Derek Jeter to the minor leagues? Because that's where some team executives thought Jeter belonged. All these years later, with Rivera and Jeter headed for the Baseball Hall of Fame, it may sound laughable. But in late March 1996, it nearly happened.

One voice was loudest in preventing a disaster that would have changed the course of Yankees history and probably altered the narrative of late-twentieth-century baseball.

While Gene Michael had indeed engineered the last trade of his career, the onetime slick-fielding shortstop made a final pivotal infield save for his former team. In a sharp exchange with George Steinbrenner, Michael insisted that Jeter had to be the Yankees' starting shortstop in 1996. And that would make a trade of Rivera unnecessary.

"I wasn't involved in many things when the '96 season began, but I wasn't going to let someone ruin the years we spent developing Derek and Mariano," Michael said.

When spring training in 1996 began, the Yankees had not felt any pressure to install Jeter as their everyday shortstop. It was the likely plan, but they knew the team had a backup contingency, veteran Tony Fernández, if the twenty-one-year-old Jeter faltered. But Fernández broke his arm late in spring training, and suddenly Jeter was the team's only answer at shortstop.

George Steinbrenner was always distrustful of fledgling, developing players. In the previous five years he had been adamant about trading Bernie Williams and willing to deal Rivera, Pettitte and Posada — more than once.

Worse, by March 1996, Steinbrenner had distanced himself from Michael and jettisoned Showalter and the top executives who had shepherded the minor league operation: Bill Livesey, Mitch Lukevics and Kevin Elfering.

In their place, Steinbrenner could be easily swayed by a cadre of "special advisers" he kept on the team payroll. It was a quizzical mix of former players, managers and, in a couple of cases, men who had never played professional baseball at any level. They rotated in and out of Steinbrenner's favor.

When it came to the decision about whether Jeter was ready to start at the infield's most pivotal position, the person with Steinbrenner's ear was former Brooklyn Dodgers pitcher Clyde King, who had become an ad hoc troubleshooter for the Yankees' owner.

King, an amiable Southern gentleman from North Carolina, with the drawl to prove it, had brief stints as a manager for the Yankees, San Francisco Giants and Atlanta Braves. He was a protégé of the Dodgers' pioneering general manager Branch Rickey. King had been Steinbrenner's general manager in 1985–86 and also served as the team's pitching coach during several seasons. It's not entirely clear how King, seventy-one years old at the time, came to be Steinbrenner's oracle on Jeter in the spring of 1996, but he had convinced the owner and others in his inner circle that Jeter was not ready for such a big job. The team's Columbus minor league affiliate beckoned.

On Steinbrenner's orders, the Yankees had negotiated with the Seattle Mariners to acquire shortstop Felix Fermin, who had been benched in favor of Alex Rodriguez. Once again, Lou Piniella wanted Rivera in return for Fermin, or maybe the reliever Bob Wickman. Watson said the trade was on the table. It was up to the Yankees — yes or no.

Michael caught wind of this possibility and was irate. The ferocity of his indignation moved Steinbrenner to summon roughly a dozen coaches and team executives to Joe Torre's office for a meeting on Jeter's future. "There were a lot of people in that room, and it was a tense exchange of ideas," Brian Cashman, one of those in attendance, recalled in 2017. "Derek had struggled in the spring, and this story line emerged that 'the kid' wasn't ready. It was time to finalize the roster and time to either make that Seattle trade or not make it."

The reporters covering the team saw the gaggle of coaches and executives crowd into Torre's office and waited outside in the hallway to see what the verdict would be. "They were looking for the puff of white smoke to appear, like when the papal decision is being made," Cashman joked. "But it wasn't funny; it was intense."

King was forced to defend his position. Essentially, he thought Jeter needed more seasoning, a little extra time to mature. The Seattle trade would provide the Yankees insurance.

Cashman disagreed. "I spoke my mind but I wasn't alone. There was a lot of pushback," he said.

Third-base coach Willie Randolph, who had started for a pennant-winning Yankees team at second base when he was the same age as

Jeter, chimed in. "Derek is gifted and very confident," he said. "You've got to just support him and let him breathe."

Steinbrenner remained unconvinced. Then Michael, who had known Steinbrenner longer than anyone else in the room, stood up and faced the owner. "You promised you wouldn't do this," he said, all but shouting at Steinbrenner. "We all agreed to give Jeter at least the first half of the season. We were going to leave him alone until then, remember? Why are we even here discussing this?"

Most everyone in Torre's office had been in team meetings throughout the off-season when it was indeed decided that Jeter would be the team's everyday shortstop, even if he had a bumpy start to the season.

Michael's exhortation had left him red-faced. Steinbrenner looked at his longtime employee. "OK, I know, I know," he said with a smile. "I was supposed to stay at home in Tampa and not say a word until July."

With the tension broken, everyone in the room laughed. Michael, remembering the scene twenty years later, said: "Let's face it, no one was counting on George being silent forever. But the argument was over. Derek was our shortstop. We dumped the trade talks."

Good thing. Fermin's major league career lasted only 11 more games and he became a footnote to Jeter's history. Wickman went on to save 256 games in a 15-year career, albeit primarily for teams other than the Yankees, who beginning in 1997 no longer needed a closer because they had Rivera.

As Gene Michael liked to say: Sometimes a general manager's legacy is measured by the trades he doesn't make.

In his second at-bat on opening day in 1996, Jeter smashed a home run. That day, with David Cone protecting a slim lead in the seventh inning and a runner on base, Jeter turned his back to the infield and dashed between the sprinting outfielders Gerald and Bernie Williams to make a spectacular over-the-shoulder catch in shallow left field to preserve the first Yankees victory of the year. The following afternoon, Jeter had three hits, a stolen base and scored three runs in the team's 5–1 victory. Pettitte pitched seven strong innings for his first win of the season.

"We were off and running," Cashman said. "We didn't look back. Jeter's value and worthiness certainly did not come up again."

But the rest of the season wasn't as easy as Cashman made it sound.

Tino Martinez, for instance, seemed overwhelmed in his first month as a Yankee. He was booed mercilessly by Yankees fans who were unwilling to see Mattingly replaced. By late April, Martinez had three home runs and was hitting just .244. Sometimes when he came to the plate at Yankee Stadium, the fans would chant, "Don-nie Base-ball," in homage to Mattingly — and to mock Martinez.

The fans had long memories in other ways. Joe Torre was jeered at Yankee Stadium, too. Torre, unlike twelve of the previous thirteen Yankees managers, had no ties to the organization, and more than anyone he represented the startling change that disrupted the feel-good mood emanating from the 1994 and 1995 Yankee seasons.

But Torre understood the Yankee fans' mentality in 1996. "They're being loyal and there's nothing wrong with that," he said. "Those of us new to the uniform are simply trying to earn their loyalty."

Torre was good at that. He may not have been a Yankee, but he was a New Yorker, born and raised in the Marine Park section of Brooklyn, and he understood all of the city's influential constituencies and power brokers. He courted noted celebrities, like New Yorker Billy Crystal and Mayor Rudolph Giuliani, and welcomed them into the team's dugout before games. Their luster reflected well on the new Yankees manager.

Torre was also honest, diplomatic and had a steadfast calm. His communication skills, at all levels, were sophisticated, and his sagacious handling of the media won him allies. His desire to protect his players from criticism established a priceless credibility in the clubhouse. Torre neither lashed out at his critics nor looked worried. Instead, he waited.

But if Torre was unshakable, it still took a while for the 1996 Yankees to become a well-oiled machine. The pitching rotation was shaky at best and struggling to find a consistent rhythm. Pettitte was the staff's rock and on his way to becoming the Yankees ace at twenty-four years old. But Jimmy Key was only gradually regaining his arm strength after another arm surgery. Dwight Gooden, signed in February, was inconsistently mounting a comeback after not pitching an inning of baseball in 1995. Kenny Rogers, another free agent, had spent the previous seven years in Texas, where it's always football season and the major league baseball team is often an afterthought. In New York, Rogers was warily and stiffly trying to acclimate to pitching in the pressure cooker of Yankee Stadium. It was a rocky adjustment. Cone, meanwhile, had won four of his first five decisions but was suffering from a peculiar numbness and chill in the fingers of his right hand. Tests revealed an aneurysm in his pitching arm. Surgery kept Cone off the mound until September 2.

The responsibility for bridging the gap between the erratic starting pitching and the revived bullpen closer John Wetteland fell to three relievers: the newly acquired Jeff Nelson, Wickman and most especially to the elastic-armed Rivera, who was frequently asked to pitch as many as three innings per outing.

"Whatever role we needed, Mo could do it," Girardi, the new everyday catcher, said, using Rivera's nickname. "That first year I was with the Yankees he was multipurpose, multisituational."

Wetteland had bounced back from his disastrous performance in the Seattle playoff series, for which he blamed himself, not Showalter. "I never gave Buck a reason to be confident in putting me out there," said Wetteland, who early in 1996 led the major leagues in saves.

But with Wetteland headed to free agency after the 1996 season, everyone on the Yankees could see who the team's closer of the future would be. By late April, Rivera had made ten appearances and had an ERA of 1.27. His WHIP, which measures walks and hits per inning, was a superlative 0.84.

Still, on April 29, the AL East standings had the Yankees trailing the Orioles, a consensus pick to win the division. That day, the two teams met at Baltimore's Camden Yards for the first of what was expected to be a quick two-game series. In the opening game, Pettitte had the worst outing of his career to that point, giving up nine runs before he had registered an out in the second inning.

At that moment, the Orioles, whose lineup featured two future Hall of Famers in Roberto Alomar and Cal Ripken Jr., surely seemed like the class of the division, if not the major leagues. But the 1996 Yankees proved to be more resilient than expected. While young, the roster had been tempered in the crucible of the 1995 playoffs. Most of the players had also been on the 1994 team, which seemed World Series bound until the players' strike.

So despite the shock of Pettitte's rare implosion on the mound, the Yankees battled on. A Leyritz home run in a five-run fifth inning helped the Yankees climb back into the game, and Martinez's three-run home run in the seventh gave the Yankees a lead they never relinquished in a wild, 13–10 victory. The game took 4 hours and 21 minutes to play, which made it the longest nine-inning game in major league history at the time.

The next day saw Rogers and David Wells square off, but the two starting pitchers were long forgotten by the time the game wound into extra innings, tied 6–6. That score was unchanged when Pettitte came on in relief to start the thirteenth inning. Pettitte would hold the Orioles scoreless for three innings and pick up the win when a grand slam by Martinez blew open a taut contest in the top of the fifteenth. The game had lasted 5 hours and 34 minutes. It took nearly 10 hours to play the two games of the *short* series, but the Yankees left Baltimore in first place.

The Yankees did not run away from the Orioles, who would battle the Yankees for American League supremacy into October. But many things kept falling into place, just as they had been designed and nurtured.

One midsummer game against Boston at a teeming Yankee Stadium illustrated how well the Yankees' best-laid plans, many that were traceable to the early nineties, were coming to fruition.

Singles by O'Neill and Jeter, who would go 4-for-4, staked the Yankees to an early lead that was extended by a long home run to left field by Bernie Williams, who had become the Yankees' most versatile and potent power hitter. The multiskilled Williams, now a sinewy, sturdy twenty-seven-year-old, posed an onerous, complex challenge to opposing pitchers because they might see him as the leadoff hitter or in the cleanup spot in the batting order. As a switch-hitter who rarely left the lineup, he had acquired a keen grasp of the strike zone and walked frequently.

Williams's on-base percentage in 1996 was .391 (the team's OBP would be .360). But Williams could also drive the ball to the deepest reaches of any ballpark, and his midseason slugging percentage hovered around .600. He would finish the season with a team-leading .535 slugging percentage, bat .305 and drive in 102 runs. He would also lead the team in stolen bases (17) and home runs (29).

More than twenty years later, Williams credited his steady maturation, one begun when he was first indoctrinated in the Yankee Way as a teenager. "My production came from years of patient development. I had been schooled by many of the same people, like Buck Showalter, Brian Butterfield and Stump Merrill, since I was in the minors at eighteen years old," Williams said in a 2017 interview. "It was paying off."

Also in the game against Boston, Wade Boggs had a pivotal hit. Boggs, though thirty-eight years old, would bat .311 in 1996 with a .389 on-base percentage.

Wickman, acquired for Steve Sax in Gene Michael's steal of a trade with the Chicago White Sox in 1992, relieved a struggling Kenny Rogers in the sixth inning. Wickman had become the wingman to Rivera and Wetteland, picking up his bullpen mates whenever either needed a rest. Wetteland was on his way to 43 saves. Rivera was building a reputation as a steely, dark-eyed relief assassin. Twice, Rivera had consecutive score-less-inning streaks of 23 innings or more.

Wickman, Rivera, Wetteland and Jeff Nelson all pitched against the Red Sox, who scratched out just one run against the Yankees bullpen quartet. The Yankees cruised to an easy victory, boosting their lead in the AL East to four and one half games.

And there was also a bit of theater during the contest. O'Neill kept teammates amused by breaking his bat over his thigh when a line drive he had smoked to right field was caught for an out. O'Neill entered the dugout and, using one of the shards of his splintered bat, destroyed the team water cooler. "I've got to start getting some hits," he said afterward.

At the time, O'Neill was leading the American League with a .352 batting average.

Gerald Williams, the usual Yankees left fielder and a valued teammate with a variety of skills that did not always show up in the box score, threw out a Red Sox base runner trying to advance to third base on a caught fly ball.

Jorge Posada did not play in the Boston game, although he was on the bench — one of about 30 games Posada spent with the Yankees. Torre, with the encouragement of his vocal bench coach Don Zimmer, had thrown his support behind Joe Girardi as the team's catcher, even though some in the organization thought Posada's development was being unfairly stunted. "Posada was ready for the majors in 1996. It just took the big league club a year or more to see that," said Stump Merrill, the AAA Columbus manager that year.

The advancement of Posada, twenty-four at the time, was hampered by the absence of Bill Livesey and Mitch Lukevics, the executives who had signed him and brought him along in the minors. He had lost some of his biggest advocates. Posada's last minor league season was nonetheless productive, as he drove in 62 runs in 106 games. He had something highly unusual for a catcher, a .405 on-base percentage. Posada would be Girardi's backup in the next season, and by 1998 became the full-time Yankees catcher (and frequent All-Star), a job he did not relinquish until he retired in 2011.

The 1996 Yankees lead in the AL East grew to 12 games by the end of July, then shrank to four games on the last day of August, after they lost 14 of 20 games late that month. Torre remained a tranquil presence, disinclined to make substantial changes. "We'll keep trotting out the guys who got us into first place," Torre said. "They'll be the ones who keep us there."

And just like that, Pettitte stopped the bleeding with a solid victory on August 31. In 1996, Pettitte compiled a 13-3 record when he pitched after a Yankees loss. He would win five of his last six decisions and become the first homegrown Yankees pitcher to win 20 or more games since Ron Guidry did it in 1985.

In September 1996, the Orioles stayed close to the Yankees but never seriously threatened to take over the top spot in the AL East, which the Yankees won with a 92-70 record. It was the Yankees' first full-season division title since 1980. Jeter would hit .314 and win the American League Rookie of the Year Award. O'Neill cooled off in the last six weeks but still drove in 91 runs and hit 19 homers. Leyritz was a pesky clutch hitter off the bench who drove in 40 runs.

Jimmy Key rebounded after losing five of his first six 1996 starts to win 11 of his next 17 decisions. More importantly, Key pitched nearly 170 innings after pitching about 30 innings in the previous injury-riddled season. Dwight Gooden, who pitched a no-hitter in May, posted an 11-7 record even if his earned run average was 5.01. Kenny Rogers had a 12-8 record, although big crowds and crucial games still seemed to unnerve him. David Cone had returned from arm surgery to post a 3-1 record in September.

The Yankees were a good team with few blatant weaknesses. Imbued with the talent of a stocked minor league system that had indoctrinated its developing players with the same baseball tenets, they had the vibrancy of youth and conviction in the merits of their methodical training and baseball education. Moreover, those young players were battle tested because they had spent most of their minor league careers competing for, or winning, championships under managers named Merrill, Showalter, Sherlock and Butterfield.

The 1996 Yankees also had a deft mix of seasoned veterans — players primarily and adroitly acquired by Gene Michael across many seasons. The Yankees may not have won a World Series for eighteen years, but they had been edging closer every year. In prominent ways, the bitter disappointment of the past two seasons had left scars on the 1996 team. But the Yankees had also been hardened by those experiences.

"We headed into the '96 playoffs quietly confident," O'Neill recalled. "The '95 playoff series in Seattle had changed us. We had a little chip on our shoulder because we still believed we should have won the whole thing in 1994 and probably gone farther in '95, too.

"We knew how far we had come from the early 1990s. But I don't know if anyone else felt like we were going to go far in the postseason. The way '94 and '95 ended made everyone a little leery."

33

To the Mountaintop

PAUL O'NEILL WAS right about the mood of Yankees fans and those who covered the team. Not many baseball writers, in New York or across the nation, considered the 1996 Yankees a threat to win the World Series. Most didn't think they could win a playoff series.

The Yankees were the underdogs against their divisional-round opponent, the Texas Rangers, who had surged past the formidable Seattle Mariners to win the American League West. Also waiting in the path to the World Series were the Cleveland Indians, who won their division by 14½ games. The Indians were by far the most feared team in the American League. They had two future Hall of Famers in Jim Thome and Eddie Murray, plus Manny Ramirez, a likely Hall of Famer if he had not been suspended for steroid use later in his career.

As for Yankees fans, there was no question they were approaching the 1996 postseason with an uneasy caution. As usual, the home playoff games sold out in a few hours, but the fans displayed an uncharacteristic reserve born of repeated postseason frustration.

It had been fifteen long years since the franchise had won a postseason series, despite the euphoria of the 1994 season and the 2–0 lead in the 1995 playoff series against the Mariners. Just about everyone in the Yankees' orbit was unconvinced that the 1996 version of the team was destined for greatness.

But there was a team that fit that category. As the twentieth century was drawing to a close, the pitching-rich Atlanta Braves, the defending World Series champions, were the team that seemed on the verge of a dynastic period of success. When the Braves received their commemorative rings for winning the 1995 World Series, they were inscribed with a motto: "Best Team of the '90s."

As the Yankees prepared for their opening series with Texas, the two teams had distinct connections. The Rangers' manager, Johnny Oates, was a former Yankees minor league manager and player. Oates had been Buck Showalter's manager in Nashville. When Showalter told Oates he was retiring as a player in 1984, it was Oates who told the Yankees front office that they might want to offer Showalter the minor league manager's position in Oneonta, New York. The Texas general manager was Doug Melvin, the former Yankees assistant scouting director who in 1985 hid Bernie Williams in a prep school baseball camp near his Connecticut home until Williams was eighteen years old and could sign a professional contract.

In some ways, new and old worlds in the Yankees universe were colliding in the 1996 division series.

"I'm from Texas," Andy Pettitte said many years later. "And what I remember about that series is that people down there were pretty sure the Yankees were going to be overwhelmed. We weren't feared like past Yankees teams."

In the opening game at Yankee Stadium against Texas, the Yankees indeed looked overmatched in a 6–2 loss. But they rallied the next day to win in 12 innings when Jeter ended the game by dashing home from second base on a bunt and a throwing error.

Bernie Williams's home run helped the Yankees win the third game in Texas, a 3–2 victory that went down to the last strike, as the Yankees' bullpen kept the Rangers scoreless in the final four innings. The Yankees had gained a crucial edge in the best-of-five series.

The next day, Williams, who hit .474 in the series, slammed two more homers as the Yankees broke open a tied game in the later innings to win, 6–4. After a fifteen-year wait, the Yankees had finally won another postseason series.

Jeter had seven hits in the four games, second baseman Mariano Duncan drove in four runs, and six Yankees relievers pitched 20 innings and yielded just two runs.

But most of the media focus was on Williams, the center fielder who now looked worthy of patrolling the same ground once trod by DiMaggio and Mantle. "Bombs Away Bernie!" the *New York Daily News* backpage headline bellowed on the morning after the Yankees advanced to the American League Championship Series. Another headline read, "Burn

Baby Bern," which was also the home run call concocted for Williams by the Yankees' longtime radio broadcaster John Sterling. It would become a staple of the team's broadcasts for another decade, during which Williams would hit 208 regular-season and 22 postseason home runs.

The Yankees' ALCS foe was a shocker, as the wild-card-berth Orioles upset the mighty Cleveland Indians, who went home after winning 99 regular-season games.

The first game of the ALCS was notable, and ultimately renowned, for Jeter's eighth-inning home run, which famously fell into the hands of twelve-year-old Yankees fan Jeffrey Maier, who appeared to reach into the field of play to snag the ball. The disputed home run tied the contest, which went into extra innings. Less remembered is that Mariano Rivera held the Orioles scoreless in the tenth and eleventh innings in relief of Wetteland. That allowed Williams — who else? — to win the game with a leadoff, walk-off homer in the bottom of the eleventh.

The teams traded victories in the next two games. In the fourth game of the series, O'Neill and Williams, who would be named the series' Most Valuable Player, each slugged two-run homers. Darryl Strawberry added two home runs in an 8–4 victory that put the Yankees up 3-1 in the series.

The next day, the Orioles were vanquished on a warm evening at Camden Yards, with Pettitte giving up just three hits and two runs in eight innings. The game ended in a dramatic, changing-of-the-guard moment when Cal Ripken Jr., the American League's preeminent shortstop since 1983, bounced a ground ball into the hole on the right side of the infield. Jeter, who was four years old when Ripken played his first professional game, chased it down, pivoted and fired a strong throw across the diamond that just beat Ripken, whose postseason career ended with a jarring, futile, head-first slide into first base.

Leyritz homered in the game, as did Cecil Fielder, a veteran, powerful slugger who would have a stellar postseason for the Yankees.

The talented Yankees farm system had been instrumental in the acquisition of Fielder in July 1996. The Yankees traded Matt Drews, a six-foot-eight pitcher who had been the team's first-round draft pick in 1993, to the Detroit Tigers along with outfielder Rubén Sierra for Fielder. Drews did not have the career he imagined and never made the majors. Fielder proved to be a valuable power hitter for the Yankees for parts of two seasons.

But in mid-October 1996, with the Orioles defeated in five games, Fielder was most beloved in New York for helping the Yankees earn their first American League pennant since 1981. Finally and happily, Yankees fans were no longer fretting about the bad postseason karma that had seemed to accompany the franchise in 1994 and 1995.

Then the World Series against the Atlanta Braves began.

In the opening game, the first at Yankee Stadium since Reggie Jackson, Lou Piniella and Dave Winfield were Yankees, Pettitte was hammered in a 12–1 loss. "I felt certain I had blown the whole series and let everyone down — teammates, fans, my family, just about everyone," Pettitte said years later of his inaugural World Series start.

The second game was not much better for the home team. Atlanta's Greg Maddux shut out the Yankees, 4–0, with Key taking the loss.

The series shifted to Atlanta for the next three games, with the Braves needing only two victories to win back-to-back championships and at least partly live up to the slogan etched inside their World Series rings.

Before the third game of the series, an Atlanta newspaper columnist, Mark Bradley, insisted that the series with the "overmatched" Yankees was over. "We are no longer watching a competition," Bradley wrote. "We are witnessing a coronation."

And that's when things really got interesting.

The Yankees won Game 3 in Atlanta, 5–2, but not before Torre, in a near repeat of the situation facing Buck Showalter one year earlier inside the Kingdome, endured a gut-wrenching decision about whether to replace a tiring David Cone with the game on the line.

Once again, Mariano Rivera was available in the bullpen as Cone, trying to protect a one-run lead, loaded the bases. Exhausted, Cone was faltering, and Torre knew that if the Yankees fell behind in the series by three games, there was little chance they could come back with four consecutive victories.

But like Showalter before him, Torre had faith in Cone's experience and guile. Rivera remained in the bullpen. This time, Cone got out of the inning with the Yankees still ahead.

Showalter and Torre had made the same decision in a taut playoff game. For Showalter, it probably cost him his job. For Torre, it might have been his salvation on the job.

Rivera came on in the next inning and held the Braves scoreless. In the eighth inning, Jeter singled and Bernie Williams, batting left-handed, stroked a home run to deep right field for a three-run lead the Yankees never relinquished.

Williams clubbed his homer using Joe Girardi's bat. As Joel Sherman reported in his 2006 book, *Birth of a Dynasty: Behind the Pinstripes with the 1996 Yankees,* it was another case of "Bernie being Bernie," as his teammates liked to say. Williams had left for the road trip to Atlanta without packing any of his bats.

In Game 4 the next night, Kenny Rogers looked rattled, and pitched like it, as the Braves took a 6–0 lead into the sixth inning. But Jeter and Williams each reached base and scored on Atlanta defensive misplays. By the eighth inning, the Yankees had trimmed the Atlanta lead to 6–3 when two singles brought backup catcher Jim Leyritz to the plate as the tying run.

Twirling his bat, Leyritz battled Atlanta's hard-throwing Mark Wohlers for nearly three minutes, until Wohlers threw a hanging 2-2 slider that Leyritz lofted toward left field. The drive carried just beyond the wall and tied the game, instantly silencing a raucous home crowd.

The thirty-two-year-old Leyritz had already been on the scene, and in the middle, of a host of prominent moments in Yankees history.

Since he signed as an undrafted amateur free agent in 1985, he had frustrated scores of Yankees minor league coaches and managers. That group included Showalter, who managed him with three different minor league teams — and won a championship with Leyritz in each season. Leyritz, the part-time, converted catcher, always seemed to find a way to contribute in myriad ways.

He had also played a major role in Andy Hawkins's lost no-hitter in Chicago. He had hit the dramatic, fifteenth-inning home run that put the Yankees ahead by two games in the 1995 division series, and he was the catcher fielding the baseball a millisecond too late as Ken Griffey Jr. scored the series-clinching run that eliminated the Yankees and ultimately led to an off-season of upheaval and firings.

But on October 23, 1996, Leyritz tied the fourth game of the World Series with a stunning home run that so flustered the incandescent Braves that they never recovered — perhaps forever, since the powerhouse team assembled in Atlanta never won another World Series.

Two innings after Leyritz's home run dropped over the left-field fence, Wade Boggs, as a pinch hitter, drew a bases-loaded walk for the winning run in the tenth inning. John Wetteland gave up a single in the bottom of the inning but retired the final Braves batters for his second save of the series. The Yankees' six-run comeback was the second largest in World Series history. Only Connie Mack's 1929 Philadelphia Athletics had rallied from further behind.

In the next game, the Yankees' starter was Andy Pettitte, and he was determined to earn redemption. "I couldn't believe I was getting the chance to make up for how bad I pitched in my first World Series game," he said. "I wasn't going to mess it up again."

In the fifth game of the series, and the final game at Atlanta–Fulton County Stadium—the Braves were moving to Turner Field in 1997—Pettitte outdueled Atlanta's ace, John Smoltz, as the Yankees won, 1–0. The lone run of the game scored on another Braves defensive mistake when the four-time Gold Glove center fielder Marquis Grissom dropped a routine fly ball. (The Yankees were no longer cursing their bad playoff karma.)

Atlanta's best scoring opportunity in the game came in the sixth inning when two singles put Braves runners at first and second base with no outs. Atlanta second baseman Mark Lemke bunted, but Pettitte dashed off the mound to corral the ball bare-handed and in one motion threw to third base to get the force out. The next batter was Chipper Jones, the first overall pick of the 1990 amateur draft.

Pettitte flummoxed Jones with a sharp, inside slider, which Jones tapped back to the mound. Pettitte nimbly pounced on the grounder and threw to second base to begin an inning-ending double play.

Pettitte pitched into the ninth inning, although Wetteland was needed to get two outs in that dicey inning. With two Braves on base, the victory was not assured until Paul O'Neill, limping noticeably from a strained hamstring, ran down and snagged a deep drive near the wall in right-center field for the game's final out. O'Neill barely got to the ball in time, and he slapped his right hand and glove against the padding of the wall at the end of the play. The catch meant that John Wetteland had saved each of the three games in Atlanta.

Everything seemed to be falling into place for the 1996 Yankees. Pettitte outpitched Smoltz, who had lost only once in 17 previous postseason appearances.

The series returned to Yankee Stadium, where Maddux and Key would be the Game 6 starting pitchers. In December 1992, Gene Michael was certain he had persuaded Maddux, who was a free agent after several stellar seasons with the Chicago Cubs, to sign with the Yankees. Maddux had been wined and dined and feted at a Broadway show. When Maddux left New York, Michael thought he had a done deal.

Maddux shocked the Yankees by signing with the Braves. That winter, Michael instead turned to Key, who left Toronto for a four-year Yankees contract. Since then, Key had won 49 games for the Yankees, but most notably, he had been a crucial, early figure in the cultural makeover of the team's clubhouse initiated by Michael and Showalter. Key had helped significantly reshape the roster in ensuing years by enticing O'Neill, Boggs and Cone to play for the Yankees. He had set a tone with his professionalism and with his even comportment under pressure.

How cool was Jimmy Key in big moments?

In the hours before his start in the sixth game of the 1996 World Series, with a championship on the line, he had proposed to his longtime girlfriend, Karin Kane. Key was apparently not worried that later that Saturday night he might be celebrating his engagement despite an ill-timed defeat on the mound of so pivotal a game. "Actually, I figured it would be a fun way to always remember a World Series victory," he later said.

Key gave up just one run and five hits in nearly six innings of work that night. By then, a triple by Girardi and RBI singles by Jeter and Williams had put the Yankees ahead, 3–1.

The bullpen did its job, including Rivera, who pitched two scoreless innings while facing only seven batters. In the postseason, Rivera had allowed one run in 14⅓ innings. Throughout the regular season and playoffs in 1996, he had given up one home run in 122 innings and struck out 140.

The ninth inning was turned over to Wetteland, and the Braves cut the Yankees lead to 3–2. With two outs, Atlanta had runners on first and second base with Mark Lemke at the plate.

The home crowd was on its feet — roaring, jubilant, nervous and ready to erupt. In their souls, Yankees fans instinctively feel a direct connection to all of the franchise's many championship teams. To be a Yankees fan is to be part of a lineage that dates back to the World Series teams of Babe Ruth, Joe DiMaggio, Yogi Berra, Mickey Mantle and Thurman Munson.

But it had been 18 seasons since the last Yankees championship.

The Yankees had won 22 World Series to that point in the twentieth century. But the intimate link to those prolific Yankees teams was growing frayed. There had been too many bad teams, too many indifferent teams and too many good teams that had nonetheless fallen short in October.

The franchise desperately needed a twenty-third championship. With two outs in the ninth inning on October 26, 1996, Yankees fans cheered and stomped until the old Yankee Stadium, whose foundation was poured months before the team's first championship season of 1923, began to shake and sway.

Swinging at a 3-2 pitch, Lemke lofted a soft fly ball in foul territory behind third base and a few feet from the first row of the grandstand. Third baseman Charlie Hayes backpedaled until he was standing beneath the pop-up. After the humiliating 1991 Yankees season, in one of Gene Michael's first trades, Hayes was acquired for a minor league pitching prospect. The Yankees lost Hayes a year later in the expansion draft when Michael gambled by leaving him unprotected. But the Yankees never forgot about Hayes's poise and unruffled manner in the high-pressure New York environment, and in 1996 they reacquired him for another minor league pitching prospect.

As Hayes waited underneath Lemke's foul ball, Michael was watching from a mezzanine-level private box. "I was really glad it was Charlie," Michael said years later. "You go after reliable guys like him because they're the ones you want the last out hit to — because they'll catch it."

A second before the ball dropped into Hayes's glove, Derek Jeter jumped straight into the air with both arms raised over his head.

Bernie Williams was sprinting in from center field. When Hayes squeezed the final out of the game, Wetteland raised his right index finger over his head. One of the first to embrace him from behind was Williams. Rivera, charging from the dugout, was not far behind.

There was soon a pileup of Yankees in the center of the diamond. Paul O'Neill leaped awkwardly on top of the first-base side of the celebration and did a somersault that left him lying in the grass at the feet of Andy Pettitte on the third-base side of the infield.

In the dugout, Torre, who had been a steadying force since midsummer, was mobbed by his coaches. Torre had waited 4,278 games as a player and manager to be part of a World Series champion.

It was a Saturday night in New York City, and the festivities were just getting started. Police officers on horseback had formed a cordon around the edges of the field to keep the fans away from the players.

One of those mounted police was Lieutenant Jim Higgins, a Bronx native and Yankees fan whose grandfather, another New York mounted policeman, had brought him to Yankees World Series games in the 1960s. "I was watching Derek Jeter going nuts on the field when someone tapped me on the back," Higgins recalled in 1998. "It was Wade Boggs, and he asked, 'Can I get up on your horse?'"

Giving horseback rides was against police regulations except in emergencies, but Higgins considered Boggs's request a special circumstance, and he helped Boggs onto the back of his 1,400-pound gelding, Beau. Boggs, despite a lifelong fear of horses, took a ride around the ballpark until Higgins dropped him off at home plate.

At roughly the same time, spurred by Torre, Jim Leyritz gathered his teammates and suggested the entire team take a victory lap. Led by Leyritz, the only player still on the roster from the 1990 Yankees, the champion 1996 Yankees waved and saluted fans in a playful jog around the stadium's warning track.

David Cone remembered running up to O'Neill and shouting: "Do you believe this? It's almost like this season was destined to happen."

George Steinbrenner was being hugged by family and friends in a private box. His son Hal saw something he had never seen before: tears in his father's eyes. "I had never seen him cry, but eighteen years is a lot of waiting," Hal Steinbrenner said in 2017. "He had faced a lot of criticism in many of those years. And he knew that; he read the newspapers. I never asked him, but it had to be a good feeling for him.

"It was tears of joy. But tears are tears. I just think that it was that emotional. And a great, great moment."

Gene Michael celebrated in his mezzanine suite with some other members of the front office. While Boggs was taking his first trip on a horse, Michael was pointing at him on the field and laughing along with everyone else. Then he retreated to his office overlooking the field with a handful of other executives of the team. The group helped themselves to a bottle of champagne, as well as other, stronger libations. "We had a pretty good party — that was a fun night," Michael said with a chortle.

He eventually made his way down to the clubhouse, but he didn't remain there long. "I wanted to congratulate Joe and some of the guys, but you know, that was their moment, not mine," Michael recalled in a 2017 interview. "But it was wonderful to see us back on top after all the really hard, really long, losing years."

Michael paused as if trying to summon every recollection from that night in 1996. "Later, there was a time to think about everything that was done from 1990 up until that moment — and all the people who were a part of that," he said. "The '96 team did a great job, that's all on them. And on that night, you're just all smiles. But there's always so many things that go into a championship. I knew that. We all knew that."

Meanwhile, Brian Cashman, Michael's assistant since the early nineties, made a note to himself about a phone call he wanted to make the next day.

"At about 8 a.m. on that Sunday morning after the '96 Yankees won the World Series, my home phone rang and it was Brian Cashman," said Bill Livesey, the Yankees' director of player development and scouting from 1990 to 1995. "He called to thank me. And that made me feel pretty good."

Don Mattingly watched the clinching game of the series on television. But more than twenty years later, when Mattingly was asked where he had been when the Yankees won their first championship since 1978 — or eight months before he was drafted by the team — he said he could not remember. But, Mattingly said, "I was so happy for those guys on the '96 team; they finally got there and won it. And that was great. Those were some of my really good friends.

"At some point, you have some thought that, you know, that didn't happen for you. But not for too long. I was happy for them. It was a good thing."

Mattingly went on to become a coach for the Yankees under Torre and the manager of the Los Angeles Dodgers and Florida Marlins. Over the next five to ten years, he conceded, whenever he ran into Buck Showalter, the two men would exchange a knowing look, a silent recognition of their shared past. "Nothing is said. Nothing needs to be said."

They were vital cogs in the last baseball dynasty of the twentieth century. They just weren't there for those Yankees championships.

Buck Showalter was at home in Arizona on the final night of the 1996 World Series. He watched the games and saw what he expected to see. "Paul or Bernie would get a big hit and I'd say to myself, 'Yep, there it is; that's what I thought would happen,'" Showalter said. "I saw Andy Pettitte pitching shutout innings, and I thought, 'Yep, that's him.'

"It was the same with Mariano and Derek. You say, 'See, that's why we didn't trade those guys in all those years.' I wasn't surprised by what occurred at all. So all that was good to see. I was pleased."

Showalter leaned back in his chair and folded his hands across his chest. "Now I know what you're thinking — that I'm just saying what I have to say," he said. "But you have to believe me when I tell you this: It was not painful to see the Yankees do well. It makes you feel good that you were able to project that. That's what we went through the tough times for."

Showalter, however, acknowledged that watching those World Series games was a personal, poignant journey. "Yeah, I remember watching each game in private," he said in 2107. "I was in the house watching by myself. I'm sure people wonder if I was thinking about whether that should have been me in the Yankees' dugout. People say it's human nature to think that. But I'm telling you the truth when I say I didn't have that emotion. I didn't. I remember feeling proud of them.

"Life isn't fair. It's also too short. You can't go around feeling the wrong way about something good that happened. We all had a role in it. I was happy about that."

But when the final out settled into the glove of Charlie Hayes, Showalter did not watch what transpired next. The job was done. Showalter shut off the television and left the room.

The Yankees celebration went on late into the night. Two days later, there was a ticker tape parade through lower Manhattan's Canyon of Heroes. Along the same avenue that had once paid tribute to everyone from Jesse Owens to Apollo astronauts to the freed hostages from the American embassy in Iran, the Yankees were feted by more than three million people. It was a joyous, animated and exuberant throng.

It was, notably, a youthful crowd, as most of the people lining the streets were in their twenties and thirties. A new generation of Yankees fans now had a World Series victory that was theirs alone, as well as a team made in their image.

The twenty-two-year-old Derek Jeter was about to become an incandescent figure in the sport. Rivera, twenty-six, would soon establish himself as the greatest reliever, and one of the most dominant pitchers, of all time. The connection to the long lineage of Yankees championships was reborn with new homegrown stars. And the party was just beginning.

The Yankees empire, mocked as a wasteland in 1990, had made it all the way back to baseball's promised land. The resurrection was complete. The worst Yankees teams in history had evolved into the best team in baseball — with much more success to come.

The phoenix had risen from the ashes.

Epilogue

THE YANKEES, in a surprise, did not win the 1997 World Series. They were dispatched in the American League Division Series by the Cleveland Indians after Mariano Rivera gave up a shocking, late home run in what would have been the series-clinching victory.

It proved to be a brief setback. From 1998 to 2000, the Yankees won three more World Series, in consecutive years, something accomplished only three times previously in major league history. In fact, in the final quarter of twentieth-century baseball, the Yankees' dominance — four World Series victories in five years — was unmatched in baseball. No team had done it since the Yankees of the early 1950s.

But the late-nineties Yankees were not just consistent winners. They were often spectacularly prolific. The 1998 team, for example, won 114 regular-season games and had an 11-2 postseason record, including a World Series sweep of the San Diego Padres.

The next year, the Yankees were even better in the playoffs, losing only once and sweeping the Atlanta Braves in the World Series. In 2000, in the first New York subway series in forty-four years, the New York Mets and Yankees met for five high-energy, riveting games. But again, the Yankees were crowned baseball's best.

"Once we got on a roll and really learned how to win the big games," Paul O'Neill said, "it became like a collective will. Don't get me wrong, it was never easy, but we had a history together. So many games going back so many years."

In this period, only in 2001 did the Yankees falter in the World Series, losing in seven games to the Arizona Diamondbacks. One year earlier, Buck Showalter had been fired as the Diamondbacks' manager.

Overall, the Yankees were in the playoffs every season from 1995 to 2012 except one. In what came to be known as the Core Four era of Jeter, Posada, Rivera and Pettitte, the Yankees also won a fifth World Series, in 2009.

The Yankees, the butt of jokes in 1990, did more than regain their footing on the field. They once again became the most influential sporting brand in North America, if not the world. Advertisers and corporate sponsors rediscovered the worth and power of a vibrant, prosperous championship team playing its home games at Yankee Stadium.

And the run of success had ensured that the team's home would continue to be in New York, as city officials agreed to build a new Yankee Stadium across the street from the original one, a palace that opened in 2009.

"A lot of things went right for the franchise year after year, and there's no doubt that you can trace it all to the first successful teams of the mid-1990s," Hal Steinbrenner, who took over the day-to-day control of the team in 2008, said. "And by that I mean the 1994 and 1995 teams as well. There is a continuum, even if the big breakthrough wasn't until 1996."

The majority of the protagonists in this now famous Yankee renaissance have existed on both sides of the 1995–96 divide for more than twenty years. Some, like tragic heroes in a Shakespearean drama, saw their Yankee experience end with the devastating 1995 playoff loss in Seattle. They never directly reaped the benefits of their hard work and foresight. The ticker tape parade confetti never cascaded onto their shoulders.

But others continued with the team and lived through the prosperity, as did some who did not arrive until 1996. And yet, their perspectives, with varying degrees of satisfaction or accrued acceptance, are generally similar.

Don Mattingly, for instance, is proud to have been part of what he called "the building blocks of a dynasty." "You could see what was coming," he said. "I doubt any of us who left after 1995 were too surprised. It is unfortunate that Buck wasn't there to see it finish out."

But Mattingly, who coached for Torre for four seasons beginning in 2004, added, "I also saw that when Joe came along he was the perfect guy for that spot — a group ready to go."

Torre, who was inducted into the Baseball Hall of Fame because of his four championships as manager of the Yankees, is unequivocal that his initial success was predicated on the foundation laid before he took the job. "I certainly fell into it and inherited some good people who were used to winning at that point," he said in a 2014 interview. "But there's a reason for everything that happens."

Torre's remarks led to a follow-up question: If there had not been a players' strike in 1994 and the high-flying Yankees had won the World Series that year, would Torre be the manager in 1996? "No, I don't believe I would've been," Torre answered. "But if they had won in '94, then maybe '95 doesn't turn out the way it did. Maybe I never manage the Yankees. Who knows what happens?"

Paul O'Neill agreed. "Sometimes I wonder if we had to go through the setbacks to accomplish everything else," he said. "Maybe we don't win in '96 if we don't lose in '95."

It is a lingering question: Would things have played out the same for the Yankees if Showalter had remained the manager in 1996 and beyond? Would there still have been a last, late-twentieth-century Yankees dynasty?

Willie Randolph, who coached for Showalter but also stayed on as Torre's third-base coach for the next nine seasons, thinks not. "It's a tough question, but with all due respect to Buck, I really feel like Joe was probably the one we needed at that time," Randolph said. "I think he's the only one who could have done what he did. Because it wasn't just 1996, it was every year after that for a long time. Joe being a New York guy and being around for a lot of years, he understood how to handle all the different parts of the job that kept changing."

At the same time, Randolph is certain Torre's path to success would have been rocky and perhaps impassable without the way having been cleared for him before 1996. "Buck, Stick Michael, the scouts, the minor league managers and the big league coaches built that team from the ground up, and most of all, they had to absorb that really tough loss in 1995," Randolph said. "And I'm a firm believer that devastating disappointment is a great teacher for champions. Every championship team usually has to endure some serious heartache and heartbreak before winning it all.

"That's what Buck, Stick and the 1995 team did for the franchise. They took that bullet. The bad taste it left in everyone's mouth became the motivation for reaching higher the next season and all the seasons after that."

Showalter, meanwhile, has always given Torre the credit. "Joe took it to another level," he said. "I don't know if I could have done what Joe did."

George Steinbrenner, who made the decision to switch from Showalter to Torre, and then changed his mind, told me in a 1997 interview at his Tampa hotel that he regretted how he handled Showalter's exit. But in retrospect, he was not second-guessing himself either.

Steinbrenner could still smile and frown at the same time.

"I regret how it played out at the time," he said. "But sometimes things don't go as smoothly as you want them to go. It happens. I do wish it had been easier on everyone. But Buck is in a great place right now. He's going to do great things, you'll see. And we won the World Series with Joe." Steinbrenner shrugged his shoulders and threw up his hands as if to say, What do you want me to say?

He added, "That's how it worked out."

As the Yankees' World Series victories and playoff appearances accumulated in the succeeding seasons, and with Steinbrenner having sworn off the tabloid spotlight years earlier, the owner who had been bitterly lampooned for his bombastic ways took on the aura of a beloved patriarch.

It was a welcome metamorphosis for many in his inner circle, including those he had once warred with, like Gene Michael. "New York began to love him," Michael said. "As much as they hated him for a while, people forgave him. It was because of all the winning teams and because he stayed away from harassing people publicly.

"It helped his image and everything else. And he knew that. He knew that among Yankees fans he was now beloved. At the end of his life I was happy he knew that."

On a stage in the locker room in the wake of the team's 1998 World Series, Steinbrenner wept uncontrollably when handed the trophy signifying the victory. The hearts of Yankees fans melted. This was the Boss?

A few years later, Steinbrenner was standing on a makeshift platform in Yankee Stadium's left field, conducting a television interview half an hour before a home season-opening game. Fans in the nearby outfield bleachers spotted him and began chanting, "Thank you, George!"

Although he was wearing dark sunglasses, viewers could see the tears roll down Steinbrenner's cheeks on live television.

By 2006, Steinbrenner, beset by a series of health problems, withdrew from public appearances. He relinquished his substantial input in the team's affairs by 2008. Ten days after his eightieth birthday, in 2010, Steinbrenner had a heart attack at his Tampa home and died in a local hospital.

The tributes poured in, especially from the thousands that his philanthropy had benefited.

"I'm sure people can debate parts of his legacy," Hal Steinbrenner said of his father. "I'm know I'm biased, but I don't know if he gets enough credit for what he did across the decades with the Yankees. Go back to 1973 and see where the team was then and where it is now."

Gene Michael, who in 2017 joked that he wished he could have dinner with Steinbrenner again so he could "tell him off one more time," agreed that Steinbrenner's imprint on the Yankees would be perpetual. "He made me get my hair cut as a player in 1973 and we still have that policy on long hair, right?" Michael said with a grin. "George doesn't go away."

After he was pushed out as general manager in 1995, Michael took on a variety of roles in the Yankees organization. Initially called the director of scouting, he became more like a guru who was consulted on everything from major league trades to the outfield wall dimensions of the new Yankee Stadium.

"A fountain of knowledge because he had done it all — player, coach, manager, general manager, scout," said Randolph.

Michael, who had moved to the Tampa area, was still assessing talent and advising the Yankees on September 7, 2017, when he died of a heart attack. He was seventy-nine.

Buck Showalter, who was managing the Orioles, was driving to Baltimore's Camden Yards for a game against the Yankees when his wife, Angela, called with the news of Michael's death. "There are moments in your life when you hear something and you just have to stop whatever you're doing to gather yourself," Showalter said. "And that was one of them. I had to pull the car over and just cry right there.

"So many memories. So many things I would have thanked him for one more time."

Michael's funeral was held three days later at the Calvary Baptist Church in Clearwater, Florida, and a host of players attended, including Derek Jeter and Bernie Williams.

Brian Cashman, who spoke at the funeral, told the congregation:

"Gene was someone who saw something in everybody that was good. He wanted to help everyone somehow."

And Cashman recalled Michael's self-assurance during the most adverse times. "When I think back to the darkest days in the early 1990s," he said, "I can still hear Stick saying, 'Don't worry, we'll get this fixed up.' He had a plan.

"There weren't a lot of believers at the time. But he convinced those of us working with him. We followed him and he turned out to be right."

Michael had remained close with Showalter, whose nomadic baseball journey took him to managerial jobs in Arizona, Texas and Baltimore. "Whenever I came to New York or Tampa, Stick would always arrange to get together, or he'd poke his head into my office for twenty minutes," Showalter said. "And if things were going bad, that's when I could really count on him to reach out to me."

As an example, Showalter remembered the day he was fired by the Diamondbacks in 2000. The team had an 85-77 record, and one year earlier, in the expansion franchise's second year of existence, the Diamondbacks had won 100 games and the National League West championship.

Michael was among the first to call. "What a bunch of horseshit," he said into the phone. "They should be kissing your ass for having any chance to win after only two or three years. Nobody's done that." Michael also told Showalter he could have his pick of another two or three major league managerial jobs if he wanted them.

But Showalter wanted a break from the dugout to ponder his next move. He took a job as a postgame analyst with ESPN.

And that's how Showalter happened to be perched in a makeshift television studio just beyond the outfield walls of Bank One Ballpark in Phoenix on November 4, 2001, as the Yankees and the Diamondbacks prepared to play the seventh game of the World Series.

By the end of the night, one team would be celebrating. It would be either the team Showalter helped build into a perennial World Series contender in the early to mid-1990s in New York or the franchise he helped create in the Arizona desert from 1996 to 2000.

Or as Showalter quipped to reporters before the game, "Somebody told me I'm going to watch someone else walk my daughter down the aisle again."

That game would later be chosen by *Sports Illustrated* as the best postseason game of the decade, with starters Roger Clemens and Curt Schilling pitching into the late innings of a 1–1 game.

Randy Johnson, ever the Yankee killer, made a crucial relief appearance for Arizona despite having pitched the night before. In the end, in the bottom of the ninth, Luis Gonzalez of the Diamondbacks lofted a bloop single over a drawn-in Yankees infield to drive in the series-clinching run against Mariano Rivera.

Showalter talked on the air for ESPN for about forty-five minutes, then left to walk back to his hotel, which was about four blocks from the ballpark. "I was walking through all these fans celebrating in the streets," he said. "Arizona had never won a professional championship in any sport. It was like Mardi Gras out there."

He passed through the crowds unnoticed.

The next day, one of his colleagues on the ESPN broadcast, the former major league infielder Harold Reynolds, called with a question: "Do you think anybody got what you were going through last night? After the game, that had to be pretty intense."

Replied Showalter: "It's OK. I've had practice at this."

But years later, Showalter believed it helped him. "It made it a lot more natural," he said, sitting in his Dallas home office. "I could see firsthand how much it meant to everybody — the Yankees fans, the Arizona fans — all the people that had embraced me in those places. I was part of the process, not separate from it."

Sitting in the stands of the Yankees' spring training complex in 2017, Gene Michael said he knew how Showalter felt. "You're left with the positives," he said. "Some people work just as hard and get nowhere. You have to see the whole picture. Look where we ended up."

On Saturday, June 22, 2014, the Yankees held their sixty-eighth annual Old-Timers' Day. Before a benevolent, appreciative crowd, scores of retired Yankees were introduced in a grand on-field ceremony. A brief old-timers' exhibition game preceded a regular-season game. It was always a hot ticket and 2014 was no different, with 47,493 fans flocking to Yankee Stadium.

On that day, the Yankees' regular-season opponent was Showalter's Baltimore Orioles.

Showalter had not been in uniform at Yankee Stadium for Old-Timers' Day since he was the Yankees' manager in 1995.

During the pregame festivities, Gene Michael, wearing jersey number

17 as he had as a player, emerged from the home dugout to join all the other Yankee old-timers already congregated on the field.

But before joining the other honorees, Michael jogged over to the visiting dugout. Showalter stood to meet him on the top step. Michael and Showalter hugged, as several generations of Yankees and Yankees fans watched, and applauded.

Acknowledgments

One of my mentors, the late Pulitzer Prize–winning *New York Times* sports columnist and author Dave Anderson, told me years ago that writing a book was like scaling a distant mountain peak. "A long, step-by-step climb," Dave said. "But, when you're done, the view from the top is great."

I would add that step by step you have to rely on so many others for a boost in the journey to the top.

In recognition of that, my first thank-you goes to the dozens upon dozens of players, coaches, managers and team executives in baseball who consented to be interviewed for this book across nearly two years. Baseball is a community, and there is a reason why baseball locker rooms are called clubhouses. The term reflects the usually sociable atmosphere of those quarters, especially before games and during spring training, which is when I did all of my interviews.

Over and over, I asked people to recall their times from 1990 to 1995, at home and on the road, in clubhouses, hotels and dugouts around the country in an attempt to retrace the story of those Yankees teams. I was fortunate that so many were happy to be transported back in time.

Buck Showalter sat for several long interviews and was always thoughtful, perceptive and funny in his recollections. His wife, Angela, did the same, offering her own valuable, off-the-field perspective.

Gene "Stick" Michael, one of the wisest, wittiest and most popular men in baseball, was gracious with his time, taking me back to his childhood and on into the twenty-first century of major league baseball, too. In the more than thirty years I knew Stick, every conversation was illuminating, entertaining and somehow made you walk away feeling a little more cheerful. Stick died unexpectedly in September 2017. In one of our final conversations, he told me he was looking forward to reading this book.

"So don't screw it up," he said with a laugh.

I'm going to miss hearing his critique.

I am in debt to many lifelong baseball men who willingly recounted their memories, sometimes in multiple interviews, including Bill Livesey, Mitch Lukevics and Brian Cashman.

Hal Steinbrenner, George's son and now the Yankees' chief executive, does not accede to many prolonged interviews, but he amiably agreed to a lengthy, revealing talk about the early nineties and the impact of those days on his father and the team — then and now.

Susan Canavan, my editor at Houghton Mifflin Harcourt, enthusiastically threw her support behind the book's premise from the very beginning, a boost like no other. She also helped develop some of the dominant narrative themes: revival, ingenuity, perseverance in adversity. That is one of the reasons that so many authors love working with Susan. Also at Houghton Mifflin Harcourt, I had the benefit of scrupulous, deft editing by Larry Cooper and the dedicated assistance of Jenny Xu and Mary Cait Milliff. My longtime friend and *New York Times* colleague Patty LaDuca pored over the manuscript to check facts and offer insight on improvements.

My agent, Scott Waxman, once again did what he does best: listened, gave sage advice, then quietly and efficiently made sure a prospective book became a reality.

Jeff Idelson, the president of the Baseball Hall of Fame, and others at the hall, especially communications director Craig Muder, and John Horne and Cassidy Lent in the research library, leaped through various hoops to help me access their vast files of research and photos.

The Yankees' Jason Zillo, though ceaselessly on the move, still managed to line up interviews for me or find someone's phone number whenever I asked. Kristen Hudak with the Baltimore Orioles offered similar assistance, as did Peter Chase of the Chicago Cubs.

As an aside, I just want to say that I don't know how anyone wrote baseball nonfiction before the advent of baseballreference.com. It is a research tool so instantly valuable, it almost seems like a magician's trick.

My editors at the *New York Times* have always helped guide my career. I'm very fortunate to have been recruited to the paper in the mid-1990s by the one and only Neil Amdur. His successors as sports editor, Tom Jolly and Jason Stallman, helped make me a better reporter and writer, as has one of their colleagues, Randy Archibold. Jeff Roth, the *Times*'s photo morgue maven, was of great help when I begged for his wisdom.

Covering baseball in the 1990s, I was surrounded by scribes who went on to become some of the best-known baseball faces, voices and writers in the country, including Jack Curry, Michael Kay, Bill Madden, Ian O'Connor, Joel Sherman, Claire Smith and Tom Verducci. In my research for this book, it's been edifying and a pleasure to go back and read how intrepid and clear-sighted their work was even when the Yankees were going bad. Like the team they were covering, perhaps we all should have seen the greatness coming.

On a separate note, Michael Kay's thoughtful *CenterStage* interview show, where scores of Yankees have appeared, became must-see television.

As she has done for my previous books, my wife, Joyce, took over as chief researcher without being asked. She produced and cataloged a treasure trove of material — thousands of newspaper stories, correspondence, videotapes and photos. I start with the idea for a book, and Joyce's research makes the words come alive on every single page.

My children, Anne D., Elise and Jack, were frequently enlisted into the project, contributing in myriad ways, including brainstorming a book title. As the youngest and the only one still in college and (sort of) living at home, Jack was put to work assembling a detailed, methodical timeline of every major event or substantial occurrence in baseball from 1990 to 1995. I bet he's now the rare fan his age who truly grasps how much wild-card playoff teams changed the face of baseball.

Most of all, I am forever grateful for a family that willingly treats any major project within the household as a project for all of us.

That's how you get to the mountaintop.

Notes on Research and Sources

It would make a terrific story if I said I knew, while covering the 1990 New York Yankees, that they would someday ascend from a woeful, last-place team to World Series champions. That wouldn't be true.

Even in the fall of 1996, standing on a platform truck with other reporters as we cruised through the ticker tape parade celebrating the Yankees' first World Series victory in fifteen years, it did not dawn on me that the last great baseball dynasty of the twentieth century was about to materialize.

So I did not recognize the fodder for this book as it was happening. But that's the point, isn't it? No one truly saw it coming.

What I can say is that day by day, I was around those 1990s Yankees, first as a traveling newspaper beat writer assigned to the team and then as a sports columnist. As early as the mid-eighties, it was my job to develop close professional relationships with many of the principals in this book, like Gene Michael and Buck Showalter, whom I met days into his first managerial job on a dusty upstate New York diamond in 1985. As for George Steinbrenner, covering him was almost a beat unto itself, and like many writers covering the Yankees in that period, for me it was almost a daily ritual to leave a message at Steinbrenner's Tampa office requesting a return call.

This was especially true for someone based at a newspaper syndicate in northern New Jersey, where Steinbrenner was threatening to build the new Yankee Stadium. From 1985 to 1996, I conducted hundreds of interviews with Steinbrenner, including visits to his Tampa hotel during his baseball exile and in his private plane as he reviewed construction sites for a New Jersey stadium.

I explain these many decades-long relationships to make the point that much of the reporting for this book I did personally in the early 1990s and later as a reporter at the *New York Times,* even if I did not know it would someday lead to a book. Whether it was recounting the toxic atmosphere of the 1990 Yankees' clubhouse or the buoyant electricity of the team's 1994 revival or the palpable despair in the Yankees' losing locker room after their fateful playoff loss in Seattle, as an author, I had the benefit of having been there.

At the same time, those experiences and observations were only a starting point. When I began my research in 2016, I went back and interviewed all the principals for days at a time. I was not surprised that their memories of those days were crisp, potent and edifying. But I'll add that twenty to twenty-five years of hindsight also informed them with new perspectives. Moreover, people sometimes tell stories about a certain episode or an individual more fully, or without inhibition, when they are removed from the situation by two decades or more. The book was made better in countless ways by those added nuggets and new details.

Luckily, I discovered that virtually everyone I approached for an interview was eager to revisit the subject, as if they had come to recognize what a unique period of baseball history it represented. Dozens of former players, coaches, managers, team executives, scouts — as well as associates of Steinbrenner and members of his family — happily reconstructed meetings, deliberations and hot-tempered, red-faced arguments about how the daunting 1990 rebuild would have to take place. I would ask for a twenty-minute interview and end up with a ninety-minute tape recording.

In time, I spoke with about 140 people, a diverse group that included sports agents, trainers, clubhouse managers, television and advertising executives, security workers, broadcasters, athletic trainers and fans.

These conversations fleshed out what I learned, or relearned, by scouring the voluminous archives of New York–area newspapers, which published thousands of articles about the 1990–95 Yankees. Back then, eight daily papers assigned traveling beat writers and columnists to the Yankees. I am indebted to the vast, meticulous digitized archives of those papers, particularly the *New York Times,* and to the New York Public Library for keeping a deep record of the content of various periodicals that published articles about the Yankees.

The research into those seasons informed countless interviews and were the lifeblood of dozens of rich reporting threads found in other places, from Sherman Oaks, California (where Jack McDowell went to high school), to Kalamazoo, Michigan (where a tour of Derek Jeter's high school and childhood neighborhood proved fruitful).

The Baseball Hall of Fame Library was also a nearly boundless resource, with thick files about players, managers and owners. The library is also a unique research opportunity, because visiting players will often sit at a library desk and in their own handwriting jot down accounts of their careers or fill out Q and As. That kind of authenticity is hard to find elsewhere.

The following is a list of people interviewed once or multiple times for this book. The list excludes some team officials, baseball executives and players who asked to remain anonymous because they were relating scenes they did not feel comfortable speaking about on the record while they were still employed by the Yankees or another major league team.

David Abate, Jim Abbott, Jesse Barfield, Brian Boehringer, Wade Boggs, Bobby Brown, Brian Butterfield, Brian Cashman, Chris Chambliss, Mike Christopher, Royal Clayton, Tony Cloninger, Wayne Coffey, David Cone, Billy Connors, Mark Curran, Russ Davis, Dennis Delvecchio, Bucky Dent, Lou D'Ermilio, Mariano Duncan, Kevin Elfering, Troy Evers, Todd Ezold, Tony Fernández, Mike Gallego, Bob Geren, Joe Girardi, Dwight Gooden, Dallas Green, Harvey Greene, Tom Grieve, Dick Groch, John Habyan, Ron Hassey, Andy Hawkins, Charlie Hayes, Rickey Henderson, Sterling Hitchcock, Steve Howe, Jeff Idelson, Dion James, Derek Jeter, Tommy John, Jimmy Jones, Scott Kamieniecki, Bill Kane, Michael Kay, Pat Kelly, Jimmy Key, Joe Klein, Dave LaPoint, Tim Layana, Jim Leyritz, Bill Livesey, Graeme Lloyd, Chris Lombardozzi, Mitch Lukevics, Jason Maas, Billy Martin Jr., Tino Martinez, Don Mattingly, Jack McDowell, Doug Melvin, Stump Merrill, Hensley Meulens, Monk Meyer, Gene Michael, Gene Monahan, Bobby Murcer, Sam Nader, Jeff Nelson, Paul O'Neill, Paul Pearson, Tom Pedula, Pascual Pérez, Andy Pettitte, Lou Piniella, Luis Polonia, Jorge Posada, Nick Priore, Tim Raines, Ed Randall, Willie Randolph, Dody Rather, Harold Reynolds, Rick Rhoden, Dave Righetti, Mariano Rivera, Rubén Rivera, Phil Rizzuto, Deion Sanders, Scott Sanderson, Steve Sax, Glenn Sherlock, Angela Showalter, Buck

Showalter, Russ Springer, Andy Stankiewicz, Mike Stanley, George Steinbrenner, Hal Steinbrenner, Hank Steinbrenner, John Sterling, Darryl Strawberry, David Sussman, Bettie Taylor, Brien Taylor, Wayne Tolleson, Joe Torre, Kevin Trudeau, Shane Turner, Bobby Valentine, Randy Velarde, Fay Vincent, Suzyn Waldman, Bob Watson, David Weathers, Earl Weaver, John Wetteland, Roy White, Bernie Williams, Gerald Williams, Ron Wilson, Dave Winfield.

Bibliography

Anderson, Dave. *Story of the New York Yankees from 1903 to the Present.* New York: Leventhal Publishers, 2012.

Appel, Marty. *Now Pitching for the Yankees: Spinning the News for Mickey, Billy, and George.* Toronto: Sport Classic Books, 2001.

———. *Pinstripe Empire: The New York Yankees from Before the Babe to After the Boss.* New York: Bloomsbury, 2012.

Coffey, Frank. *The Wit and Wisdom of George Steinbrenner.* New York: Signet, 1993.

Geivett, Bill. *Do You Want to Work in Baseball? Inside Baseball Operations.* Self-published, 2016.

Jeter, Derek, with Jack Curry. *The Life You Imagine: Life Lessons for Achieving Your Dreams.* New York: Crown, 2000.

John, Tommy. *T.J.: My 26 Years in Baseball.* New York: Bantam Books, 1991.

Kaat, Jim, and Greg Jennings. *If These Walls Could Talk: Stories from the New York Yankees Locker Room, Dugout, and Press Box.* Chicago: Triumph Books, 2015.

Madden, Bill. *Steinbrenner: The Last Lion of Baseball.* New York: HarperCollins, 2010.

Madden, Bill, and Moss Klein. *Damned Yankees: A No-Holds-Barred Account of Life with "Boss" Steinbrenner.* New York: Warner Books, 1990.

Mahler, Jonathan. *Ladies and Gentlemen, the Bronx Is Burning: 1977, Baseball, Politics, and the Battle for the Soul of a City.* New York: Farrar, Straus and Giroux, 2005.

Murcer, Bobby, and Glen Waggoner. *Yankee for Life: My 40-Year Journey in Pinstripes.* New York: Harper, 2008.

Negron, Ray, and Sally Cook. *Yankee Miracles: Life with the Boss and the Bronx Bombers.* New York: Liveright, 2012.

O'Connor, Ian. *The Captain: The Journey of Derek Jeter.* New York: Houghton Mifflin Harcourt, 2011.

Pennington, Bill. *Billy Martin: Baseball's Flawed Genius,* New York: Houghton Mifflin Harcourt, 2015.

Pepe, Phil. *Core Four: The Heart and Soul of the Yankees Dynasty.* Chicago: Triumph Books, 2013.

Piniella, Lou, and Maury Allen. *Sweet Lou.* New York: Putnam's, 1986.

Posada, Jorge, with Gary Brozek. *The Journey Home.* New York: HarperCollins, 2015.

Prato, Greg. *Just out of Reach: The 1980s New York Yankees.* Self-published, 2014.

Randall, Ed, Ken McMillian, and Bruce Markusen. *Amazing Tales from the New York Yankees Dugout.* New York: Sports Publishing, 2012.

Randolph, Willie. *The Yankee Way: Playing, Coaching, and My Life in Baseball.* New York: HarperCollins, 2014.

Rivera, Mariano, with Wayne Coffey. *The Closer.* New York: Little, Brown and Company, 2014.

Sherman, Joel. *Birth of a Dynasty: Behind the Pinstripes with the 1996 Yankees.* New York: Rodale Press, 2006.

Stout, Glenn, and Richard A. Johnson. *Yankees Century: 100 Years of New York Yankees Baseball.* Boston: Houghton Mifflin Harcourt, 2002.

Thorn, John. *Glory Days: New York Baseball, 1947–1957.* New York: HarperCollins, 2008.

Torre, Joe, and Tom Verducci. *The Yankee Years.* New York: Doubleday, 2009.

Vancil, Mark, and Alfred Santasiere. *Yankee Stadium: The Official Retrospective.* New York: Pocket Books, 2008.

Vincent, Fay. *The Last Commissioner: A Baseball Valentine.* New York: Simon and Schuster, 2002.

Winfield, Dave, and Thomas Trebitsch Parker. *Winfield: A Player's Life.* New York: Norton, 1988.

NEWSPAPERS/WIRE SERVICES

Arizona Republic
Associated Press
Atlanta Constitution
Baltimore Sun
Bergen Record
Boston Globe
Boston Herald
Chicago Tribune
Cleveland Plain-Dealer
Dallas Morning News
Detroit Free Press
Detroit News
Fort Lauderdale Sun-Sentinel
Hartford Courant
Kalamazoo Gazette
Los Angeles Times
Newark Star-Ledger
Newsday
New York Daily News
New York Post
New York Times
Reuters
San Francisco Chronicle

Seattle Times
Tampa Tribune
Toronto Star
USA Today
Washington Post

MAGAZINES

Baseball America
Esquire
Forbes
GQ
Parade
People
Sporting News
Sports Illustrated
Time

VIDEOS/BROADCASTS

CenterStage with Michael Kay, Jim Abbott, YES Network, 2012
CenterStage with Michael Kay, Derek Jeter, YES Network, 2004 and 2017
CenterStage with Michael Kay, Andy Pettitte, YES Network, 2010
CenterStage with Michael Kay, Jorge Posada, YES Network, 2008
CenterStage with Michael Kay, Willie Randolph, YES Network, 2013
CenterStage with Michael Kay, Mariano Rivera, YES Network, 2014
CenterStage with Michael Kay, George Steinbrenner, YES Network, 2005
CenterStage with Michael Kay, Bernie Williams, YES Network, 2009
ESPN SportsCentury, Derek Jeter, ESPN, 2003
Game broadcast clips, 1990–1996: Baseball Network, Fox, MSG Network, NBC
Stadium Stories with Jayson Stark, Buck Showalter, 2018
YES Network, *Remembering Gene Michael,* 2017

Index